The Other Movement

CONTEMPORARY AMERICAN INDIAN STUDIES
Heidi M. Altman, *Series Editor*
J. Anthony Paredes, *Founding Editor*

The Other Movement

Indian Rights and Civil Rights in the Deep South

Denise E. Bates

THE UNIVERSITY OF ALABAMA PRESS

Tuscaloosa

Copyright © 2012
The University of Alabama Press
Tuscaloosa, Alabama 35487-0380
All rights reserved
Manufactured in the United States of America

Typeface: Caslon

∞

The paper on which this book is printed meets the minimum requirements of
American National Standard for Information Sciences—Permanence of Paper for
Printed Library Materials, ANSI Z39.48-1984.

Library of Congress Cataloging-in-Publication Data

Bates, Denise E.
    The other movement : Indian rights and civil rights in the deep south / Denise E.
Bates.
       p. cm. — (Contemporary American Indian studies)
    Includes bibliographical references and index.
    ISBN 978-0-8173-1759-1 (cloth : alk. paper) — ISBN 978-0-8173-8594-1 (electronic)
1. Indians of North America—Civil rights—Southern States. 2. Indians of North
America—Southern States—Government relations. 3. Indian activists—Southern
States—History. 4. Civil rights movements—Southern States—History. 5. South-
ern States—Race relations. 6. Southern States—Politics and government. I. Title.
    E78.S65B39 2012
    323.1197075—dc23
                                                                        2011029909

Cover: Calvin McGhee and President John F. Kennedy, 1962. (Courtesy of the Alabama Department of Archives and History, Montgomery, Alabama.)

Contents

List of Illustrations   vii

Preface   ix

Acknowledgments   xvii

Indian Groups and Organizations of Alabama and Louisiana
xviii

Key People   xix

1. Back on the Map: The Emergence of a Deep Southern Indian
   Rights Movement   1

2. "We'll Do It in the Spirit of Brotherhood": Inter-Tribal Politics
   and the Challenge of Centralizing Representation   41

3. Acknowledging Indians in a Bipolar South: Shifting
   Racial Identities   70

4. Starting from Scratch: Struggling to Improve Indian Lives   99

5. A Regional Makeover: Tourism and How Indians Remade
   the South   141

Conclusion   172

Appendix: Other Tribes of the South   177

Notes   181

References   233

Index   249

Illustrations

1. Alabama Indian communities   xv

2. Louisiana Indian communities   xv

3. Coushatta tribal members at a gathering, circa 1971   13

4. Ruth Loyd Miller, 1922–2005   15

5. Calvin McGhee and President John F. Kennedy, 1962   25

6. House of a Louisiana Indian family at Bayou Grand Caillou, circa 1920s   103

7. Exhibit on Louisiana Indian history in Baton Rouge, 1971   148

8. Indian festival on the streets of Baton Rouge, 1983   155

9. Louisiana American Indian license plate   169

10. Alabama Bureau of Tourism and Travel brochure published in 2002   170

Preface

It is curious that after all that has been written about the dramatic changes that the American South underwent in the second half of the twentieth century, very little has been written about the transformative role that American Indians played in this process. Throughout the 1950s and 1960s, the region was a hotbed of political activity as the media regularly captured images of organized marches, sit-ins, and animated speeches delivered by such leaders as Martin Luther King Jr. and Stokely Carmichael. While the nation remained riveted by this revolution in race relations that marked the decline of Jim Crow and the passing of the civil rights acts, American Indians across the South created a social and political movement all their own. Articulate and persistent Indian leaders transcended the historical silencing that had characterized their existence in a region where most of the population believed that Indian people had been forcibly removed, had been integrated beyond recognition into the populous, or were quietly eking out an existence in the margins of society. A region once bound by a biracial identity thus witnessed a revival in Indian awareness, spawning the development—or redevelopment—of tribal governments that became increasingly vocal in their efforts to assert political authority and rally public support. As a result of this increased visibility, complicated and reciprocal relationships developed between southern state governments and Indian communities. Without examining these relationships, we cannot claim to fully understand the extent of the South's transformation.

As much as this is a story about the South's transformation, it is also a story about Indian activism. The southern Indian movement began as early as the 1950s with localized efforts to gain access to schools and combat racial violence. However, it wasn't until the 1970s that southern states broke out of their pattern of largely ignoring their Indian residents.[1] During this decade southern politicians found themselves in precarious positions as a result of shifting racial politics. This shift—coupled with the increased public awareness generated by the activities of Indian activists on a national scale—created an opportunity for southern Indian leaders to draw attention to the problems of discrimination, high poverty levels, unemployment, low educational attainment, and poor living conditions that their communities faced. As a result, they negotiated the development of state Indian affairs commissions to serve as forums in which to address these problems and function as liaisons between tribal governments and state and federal agencies. In 1971 North Carolina led the charge within the region by establishing an Indian affairs commission, followed by Louisiana (1972), Florida (1974), Alabama (1978), South Carolina (1979), Virginia (1982), Tennessee (1983), and Georgia (1995).[2]

While the state Indian affairs commissions were intended to serve many practical functions—such as assessing the needs of Indian communities, locating resources, and educating the public—their existence became highly politicized. What motivated southern state legislators to recognize Indian groups, many of which the federal government would not? Who should comprise the leadership of the commissions? Should these state agencies determine Indian legitimacy? What criteria should they use? What did state recognition really mean and how did it reflect shifting notions of race in the South? These are just a few of the questions that were openly debated during commission meetings, at tribal gatherings, in local newspapers, and even in courtrooms.

Is this story unique to the South? Yes and no. Like other regions throughout the country, the South has a distinct identity that is defined by its history, politics, and people. The growth of interdisciplinary programs in Southern Studies, as well as the robust collection of scholarship that examines the unique attributes of the region, serve as testaments to the region's distinctiveness.[3] Furthermore, the historical federal-state tensions paired with its colorful cast of political characters who made, enforced, or supported racially discriminatory policies toward African Americans only to later, in many cases, support Indian rights makes this an interesting story to unravel. The course of southern Indian history certainly didn't follow a predictable path in any case. William Harlen Gilbert Jr., who issued a report to the Smithsonian Institute in 1948 claiming that southern Indians were on their way to extinction, would have been stunned to discover that twenty years later these same groups comprised the largest percentage of petitioners for both state and federal recognition in the nation.[4]

While I argue that the southern Indian movement had some regionally unique attributes, many of the challenges southern Indians faced were not theirs alone. As Vine Deloria Jr. has identified, the 1960s marked a time of retribalization of people as they became increasingly politically aware.[5] Indian groups were formed—or re-formed—from California to New England and everywhere in between. Many of these groups also engaged in negotiations with their respective states, and many were even involved in forming state commissions. Perhaps the most frustrating shared experience by non–federally recognized groups nationally, however, was engaging in the tedious—and sometimes demoralizing—task of applying for federal recognition. For hundreds of groups in the South and elsewhere, having to produce documentation to prove their Indian identities after decades of marginalization is one of the biggest ironies of this story.

As much as I would have enjoyed relaying the evolution of the Indian movement in every southern state, I resolved to focus on two: Alabama and Louisiana. Both states were sites of tremendous political activity during the civil rights era, and each experienced increased Indian visibility and tribal reorganization in the decades to follow.[6] According to the U.S. Census Bureau, the American Indian population in Alabama in 1990 was more than twelve times the 1960 population.[7] Reflecting this upward trajectory, the Louisiana Indian population was more than five times as large in 1990 than it had been in 1960.[8] Although many causes can explain the dramatic population increase, such as higher birthrates and lower infant mortality, the largest shift occurred when people were allowed to self-identify their racial backgrounds for the first time.

In addition to the economic, political, and social factors that shaped the development of tribal-state relationships, Alabama and Louisiana also make interesting case studies because of widespread inter-tribal efforts—led by charismatic leaders—to coalesce the isolated interests and needs of diverse Indian groups for the first time. Alabama's seven state-acknowledged tribes and Louisiana's eight recognized groups varied in appearance, cultural maintenance, and degree of public acceptance in their claims to Indian identity.[9]

Tribal governments within each state also differed in political status. For example, in 1970, the Chitimacha of Louisiana was the only federally acknowledged tribe in either state. Unlike other tribes living in Louisiana, the Chitimacha maintained a continuous residence on their ancestral lands at Charenton on Grand Lake.[10] As the first tribe to become recognized by the Louisiana state legislature in 1972, the Coushatta of Elton received re-recognition by the federal government a year later. This allowed them to resume their previous federal relationship that had been severed in the 1950s during the Indian Termination era.[11]

Although the secretary of the interior gave the Coushatta federal status under provisions of the Wheeler-Howard Act,[12] other groups in the two states faced the challenge of adhering to the new regulations of the Bureau of Indian Affairs. Beginning in 1978, an unrecognized group had to present evidence confirming its status as a tribe from historical times to the present. Despite the difficulty in documenting tribal history, Indian groups in Alabama and Louisiana saw success early on. The Tunica-Biloxi of Louisiana,[13] for example, gained federal recognition in 1981, and then the Creek Nation East of the Mississippi—commonly referred to as the Poarch Band of Creek Indians—became the first and only tribe in Alabama to obtain federal recognition in 1984.[14]

While the Coushatta, Tunica-Biloxi, and Poarch Creek managed to gain federal recognition, other groups did not have the same experience, especially since their Indian identities were called into question. The most well-documented cases were those of the MOWA Choctaw of Alabama[15] and the Houma of Louisiana,[16] both of which boasted the largest membership in their states. Each group had obtained state recognition, but they ultimately failed to gain federal recognition because authorities claimed that the modern communities descended from racial amalgamations that made it impossible to discern undiluted Indian identities. Both instances illuminate the complex nature of race and reveal the conflict between federal and state determinates as to what constitutes a tribe.

In addition to federal recognition—or a lack thereof—Indian groups in both Alabama and Louisiana held other distinguishing characteristics, including the level of connection they maintained with their federally recognized relatives in other states. The Jena Choctaw of central Louisiana, for example, maintained strong ties with the Mississippi Choctaw, who even supported the Jena petition for federal recognition. The request, Chief Phillip Martin of the Mississippi Choctaw argued, should be "an open and shut case because of their direct linkage to the Choctaws of Mississippi."[17] The fact that a community of about 150 people also maintained their language and traditions made the Jena Choctaw's claim more compelling—as proven by their federal acknowledgment in 1995.[18]

The Jena was not the only group to break away from the larger Choctaw Nation only to resurface in Louisiana. Just southwest of the Jena, the Clifton Choctaws reside in an isolated stretch of Rapides Parish.[19] The Choctaw-Apache Community of Ebarb, who live in the area of Zwolle, also broke away. Because of their surnames and Catholic faith, outsiders thought they were Spanish until the Indian movement offered them an opportunity to more clearly define themselves to the public.[20] The Louisiana Band of Choctaw was the fourth, and final, group of state-recognized Choctaws. Unlike their rural counterparts, this small community is now located mainly in the suburbs of Baton Rouge; its members migrated from various rural Choctaw communities in both Louisiana and Mississippi.[21]

While the Jena Choctaw had an ongoing relationship with the Mississippi Choctaw, Alabama's Jackson County Cherokee—renamed the Cherokee Tribe of Northeast Alabama (CTNA) in 1983—attempted to reconnect with the federally acknowledged Eastern Band of Cherokee after being disconnected from them for more than a century. Remaining nearly undetected in northeast Alabama in the years following Removal, the Jackson County Cherokees officially organized in 1981.[22] Other Cherokee groups also found their voices within the Indian movement. The United Cherokee Tribe of Alabama, for example, first organized in Daleville in 1978. By 1980, however, disenchanted members of the tribe broke away to form the Echota Cherokee Tribe. With a tribal headquarters in Shelby County, the group represented Cherokees across the state and many members outside Alabama.[23] As the Jackson County Cherokee and the Echota Cherokee populations steadily grew, the considerably smaller Cherokees of Southeast Alabama organized in Houston County in 1982.[24]

Descendants of Alabama Cherokees who avoided Removal were not alone in reorganizing during the 1970s and 1980s. A massive Creek resurgence also emerged. Although most attention focused on the Poarch Creek, the state of Alabama also recognized the Star Clan of Muscogee Creeks and the Ma-Chis Lower Creeks. The Star Clan first organized in Pike County in 1975 under the name of Eufaula Star Clan.[25] A decade after the Star Clan organized, the Ma-Chis Lower Creeks of Coffee County developed under the guidelines of the Alabama Indian Affairs Commission and became the first tribe in the state to organize under the new criteria.[26]

These fifteen tribal communities reveal the internal diversity that exists within southern tribes, and their unique stories can easily sustain in-depth studies of their own; however, that is outside the scope of this book. Instead, my intent is to look at how the leadership of each of these communities interacted with one another, Indian advocates, and state government officials as participants, contributors, and shapers of a movement that brought Indian affairs into the forefront of state politics.

The Alabama and Louisiana state archives hold an abundance of legal documents, meeting transcripts, personal correspondence, news clippings, memos, briefs, and hand-scribbled notes that—along with other sources pulled from various archives and universities—collectively comprise the mosaic from which this book unfolds. Although certain groups and individuals are woven into the discussion more prominently than others, this is not intended to assign more importance to their efforts over those of others. Examples were chosen based on the authority and veracity of the evidence to illuminate the development of tribal-state relationships within each state. The course that Indian affairs took in both of the examined states was the result of the work and input of many—from the tribal leaders who traveled to the state capitols for meetings in the governors' offices to the Indian mothers who wrote letters to the Indian commissions asking for assistance. There were also numerous non-Indian legislators, lawyers, historians, anthropologists, writers, and advocates who supported the Indian movement with their time and talents. Every one of them made an impact in what the Alabama journalist Marie Cromer has so eloquently described as a "rebirth of Indian awareness and acceptance, arising like the legendary Phoenix from the ashes of [Indian] removal, abandonment, and discrimination."[27]

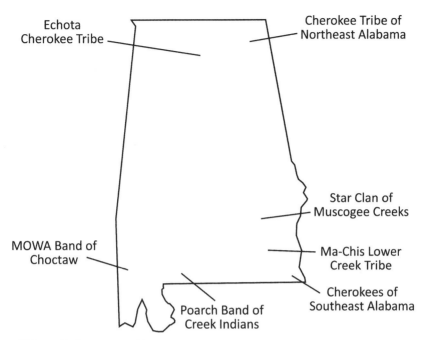

Echota
Cherokee Tribe

Cherokee Tribe of
Northeast Alabama

Star Clan of
Muscogee Creeks

MOWA Band of
Choctaw

Ma-Chis Lower
Creek Tribe

Cherokees of
Southeast Alabama

Poarch Band of
Creek Indians

1. Alabama Indian communities.

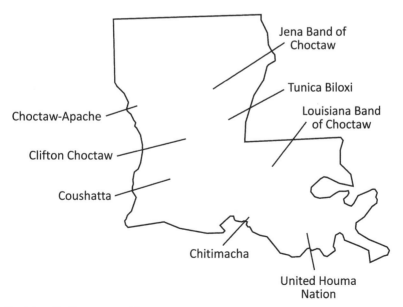

Jena Band of
Choctaw

Tunica Biloxi

Louisiana Band
of Choctaw

Choctaw-Apache

Clifton Choctaw

Coushatta

Chitimacha

United Houma
Nation

2. Louisiana Indian communities.

Acknowledgments

Like any other "labor of love," this book would not have been possible without the support of numerous people and institutions. The National Academies and the Ford Foundation provided the bulk of funding I needed to conduct my research, along with the Louise Foucar Marshall Foundation, the Michael Sweetow Endowment, the William Hesketh Endowment, and various other travel grants supplied by the Department of History at the University of Arizona.

I would like to particularly acknowledge the aid and generosity of Norwood Kerr, Meredith McLemore, and Debbie Pendleton of the Alabama Department of Archives and History, Bill Stafford and Florent Hardy of the Louisiana State Archives, and Charlene Bonnette from the State Library of Louisiana, who provided me with valuable assistance in my research. I would also like to extend my gratitude to Bonner Miller Cutting, whose enthusiasm about my book and its coverage of the work that her mother did made it all worthwhile.

Katherine Morrissey, K. Tsianina Lomawaima, Karen Anderson, and Roger Nichols all offered their wisdom and critical insight on the manuscript as it took shape. They kept me on my toes throughout the research and writing process and helped me grow intellectually. While at the University of Arizona, I had the great fortune to develop friendships with numerous individuals who served as sounding boards for my ideas and initial chapter drafts. I will be forever grateful to Margaret Vaughan, Cherstin Lyon, Martiza de la Trinidad, Meghan Winchell, Angelica Lawson, Cynthia Gonzales, and Ziad Abi-Shakra.

My current colleagues at Arizona State University have also offered their encouragement throughout the revision process. In particular, I would like to thank Kelly Nelson, Jessica Hirshorn, Stephanie deLusé, and Kevin Ellsworth.

I would like to express my appreciation to the reviewers of my manuscript for their thoughtful assessments and important suggestions. I am also grateful for Joseph Powell and the rest of the staff at The University of Alabama Press for their guidance and belief in this project.

This book would not have been possible without the support of my family, who made many sacrifices for me to complete this project. Thank you, Kevin, for running the household on days when I rarely got up from my desk. I also appreciate all the time you took to read every page I wrote to give me feedback and motivation to continue pressing on. And thank you, Claire, Aidan, and Lila, for being a constant source of joy even in the most stressful of times. I would also like to thank Allen and Naomi Barber, Larry, Alice, and Kim Bates, and John Gatturna for their love and support, as well as my grandmother, Wanda Light Tully, for fostering my love of history and encouraging me to tell a story that has such deep meaning to our family.

Last but in no way least, I would like to acknowledge the numerous people whose work and sacrifice fill the pages of this book. Your efforts will never be forgotten.

Indian Groups and Organizations of Alabama and Louisiana

As the political landscape continues to evolve beyond the scope of this book, additional Indian communities and organizations may have formed or been recognized by their respective states and thus joined the ranks of the groups listed below.

Alabama

Poarch Band of Creek Indians (or the Creek Indians East of the Mississippi)
MOWA Band of Choctaws
Echota Tribe of Cherokee
Jackson County Cherokee (or the Cherokee Tribe of Northeast Alabama)
Star Clan of Muscogee Creeks
Ma-Chis Lower Creeks
Cherokees of Southeast Alabama

Agencies and Organizations

Southwest Alabama Indian Affairs Commission (SAIAC)
Alabama Indian Affairs Commission (AIAC)

Alabama Inter-Tribal Council (AITC)
Society for the Preservation of American Indian Culture (SPAIC)

Louisiana

Chitimacha Tribe
Coushatta Tribe
Jena Band of Choctaws
Tunica-Biloxi Tribe
United Houma Nation
Clifton Choctaw Tribe
Choctaw-Apache Community of Ebarb
Louisiana Band of Choctaw

Agencies and Organizations

Louisiana Office of Indian Affairs (LOIA)
Louisiana Inter-Tribal Council (ITC)
Indian Angels, Inc.
Louisiana Indians for Equality (LIFE)
Institute for Indian Development

KEY PEOPLE

The following is an alphabetical list of some of the key people in the development of the Indian rights movement in Alabama and Louisiana who appear throughout this book.

Alabama

Roger Creekmore: Appointed to represent the non–tribally affiliated Indians within the newly structured Alabama Indian Affairs Commission (AIAC) in 1984.

Marie Cromer: Editor of the *St. Clair News Press* who lobbied the Poarch Creek for equal representation of other tribal groups in the Southwest Alabama Indian Affairs Commission (SAIAC).

Tommy Davenport: Star Clan of Muscogee Creeks leader who advocated for a democratically representative SAIAC and against the Poarch Creek's state recognition criteria. He represented his tribe in the newly created AIAC as the first vice-chairman.

Pat Davis: State representative who sponsored the Davis-Strong Act to replace the exclusionary Mims Act of 1978. She was later appointed as a state representative on the new AIAC.

Jennie Lee Dees: Poarch Creek administrator and the first executive director of the AIAC.

B. J. Faulkner: United Cherokee Tribe of Alabama leader until the group split into two factions, one of which was the Echota Cherokee Tribe.

Darla Graves: MOWA Choctaw tribal member and the state's first tribal development coordinator who later became the executive director of the AIAC.

Leonard Hudson: Retired pharmacist who was appointed by the governor as chairman of SAIAC.

Guy Hunt: Republican governor from 1987 to 1993.

Fob James Jr.: Democratic governor from 1979 to 1983; Republican governor from 1995 to 1999. He first funded the AIAC only to pull the funding as inter-tribal tensions mounted.

Reo Kirkland: State senator who supported the Poarch Creek and SAIAC.

H. L. "Lindy" Martin: Jackson County Cherokee leader who advocated for a democratically representative SAIAC. He stressed tribal economic development and represented his tribe in the AIAC.

Jacqueline Anderson Matte: Historian and teacher from Washington County who documented the history of the MOWA Choctaw.

Calvin McGhee: Poarch Creek leader who generated national attention for his community and other Alabama Indians in the 1950s and 1960s.

Houston McGhee: Poarch Creek leader who continued the legacy of his father, Calvin, in improving the conditions of his community by forging a relationship with the state government.

Maston Mims: State senator who introduced a bill to the legislature—called the Mims Act—in 1978 that created SAIAC.

James E. Ray: State representative who was chosen to head a special committee to write legislation to counter the Mims Act.

Joseph Stewart: Echota Cherokee leader who represented his community in the newly created AIAC.

Frances Strong: State legislator who sponsored a bill, the Davis-Strong Act, to replace the exclusionary Mims Act of 1978. She was later appointed as a state representative to the new AIAC.

Eddie Tullis: Poarch Creek leader who initiated the establishment of the Poarch-dominated SAIAC in 1978. He advocated for a formal state recognition process that did not involve legislators.

J. E. Turner: State representative who defended the 1979 MOWA Choctaw state recognition bill.

George C. Wallace: Democratic governor from 1963 to 1967, 1971 to 1979, and 1983 to 1987. He approved the creation of SAIAC under his administration.

Deal Wambles: Cherokees of Southeast Alabama leader who represented his tribe in the new AIAC.

Framon Weaver: MOWA Choctaw leader who advocated for a democratically representative SAIAC. He represented his tribe in the new AIAC.

Gallasneed Weaver: MOWA Choctaw leader who was appointed as the first chairman of the new AIAC.

Jane L. Weeks: Executive director of the AIAC in 1990.

Diane Weston: Echota Cherokee leader who advocated for a democratically representative SAIAC.

Louisiana

John Billiot: Houma leader and founder of the political action group Louisiana Indians for Equality (LIFE).

Richard Brazan: Legal consultant to the Louisiana Office of Indian Affairs (LOIA).

David Broome: Louisiana Band of Choctaw leader who supported the leadership of Clyde Jackson as director of LOIA.

Jeanette Campos: Served as the executive director of the Louisiana Inter-Tribal Council (ITC).

Steve Cheramie: Houma community leader.

Daniel Darden: Chitimacha tribal leader and businessman.

Bruce Duthu: Houma community member who served as director of the Dartmouth College Native American Program.

Edwin Edwards: Democratic governor from 1972 to 1980, 1984 to 1988, and 1992 to 1996. LOIA was first established under his administration.

John Faine: Professor in the Department of Sociology, Anthropology, and Social Work at Western Kentucky University. He wrote reports on several Indian communities in the state.

Margrett Fels: Journalist and Indian advocate who wrote articles about the state's Indians in several newspapers and magazines.

David L. Garrison Jr.: First commissioner of LOIA.

Helen Gindrat: Houma leader and executive director of LOIA from 1980 to 1983.

H. F. "Pete" Gregory: Anthropology professor from Northwestern State University who worked with tribes across the state for over twenty years to educate the public on Indian cultures and history.

Clyde Jackson: Jena Band of Choctaw leader and board member of the ITC. He succeeded Helen Gindrat as executive director of LOIA in 1983 and co-founded the Institute for Indian Development.

Jerry Jackson: Jena Band of Choctaw leader who advocated for a change in state policy to give American Indians a minority status.

Fred Kniffen: Geography and anthropology professor at Louisiana State University who served on the board of LOIA as an expert on American Indians.

Ruth Loyd Miller: Legal advisor to Ernest Sickey, who helped initiate the creation of LOIA.

Peter Mora: Succeeded Ernest Sickey as commissioner of LOIA.

Sarah Peralta: Founded the Baton Rouge–based organization Indian Angels, Inc.

Roy Procell: Choctaw-Apache leader who worked to secure better employment opportunities and better health care in his community.

Buddy Roemer: Republican governor from 1988 to 1992.

Odis Sanders: Louisiana Band of Choctaw leader.

Ernest Sickey: Coushatta leader who served as the first Indian commissioner of LOIA.

David Treen: Republican governor from 1980 to 1984 who made the first substantial monetary commitment to LOIA.

Diana Williamson: Chitimacha tribal member who was appointed assistant director of LOIA in 1984 and executive director in 1986.

The Other Movement

1
Back on the Map

The Emergence of a Deep Southern Indian
Rights Movement

In 1970, Ernest Sickey, a father of three in his late twenties and leader of
Louisiana's Coushatta Tribe, appeared at attorney Ruth Loyd Miller's private
practice office with his family, pleading for legal assistance on behalf of his
community.[1] The approximately 250 Coushatta of Allen Parish had endured
almost twenty years of federal neglect. This neglect began in 1953 when the
Bureau of Indian Affairs (BIA) ended its trusteeship of Coushatta land, held
since 1898, and began depriving the tribe of services.[2] With no formal action
by the federal government to terminate the Coushatta, they fell into a state
of limbo and what a news editorial described as "crude brutality." In fact, in a
survey taken of thirty-eight Coushatta families in the early 1970s, thirty-three
had annual family incomes below $3,000, and none was above $5,000.[3] With
such staggering statistics, it's no wonder that Sickey wanted to help his community. His determination touched Miller, who was previously known for
her passionate support of challenging injustices committed against women.
Miller agreed to help Sickey by using her political connections to forge a relationship between the state of Louisiana and the tribal communities of the
Coushatta, Chitimacha, Houma, and Tunica.[4] The creation of this historic
partnership between Sickey and Miller was the spark that fueled the development of a new Indian movement in Louisiana, one that had already ignited
elsewhere throughout the South.

While Ernest Sickey fought for the betterment of the Coushatta and other
Louisiana Indians, Chief Houston McGhee of the Creek Nation East of the
Mississippi was just a few hundred miles away building Alabama's own Indian movement. Unlike Sickey, McGhee did not need to forge new ground
but instead followed in the footsteps of his father, Calvin McGhee, who was

called the "Martin Luther King of the modern Creek movement" because of his success a few decades earlier in fighting for Creek rights and better educational opportunities.[5] The younger McGhee brought monetary aid to his impoverished and federally ignored community and, like Sickey, petitioned the state government for assistance. In a 1974 letter to Governor George C. Wallace, Houston McGhee asked for the state's help in obtaining some land and access to federal Indian services. He cleverly argued that "if federal services become available to Indians in Alabama, it could relieve a number of public burdens for welfare, education, and economic development."[6] This line of reasoning struck a chord with Wallace, who not only gave his support to McGhee's efforts but also played a crucial role in following in the footsteps of Louisiana by developing a formal relationship between the state government and the local Indian population.

The leadership and foresight of Sickey and McGhee promoted massive changes for the Indian people of Louisiana and Alabama. Their actions represented a new chapter in the development of tribal-state relations that evolved throughout the Southeast. Indian groups became increasingly vocal in their efforts to gain greater public recognition and more privileges as Indians despite their essential invisibility maintained through years of racial discrimination and marginalization. The region-wide Indian rights movement developed against the backdrop of a changing national economic and social environment, which mobilized people both physically and politically. This chapter examines this shift in the South—and more specifically in Alabama and Louisiana—by examining the context in which Indian interests were able to intersect with state politics—in sometimes unexpected ways—through the development of state Indian affairs commissions.

A Nation in Transition: Making Sense of It All

In order to effectively understand the significance of the dramatic turn that Indian affairs took in Alabama and Louisiana, we must first look at the big picture. What factors preceded Sickey's decision to seek legal assistance in reaching out to the state legislature or McGhee's bold confidence in writing directly to the governor? Although Indian families throughout both states had been struggling for decades, what prompted Indian leaders to finally transcend their marginalized status and demand resources? The response is multilayered—if not complex—because it involves cultural, social, political, and economic shifts at both the regional and national levels.

A major catalyst that fueled the development of the southern Indian rights movement was the changing federal Indian political environment. American Indians endured a legacy in which the federal government attempted to forcibly relocate them from their homelands and either left them without the "protection" of the federal trust relationship or subjected them to a stream of federal Indian policies intended to assimilate and culturally and politically obliterate them. The impact of the termination policy of the 1950s and 1960s, for example, although only directly affecting a small number of tribal communities, "aroused tremendous fear and hostility throughout Indian country."[7] As the legal scholar Stephen Cornell argues, it was the shared anxiety over cold war Indian policies—in addition to the experiences of World War II Indian soldiers—that paved the way for Indians to conceive of themselves as a nationally unified group and begin speaking the language of sovereignty, economic justice, and cultural preservation.[8]

In response to the federal government's drive to abrogate its trust responsibilities to tribal nations, the National Congress of the American Indian (NCAI) was established to address the hostile turn that federal Indian policy had taken. This pan-Indian organization held its first convention in 1944 with delegates from more than fifty tribal communities. Over the next several years, the NCAI drew the attention and the eventual membership of nearly all tribes in the United States—including some of the previously isolated communities of the South.[9] Tribal representatives came together within the NCAI to monitor federal Indian policy and to encourage "unity and cooperation among tribal governments for the protection of their treaty and sovereign rights."[10]

Laurence Hauptman and Jack Campisi argue that by the 1960s "many eastern Indians viewed the NCAI as too conservative, too much aligned with the BIA, and too opposed to eastern Indian interests, including federal recognition efforts."[11] As a result, the 1961 American Indian Chicago Conference (AICC) was called to address the interests of a broader range of tribal groups. The AICC, which was held at the University of Chicago, proved to be another turning point in southern Indian activism when delegates from unrecognized—and predominantly isolated—tribal groups were invited to attend this nationwide conference, at which they were encouraged to come up with solutions to their own problems. Sol Tax, an anthropology professor and conference coordinator, was astounded when more than 450 Indian delegates—from reservation and non-reservation communities—became "somewhat of a community" as they realized that they shared common problems. Conference delegates asserted themselves as "angry Indians" with inherent sovereign rights that had been threatened and eroded by the federal policies of the

1950s.[12] As a result, the delegates of the AICC drafted the *Declaration of Indian Purpose*—a document that thirty-two Indian leaders delivered to President John F. Kennedy the following year during a noon ceremony on the White House lawn.[13] The *Declaration* emphasized Indian self-determination—a theme Kennedy didn't fully embrace when he interpreted the document as one that simply demonstrated that Indian services were still inadequate and that the federal government had a great deal of "unfinished business" to tend to. It was not until after Kennedy's death, when Lyndon Johnson took office and launched his War on Poverty, that Indian groups began to develop programs designed to realize the vision outlined in the AICC document.[14]

The influence of the AICC reached the South. Alabama's Poarch Creek leader, Calvin McGhee, shared experiences and strategies with other Indian leaders when he traveled to Chicago with his wife and at least four other Creeks from Alabama and Florida. He could not believe there were "so many Indians in the same boat."[15] According to the conference roster, southern Indian groups were well represented, with delegates from the Alabama Coushatta of Texas, the Louisiana Choctaw, the Mississippi Choctaw, and the Virginia Cherokee. From North Carolina there were representatives who were Cherokee, Lumbee, and Haliwa.[16] The Louisiana Houma also sent two delegates, who later returned to inspire the political and social development of their community.[17] Not only did the AICC draw the attention of federal policymakers, it also gave legitimacy to the needs of the underrepresented groups in the South that were drawn into the larger arena of Indian political activism, information sharing, and inter-tribal collaboration.

The 1970s marked a time when Congress carefully examined its obligation to Indian tribes and reimagined the future of the federal-Indian relationship. In 1975 the Indian Self-Determination and Education Assistance Act was passed and, although its purpose has been heavily debated, the common interpretation is that it was intended to empower tribes by ridding them of federal domination and allowing them to administer federal Indian programs themselves.[18] The same year that the act was passed, Congress created the American Indian Policy Review Commission (AIPRC)—made up of legislators and Indians of varying political statuses—to issue recommendations on the course that Indian affairs should take. Significantly, the commission emphasized supporting tribal self-governance, offering services to terminated or unrecognized tribes, and limiting the role of the BIA. Although not all of the ambitious recommendations issued by the commission were implemented, its influence helped shape the course that recognition policy took as Congress created a task force to look into the claims of terminated and non-federally recognized tribes. The many hearings held by the task force across the country served as forums for unrecognized Indians to lodge complaints about governmental injustice, which ultimately resulted in a series of more recommendations, one of which was the establishment of an "Office of Acknowledgment" within the Department of Interior.[19]

As Anne McCulloch and David Wilkins argue, "Federal recognition is the primary method used by tribes to affirm their existence as distinct political communities within the American system."[20] Federal recognition also gives tribes access to federal resources that serve communities in the areas of health, education, social services, and economic development. When the BIA established a process to acknowledge previously unrecognized tribes in 1978, the leaders of such tribes across the nation saw an opportunity to improve the status of their communities. As a result, petitions poured in. Although this seemed to be a good opportunity for Indian groups, the process met much criticism because of its stringent criteria that rely on documentation that many groups, particularly in the South, lack. It is a highly contested process that is subjective, complex, and politicized. The very definitions of "tribe" and "Indian" are problematic and put researchers for the Branch of Acknowledgment and Research (BAR) into a never-ending quandary of how to avoid consistently issuing contradictory findings. The fact is that a singular definition of these terms simply cannot be consistently applied to all Indian groups. As Alexandra Harmon illustrates in her examination of groups in the Puget Sound region, Indian identity is part of a political and historical process that often reflects changing social conditions.[21] Studies conducted on the Lumbee of North Carolina and the Mashpee of Massachusetts, which served as test cases for what constitutes an Indian tribe under U.S. law, offer valuable insight into the challenges of the process faced by groups whose Indian identities were questioned.[22] The issues raised in these studies reflect the challenges that other groups throughout the Southeast faced in their efforts to obtain federal recognition despite their "mixed" ancestries.[23]

Despite the headaches—and heartaches—that the federal acknowledgment issue brought to many Indian communities, it is within this context of tribal resurgence and self-determination that the southern Indian rights movement developed. Kevin Bruyneel has deemed this a "claim for postcolonial nationhood" that was born out of a politically vibrant period in which "indigenous political actors faced the tension of having to construct and express their politics betwixt and between a civil rights framework."[24]

It was amid this movement toward tribal preservation and resurgence and the push to assert their political existence that southern Indians began to find their own voices through inter-tribal coalition building. In 1972, the Coalition of Eastern Native Americans (CENA) was formed to encourage marginalized groups in the East to seek recognition from state governments and the U.S. government. Although CENA did not survive the decade, Helen C. Rountree notes that "it showed Native Americans throughout the eastern United States that their local experiences with prejudiced non-Indians were normal, not isolated instances peculiar to only a few places." CENA also educated tribal leaders in how to apply for federal grants offered through other departments outside the BIA.[25] Other inter-tribal endeavors, such as the United Southeastern Tribes, Inc., and the Lumbee-run Indian Information Project, helped southern Indian groups capitalize on the evolving federal Indian policy of the 1970s and 1980s that emphasized self-determination and resulted in a growing political awareness, land claims, and gains in the areas of education and social welfare.[26]

Southern Indian groups varied widely in their appearance and degree of cultural maintenance. Their social patterns ranged from closely knit and insular to scattered and politically disconnected. Despite the ability of some southern indigenous communities to sustain an internal cultural identity, within the larger southern culture all of these groups were subject to a biracial social structure that relegated anyone who was identifiably non-white to the bottom of the social ladder, denying them access to white resources and public spaces. The broader tensions that developed as a result of institutionalized racism in the form of Jim Crow laws provided part of the unique social and political context from which Indian affairs in Alabama and Louisiana evolved, arming tribal leaders with new opportunities and helping shape their motivations and decisions.

Scholars of the American South in the mid-twentieth century have long recognized that "a movement for equal rights for African-Americans worked a revolution in southern race relations."[27] The southern black freedom struggle, or civil rights movement, invited national attention to the region's racial tensions, demanded the desegregation of public spheres, and pressured local, state, and federal governments for policy reforms to challenge directly the system of white supremacy.[28] Over the past twenty years, much research has expanded our understanding of the civil rights struggle by examining the roles of individual activists and adding new dimensions to the study of social justice while emphasizing the complexities within the movement.[29] In addition to scholarly attempts to understand the black freedom struggle, the major television documentary series *Eyes on the Prize: America's Civil Rights Years* proved influential by offering a widely accepted trajectory of events that came to define the movement.[30] Even with the expansion of civil rights history in this new direction, many holes remain in our understanding of how the movement altered race relations beyond the black-white racial paradigm.

Like African Americans, Native Americans nationally issued a similar list of civil rights complaints, including prison sentences that were more severe for Indians than for whites and limited access to state and county welfare assistance programs. Across the Jim Crow South, Indians were often forbidden admission to white schools, and they frequently avoided black schools. As a result, some Native people had no access to public education, while others sent their children to "special" Indian schools. Many of these schools were "small, poorly equipped, poorly taught and poorly attended."[31] Yet at the same time these schools often served as community centers and important symbols of Indian identity.

As a result, southern Indians responded with mixed emotions to the demands and actions of black civil rights activists to integrate public schools. For example, the Lumbee of North Carolina fought vehemently to maintain their separate schools.[32] At the same time, the Poarch Creek of Alabama, the Houma of Louisiana, and the Four Holes community of South Carolina recognized the substandard facilities and educations the schools provided and directed efforts toward school integration.[33] As Helen Rountree points out in her survey of Virginia Indians, "The civil rights era destroyed a major symbol of identity among Virginia Indians through the closing of the tribal schools. Yet the era's positive effects on Indian lives have been greater than any of the Indians dared to hope for at the time. With much expanded opportunities for education and employment, Indian people all across Virginia have moved into higher economic brackets, with consequent improvements in their health, their morale, and their general standard of living."[34] Improving educational opportunities became a central issue for many Indian groups whose struggles developed concurrently with those of their African American neighbors.

The varying strategies employed by black civil rights activists influenced the strategic approaches adopted by Indian activists on a national scale. As the legal and social justice scholars Vine Deloria and Clifford Lytle point out, the National Association for the Advancement of Colored People (NAACP) and the American Civil Liberties Union (ACLU) set a successful precedent by "using the courts as an avenue by which to promote their interests."[35] Indian activists also retreated from localized and private concerns and grew more public and unified through inter-tribal organizations. In 1970, Indians gained their own legal advocacy group when the Native American Rights Fund

(NARF) began operations with the intent of promoting Indian human rights through a variety of means. Also, some of the more militant segments of the larger civil rights movement inspired many Indian activists. According to Alvin Josephy, the National Indian Youth Council constructed the rhetoric of "Red Power" as a reference to the "Black Power" Movement in their efforts to promote the equal rights of Indians.[36] Many southern Indian activists—particularly those residing in urban centers—found guidance in the American Indian Movement (AIM) and other militant pan-Indian organizations and began staging public demonstrations similar to those seen nationally throughout the 1960s and 1970s.[37]

The black civil rights movement helped create a space for other non-white southerners to enter the political arena; however, there were some significant ideological differences between the Indian rights movement and the black civil rights movement. In fact, Kirby Verret, a Houma tribal leader, recalled that Indian activists "generally remained apart from the African American struggle, fearing they would become lost within its larger goals."[38] Although the black civil rights movement was not driven by a monolithic vision or set of tactics, its general goal was civil rights.[39] With the exception of black separatist groups, the Indian rights movement, on the other hand, ultimately sought sovereign rights. While racially defined non-white groups attempted to gain rights and power they had not previously possessed, Indians worked to reclaim a sovereign status that the federal and state governments had usurped. Tribal leaders' first responsibility, Winfrey argues, "was to make the tribe as powerful as possible, then once that was achieved, more programs could be undertaken to help the people in the tribe."[40] Despite an emphasis on tribal sovereignty, however, the principles of individual civil rights were extended to Indian country through the 1968 Indian Civil Rights Act, which required tribal governments to adhere to the basic tenets of the Bill of Rights—including the freedoms of speech, press, and assembly, and the right to a speedy trial.[41]

Ideological differences between the movements were not solely what set them apart. Early on, the black civil rights movement inadvertently served to further marginalize Indians by reinforcing the biracial image of the region. When Americans thought about political unrest and racial oppression in the South, they recalled media images of tensions between African American and white southerners. As a result, Native activists felt the added strain of gaining visibility before any real change could be achieved.[42] In addition, referring to the South as "biracial" denied not only miscegenation but the multiraciality of the region. More specifically, it gave credence to the popular notion that through genocide, assimilation, and Removal the South entered the twentieth century free of any Indians.[43] As a result, southern Indian activists found themselves even further apart from black activists because of their invisibility, which forced them to expend a great deal of energy to bring Indian issues to the attention of legislators and the public.

For southern Indian groups, disassociating themselves from the black civil rights movement was more than just an ideological goal. The anthropologist J. Anthony Paredes, a longtime supporter of the Poarch Creek, notes the efforts of Indian leaders to distinguish between the two movements. He attributes these efforts to fears of racial violence rather than fundamental differences in ideology, however. Paredes says that during the civil rights movement "new fault lines became evident in the racial system of the South [and] many Indians sought even more to distance themselves from any identification with blacks." To demonstrate this threat, Paredes recounts the brutal 1964 slayings of civil rights workers Michael Schwerner, James Chaney, and Andrew Goodman near the Mississippi Choctaw reservation. According to some accounts, reservation residents first encountered the burned-out car and "salvaged what they could from the wreck and moved on without becoming involved in the incident."[44]

The pervasive black-white racial classification of the post-bellum South is also reflected in sparse scholarship on southern Indians, particularly in the Deep South. Scholars often point out that "because the Indians do not fit into the accepted racial categories, they are more difficult to study than the blacks and the whites."[45] The works that do address southeastern Indian groups in the twentieth century are predominantly by anthropologists. In particular, three collections of essays—one compiled and edited in 1979, another in 1992, and a third in 2001—serve as the main body of literature on Indians of the post–civil rights South.[46] In addition to the essay collections, much of the scholarship on Southeast Indians are ethnographies and political histories on a few groups—such as the Lumbee of North Carolina,[47] the Houma of Louisiana,[48] the Seminole of Florida,[49] the Muskogee Creeks of Georgia and Florida,[50] and the MOWA Choctaw of Alabama.[51] General historical surveys of Indian groups in Alabama and Louisiana were also published in the 1980s.[52]

Although, in some instances, the black civil rights movement served to further marginalize the Indian rights movement, in other cases it offered some unintended benefits. The white backlash to the civil rights movement that developed among many southern politicians favorably shaped their responses to Indian activism. The political career of Senator Sam J. Ervin Jr. of North Carolina demonstrates this well. Ervin, a southern Democrat, coauthored the

1956 "Declaration of Constitutional Principles," also known as the "Southern Manifesto," in which he argued that federal civil rights legislation was unconstitutional because it protected the rights of only one segment of the population. More important, he resented the federal government's imposition and thought that states and local governments should handle racial matters. It was not until Ervin's appointment to the Senate Judiciary Subcommittee on Constitutional Rights that he directly impacted the course of civil rights legislation by killing or delaying a series of bills that came to the committee between 1957 and 1968. By the time Ervin became the subcommittee chairman in 1961, his strategy to halt the progress of black civil rights had evolved to include helping Indians as a "more deserving" group. Perhaps because of his deeply rooted racism, as well as the influence of Dr. Helen Maynor Scheirbeck, a member of his staff and a Lumbee Indian, Ervin furthered Indian rights while simultaneously rejecting black rights. Whatever his motivations, Ervin's work, which included an extensive study on the legal and economic status of about two thousand Indian groups, laid the groundwork for the 1968 Indian Civil Rights Act.[53]

Across the South, politicians supported Senator Ervin's position on civil rights as they also saw that southern states had much to gain from tribal-state relationships. According to Dewey Grantham, the civil rights movement created bitter sectional conflict in which "attitudes of northern and southern whites became steadily more polarized."[54] I argue that because of this renewed sectional defiance southern states were primed to take on a role in Indian affairs traditionally occupied by the federal government. Although state Indian affairs commissions had neither the power nor the resources of the BIA, Alabama and Louisiana developed a "state trust" responsibility with groups that had not previously had federal assistance. Through the commissions, the states provided funding, contracts for tribal-resource development, administrative guidance, and an alternative option for Indian groups to become legally recognized as both "minorities" and "tribes."[55]

As southern states reemphasized their historically based tensions with the federal government through their involvement in Indian affairs, they also recognized that a shift in southern politics following World War II had defined the terms of these tensions. Following the Voting Rights Act of 1965, southern politicians identified the need to appeal to non-white voters as the region underwent drastic changes. Moving from traditionalism to entrepreneurial individualism, the Republican Party challenged, if not destroyed, one-party politics in the region.[56] African Americans liberalized the southern Democratic Party by joining it in record numbers and becoming a part of the political machinery in many locales. As a result, conservative whites jumped to the Republican Party or joined the ranks of George Wallace and the American Independent Party. Although Wallace was eventually forced to remove himself from presidential politics because of an assassination attempt, he left a conservative influence on the American political environment that was eventually solidified by the 1980 presidential election of Ronald Reagan.[57]

Over the course of this period of southern Indian history, as the Florida Seminoles laid the foundation for Indian gaming and the North Carolina Cherokee and Mississippi Choctaw set precedents in tribal tourism ventures and economic development, Indian activists from unrecognized groups had to forge their own paths by carving out government-to-government relationships with their respective states. The similarities in the development of these relationships across the South cannot hide the fact, however, that each state has a unique story, one shaped by its politics and the activist strategies employed by the Indian leaders heading the charge.

Louisiana Indian Activism and the Creation of the Office of Indian Affairs

"Sickey Waves No Flags in Indian Rights Move" read the 1972 headline of a news article that carefully painted the picture of a soft-spoken, unassuming man who did not want to create any major political waves in his fight for the social and economic advancement of Louisiana Indians.[58] Sickey argued that "the state for too long has ignored the concerns of its Indian population and has done little to help them towards self-determination and self-sufficiency."[59]

Sickey's timing proved impeccable. He enlisted the aid of lawyer Ruth Loyd Miller and regularly gave interviews to newspaper reporters during a time of flux in Louisiana state politics. The 1971 election of Democratic governor Edwin W. Edwards—a French-speaking Cajun Catholic—was the direct result of a strong black vote, which had become a "decisive influence" following the collapse of Jim Crow. Unlike his predecessor, Governor John J. McKeithen, Edwards had no segregationist past to live down. He was deemed a "race-less governor [who] had been accustomed to treating blacks as significant political players." As a result, he received more than 90 percent of the black vote in the race against Republican David Treen. Edwards positioned himself as a representative of the falling old racial order. By 1972 the state legislature abolished the segregation-supporting State Sovereignty Commission and repealed eleven segregation laws. In addition, voters elected the first African American woman as a state representative.[60] With a receptive governor who promised to make a formal commitment to "minority issues," the time was ripe for someone to bring Louisiana's Indian interests to the governor's attention.

Sickey seized his opportunity and set out to create a new public image of Louisiana Indians as people who wanted to work for their own betterment. He was determined to show the importance of "the contribution the Indian can make to Louisiana society and economics." He advocated for an orderly form of activism in which Louisiana tribes could present a clear and specific set of needs to the state legislature. Local newspapers captured images of Sickey shuffling papers at his desk or attending meetings with state officials in a suit and tie.[61] His professional appearance matched his approach, as he commented to one reporter, "We must do our homework and be able to present a clear case."[62] This businesslike approach to promoting change was calculated, and as Sickey's Coushatta community could attest, extremely effective.

The Coushatta were no strangers to uncertainty. Driven from their homeland in the Tennessee River country of Alabama in the late eighteenth century, they led a nomadic lifestyle over the next two hundred years as they traveled through Georgia, Alabama, Mississippi, Louisiana, and Texas. By 1884 the group had divided and some made their permanent residence in Allen Parish, Louisiana, where the federal government placed 160 acres of land in trust for them in 1898. Then, in the 1930s, the BIA established an elementary school in the community. Following their unofficial termination in 1953, the Coushatta suffered the ill effects of landlessness, and without the sparse federal services that they had received earlier, poverty rose substantially and education levels fell to an all-time low. In 1965, the Coushatta made an initial effort toward redevelopment by establishing a tribal arts and crafts business called the Coushatta Indians of Allen Parish, Inc. By 1973, a more organized group called the Coushatta Alliance began administering tribal affairs under Sickey's leadership. Despite their uncertain history, the group managed to maintain a sense of cohesion and identity as a tribe, which made them a prime group to pave the way for the Indian rights movement in Louisiana.[63]

A graduate of the Academy of Radio and Television in Houston with degrees in broadcasting and public relations, Sickey drew upon his public speaking skills to focus attention on the challenges facing his community and the greater Louisiana Indian population. Most notably, he rallied the support of many non-Indians through the rhetoric of traditionalism. He emphasized the Coushatta's status as the "only full blooded tribe in the state" that had re-

3. Coushatta tribal members at a gathering, circa 1971. (Courtesy of the State Library of Louisiana.)

tained its native language and cultural traditions. This claim played heavily in his success in recruiting aid from non-Indian groups. For example, the Calcasieu Marine Nation's Bank donated money to establish a Coushatta cultural center and craft shop, and the Allen Parish Police Jury assisted the tribe by building a baseball park.[64] Sickey, who spoke both Coushatta and Choctaw, the languages of his parents, captured the interest of reporters by disconnecting his home telephone line. As one article reported, "It was one of the white man's inventions he just didn't need."[65] The articulate Sickey appealed to the sentiments of Ruth Loyd Miller, who was impressed by his mission to preserve his community's "traditional" lifestyle while also promoting economic development.[66] In a handwritten letter to an unspecified state senator, Miller echoed Sickey's plan, explaining: "Our goal of course is to help the Indian tribes realize some economic advantages from their traditional skills and to make progress in other areas too."[67]

For the Coushatta, teaching basket-weaving skills was the starting point in encouraging Indians to become more economically self-sufficient by selling their work to tourists.[68] Sickey sought to temper the fears of politicians who expressed concerns over an excess of "hand outs" to the state's poor population. He explained that Indians were "not asking to be given anything—only to work for our own betterment with the skills the Indians possess."[69] The Coushatta Craft Association was established as "an important source of revenue for homemakers and other underemployed members of the tribe," and, after collaborating with museums around the state to feature an exhibition of Coushatta baskets, many weavers tripled their prices so that they could make a living from their craft.[70] Through the traditional craft of basketry, Sickey married a cultural art form with the market economy and simultaneously generated non-Indian interest and support.

Sickey's decision to enlist an attorney to serve as an advocate and counselor for the Louisiana Indian rights movement reaped lasting benefits. Ruth Loyd Miller personally approached Governor Edwards in 1972 about establishing a state office of Indian affairs. She played upon his image as an advocate of minority rights, convincing him to sign an executive order establishing the Louisiana Office of Indian Affairs under the governor's office. Although this was a historic act, Edwards's commitment was mostly symbolic, as he failed to provide the funding needed for such an operation.

The scarce resources available for the development of an Indian affairs commission did not deter Miller, however. Recalling the passion of Indian reformers from earlier decades, Miller made the "Indian plight" her own as she continued to invest her time in erecting the commission. She wrote to John Cade of the governor's office, "You cannot imagine the distress our Indians undergo."[71] Miller's possessive discourse reflected her efforts to refashion the Louisiana Indian rights movement, placing advocates such as herself at the forefront. She anticipated criticism about her role in forming the commission and fiercely defended her actions. "There is no need for any noses to get out of joint in this program," she wrote to Governor Edwards. "The status of the American Indian and our Louisiana Coushattas has been static for hundreds of years. Anyone who desired to take the initiative has had plenty of time to have done so."[72]

Miller made the creation of the commission something of a philanthropic cause. Without sufficient fiscal support from the state, some creative planning was required if the commission were to become a reality. Miller identified a prime candidate to become the first commissioner: David L. Garrison Jr., a twenty-seven-year-old oil man and Bel family heir from Lake Charles. Miller wrote that he was "refreshingly rich . . . [and] will spare no personal expense or effort to assure the success of the project." Miller's ongoing position

4. Ruth Loyd Miller, 1922–
2005. (Courtesy of the family
of Ruth Loyd Miller.)

as the secretary-treasurer of the Jennings Gas Company, founded in 1960,
placed her in a prime position to interact with some of Louisiana's wealthiest
people and persuade them to contribute to the "Indian cause."[73] She set out
to impress the governor with her influence by mentioning her ability to procure the use of a jet for the commissioner to travel to Washington to lobby
for Indian issues.[74] Then, understanding the governor's political sensibilities,
Miller pushed even further by declaring that Garrison's appointment will "be
a most popular cause" and that it "will be a credit to your administration."[75]
The assertive Miller even took the liberty of drafting a letter for the governor to send to Garrison, which stated: "I am asking you to undertake a great
task for which there is no budget. I will consider it a personal favor to me if
you will accept. . . . I believe you possess all the attribution of personality and
character, intellect and enthusiasm to 'put this package together' in such a
way that it will show Louisiana is concerned with the welfare and happiness
of all its people."[76] Garrison was a strategic choice as the first commissioner
not only because of his wealth but also because of his family's historic connection with the Coushatta. His family's property completely encircled the
Elton Coushatta community. Miller astutely pointed out that "without Bel

family interest and cooperation the Elton settlement would be handicapped in all development programs."[77]

Miller's organizational suggestions did not end with the appointment of Garrison. She made it clear to the governor that the commission should remain small and manageable and answer directly to his office. She suggested that Garrison's appointment be accompanied by the naming of Ernest Sickey as the Indian consultant. Clearly impressed by Sickey, she later recalled that he "was, incidentally, one of the few Indians with some education who could handle the work—could give up his $10,000 a year job in Eunice and work full time for the Indian tribes."[78] After a great deal of effort, the State Department of Economic Opportunity funded Sickey's position, making him the first Indian in Louisiana's history to work in coordinating Indian affairs.[79] Miller wasn't finished making her requests. She pushed the governor further when she asked him to officially appoint herself and Edwin Hunter as legal advisors to the commission. She also asked that Garrison be given full discretion to appoint others to the commission.[80] When Governor Edwards complied, Garrison appointed William T. Dion, J. D. Langley, Archie Vilcan, Fred B. Kniffen, and Mike Duhon to the commission. He was particularly "delighted" that Fred Kniffen, a geography and anthropology professor at Louisiana State University, agreed to serve. It was Garrison's hope that "his expert knowledge and long association with Louisiana Indians will be invaluable to the Commission."[81] The emphasis on academic experts for the first commission was perhaps intended to lend some legitimacy to the newly formed agency, and although it seemed to set up a paternalistic precedent, it proved to have some immediate benefits when the Gulf South Research Institute (GSRI) was commissioned to study the status of Louisiana's Indian groups. The results of this study provided the commissioners with critical information on the demographics and needs of the state's Indian populations, laying the foundation for the direction that the commission would take.[82]

When Garrison accepted his appointment, it became clear that Miller's enthusiasm for Indian affairs was contagious. Garrison immersed himself in his new role as Indian commissioner, spending over $30,000 of his own money and keeping the position for two years (a year longer than originally planned).[83] In a letter to Governor Edwards, Garrison demonstrated the level of his commitment: "As I come to know our Indians better, I see their needs, feelings, and dreams more clearly. Louisiana needs these people. They offer an unique culture, largely unknown, of great social value. Many businesses are attracted to Indian communities because their workers are non-migratory. Tourism is a natural resource for them. Their craft and art is appreciated the

world over. They intensely love this State, in part because they are natu-
rally patriotic and in part because they were here before even my Acadian
ancestors."[84] Garrison's emphasis on business, tourism, and patriotism reinforced elements of Sickey's vision of how Indians should be represented to
the public—as an integral part of the state.

Ruth Loyd Miller also continued to advertise the commission by appealing to the emotions and sensibilities of special interest groups. In her capacity
as legal advisor, Miller wrote to the Louisiana Political Educational Council that the commission needed their monetary help in fulfilling a mandate to
preserve tribal cultures. "Indians are a minority people," Miller wrote, "more
minority than anybody, and dependent on the concern of the majority and
its spirit of fair play."[85] Miller's plea to the council's members attempted to
chip away at the mind-set that African Americans were Louisiana's only minority group. She de-emphasized issues of tribal sovereignty, which set Indian groups apart from any other group, and focused on their economic status as minorities—a concept that was more familiar to Louisianans who had
little exposure to Indian issues.

As the faces of Louisiana's Indian affairs, Ernest Sickey and David Garrison appeared on the front page of the *Jennings Daily News* on March 25,
1975. They each had a specific role in the development of the commission.
While Garrison, aided by Miller, took on the organizational tasks, Sickey remained in the background monitoring the situation closely. Having set the
wheels in motion by enlisting Miller and Garrison to take care of all the governmental and legal issues, Sickey positioned himself as the commission's
liaison to Indian communities. As one newspaper described him, "In many
ways, Ernest Sickey is as unique as his language. He has managed to retain
his tribe's cultural identity and at the same time enter easily into the 'mainstream'—the white man's world."[86]

With Garrison's help, Sickey successfully placed the needs of the Coushatta at the forefront of the commission's initial activities. As Miller later re-
counted, "David [Garrison] was constantly camped on [Congressman] John
Breaux's doorstep—and finally through unwavering persistence secured the
[state] recognition [of the Coushatta]."[87] In May 1972, the legislature passed
a resolution placing the Coushatta in the status of a "state recognized tribe."
The resolution also called upon the BIA "to speedily give formal recognition
to the Coushatta Indian Tribe, to acknowledge that the rights of the Coushatta are no less, if not greater, than that of other Indian tribes in the United
States, and to thereupon take appropriate executive and or congressional action." The Coushatta case set a precedent, implying that state recognition was

a formal proclamation of state support for federal recognition. The success of this case was also the commission's first step in helping define the parameters of tribal-state relationships in Louisiana.

To aid the Coushatta, Garrison also garnered help from some of the legally focused inter-tribal organizations—the Association on American Indian Affairs and the Native American Rights Fund—to draft dossiers and help develop legal rights for the Coushatta. Then, to increase the likelihood that the Coushatta would regain federal recognition, he raised money to purchase ten acres for the tribe so that they could become "attached" to a piece of land large enough to support the community. The land would later be placed into federal trust and then business, industry, and tourism would improve and federal grants for welfare, health, and education would become more readily available.[88] Garrison's tactics, which mirrored Miller's approach in generating supporters, became the primary method used in furthering the commission's objectives. He even noted in an official statement published in the local *Daily News* that the federal government had a "legal and moral obligation to recognize Coushatta Indians and . . . this commission is continuing its effort to aid these people [to] find the justice they deserve."[89]

In June 1973—just fourteen months after Garrison approached the BIA— the Coushatta were successfully re-recognized by the federal government and efforts were under way to create a Coushatta reservation.[90] The short amount of time this process took was seen as a great feat, especially because this was only the second time a tribe had gained recognition solely through administrative channels.[91] Sickey's strategy proved successful, and, as he stated in a public awareness brochure, "we are no longer a group of homeless people, but the Coushatta Tribe of Louisiana. This struggle has made us stronger and our victory will open a way to justice and a better way of life."[92]

Although the Coushatta benefited the most from Garrison's efforts, the larger Louisiana Indian population—over five thousand identified by 1974— was also in line to benefit from the precedent that the Coushatta case set.[93] For example, in March 1974 approximately sixty Choctaws of Jena in LaSalle Parish held a meeting to discuss tribal organization. With the help of Garrison and Sickey, the group established a tribal governing body and selected leaders. The commission pledged to provide the Jena Choctaw with technical assistance in their efforts to acquire land and to obtain resources and assistance from state, federal, and private sources. Also in that same year, the Chitimacha began planning the construction of a craft workshop. Like the Coushatta, the Chitimacha hoped to boost their economic opportunities by selling crafts to tourists traveling to their reservation. The commission then provided technical support to the Houma in their efforts to develop a shrimp co-op run by an "all Indian board."[94] The commission served the needs of Indian groups in a variety of ways as it became a source of both empowerment and contestation over the course of the decade.

While Miller and Garrison enjoyed some success from lobbying state legislators, BIA officers, and the general Louisiana populace on behalf of the Coushatta and other Louisiana Indians, Sickey worked among Louisiana tribes to strengthen the Indian movement. Garrison readily acknowledged the crucial role that Sickey played as the Indian consultant to the commission. He wrote: "Sickey has met with complete success to date. . . . Fluent in two local Indian dialects and well received in all Indian communities, he offers much promise to the Commission in its attempt to serve the Indian communities."[95] Sickey demonstrated the extent of his support when he launched plans to create a state Inter-Tribal Council in 1972 to promote Indian self-determination. The Inter-Tribal Council drew the widespread favor of Louisiana legislators because of its potential to tap into federal resources and, as Governor Edwards described in a formal statement, relieve the fiscal burden on the state.[96]

Through an inter-tribal coalition, even Indian groups that lacked federal status as Indians—and therefore were denied the resources that came with federal acknowledgment—could merge their populations and use their shared economically impoverished status to qualify for financial assistance.

Eventually incorporated in 1974, the Inter-Tribal Council (ITC) of Louisiana served four Indian groups—the Houma Alliance, the Chitimacha, the Jena Band of Choctaws, and the Coushatta—that came together as a "formal unit" to apply for grants. In addition to his responsibilities as the full-time chairman of the Coushatta Tribe and the Indian consultant to the commission, Sickey served as ITC chairman and oversaw efforts to improve education, mental health, public relations, and economic opportunities for the communities represented by the ITC. Sickey believed that LOIA was necessary, but he thought the ITC would promote real change for Indian people in Louisiana. He declared, "It was the first Indian effort of its kind in the state and was built on the fact the cooperation amplifies human capabilities. In other words, what one person can do, two working together can do better."[97] Like so many other Indian leaders across the nation, Sickey saw inter-tribal cooperation as the key to success; however, he focused his efforts within the confines of the state by specifically working to address the needs of Louisiana's Indian population. Employing "sound management concepts while still maintaining an Indian identity" was the essence of his approach.[98]

Louisiana's Indian rights movement proved to be just as complicated and diverse as the black civil rights movement when urban Indian activists began sharing the media spotlight with Ernest Sickey. While Sickey set out to distinguish the Indian rights movement from some of the more overtly radical activities of black civil rights activists who still had the South reeling, other Indian activists began staging their own public demonstrations. The 1969 media coverage of the occupation of Alcatraz Island by Indian activists left a lasting impression on Sarah Peralta, a Louisiana Choctaw-Apache, who with her two daughters traveled to San Francisco to participate in the event. Upon their return, they organized a Baton Rouge–based pan-Indian group called the Indian Angels, Inc., to lend support to AIM, while directing the attention of Louisiana politicians and the public to the needs of the state's urban Indian population.[99] The Indian Angels included Native people from various backgrounds, who formed the American Indian Center to provide counseling and assistance to Indians. They also served as Louisiana's main connection to the national Indian movement by serving as a type of welcoming committee by hosting powwows and luncheons for Indian visitors from other states.[100]

The Indian Angels used public demonstrations and marches to the governor's mansion, donning "war paint" and brandishing American flags, to get the attention of reporters and politicians.[101] In a 1983 interview with a newspaper reporter, Peralta was presented with a photograph taken during the organization's first parade to the state capitol building in 1970. It clearly struck a nerve when she instructed the reporter: "Look at this picture closely. Do you see anything missing? See, there are no people watching, just the Indians marching down the street. The stores closed their doors and locked them when they saw a bunch of Indians parading down Third Street. Any other parade route is lined with spectators, isn't it? I don't have to tell you about it. This picture shows what happened. The people disappeared when the Indians came. Yes, we still felt discrimination even in 1970."[102] Peralta's more radical form of activism clearly made many Louisianans uneasy during a time when racial tensions were already high. She thrived on this uneasiness, however, and organized many more demonstrations following the 1970 incident.

True to her AIM influence, Peralta took the pan-Indian ideology to heart when she regularly spoke on behalf of all Louisiana's Indians.[103] Perhaps the most damaging claim to the efforts made by Sickey, Garrison, and Miller was Peralta's repeated declaration that Louisiana Indians had little faith in the state's ability to take Indian affairs seriously.[104] This claim created a great deal of tension between Peralta and many tribal leaders—particularly those from the Chitimacha, Choctaw, and Coushatta communities who worked to strengthen tribal-state relationships. They felt that the Indian Angels were too radical and did not work for the best interest of all of Louisiana's tribes. While members of the Indian Angels demonstrated on the streets of Baton Rouge wearing war paint and feathers, many tribal leaders from elsewhere in the state were reluctant to associate themselves with the group and their aggressive strategies.[105] As a result, when the Indian Angels invited Garrison to their powwow in 1972, he had to turn down the invitation because, as he explained to the governor, "[T]he commission's approval and recognition of their organization would risk alienation of the majority of Indian tribal leadership with the Indian Affairs Commission. Rather than jeopardize the enthusiastic support of these tribal governments, I have informed Mrs. Peralta, Indian Angels Secretary, that I shall not attend their Pow-Wow, lend support to their activities, nor recommend that you [Governor Edwards] or the Mayor of Baton Rouge lend their pictures or support to the Pow-Wow."[106]

Although Peralta maintained a strong presence in Indian affairs through 1981, tribal leaders made a coordinated effort to prevent her from being appointed by the governor to the commission. A handwritten note on behalf of several tribal leaders to the governor's assistant John Cade, stated, "we do not recommend Ms. Sara[h] Peralta of the American Indian Center because of her militant behavior which we feel is an embarrassment and hindrance to the orderly advancement of the Indian people in our state."[107] Ultimately, the Indian Angels succeeded in promoting their interests to the media, but they failed to create the pan-Indian movement that they had envisioned. In fact, tribal leaders often viewed with suspicion other urban-based organizations across the South that drew from the militant tactics of AIM.[108]

Members of the Indian Angels became the "war-painted" faces of the more radical segment of the Louisiana Indian movement, which was often juxtaposed with Sickey's businesslike image. While Peralta thrived on the media attention she received through public demonstrations, Sickey measured his actions and words and expressed distaste for Peralta's tactics, which he believed served to place Indians on exhibition.[109] The tension between the two starkly different approaches to promoting Louisiana Indian rights often appeared in the local newspapers, creating some confusion among the public.

Despite their different approaches, and perhaps because of them, the combined efforts of Sickey and Peralta ultimately helped carve out a political niche for Louisiana Indians within the state government and public mindset. Sickey's bureaucratic form of activism proved appealing to non-Indian advocates, who—like Ruth Loyd Miller—had little patience for the strategies demonstrated by the Indian Angels. Miller felt that Peralta had no real direction, yet she was "always around screaming about something." From Miller's perspective, Sickey was the real hero in the Louisiana Indian rights movement. She singled him out and credited him with "working so valiantly for the Indians long before the state put forth any effort and assistance on behalf of the Indians." She noted, "Perhaps Sickey's success can best be measured by the fact that everyone now wants to get in the act and *Help the Indians*."[110] Sickey himself recognized his own role in the movement but, as he expressed to a reporter in 1980, "my greatest desire was to come back to my own people."[111]

While Sickey slipped into the governor's office through the backdoor, the Indian Angels were busy pounding on the front door. As the first state Indian affairs commissioner, Garrison recognized the impact that the Indian Angels had on getting people's attention. "Personally," he wrote the governor, "I feel that the Indian Angels were instrumental in gaining early recognition and opening doors for Louisiana Indians."[112] Garrison's perspective was reiterated by the historian Mark Miller, who also credits the Indian Angels with pressuring Governor Edwards into establishing the state Indian affairs commission.[113] Indeed, the two different forms of activism reveal that the Indian rights movement was not monolithic and required multiple strategies in order to get the attention of the legislature and the public at large to promote change.

Alabama Indian Activism and the Creation of the State Commission of Indian Affairs

The development of the Alabama Indian rights movement, along with the establishment of a formal relationship between Indian groups and the state, was the product of Calvin McGhee's vision and foresight that began in the 1940s. McGhee was a charismatic dirt farmer and descendant of the "friendly Creeks" who provided aid to the United States against other Creeks during the Creek War (1813–14). This group was "permitted" to stay behind during the Removal period only to be abandoned and forgotten by the federal government and viewed as "objects of suspicion, prejudice, and discrimination by certain elements of local white society."[114] As a result, these Poarch Creeks occupied a marginal economic and social status until McGhee changed the course of Alabama Indian history by igniting what the *Tampa Times* called "the birth of the modern Creek Nation East of the Mississippi."[115]

Like many other isolated Indian groups throughout the South, the Poarch

Creek community near Atmore, Alabama, suffered the ill effects of racial segregation. Creek children attended a grammar school specifically provided for them; however, they were prohibited from attending the all-white high school and obtaining a higher education. McGhee—more commonly known as "the Chief"—had only a grammar school education himself when he announced plans to provide better opportunities for the next generation of Creek children. In 1947 he "decided he would no longer abide the ramshackle wood-frame schoolhouse provided for the children of his Creek community," so he filed suit against the Escambia County school board for failing to provide an adequate education to Poarch Creeks. McGhee hired attorney Lenore Thompson, a seventy-year-old lawyer who went to work for the Creeks because he felt that "someone in my lineage ought to do something for them." Thompson's great-grandfather had commanded a militia that drove many Creeks off their lands. The attorney admitted that it was partially a sense of ancestral guilt that prompted him to endure the cold shoulder from the Escambia school board members and merchants who resisted the political and social advancement of the local Creek community.[116]

When no immediate results came from local displays of civil rights–inspired activism—such as holding meetings with the school board and linking arms in the street to block the high-school-bound school buses—McGhee felt that he had to intensify his efforts. He went to Montgomery to initiate contact with the state legislature. When he arrived unannounced at Governor "Big Jim" Folsom's office, McGhee was invited to explain his problem as the governor ate a brown bag lunch at his desk. Although the anthropologist J. Anthony Paredes argues that Governor Folsom gave McGhee's grievances a "sympathetic hearing," the outcome of the "lunch meeting" reflected Folsom's unwillingness to make any immediate changes to the existing racial order.[117] In fact, the governor sought to divert the "Indian problem" from the state's jurisdiction by recommending that McGhee seek the services of a lawyer who was willing to take the issue to federal court.[118]

McGhee took the governor's advice and sought additional legal aid by hiring attorney Hugh Rozelle, who helped refashion the Alabama Indian movement in Alabama into one that would see many successes over the next several years. Rozelle's attempt to negotiate with the Escambia County school board revealed the deeply held racist views that Poarch Creeks faced when the high school principal echoed the sentiments of the greater school board by telling Rozelle that "those Indians are not going to come to our school!"[119] Yet by 1950—while Alabama's African American residents continued to be subjected to racial segregation—the Escambia County school board reluctantly agreed to replace the old Indian grammar school with a new county school and begin busing Creek children to local white high schools.[120] Paredes argues that this act reflected Alabama's racial hierarchy, which placed Indians below whites but above African Americans. From the perspective of many Poarch Creeks, however, they suffered just as much as if not more than African Americans from white discrimination. It was this distinction that made Poarch Creeks feel disconnected from the black activists.[121]

McGhee's lawsuit—which had a specific and localized focus—had a far-reaching impact as Alabama Creek people rallied around the central issue of educational advancement. Newspapers reported that during this struggle, "the Creeks in Alabama began to feel like a tribe again, and [McGhee's] movement spread to Florida and Georgia and encouraged descendants of other eastern tribes to rise up and be recognized again."[122] Then in 1950, when McGhee again positioned himself for another battle—this time to seek payment for millions of acres taken from Creeks during Removal—the Poarch Creek held a mass meeting and officially reorganized as a tribe, naming Calvin McGhee as their leader.[123] The group initially called themselves the Perdido Band of Friendly Creek Indians of Alabama and Northwest Florida; however, the name was later changed to the Creek Nation East of the Mississippi and then a second time to the Poarch Band of Creek Indians. Because of the official organization of the group and the strong relationships forged with the Creek communities of Georgia and Florida, McGhee created a political force that caught the attention of southern politicians, who became increasingly aware of their Indian constituency. He even oversaw political rallies for candidates at the local and state levels, making his endorsement valuable to many political campaigns.[124]

McGhee's leadership served to reestablish the Poarch Creeks after more than a century of neglect. He believed that his community's power lay in their degree of visibility, so he made many personal and financial sacrifices to connect the Poarch Creek with the national inter-tribal movement. In 1961 he attended the American Indian Chicago Conference and was among the delegates who delivered a copy of the *Declaration of Indian Purpose* to President Kennedy the following year. According to McGhee's daughter-in-law, Olivette McGhee, Kennedy was intrigued by McGhee and even commented that "he never heard of a blue-eyed Indian."[125]

As figure 5 demonstrates, McGhee believed that he had to wear Plains Indian regalia during public appearances in order to be taken seriously. He wanted to leave a lasting imprint in the minds of legislators and the larger public and show them that Alabama was not devoid of an Indian population.

5. Calvin McGhee and President John F. Kennedy, 1962. (Courtesy of the Alabama Department of Archives and History.)

When asked about his impressions of McGhee, former Alabama congressman Jack Edwards recalled, "First, he was proud of his heritage; there was no question about that, and secondly, I believe he understood what he was about so well. He used that headdress for meetings with me and other congressmen over the years to impress upon them the seriousness of what he was about. It was done in a very formal way—not in jest at all—and he got our attention almost single-handedly. I think wearing that headdress was an integral part of his effort."[126] Although McGhee's strategy was not fully accepted or understood by everyone, he was one of many Indian leaders across the South who felt that he had to portray his Indianness publicly to ensure "racial and political legitimacy."[127] His adoption of Plains Indian cultural symbols also linked him to the national Indian movement, which—as seen with the NCAI—

drew upon the same symbols to create a unified "Indian" image in their public relations campaigns.[128]

Following McGhee's death in 1970, his son Houston McGhee carried on his legacy by envisioning the Creek communities of Alabama, Georgia, and Florida as part of "one family." Refusing to allow state boundaries to separate the groups, he established an official alliance by convening a meeting in 1973 to create the Tri-State Creek Council. Poarch was deemed the eastern Creek capital with Houston McGhee as the Principal Chief of the Alabama Creeks, Neal McCormick the Principal Chief of the Georgia Creeks, and Wesley Thomley the Principal Chief of the Florida Creeks.[129] The hope was that a "strength in numbers" approach would help spur social and economic development within all three communities.

In addition to forming the Tri-State Council and leading the eighteen-member Poarch Creek Council that represented approximately 1,300 people, Houston McGhee picked up where his father had left off in forging relationships with local and state governments. With the eventual closing of the Creek Indian School in 1970 because of federal pressures toward integration, Poarch Creek community members felt that they had lost an important marker of their identity. As a result, they set out to raise funds from the state and other entities to acquire the school land for a cultural center and recreational complex. The complex would create jobs and serve as a tourist attraction. Under Houston McGhee's leadership, the Creek Nation East of the Mississippi tempted local politicians and businessmen with this potential revenue-generating venture, which would benefit the surrounding non-Indian community. Some businessmen even joked about the possibility of creating an "Indian Disneyland." Although they were not able to raise all of the funds necessary to purchase the land initially, the tribe did establish a new local tradition. In 1971, the first Thanksgiving Homecoming Powwow drew non-Indian spectators from miles around, who began to redefine the area's identity to include the once long-ignored Indian population.[130]

Compared to his father, Houston McGhee was described as an "almost non-existent leader" because he did not display his "Indianness" publicly and generally avoided the news media.[131] During the elder McGhee's lifetime, the isolation of and discrimination against the Poarch community discouraged tribal members from having contact with non-Indians; however, by the time Houston became the tribal leader this was no longer the case. Under Houston's leadership, the tribe managed to build relationships with the local mayor, the chairman of the Escambia County Commissioners, and the chairman of the local Community Action Corporation.[132]

As occurred in Louisiana, the shifting politics of race in Alabama following the black civil rights movement provided an opportunity for Indians to claim a formal political space within the state government. One of the most visible representatives of these shifting racial ideologies was Alabama's governor, George C. Wallace, who in his 1963 inaugural speech said, "I draw the line in the dust and toss the gauntlet before the feet of tyranny. And I say, Segregation now! Segregation tomorrow! Segregation forever!"[133] Yet by his third term, which began in 1975, Wallace was a different man; his inaugural featured a black choir, and he promised to "represent all our citizens . . . black or white."[134] The man Martin Luther King Jr. once deemed "the most dangerous racist in America" had a change in perspective following a 1972 assassination attempt that left him a paraplegic.[135] Soon after, Wallace represented himself as a sorrowful man who sought forgiveness from those he had wronged in an attempt to "get right with [his] maker."[136]

Wallace's public transformation gave the impression that he cared about Indian issues, and this perception was reflected in the mail he received from Alabama's Indian residents, who put pressure on him to involve the state in Indian affairs. He received letters that complained, "My ancestors from the very beginning have been mistreated and rejected. . . . Something needs to be done . . . I pray that you will look into the Indian problems and try to get something done for my people."[137] Not all of the letters were so general in their complaints; others had more specific requests. Wallace's archive reveals a series of hand-scrawled letters from elderly Indians, such as one sent in 1978 by Ada M. Godwin of McKenzie who wrote: "My daddy was a full Blooded Indian. He was borned 1850. You know when the white man took over America they drove the Indians back and took over. The government has to take care of us Indians. I would like for you [to] get my shair for me. I want my pay in a lump. I want to hear from you right away."[138] These letters reflect a significant shift in the attitudes of many Alabama Indians who began making direct contact with the governor in the hopes of having their needs addressed in a systematic way. The letters also demonstrate a belief in the governor's authority over Indian affairs, an authority that made the emergence of a tribal-state relationship seem imminent.

The increased visibility of Alabama Indians also incited racial commentary. Wallace received letters revealing how the resentment against African Americans resulted in a push to emphasize Indians as the favored minority of the South. For example, a 1971 letter from "a concerned taxpayer" expressed resentment that public funds were preserving African American history by building museums. Hugh Shadduck argued, "If any minority group should have recognition and aid, it is the American Indians, who are victims of the most shameful treatment on the part of the Federal Government. . . . The American Indians have contributed greatly to our civilization and to the formation of the character of the white American pioneer. Compared to them, the contributions of the Negro are negligible. Indeed, the history of the great majority of American Negroes can be summarized in three words, 'they were slaves.'"[139] By privileging the contributions and needs of Indians above those of African Americans, Shadduck reinforced the racial hierarchy of earlier decades. His letter also demonstrates the pressures on Wallace, who could never quite escape his racist reputation.

Wallace launched the state into the domain of Indian affairs for numerous and complex reasons. The increased visibility of the state's Indian population coupled with the pressure generated by the letters that flooded into the governor's office demanded attention. Wallace, who once "played Indian" in front of a crowd of his campaign supporters by donning a feathered bonnet and performing a "war dance" around a ballroom, saw the opportunity to redefine the state's blemished image by emphasizing the romantic notion of "Alabama's indigenous identity."[140] Also, it is possible that despite Wallace's newfound public attitude toward race, the civil rights movement served to renew the sectional defiance of southern states. Lingering hostilities made taking over a position traditionally occupied by the federal government—such as the authority over Indian affairs—an appealing opportunity for many southern politicians such as Wallace, who could not pass up a chance to assert the rights of their respective states.

Whatever his reasons, Wallace responded favorably to Houston McGhee's 1974 letter asking for assistance in obtaining the surrounding property that the Poarch Creek Indian School in Escambia County sat on. When the state transferred the school and land title to the Escambia County school board, McGhee's goal was to have the school and land officially restored to the state on behalf of the tribe.[141] The hope was that the land would be turned into federal Indian trust land and that ultimately the Poarch Creek would become federally recognized.[142]

Houston McGhee demonstrated his political acumen when he reassured Wallace that the Poarch Creeks supported him. "We have come to you," McGhee wrote, "because of the special confidence which we have always placed in your friendship and goodwill." He then pointed out all of the benefits the state would reap if Wallace were to support them in their efforts to obtain land and federal recognition: "It could ultimately inject additional money into the State's economy [and] equalize the status of Alabama and Escambia County with that of other States and counties with Indian populations. As federal Indian economic development and loan funding became available, it would enhance the feasibility of an Indian Tourist and Cultural Center for Escambia County, which could provide substantial new jobs and income to this part of the State. The development of our Creek Indian Community will enhance and enrich the cultural heritage of Alabama for all her citizens."[143] Similar to the tactic Sickey used in relating to Governor Edwards in Louisiana, McGhee addressed Governor Wallace's economic concerns. Wallace frequently spoke out against the greed of the rich and the demands of the "undeserving poor" whom he thought abused the nation's welfare system.[144] McGhee played upon these prejudices by mentioning how the acquisition of the land would enable the Poarch Creek to help themselves economically and how it could potentially serve the needs of the state.

It worked. To show his support, Wallace sent a letter to the Escambia County Board of Education, asking that they turn the Creek school land back over to the state. He stated, "I believe that it would be good for both Escambia County and the State of Alabama for the Federal Government to recognize the Creeks."[145] The governor's assistant legal advisor, Curtis Reding, expanded on the state's position in a letter to Dr. Ted Mars, the Chief White House Advisor on Indian Affairs. Reding pointed out that the acceptance of the Poarch Creek land into federal trust was "a fitting way to preserve the native American heritage of our State."[146] By September 1975 the board of education had complied with Wallace's request, and the land was turned over to the state on behalf of the Poarch Creek.[147] In his negotiations with the federal government, Wallace was intent on preserving the state's interests, and he clarified his position by asking not only that the federal government place the property into trust for the Poarch Creek but that the agreement include a provision to reserve mineral rights for the state.[148]

The activism of Calvin and Houston McGhee influenced the emergence of another strong Creek group. The Star Clan of Muscogee Creeks—also known as the Troy Creeks—demanded state attention about the same time that the Poarch Creek became less visible and more insular in their efforts toward community development. While Houston McGhee was busy planning for the development of a tribal complex on the grounds of the old Indian school, the Star Clan of neighboring Pike County forged a relationship with Alabama state senator Wendell Mitchell, who sponsored a bill in 1976 creating the Alabama Creek Indian Council.[149] The council was the earliest attempt to establish an Indian affairs commission that would serve as a liaison between an Indian community and the state government. The exclusion of the Poarch Creek from this council created tension between the two Creek communities that erupted in the public arena over the next couple of years.

It was not until the enthusiastic Eddie Leon Tullis became tribal chairman in 1977 that the Poarch Creek once again became publicly visible—but this time as a separate, distinct group and not as part of the Tri-State Creek Council.[150] Unlike Calvin and Houston McGhee, who envisioned one large Creek family, Tullis took a more isolationist approach as the new Poarch Creek leader. He believed that the Poarch Creek would be given more legitimacy as a tribal government if they formed a distinct community. Former members of the Tri-State Council saw Tullis's decision as a betrayal, one that "brought an end to political solidarity" with the Georgia and Florida Creek communities.[151] Yet, despite the hard feelings that Tullis created, he initiated the beginning of a more clear-cut relationship between the state of Alabama and the Poarch Creek community. The Tri-State Council complicated the potential for effective tribal-state relationships to be developed because of the difficulty in navigating through all of the competing states' interests involved in such a dynamic relationship.

Even though Tullis did not share the vision of the Tri-State Council, his leadership principles—like those of his predecessors—echoed the inter-tribal cooperation doctrine of the NCAI and AICC. Like Calvin McGhee, Tullis used national and regional Indian organizations as a way to legitimate his local efforts. Soon after becoming tribal chairman, Tullis was elected president of CENA, and in 1979 he was elected vice president of the Southeastern Region of the NCAI.[152] Through his involvement in national inter-tribal organizations, Tullis became an influential force in formulating the criteria that Indian groups had to meet to become federally recognized—a position that would ultimately benefit the Poarch Creek.[153]

Tullis also challenged the Alabama Creek Indian Council. At a public hearing in March 1977, Tullis spoke on behalf of the Poarch Creek in an event that one reporter deemed "verbal warfare" between the Poarch Creeks and the Star Clan of Muscogee Creeks.[154] Tullis argued that a state Indian affairs commission should represent all Indians in the state and that "[t]he 1976 Act did not go far enough to set up the mechanics for getting federal funds and applied only to the [Star Clan] Creeks. We think we will find small isolated groups of Choctaws and Cherokees [in the state]."[155] The Pike County superintendent of education spoke in favor of maintaining the Creek Indian Council, claiming that a new commission would cost the state about $20,000 a year, while the council "works free with no funds provided."[156] Although Tullis emphasized representation, the majority of the debate focused on the potential economic benefits of the commission as the procurer of federal funds that would relieve the state's financial burden. Supporters of the existing council argued that the Star Clan of Muscogee Creeks were already experienced in obtaining federal grants; they had been receiving Indian education money since 1972. Similarly, advocates for Tullis's proposed commission held that the Poarch Creek were also skilled at acquiring grants, but what set them apart was their historically strong leadership. In the end, the debate deadlocked; upon hearing the arguments, the Senate Finance Committee temporarily suspended any action until they could further explore the possibilities.[157]

By May 3, 1978, Tullis's efforts to create an agency that would represent the interests of Alabama's Indian population were realized when the Southwest Alabama Indian Affairs Commission replaced the Creek Indian Council through the passage of the Mims Act (No. 677). In an ironic twist, the Poarch Creeks once again benefited from the actions of someone who had a past link to them. Senator Maston Mims, whose ancestors had been killed by Upper Creeks during the so-called Fort Mims massacre at the beginning of the Creek War, sponsored the bill and overlooked the Creek Indian Council when he stated that the new commission was an attempt to reconcile history. As he stated to one reporter, "I believe it's time we recognized native Americans."[158]

The new commission, which was intended to be more representative of the Indians throughout the state, actually targeted the Poarch Creek as the main representative of the entire Alabama Indian population. Instead of creating a new representative commission, the Mims Act simply established the council of the Creek Nation East of the Mississippi as the actual state commission itself.[159] Much to its disappointment, the Star Clan of Muscogee Creeks, as well as the various groups of Choctaws and Cherokees Tullis had mentioned in the public hearing, were excluded from the new commission.

Not unlike the benefits that the Coushatta saw from the establishment of the Louisiana commission, the Poarch Creek Council's direct access to the state government proved beneficial. By 1979, the Creek Nation East of the Mississippi was receiving funding or services from the Department of Labor (which sponsored an Indian Comprehensive Education and Training Act [CETA] program), the Office of Human Development, the Community Services Administration (which provided a statewide Food & Nutrition Program, Emergency Energy Assistance Program, and a Headstart Program), State Adult Basic Education funds for teachers, the South Alabama Regional Planning Commission, and the Alabama Committee for the

Humanities.[160] In addition, with the state's official support, the Poarch Creek petitioned the federal government for recognition. Calvin McGhee's visibility campaign years earlier bore fruit when the community inadvertently gained an ally in Dr. Ted Mars, who was from Alabama. A letter from Barry Margolin, an Indian legal aid, to Curtis Reding indicated that Dr. Mars "was familiar with the Creek community around Atmore and expressed a personal interest in helping to move their petition through the Interior Department."[161] The support of George Wallace and Dr. Mars, as well as the capable leadership of Tullis, led the Poarch Creek to become the fourth southeastern Indian nation—and the only Alabama group—to become federally recognized on August 11, 1984.[162]

Although the Poarch Creek reaped most of the benefits from this new relationship with the state, other tribal communities were also impacted by the early work of the commission, which began applying for grants. After only one year, the Poarch Creek–run commission provided services to more than four hundred families in the Choctaw community in Mobile and Washington counties, and helped forty-two people find jobs and support services. The commission even maintained a full-time outreach office in Washington County to be closer to the Choctaw.[163] By 1979, other outreach efforts were under way, but the penniless commission drew little attention until Governor Fob James first provided discretionary funds through CETA in 1980.[164] This money allowed the commission to set up an office in Montgomery for a more centralized location as the representative of Alabama's Indian population, as well as to gain easier access to state legislators.

The establishment of the Southwest Alabama Indian Affairs Commission and the strong leadership of the Poarch Creek resonated throughout the state as other Indian groups became more visible in their efforts to (re)organize politically. For example, the United Cherokee Tribe organized officially in 1978. It was followed by the MOWA Choctaw, who incorporated in 1979, the Jackson County Cherokees in 1981, and the Cherokees of Southeast Alabama in 1982. Despite Tullis's argument years before for the abolishment of the Alabama Creek Indian Council in favor of a more representative state commission, other tribal groups across the state found that the Poarch Creek's interests dominated state Indian affairs, an issue of contention for years to come.

As in Louisiana, the southern Indian movement in Alabama resulted in a formalized relationship with the state government. This was not a relationship that developed overnight, however. It took the efforts and talents of three Poarch Creek leaders to gain visibility and acceptance as a tribal nation. As the black civil rights movement took shape, the Poarch Creek emerged from obscurity as Calvin McGhee fought for better educational opportunities for his people. Like Sickey, McGhee sought the aid of attorneys, but he placed himself in the forefront of the movement by meeting face-to-face with the governor and interacting with national pan-Indian organizations. While the elder McGhee did not live to see the establishment of a formal state Indian affairs commission, by uniting eastern Creek groups and demanding the attention of politicians and the larger public, his form of activism laid the groundwork for change.

Houston McGhee—although a more reticent leader—inherited his father's vision of a united Creek nation. He also brought Alabama Indians a step closer to establishing a formal partnership with the state government by initiating a productive relationship with Governor Wallace. The early public exposure of the Poarch Creek through the skillful use of the media and political maneuvering laid the foundation for Tullis's aggressive leadership and served as a blueprint for other unrecognized southern Indian groups. After helping establish the Southwest Alabama Indian Affairs Commission, Tullis guided the Poarch Creek through federal recognition and helped define the tribe more as a tribal nation and less as an underrepresented fringe group hidden away in the Deep South.

Forging New Ground: Developing Tribal-State Relationships

Why did southern states recognize Indian groups when the federal government would not? This question is even more intriguing given the contentious tribal-state relationships that existed in the region during the Removal period of the nineteenth century.[165] Without the power struggles centering on issues of jurisdiction, taxation, and competition over natural resources that often defined tribes' relationships with their state governments within a federalist system, non–federally recognized southern Indian groups forged a different type of relationship—a mutually beneficial one.[166] Southern state legislators were motivated to enhance connections with Indians for a multitude of reasons. For one, they were driven by a public relations strategy following the Voting Rights Act of 1965, which meant they had to appeal to non-white voters. Legislators also supported Indians in waging a racialized critique of African Americans in the wake of the civil rights movement, refashioning the southern identity by emphasizing its indigenous roots, and asserting states' rights by assuming federal responsibilities. In certain cases, legislators and Indian advocates supported the movement out of an honest sense of ancestral guilt over how Native people were treated in the South.

While state Indian commissions provided a forum for these mutually bene-ficial relationships to evolve, these agencies did not always serve this purpose. In fact, state Indian affairs commissions came rather late to the South com-pared to those in other states. In 1949 North Dakota was the first state to es-tablish such a commission in anticipation of Indian termination. The state wanted to "prepare itself for assuming Indian services costs when the federal government terminated the state's tribes." Throughout the 1950s and 1960s, western and northern plains states followed North Dakota and organized In-dian commissions to answer the federal drive to rid itself of its trust responsi-bility. With the decline of the termination policy, state commissions began to expand their roles as liaisons between various agencies and Indian groups and in many cases promoted cultural and religious maintenance and tribal eco-nomic self-sufficiency.[167] The distinct difference between southern commis-sions and those that had been established in other states, however, was that from the beginning southern states had created commissions so tribal com-munities could leverage resources previously unavailable to them.

In southern states, where non–federally recognized Indian groups were the majority, a relationship with state governments offered tribes a unique posi-tion from which to negotiate power. Without a formalized relationship with the federal government, determined Indian activists such as Sickey, Peralta, the McGhees, and Tullis invited Louisiana and Alabama into the federal-ized domain of Indian affairs. Because states traditionally presented tribes with the greatest threat to their sovereignty and resources, a great deal of un-easiness arose among many leaders of federally acknowledged tribal nations, who were adamantly against state involvement in Indian affairs.[168] Wilma Mankiller, the Principal Chief of the Oklahoma Cherokee Nation, went so far as to send Alabama governor Guy Hunt a letter arguing: "While many state governments in the history of our country have had incidental dealings with various Indian tribes over the years it is a recognized canon of American Indian law that it is the federal government that is vested with the sole au-thority to deal with and regulate American Indian tribes on a government to government basis."[169] The numerous unrecognized groups in the Southeast would not have argued with Mankiller's sentiment; after all, the (re)establish-ment of a government-to-government relationship with the federal govern-ment was most often cited as a tribe's ultimate goal. In the cases of the Cou-shatta and Poarch Creek, however, tribal-state relations proved to be valuable in promoting change while on their journeys toward receiving acknowledg-ment from the federal government. Although these relationships varied from state to state, they allowed tribal groups to forge strong networks with local, state, and national agencies while advocating for cultural preservation and re-vitalization, economic development, and the implementation of community services.

Establishing the parameters of a tribal-state relationship was a difficult task, and many southern Indian leaders had to look outside their own states for guidance. While the Southwest Alabama Indian Affairs Commission looked to the North Carolina Indian Affairs Commission for inspiration,[170] the Louisiana Office of Indian Affairs looked to inter-tribal councils found throughout the South as models on which to build.[171] Most southern states also became involved in the national Governors' Interstate Indian Council, which held annual conferences to educate state legislators and tribal leaders about creating strong tribal-state relationships.[172]

The impact of the Governors' Interstate Indian Council, specifically on the Alabama commission, was undeniable. Viola Peterson, a Miami Indian from Michigan and council chairperson, contributed her insights to a 1981 Alabama Indian affairs newsletter. She encouraged Indians to become more politically active, for "the day of the political sympathetic ear has gone for Indian people." Peterson advocated for a more proactive approach by building relationships with legislators, whom she argued should be informed of the needs of Indian people. The editor of the commission's newsletter reinforced Peterson's comments, providing an extensive list of names and addresses of Alabama legislators to encourage people to write letters.[173]

Negotiating new relationships with state governments often proved challenging to Indian affairs commissions and inter-tribal councils; this had to determine the degree to which they involved themselves in state politics. The question of endorsing political candidates became a particular point of contention in Louisiana when Ernest Sickey, in his capacity as chairman of the Inter-Tribal Council of Louisiana, endorsed a candidate for governor in 1979.[174] His endorsement caused concern among the tribal council of the United Houma Nation, which sent Sickey a letter stating that the Houma Tribal Council decided "there will be no public endorsement of any political candidates."[175] This issue revealed the tension generated surrounding the competing visions of Indian leaders, each with a different idea about the level of involvement to have in state politics.

The relationships forged between states and tribal groups throughout the South in the 1970s also challenged legislators to define clearly the states' roles in Indian affairs. Entering the Indian affairs domain provided southern states with the opportunity to assert their own sovereignty—especially in the aftermath of the black civil rights movement—by placing state governments in a position traditionally occupied by the federal government. Although the relationships between states and tribes were ultimately determined by the federal status of a tribal group, southern states began to push the boundaries of their authority in Indian affairs by extending state recognition to Indian groups. Many tribal communities felt that state recognition validated unrecognized groups and provided their members with the psychological benefits of having their Indian identities recognized. Although state recognition did not have the authority of federal recognition, Indian groups saw it as the first step in what could evolve into a formal relationship with the federal government.

With southern state governments defining their new role in Indian affairs, tribal leaders were able to experiment and further test the extent of state authority. For example, prior to federal recognition, the Tunica-Biloxi explored the possibility of establishing a state reservation.[176] Also, the United Houma Nation persuaded state legislators to support their petition for federal recognition.[177] In fact, supporting federal petitions became commonplace in Louisiana when Governor Edwin Edwards insisted in a letter to Congressman David Treen that "all Native American Tribes who are currently not federally recognized be immediately granted federal recognition."[178]

State support of tribal self-determination in Louisiana and Alabama was conditional. As long as tribal groups did not pose a threat to state interests, they could maintain the verbal backing of legislators. Across the nation, tribal-state relationships were often defined by the gaming issue, which fueled a tradition of hostility between states like Texas and the Indian communities living within the state.[179] Fear of the complications brought on by Indian gaming also impacted deep southern states; however, in the 1970s, concern over potential Indian land claims took center stage in defining tribal-state relationships. For example, when the Chitimacha tribe filed suit in 1977 to gain eight thousand acres of swampland, it created a panic among Louisiana legislators and private landholders. The tribal attorneys publicly declared: "It's not in our clients' interest to cause any distress for the small property owners. . . . Our clients are not merciless landgrabbers."[180] Despite this reassurance, Sickey observed that "the recent land claims may have thrown a scare into the attorney general's office."[181] This scare led state legislators to take more conservative positions on Indian affairs.

Alabama's conditional support of its Indian populations can also be observed in the state's creation of American Indian Heritage Day—on a day that was already a state holiday. As Senator Jimmy Holley, a co-sponsor of the holiday bill, reasoned, "it won't cost the state government any additional money."[182] This was not the first time that Alabama extended such a shallow gesture in honoring the memory of the state's non-white residents. In 1984, the legislature passed a long-overdue bill recognizing the birthday of civil rights leader Martin Luther King Jr. on the third Monday in January, a day that was already a state holiday reserved to celebrate the birthday of Confederate general Robert E. Lee.

Although great strides were made in the development of state Indian affairs commissions in Alabama and Louisiana, the willingness of both states to uphold their commitments came into question when they failed to provide the funding necessary to sustain the commissions. Louisiana governor Edwin Edwards openly took credit for creating the commission, yet he was unwilling to make a monetary commitment to maintaining it.[183] Arguably, however, Ruth Loyd Miller misled him to believe that the commission would be self-sustaining with her repeated comments on Garrison's great personal wealth and his ability to fund the operation of the commission.[184] Garrison, on the other hand, had a different perspective on the budgetary issue. In a letter to Governor Edwards in March 1973, Garrison responded in distress upon hearing that there was no state funding available for the commission. He complained that he had already spent $4,000 of his own money on travel expenses alone in order to do his job—and this did not include the thousands of dollars of personal funds he had spent on office-related expenses necessary for running the commission. Garrison was initially identified by Miller and appointed by the governor with the assumption that he would spare no expense in operating the commission through his own means and without financially burdening the state budget. But after two years enough was enough. Garrison commented on the extensive work that he and Ernest Sickey had put into the commission: "As this now occupies approximately 80 hours a week of our time, we need to know if we shall be paid to continue your Indian Affairs work. Expenses and a small staff are necessary, too, as outlined in our budget. We are aware that funds are tight because you have not given us any."[185] Garrison then challenged Governor Edwards "[to] consider the commitment you wish Louisiana to make to Indians. . . . We have begun many programs and done much good already. The Indians are enthusiastic and cooperative. I feel we can have tremendous impact on this minority group with little cost to the State. A special effort here should pay great rewards. The Alabama-Coushatta Reservation in Texas showed a profit of $50,000 for 1971 and 1972. Let us try that here."[186] Edwards evidently heard Garrison's concerns, as Garrison told Miller in a handwritten note just a few months later that "we shall have a budget after all."[187] Although the Louisiana commission was eventually given an operating budget, the state still failed to make a significant monetary commitment and over the next decade functioned on very little money.[188]

The creation of the Southwest Alabama Indian Affairs Commission also proved to be more of a symbolic gesture than an explicit commitment. After the 1978 passage of the Mims Act, the commission still lacked funding, and it became inactive. More than two years passed before Governor Fob James realized the importance of the commission and began funding it in 1981 with the governor's special grant from CETA. Yet funding continued to be unstable and commissioners had to deal with repeated budgetary cuts that forced them to be creative in order to keep the commission on its feet. Commission members made cooperative agreements with various state agencies and found alternative funding, such as the VISTA volunteer program, the CETA Summer Youth Employment Program, and private sources.[189]

With Ronald Reagan's election in 1980, the dynamics between states and tribes would undergo a shift and Republican candidates would win the governorships of both Louisiana and Alabama in 1980 and 1987, respectively.[190] Instead of administering grants through federal agencies, plans were under way to create a new system that issued block grants to states, which then assumed the discretion of their dispersal. This experience was both a stressful and empowering one for Louisiana and Alabama Indian groups, whose relationships with state governments became even more important. Many southern Indian leaders had doubts about this new policy and the newfound financial power that it gave the states. Even Ernest Sickey, with his many years of experience in working with the state of Louisiana, expressed grave concerns over state block grants. In a 1980 meeting he made these concerns clear when he questioned the sincerity of the governor. "We just don't know where he stands," Sickey complained. "Where does that leave Louisiana Indians in terms of being recipients of this block grant money? Do we need to create legislation establishing Indian tribes as being declared as a 51st state in Louisiana? Or do we want to stay left out as we've been for the past 200 years?"[191] Without the incentive to work side by side with tribes to tap into federal resources, states, Indian leaders feared, would ignore their needs when distributing funds.

Tribal leaders in Alabama also faced a new set of challenges as the terms of funding distribution shifted. Perhaps the most outspoken opponent of state block grants was Eddie Tullis, who found that the grants restricted tribal sovereignty by placing the state government in a more powerful position than Indian groups. He advocated for tribes to receive block grants directly so that they were not at the state's mercy.[192]

Despite these concerns, Indian leaders did not let these problems deter them from creating a better life for their people. Sickey said it best when he declared, "we as Indians have been sitting around here for two hundred years. Today we made up our minds that we want to do something; that we _are_ going to do something!"[193]

In Sum

The events leading up to the development of Indian affairs commissions in Alabama and Louisiana provide a glimpse into the strategies that Indian leaders employed throughout the 1970s in their efforts to gain a stronger political voice and greater access to resources. The marginal status of unrecognized southern groups required activists like Ernest Sickey and Calvin McGhee to fashion public personae that would generate interest in their concerns. While Sickey emphasized the traditionalism of the Coushatta, McGhee drew upon the influence of pan-Indian organizations by appropriating Plains Indian symbols. Both approaches successfully created enthusiasm among lawyers, legislators, businessmen, and concerned taxpayers. Ruth Loyd Miller, one of the most ardent Indian allies in this story, demonstrated her passion in a 1972 letter to the governor, in which she closes, "With Hopes Sincerely Jubilant [_sic_] That We Are On the Morn of a New Day For Our Indian People."[194]

Southern Indian activists also found strength through their involvement in regional and national inter-tribal organizations. While McGhee and Tullis were linked to more conservative groups such as the NCAI, Peralta and the Indian Angels demonstrated the diversity within the southern Indian movement by supporting the efforts of AIM. Southern Indian groups found that they received many lasting benefits from the exposure they generated. And, just as the national Indian rights movement resulted in more federal Indian legislation, localized southern Indian activism jump-started state Indian legislation.[195]

In the early years, Indian leaders such as Sickey and McGhee must have felt alone in their efforts. It didn't take long, however, to generate outside support for Indian issues within their states. For example, Vine Deloria Jr., the Standing Rock Sioux scholar and activist, displayed his support of Louisiana's Tunica-Biloxi in their drive for federal recognition by appearing in a 1973 documentary discussing their case. Deloria and W. J. Strickland, chairman of the Coalition of Eastern Native Americans, talked with the Tunica-Biloxi tribal council about how best to proceed in its efforts toward federal recognition.[196] Deloria later went on to write a powerful foreword to a book on Alabama's non–federally recognized MOWA Choctaw community. He told readers, "if you like this book, and there is certainly enough food for deep thought here, why not write your senators and congressmen and ask them to give the MOWA Choctaws a hand and let's get this recognition problem solved once and for all."[197]

Indian activists in Louisiana and Alabama also displayed savvy decision-making by framing their own interests in a manner that was politically appealing to lawmakers. In particular, they used economic concerns to promote tribal self-determination, as well as to offer a potential economic boost to the surrounding non-Indian communities. Sickey—and, to a lesser extent, Tullis—employed this approach, creating alliances with relevant people and agencies within the state government.

The development of the formal tribal-state relationships that emerged out of the shifting politics of race, changes in federal Indian policy, and increased southern Indian activism provided both states and Indian groups the opportunity to define the parameters of a unique partnership. As the evidence demonstrates, Indian leaders and advocates initially invested more in the development and maintenance of the Indian affairs commissions than did the state governments. Governors Edwards and Wallace gave their verbal and symbolic support—historic in its own right—but failed to commit the necessary funding. The recognition and support of Indian communities by southern state legislators, however, was a significant change compared to the treatment of tribes by state governments in decades past: legislators were now motivated to develop Indian affairs within their states for a variety of reasons. Nevertheless, tribal leaders and Indian advocates were committed to generating change, despite the additional challenges that lay ahead of them in negotiating how the commissions were to evolve.

2

"We'll Do It in the Spirit of Brotherhood"

Inter-Tribal Politics and the Challenge of Centralizing Representation

The 1980s held the promise of a new era for Alabama Indian affairs. In the extreme southern portion of the state, Poarch Creek leaders Calvin McGhee, his son Houston, and Eddie Tullis set change in motion when the 1978 Mims Act established the Southwest Alabama Indian Affairs Commission. The excitement over the commission's potential future spread to Indian communities across the state, which began lobbying for recognition and representation. This excitement, however, soon turned to frustration as Dr. H. L. "Lindy" Martin of the Jackson County Cherokees, Diane Weston of the Echota Cherokee, Tommy Davenport of the Star Clan of Muscogee Creeks, and Framon and Gallasneed Weaver of the MOWA Band of Choctaws each formally presented their community's interests in becoming part of the commission—only to be rejected. Angry that their futures were at the mercy of Eddie Tullis and other Poarch Creek tribal leaders who controlled the agency, Indian groups across the state vowed to use whatever means necessary to be included in the new movement to develop Indian affairs within the state.

"Anything other than equality is intolerable," argued Echota Cherokee representative Diane Weston just minutes into a 1982 meeting held to discuss the development of the commission. "We feel that all of the Indian people in this state are entitled to representation whether they be Choctaw, Cherokee, or Creek because we are all natives of this land."[1] Although Weston was the spokesperson for the nearly five thousand members of her community, her discontent reflected that of other tribal leaders at the meeting. With the establishment of the state Indian agency and the public's increasing interest in the region's indigenous population, the future of Indian affairs looked promising. Leaders like Weston were willing to fight to receive any benefits that could be reaped.

While Alabama tribal leaders debated about the direction of Indian affairs, the Louisiana Office of Indian Affairs also experienced growing pains. Although no legislative act placed the commission into the hands of a single tribal entity—as done in Alabama—the competing visions of tribal leaders, commission staff members, and state legislators created a challenge for the agency to unify Indian interests. Ernest Sickey, the Coushatta leader whose activism initiated the formation of the commission in 1972, felt particularly at odds with the direction in which the commission headed after he left his post as commissioner in 1976.[2] He thought that it had fallen prey to the pressures of state politics as state recognition and commission services were extended to groups whose legitimacy he thought was questionable. As in Alabama, the struggle that prompted the birth of the Louisiana Office of Indian Affairs paled in comparison to the difficult years that followed as tribal leaders fought to shape—and reshape—the commission into an agent of change.

This chapter examines the roles that internal and external pressures played in the development of Indian affairs in both Alabama and Louisiana by using the state commissions as lenses through which to view the evolution of intertribal relationships within the context of a shifting southern political culture. Both states followed the same trajectory in the 1970s as governors made political promises they failed to support with the monetary backing necessary to develop ongoing agencies. It was not until the 1980s—when Republican concerns over poverty and the elimination of welfare took center stage—that the commissions were funded in meaningful ways. The course of events in the development of the Southwest Alabama Indian Affairs Commission (SAIAC)—later renamed the Alabama Indian Affairs Commission (AIAC)—and the Louisiana Office of Indian Affairs (LOIA) unfolded at their own pace due to the diversity of Indian groups and unique political environments. The results were the same, however, as both agencies became more democratically representative of tribal interests.

This change did not happen overnight, as the whole process was often hostile. Indian groups vied for legitimacy and power as they debated the questions of who should serve as the commissions' leaders, what criteria should be established to determine who is entitled to representation, who should declare a tribe a tribe, what role the commissions should play within the state government, and what role they should play within tribal governments. These questions dominated meetings among tribal leaders, who nevertheless agreed on one fundamental point: the power of tribal recognition and commission leadership should be in the hands of Indian people themselves—except when temporary legislative intervention was necessary to balance out the power among groups. Tribes in both states saw the commissions as arenas in which to define tribal sovereignty and take the necessary steps toward self-sufficiency while carving out a political and economic niche for themselves within the state governments. Conflict developed among Indian leaders, however, as their visions of how to achieve tribal development competed. Some believed that inter-tribal cooperation in every aspect of Indian affairs was necessary, and others emphasized a more insular approach with minimal interaction with other Indian groups. Whatever the philosophies, the realities of operating a commission within the confines of the state government proved difficult. Bureaucratic obstacles, tribal politics, competitive attitudes, revolving leadership, and insecurity shaped the interactions of commission members—both Indian and non-Indian.

The Development of the Alabama Indian Affairs Commission (AIAC)

The frustration that led representatives from Alabama's diverse Indian groups to travel to an SAIAC meeting in 1982 was several years in the making. Tribal leaders planned to confront the Poarch Creek–dominated commission that continued to exclude them in the crucial process of developing a relationship with the state government. Poarch Creek leaders held strongly to their position that any changes in the representation of the commission could only occur through a formal recognition process. State legislation (the Mims Act) granted them the responsibility of running and maintaining the commission, as well as establishing criteria for recognizing Indian tribes. Eddie Tullis and the rest of the Poarch Creek Tribal Council took this responsibility seriously. They faced the difficult challenge of providing technical assistance, coordinating funding sources, and developing programs for Alabama's entire Indian population—a population with which they were not entirely familiar.

The Poarch Creek stance was not popular among other Indian groups and their leaders reminded Tullis of his persuasive and impassioned argument in 1977 against the exclusive Creek Indian Council. Weston, Martin, the Weavers, and other tribal leaders pointed out that Tullis had complained that the Star Clan of Muscogee Creeks failed to represent the interests of the broader Alabama Indian population. By 1978, he saw his wish granted when the Mims Act abolished the Creek Indian Council, creating the SAIAC. Now, six years later, these other tribal leaders wondered why history was repeating itself as they stood before the Poarch Creek–dominated commission. They questioned Tullis's original motives and asked why the new commission was just as exclusionary as the old one.[3]

Tullis, the most visible tribal leader in Alabama because of his involvement in the National Congress of the American Indian (NCAI) and the Coalition of Eastern Native Americans (CENA), defended his and the Poarch Creek Council's actions using political and economic reasons. The council, he explained, would be a vehicle enabling the state's Indians to have greater control. The intent was not to exclude other tribal communities but to take the power of recognizing Indian tribes away from the state legislature. The Poarch Creek were responsible for running the commission because of their visibility and acknowledged organization. The long-lasting political alliances the tribe had forged with influential people like Senator Reo Kirkland also worked to the group's advantage in the passing of the Mims Act. Kirkland's relationship with the Poarch Creek had been initiated by Chief Calvin McGhee, who had left an impression on a whole generation of legislators. McGhee's political activities made the Poarch Creek the most visible of Alabama's many Indian groups. The then thirty-four-year-old senator fondly remembered McGhee's 1962 meeting with President Kennedy: "When Chief McGhee was head of the Creeks down here, and I was a little bitty boy, I remember seeing his picture in the newspaper. I sat on the Capitol steps and watched the Indians all in headdress going to Washington to work to get something going for the Indians and not just the Creek Indians, for Indians all over Alabama."[4] With national visibility and respectability in their favor, Tullis argued, "[it] would have been stupid if we hadn't been put in control over the people."[5] Governor George Wallace agreed when he appointed the Poarch Creek Council to serve as the state Indian affairs commission, albeit without the state's financial backing. Wallace answered the call to create an Indian agency, but he took the most convenient and inexpensive measures to do so.

Defending their position further, Poarch Creek leaders explained the commission's 1978 needs assessment as an effort to reach Indians throughout the state. "Stand up and be counted" was the call to Alabama's Indian population. The announcement had insisted that "in order to assure equitable delivery of services," Indian people needed to identify themselves by calling the Poarch Creek Tribal Council office or dropping a referral card into a designated box.[6] In addition, the SAIAC asked volunteers to conduct surveys, but the lack of state support to fund the search restricted their efforts to the southwestern part of the state, where the Poarch Creek and MOWA Choctaw resided. Jennie Lee Dees, a Poarch Creek administrator and backbone of the newly emerged commission, coordinated the study. On its own, however, her tremendous energy was not enough to complete the study with such limited resources. As she complained in a letter to Governor Wallace, "funding has been squeezed from every available Tribal Council program, and we are heavily relying on community volunteers for conducting interviews, or surveys." Even with volunteers, a shortage of funding made it difficult for them to travel from home to home, which limited the scope of the study. Demonstrating her commitment to locate other Indian groups in the state, Dees challenged Governor Wallace to live up to his commitment to Indian affairs by funding the search.[7] Although Wallace lived up to many of the promises he made to African Americans during his last years in public office—such as appointing them to all levels of state government—he did not follow suit for his Indian supporters. The commission remained essentially inactive until 1980 when Governor Forrest Hood (Fob) James responded to the council's pleas for funding.

Poarch Creek leaders understood how fortunate they were to receive funding from a governor who was preoccupied with cutting the state budget. Like Wallace, Fob James catered his political positions to the current popular trends. A Republican-turned-Democrat-turned-Republican, he adopted many of the Reagan administration's economic policies and attempted to consolidate state agencies to reduce spending.[8] His funding of the SAIAC and subsequent support of tribal petitions for federal recognition was an investment in the future of Indian self-determination and a step toward relieving the state's responsibilities to impoverished Indian communities. To fund the agency, James dipped into discretionary funds allocated for the Comprehensive Employment and Training Act (CETA), and in the fall of 1980 the commission's new office in Montgomery opened.[9]

The celebration was short-lived when Poarch Creek leaders realized that the funding came with restrictions as the state—or more specifically, the governor's office—asserted itself into Indian affairs. Although Governor James officially appointed Jennie Lee Dees the commission's executive director, a position she had occupied before the funding came through, James also appointed Dr. Leonard Hudson, a retired pharmacist, as the chairman.[10] As a non-Indian, Hudson was expected to be a liaison between the commission and governor's office. Hudson, however, freely admitted that his role would be difficult: "When the commission was first established, the majority of the average people in Alabama, of which I was one, had no idea on earth there were any Indians in the state, much less who they were, where they were, or what they were."[11] Although the Poarch Creek Council initially supported

Hudson's appointment in their eagerness to get the commission funded, his lack of knowledge and experience in Indian affairs made his role as chairman troubling.

Even more worrisome to Poarch Creek leaders was the power struggle that developed between themselves and the new chairman. Hudson believed he represented the interests of elected state officials—not Indians. He also did not share the Poarch Creek vision of the SAIAC as an expression of tribal self-determination. Rather, Hudson argued that because the commission's funding came from the governor's office, the governor could dictate how the agency should function. As a result, Hudson answered only to the governor and came to represent a white male authority that controlled the future of Indian affairs, the very thing Poarch Creek leaders feared.[12]

With Hudson looking out for the interests of legislators who supported other Indian groups statewide, along with new funding, the commission expanded its survey of other Indian groups, using television, radio, and newspapers to reach out.[13] As a result, the new agency identified the Echota Tribe of Cherokee, the Jackson County Cherokees, the Star Clan of Muscogee Creeks, and the MOWA Band of Choctaws.[14] As tribal leaders from these groups quickly learned, however, although the Poarch Creek offered them some services, being identified was not enough to ensure their full participation in the commission. Self-identified Indian identity that could not be easily substantiated by the recognition of the federal or state governments meant little to Poarch Creek leaders. Tullis argued that for new Indian groups to share control of the commission, a recognition process must be developed so new tribes could prove their legitimacy.[15]

The issue of recognizing new tribes was a point of contention between the SAIAC and the state. Although the Mims Act intended to remove the power to recognize tribes from the state government, legislators complicated matters by ignoring the Indian commission's authority and proposed tribal recognition legislation. For example, in 1979, the Poarch Creek Council fired off a letter to Governor Fob James objecting to a proposed Senate bill extending state recognition to the United Cherokee Tribe of Alabama, a group that had officially organized a year earlier under the leadership of B. J. Faulkner, who often spoke to the media about the desecration of Indian burial sites.[16] Arguing that the group was not a legitimate tribe, the council expressed alarm at the improbably large number of individuals who appeared on their tribal rolls. When members of his own tribe accused Faulkner of fraudulently inflating the rolls in 1980, the group was unable to sustain the scrutiny and splintered into several other groups—including the Echota Tribe of Cherokees—

with multiple headquarters around the state.[17] Despite the United Cherokee Tribe's breakup, the Poarch Creek continued to invoke Faulkner's name as an example of fraudulence and the reason for the commission's enforcement of a recognition criterion.[18]

While the bill to acknowledge the United Cherokee never passed, the legislature did recognize the MOWA Choctaw in 1979. The group's population of about ten thousand attracted the attention of politicians like State Representative J. E. Turner, who defended the legislation to recognize the Choctaw.[19] Supporters had planned to introduce the bill sooner, but prior to the Mims Act in 1978, Eddie Tullis met with MOWA Choctaw leader Framon Weaver and asked him to refrain from proposing any bills until the Mims Act passed so as not to overwhelm lawmakers with Indian legislation. Tullis believed that the Mims Act would somehow immediately benefit the MOWA Choctaw as well as the Poarch Creek, but after Weaver agreed, it became clear that the Mims Act did more than just grant the Poarch Creek recognition—it also created a commission and placed the Creek in control. As an active participant in the Indian movement, Weaver felt betrayed and saw no choice but to force through a bill on behalf of the MOWA Choctaw.[20] Representative Turner, who sponsored the bill, argued that it was necessary because he believed the Poarch Creek–dominated commission likely would not grant the MOWA Choctaw recognition or representation in the SAIAC. Legislative action, therefore, was the only way the group could gain access to federal and state grants that Weaver felt the commission should share with other Indian groups.[21] Weaver himself defended Turner's bill, adding that it was the only choice for the MOWA Choctaw. "I don't feel like we have anyone on the Council or anybody on the Commission to see that we receive justice," Weaver explained. "We appeal to the legislature because we do have a voice there."[22] He even appealed to Governor James to intervene, reassuring James that his tribe was not seeking a handout but rather technical assistance and guidance in becoming more self-sufficient. He wrote, "Of particular concern to me is the critical loss my people may expect as a result of the continuation of the current Alabama Indian Affairs Commission, as established under the Mims Act of 1978."[23] Like Weaver, other MOWA Choctaw leaders felt that their Indian identities alone were not enough to provide them access to the resources necessary for community development, and they blamed the political control of the Poarch Creek over state Indian affairs.

Eddie Tullis and other members of the SAIAC were convinced that the state legislature had no business judging Indian identity. They argued that this should be the responsibility of the Indian affairs commission, which was better equipped to determine who other Indians were. With money as motivation in claiming Indian identity, commission members remained committed to protecting Indian resources by enforcing a formal recognition process, which meant that petitioning tribes, groups, or organizations had to submit proof that they had maintained traditional Alabama Indian names, kinship relationships with other recognized Indian tribes, and traditions signifying their heritage. In addition, the SAIAC requested official records or statements from petitioning groups recognizing individual tribal members as Indian, outlining historical accounts of the tribes' ancestry, and proving receipt of grants from sources designed for Indians only.[24] Tullis argued, "[W]e have to accept the fact that there are some people who want to be Indians that are not Indians, and I [can] show them to you from one part of this country to the other." Even within his own state, "under the existing rules," Tullis said, "some of these people will have trouble meeting the criteria." He went on to point out how many federally recognized tribes across the country were "really put out of shape from all these new Indians around the county."[25] It was important to Tullis that suspect groups not tarnish the legitimacy of the Poarch Creek and other groups in Alabama that asserted a rightful claim to Indian identity. Southern tribes were already battling national misconceptions and prejudices about the region, and Tullis wished to avoid having Alabama labeled as the home of "fake Indians."

Poarch Creek leaders argued that without the input of the commission in the recognition of groups like the MOWA Choctaw, state legislators hindered Indian self-determination. "I'll take my chances with Indians any day," Tullis argued. "I'd much prefer to have Indians say who is an Indian than I would the legislature." He challenged other tribal leaders to give the system a chance and promised that the commission's criteria were not as extensive or onerous as the federal criteria, which required far more historical documentation on numerous generations. Because of the arguments of Indian leaders like Weaver, Tullis reassured them that he would seek an amendment to the Mims Act to broaden the commission's representation after new groups were formally recognized. Tullis argued that it was in the Poarch Creek's best interest to identify and recognize other tribes in order to create more possibilities for the commission to tap into federal and state resources and forge relations with other tribes nationwide. He pointed out: "The more Indians we recognize in the state of Alabama, the more the Navajos look at us, the more the Mississippi Band of Choctaws look at us, the more the Rosebud Sioux look at us."[26]

Not all legislators were comfortable in the role of recognizing new Indian groups. For example, Senator Reo Kirkland supported the Poarch Creek stance that "the legislature should not be in the business of deciding who is and who is not Indian." He argued that Indian groups should work out recognition issues within the SAIAC, without relying on the legislature to work out their problems. Otherwise, he warned, "[e]very Indian will pay for it dearly if it is fought out on the floor of the legislature . . . you will . . . set back the progress the Indians have made in this State in the recent years." Airing tribal politics publicly, Kirkland said, would only cause the legislators to lose respect for tribes and be less likely to help them in the future.[27]

Although Alabama's tribal leaders recognized the validity of Kirkland's warning and even agreed that Indians should control the recognition process, most of them resented being asked to prove themselves as legitimate Indian communities to the Poarch Creek. Gallasneed Weaver, a respected leader of the MOWA Choctaw, likened the process to how "blacks feel about the Ku Klux Klan."[28] This commentary on the intimidating nature of the commission raised many questions about its ability to serve the comprehensive interests of Alabama's Indian population. The skewed power dynamics led some tribal leaders, including Weaver, to feel alienated and repelled by the commission itself. Many wondered why the Poarch Creek—who like other groups in 1982 lacked federal recognition—had become so privileged. "We have to prove ourselves daily that we're Indian people," Tommy Davenport of the Star Clan of Muscogee Creeks complained. "Now the Indians ask us to do the same thing."[29] Davenport, who felt he had even more reason to complain given the Poarch Creek drive to abolish his Creek Indian Council a few years earlier, asked why the commission was unwilling to trust the ability of tribes to monitor their own membership: "I accept everyone in my clan as Indian. I don't accept them because they say they're Indian. I check their records out, and I think the Commission should accept what I bring to the Commission. If I say they're Indian, I think they ought to be accepted as Indian."[30] The perceived lack of trust only served to divide tribal leaders further from the Poarch-dominated commission. Indians judging Indians was a matter of self-determination for the Poarch Creek, but it was humiliating for the disempowered groups.

Frustrated about having to prove their legitimacy, tribal leaders questioned why the Poarch Creek did not have to meet the same criteria for recognition imposed on other groups. In particular, Diane Weston—the Echota Cherokee representative who led the debate—was on the defensive because of Tullis's suspicious attitude toward her community's origins. Weston wondered whether the Poarch Creek would qualify under its own criteria.[31] Gallasneed

Weaver also pointed out these problems: "You want to make some rules and regulations to apply to other people, which you yourself do not meet. It would be difficult for us to appeal the decision if you rule against it, but under the law, it states that even if we met these requirements, you'd still have the right to reject us if you want to."[32] Because the hostility toward the Poarch Creek–dominated commission ran so deeply, it became painfully clear that the only way Alabama's tribal governments would unify would be if power were equalized. The Mims Act allowed the Poarch Creek the luxury of protecting its own tribal interests, but the law left other Indian groups feeling vulnerable and compelled to ban together against the Poarch Creek by appealing to legislators.

Even more damaging to the early development of the SAIAC than the schism between the Poarch Creek and other Indian groups was the role Chairman Hudson played in the conflict. As a representative of legislators who supported tribal groups in their districts, he saw himself as an advocate for the rights of Indian groups not represented on the commission and began taking action to change the power dynamics within the agency. For example, much to the shock and dismay of Tullis and other Poarch leaders, Hudson wrote to other Indian groups in the state on behalf of the commission declaring that they were now state recognized. Infuriated by Hudson's undermining of the established recognition procedures, Poarch Creek commissioners felt that he was making a mockery of the Mims Act. They immediately responded and contacted each group, reversing Hudson's actions and clarifying that he did not have the authority to recognize groups unilaterally.[33] Problems between Hudson and the rest of the SAIAC were further exacerbated when he encouraged non-represented groups to take any recourse necessary to get representation, "either legal or legislative."[34]

According to Hudson, the Poarch Creek excluded not only other Alabama Indian groups from representation on the commission but also two hundred to three hundred federally recognized Indians who had moved to Alabama from other states. He claimed to have received many phone calls and letters asking why federally recognized Indians had no representation. "They expressed a desire to be heard because their children were going to school here [and] they are making their homes in Alabama," he reported.[35] Hudson argued that the commission had no right to continue excluding federally recognized Indians. Poarch Creek commissioners resented Hudson and his efforts to remake the SAIAC. His leadership was unwanted, and Tullis was particularly agitated by Hudson's attempts to serve as a mediator between the Poarch Creek and other tribal groups. "We're getting back to the point where Indians are fighting Indians," Tullis complained, "and the white man is refereeing them."[36]

Alabama Indian affairs were in a deadlock. With the exception of Hudson, the commission was unwilling to grant representation to any group that did not go through the established procedures. At the same time, most of the Indian groups that sought representation simply refused to comply with the commission's demands. Hudson believed that the only way to rectify the situation was through legislative action, so he introduced an amendment to the Mims Act that added representatives from the MOWA Choctaw and Jackson County Cherokees to the commission. In Hudson's assessment, these tribes were two of the most politically active of the unrecognized groups. The amendment, however, failed to make the legislative calendar during the 1981 session.[37]

Soon after, tribal leaders approached Hudson with a second amendment, which proposed that the commission be renamed to reflect a broader representation of Indian groups. It suggested that the geographically exclusive "Southwest" be dropped from the name and the more general "Alabama Indian Affairs Commission" be adopted. The amendment also proposed that the commission be reconfigured by reestablishing it as an agency existing outside the Poarch Creek Tribal Council. It recommended that the commission be made up of representatives from five different groups: the Poarch Creek, the Star Clan of Muscogee Creek Indians, the MOWA Band of Choctaws, the Jackson County Cherokees, and the Echota Cherokees. In addition, the amendment addressed Hudson's earlier concern by including a position for someone to represent other Indians living in Alabama who were not native to the state.

The proposed amendment did not gain the widespread support Hudson and the non-represented Indian groups had hoped for. Throughout 1981 and early 1982, the amendment received little public attention and failed to even reach the House and Senate floors. In anticipation of the upcoming regular legislative session in April 1982, Indian and non-Indian activists staged a massive effort to publicize the amendment. Indians from across the state appealed to the media and in some cases showed up at the statehouse wearing tribal regalia to gain the attention of legislators.[38]

Their efforts did not go unnoticed; soon afterward the governor established a special committee to review the Mims Act. Representative James E. Ray, from the Star Clan of Muscogee Creeks' home of Pike County, was selected to head the committee.[39] Under Ray's leadership, the committee helped this new amendment (House Bill 780) receive a favorable vote in the

Senate Rules Committee and the House. Yet, when the bill came up for a full Senate vote, Senator Reo Kirkland—who had previously warned tribal leaders against bringing their problems to the legislature—introduced an alternative bill that quickly passed. The Kirkland bill overrode HB780 and reinforced the exclusionary structure of the existing Indian affairs commission by granting sole control to the Poarch Creek. Kirkland maintained his previous position that the Poarch Creek was the most logical group to head the agency and that other tribes should work within the existing structure to gain recognition and representation.

Angry and feeling betrayed, the other Indian groups throughout the state lobbied Governor James to veto the Kirkland bill. The hostilities between the Poarch Creek and other tribal groups in the state alarmed the governor, who not only vetoed the Kirkland bill but also withdrew funding from the commission "until the various Indian interests can agree on what they want in the way of state representation."[40] Tribal leaders across the state were stunned and the Alabama Indian Affairs Commission ceased to exist, making the future of tribal-state relations uncertain.

Abiding by Governor James's request to agree on an overall state representation structure was no easy feat for the state's Indian groups, which expressed different levels of commitment to unity. Some groups constructed their identities to embrace notions of inter-tribal cooperation, while other groups—although not opposed to unified efforts—turned their energies inward and focused on their isolated distinctiveness.

The language and symbols that tribes used to represent themselves said a great deal about who they were, how they believed others perceived them, and the direction in which they hoped to go. The Poarch Creek is a very good case in point because of the way in which their tribal business stationery changed over time to tell a story about the evolution of the tribe's status and goals. For instance, under the leadership of Calvin and Houston McGhee from the late 1950s to the mid-1970s, there was a strong emphasis on a unified Creek family that defied state boundaries. Tribal letterhead donned the seal of the Oklahoma Muskogee Creek Nation, connecting the Alabama group to their federally recognized relatives in the West. The letterhead also demonstrated attempts by the McGhees to assert the group's legitimacy as an Indian tribe by placing "Chief McGhee" prominently at the top of the page followed by a generic image of a bare-chested "Indian" with a single feather placed on top of his head.[41] By the time Eddie Tullis assumed the Poarch Creek leadership in 1978, the group's construction of tribal identity had shifted as the rhetoric of self-determination became a hallmark of the tribe's identity and their goal of obtaining federal recognition. Tullis also followed such leaders as Ernest Sickey, who once explained to a reporter that "being a tribe is a business."[42] This shift in how the tribal leadership wanted to be represented was, again, evident in the tribal stationery. For example, Tullis was identified as the chairman of the tribe, rather than the chief, and the group constructed their own tribal symbol instead of borrowing from the Oklahoma Creek Nation.[43] The Tullis administration channeled its energy inward to promote Poarch Creek tribal development, and the goal of "Seeking Prosperity and Self-Determination" was prominently stamped along the bottom of the tribal stationery.

The Poarch Creek form of self-representation was in stark contrast to that of other groups in the state. The Echota Tribe of Cherokee officially bore the philosophy of "Progress through Indian Unity" on their tribal seal and, like many other groups that lacked a land base and enduring tribal culture, the Echota Cherokee found empowerment through their connection to other tribal groups.[44] This point adds another level of understanding to why representation on the state Indian affairs commission proved so crucial to the construction of the Echota Cherokee tribal identity. It also illuminates the conflict between the Poarch Creek and Echota Cherokee in the early 1980s—one group thought that tribal development should be the result of an inward-looking process, while the other believed inter-tribal cooperation was the answer.

Even for groups that emphasized inter-tribal unity, however, the vulnerable status of unrecognized Indian groups caused them to protect themselves by emphasizing their own legitimacy and distinct political identity while pointing out more questionable groups. For example, a public dispute erupted in the early 1980s between H. L. "Lindy" Martin of the Jackson County Cherokee and other Cherokee groups in the state. Martin, who was born on the North Carolina–Virginia border to Cherokee-Powhatan parents, oversaw the development of his group's tribal council at North Sand Mountain High School in Higdon, Alabama, where he secured space to hold a large meeting. Martin's perspective on southern Indian issues was shaped over the course of his education, which took him from the Indian schools of North Carolina where he obtained a B.A. from the Lumbee-run Pembroke State University, to Alabama where he earned a master's degree from Auburn University, and then to California Western University where he received a Ph.D. When he arrived in Birmingham, Alabama, to serve as the Dean of Students at Samford University, Dr. Martin thrust himself into the Alabama Indian rights movement by founding the Society for the Preservation of American Indian Culture. While many tribal leaders appreciated the work Martin did to preserve Cherokee culture, others were insulted by his reported reference to other Alabama Cherokee groups—such as the Echota Tribe of Cherokee—as "weekend or hobby Indians."[45] Local reporters exacerbated the situation by creating a divisive wedge between the two groups. By January 1982 Martin recognized how poorly the "Alabama Cherokee feuds" reflected on Indian affairs and decided to put the issue to rest by directly addressing Joe Stewart of the Echota Cherokee, as well as other tribal leaders affected by the conflict.[46] He stated: "I am tired of other people telling us what you have said and what we have said. I love Joe Stewart and always have. Reporters indicate that we are fighting each other because his group is one kind and ours is another. I apologize for that to him and his people. . . . There are many people who have spoken for us in the newspaper. Even other legislators have told me what you have said, and I would like to come today to say in the presence of God and these witnesses that I have a deep regard for all of you and a deep love."[47] As Martin indicated, part of the conflict was played out in the media, which could only harm the broader movement. As a result, his gesture reflected more than just his emotional need to eliminate the tension between the Cherokee groups; it arose from his awareness of the benefits that all Indian groups in the state would reap if they could demonstrate a unified front.

In fact, a cooperative effort was imperative if Alabama tribes were to tap into new resources. "I think we should look to how we can work together to try to further the education fund like the Blacks have done in the United Negro College Fund," argued Gallasneed Weaver. He went on to describe a similarly constructed United Indian Fund: "Many people in the state of Alabama have said they would love to give money to a good cause united together, but they would want somebody to manage it, but since we're not united to manage it, who wants to get involved in a feud? So there are so many things we could do together, we could have a United Job Program and hire Indians. We could have our own employment service in the state of Alabama working together. We could have our own social program working together."[48] Weaver saw the big picture. The unification of diverse tribal interests was a source of empowerment in places like Alabama, where no tribal group had yet obtained federal recognition. A power-in-numbers approach, Weaver thought, could lead to long-term monetary benefits.

Despite Weaver's hopeful vision, it would remain a pipe dream as long as the commission lay dormant. After the SAIAC was defunded in 1982, and following the battle over representation that took place on the floor of the legislature, there was no longer a commission to fight over. For more than a year following Governor James's drastic solution to the hostilities between the Poarch Creek and other groups, Indian leaders throughout the state lobbied for the revival of the state commission—one that was more equitable. They were fortunate to gain the support of two state legislators: Representative Pat Davis and Senator Frances "Sister" Strong. The two women agreed to sponsor a new bill to revive Indian affairs coauthored by Echota Cherokee leader Joseph Stewart, Tommy Davenport of the Star Clan of Muscogee Creeks, Deal Wambles of the Cherokees of Southeastern Alabama, and Framon Weaver of the MOWA Choctaw. Bill No. 625, which became known as the Davis-Strong Act, would repeal the 1978 Mims Act and give official state acknowledgment to six Indian groups throughout the state.[49]

Unfortunately, Davis and Strong had minority positions within the state legislature and the bill was defeated several times in the Senate. Perhaps memories of the hostility over the former commission were still fresh in the minds of legislators who were unsure about the effectiveness of yet another Indian agency. But despite the frustrating setbacks, supporters of the bill continued to lobby the legislature, and in April 1984 the bill passed the House with only one vote of dissension. It then passed the Senate on May 1, 1984. The Davis-Strong Act created the AIAC and helped set Indian affairs back on track with a starting budget of $125,000 for a new, representative commission.[50]

The power dynamics among Alabama tribes were officially no longer skewed—although the Poarch Creek became federally recognized the same year that the new commission was established. The Davis-Strong Act established a governor-appointed ten-person commission to oversee Alabama Indian affairs under the direction and supervision of the Joint Committee on Administrative Regulations. Six tribes were officially recognized by the state under the act and instructed to submit the names of potential representatives to Governor Wallace for consideration. Soon after the new commission's inception, Wallace appointed six initial representatives: Eddie Tullis for the Poarch Band of Creek, Gallasneed Weaver for the MOWA Choctaw, Tommy Davenport for the Star Clan of Muscogee Creeks, Joseph Stewart for the Echota Cherokee, Jaynn Kushner for the Jackson County Cherokees, and Deal Wambles for the Cherokees of Southeast Alabama.[51] Many of these tribal leaders, who had been at odds with one another just a year prior, were now expected to cooperate and work toward inter-tribal unity. Also added to the new commission was Roger Creekmore, who was appointed to represent the non–tribally affiliated Indians in the state, and Loretta Pittman, a California Indian, who was appointed to represent the federally recognized Indian residents. Following the tradition of the prior commission, two additional commissioners were appointed to serve as representatives of state government. Because of their previous efforts in working with the state's Indian groups, and perhaps as a reward for their endurance in getting the new legislation passed, Governor Wallace appointed Senator Strong and Representative Davis as the final two commissioners.[52]

With the board of commissioners in place, the next few months were spent establishing the administrative foundation of the commission. Jane L. Weeks, chairwoman of the Alabama Women's Political Caucus, became the executive director. Gallasneed Weaver became the chairman and Tommy Davenport became the vice-chairman.

By 1984, Alabama Indian affairs had reverted to an embryonic stage as new leaders were thrust into the position of re-forming the commission from scratch. Yet despite their great diversity and rivalries, Alabama Indian tribes entered a new era with a fully developed sense of cohesion.

The Development of the Louisiana Office of Indian Affairs (LOIA)

Like Eddie Tullis in Alabama, Ernest Sickey had a similar vision of an Indian-controlled commission in Louisiana.[53] In fact, when David Garrison became the first LOIA commissioner in 1972, he knew it was temporary. Garrison accepted the position at Governor Edwin Edwards's request, hoping he could use his skills and influence to get the commission on its feet prior to turning it over to Indian leadership. When Garrison left his post in 1974, Sickey succeeded him. As the first Indian commissioner, Sickey did something that Garrison would not have been able to do: build a bridge between LOIA and the Inter-Tribal Council (ITC) of Louisiana.[54] This relationship helped LOIA obtain and distribute $500,000 in annual CETA funds that were channeled into the ITC for distribution to the affiliated tribes of the Coushatta, Chitimacha, Houma, Tunica-Biloxi, and Jena Choctaw.[55]

From LOIA's inception, its officials believed that "organization and unity of the tribes are very important if assistance programs are to be successful and if the cultural heritage is to be preserved."[56] Yet even with this philosophy of unity, the early years of the commission—under both Garrison and Sickey—appeared to be Coushatta-centered. Newspapers even reported the possibility of declaring that the Coushatta home of Elton be named the Indian capital of the state.[57] Although the Coushatta reaped many benefits through the acquisition of land and resources, LOIA conducted a survey to identify other Louisiana Indian groups. Unlike the Alabama commission, which issued an announcement for Indian groups to self-identify, the Louisiana commission staff personally contacted tribal leaders to identify previously unknown groups.[58] In 1972 Garrison issued a memo to known Indian leaders and government agencies asking whether anyone knew of "sizable Indian communities other than the Houma, Chitimacha and Coushatta."[59] As a result, by 1975 the commission had added the Jena Choctaw and Tunica-Biloxi tribes to its list of communities eligible for services.[60]

The first five recognized groups also happened to be the same ones unified by the ITC of Louisiana. Unlike LOIA, which did not yet have a formal recognition process, the ITC developed criteria for tribal membership based on the federal criteria for tribal acknowledgment.[61] The rationale was that if the council received federal funds from such diverse sources as the Office of Housing and Urban Development, Department of Health, Education and Welfare, Department of Labor, Office of Economic Opportunity, and the Bureau of Indian Affairs, then recipient tribes should conform to federal guidelines.[62]

By 1976 the amicable partnership between LOIA and ITC ended when Sickey resigned as LOIA commissioner to return to his tribe as chairman and to serve as chairman of the ITC. With Sickey gone from the commission, state legislators began passing resolutions to acknowledge other tribal groups that lobbied for help and support. When the Louisiana Senate recognized the Clifton Choctaws and Choctaw-Apache Community of Ebarb in 1978 and 1979, other groups looked on with suspicion. Leaders from federally recognized tribes, like Sickey, publicly questioned the origin of these previously unknown Choctaw groups. He complained that the legislature had overstepped its bounds when it granted state recognition to groups he felt had no historical or traditional claims to a tribal identity. ITC director Jeanette Campos agreed with Sickey, stating that the legislature gave new groups "a false sense of identity."[63] Sickey and Campos feared that instilling these communities with a feeling of entitlement would discourage them from developing a formal petition and proving their legitimacy. Despite these concerns, by 1980 the Apache-Choctaw Indian Community of Ebarb, the Clifton Choctaws, and the Louisiana Band of Choctaw Indians had joined the list of state-recognized groups.

While LOIA was legally mandated to serve the interests of all state-recognized tribal groups, the ITC was not. This discrepancy divided the state's Indian population. Peter Mora, Sickey's successor as commission chairman, further split the commission and the ITC when he argued against the council's recognition criteria. He maintained that rigid guidelines based on federal criteria were unnecessary and impractical for many groups that could not afford to hire a research staff to help them qualify. Council members continued to believe that these stringent criteria were vital in determining which groups had legitimate claims to resources.[64]

Mora argued that it was unfair for the ITC to represent the interests of some groups and not others. He attempted to channel CETA funds for excluded groups through LOIA. After much dispute, a representative from the granting office decided that the ITC should be the sole manager of the funds and continue to apply the necessary guidelines. This conflict put an end to the relationship that Sickey had established between the commission and the ITC. In fact, Mora minimized the council's role in Indian affairs by referring to it as simply "a CETA program," and communication between the two agencies ceased temporarily.[65] Tribal leaders later referred to this period as a dark time for Louisiana Indian affairs, one when inter-tribal unity seemed out of reach and feuds made progress difficult, if not impossible.[66] By 1979 Mora no longer wanted to deal with the persistent conflict so he took a job as a warden with the Louisiana Department of Corrections, where he worked until his death ten years later. In the meantime, the commission had come to a "dead stop."[67]

As in Alabama, a change in the Louisiana state administration revived and restructured LOIA. Following the 1980 election of Republican governor David C. Treen, the commission received its first substantial monetary commitment. Like Alabama's governor Fob James, Treen worked to eliminate the state's long-term economic and social responsibilities to its Indian population by supporting tribal development. As a result, he re-created the commission under Act 702, Senate Bill 841, within the Department of Urban and Community Affairs.[68] LOIA, as well as the newly created Indian Housing Authority, served as a link between state and tribal governments.[69] In order to serve more effectively as a liaison, the commission no longer consisted of academics and "Indian experts" who had made up the board in the early years. Rather, Treen appointed the elected leaders from each of the eight state-recognized groups.[70]

Throughout the 1980s, power did not concentrate within a single tribal entity, as was the case in Alabama. Instead, Louisiana accomplished what many Indian groups in Alabama fought for: democratic representation. Many of Louisiana's tribal leaders, however, did not like the state government's central role in Indian affairs. They harkened back to the disputes over tribal legitimacy that had divided the ITC and LOIA years earlier and wondered how the state government could fairly distribute services to all groups equally when no official system existed to determine that each group met the same criteria. The new commission addressed this concern by establishing recognition procedures intended to place this authority squarely in Indian hands.

Louisiana's process of developing state recognition criteria was an inter-tribal effort, yet leaders believed that LOIA should serve only the communities that successfully went through this process.[71] Criteria from the Alabama and North Carolina commissions served as a model, and commissioners worked closely with the Federal Acknowledgement Office to ensure that, like the ITC, state recognition criteria closely mirrored federal criteria.[72]

Louisiana's tribal leaders wanted to take the power to recognize tribes away from state legislators, whom Senator John Saunders admitted were not knowledgeable enough to determine a tribe's legitimacy.[73] Houma leader Helen Gindrat summarized LOIA's sentiment: "It's time for the tribes to get together and say this is what makes up an Indian. . . . We need to get together with the Governor so we can say that this is what a state recognized tribe is and this is what the state recognizes. It's protecting ourselves on a state recognition basis."[74] Commissioners held firm to the position that the legislature should not have the authority to extend state recognition to any group and that legislative action was merely an expression of legislators' opinions on what the status of a group should be.[75] This approach would mean that each of the eight Louisiana tribes previously recognized by the legislature would have to start over and submit an application to the commission's oversight committee for official certification.[76] The inter-tribal LOIA shared the perspective of Alabama's Poarch Creek commissioners, who believed that the power to extend recognition was a matter of Indian self-determination. This point remained essentially uncontested in Louisiana, however, because power was already shared by different tribal interests and not concentrated with one tribal government.

Another reason tribes wanted to take away the power of recognition from the Louisiana legislature was because of the restrictions the legislature wanted to place on the construction of tribal names. Because the state attorney general's office feared an onslaught of tribal land claims, it backed amending resolutions to avoid identifying a group legally as an Indian "tribe."[77] The state's attempt to control tribal identities by altering their official names from "tribe" to "community," however, was more than many tribal leaders were willing to tolerate.[78] Odis Sanders of the Louisiana Band of Choctaws—a group recognized by state resolution—advocated for the ability of tribal governments to name themselves. He argued, "I think that [it is] the time when Indians should stand up and say 'this is what I am and the hell with it.'"[79] Other tribal leaders agreed that this was another reason why recognition should be entrusted solely to the commission, not legislators.[80]

Although the commission's criteria for state recognition helped move Louisiana Indian affairs more directly into the domain of tribal governments, the process still had the potential to become overly bureaucratic. Modeling of the state recognition criteria after federal criteria concerned tribal leaders who worried that LOIA would become another agent of Indian oppression. In some cases, the commission was even referred to as the "Louisiana Bureau of Indian Affairs (LBIA)."[81] In discussing the federally modeled state criteria, one tribal representative questioned: "Isn't that sort of [mis]leading the Indian people in the state of Louisiana? Because this is supposed to be a state office, but it looks like to me it's turned out to be a federal office."[82] Commissioners faced the challenge of creating an agency that did not simply add another layer of bureaucracy but rather empowered and supported tribal self-determination.

The unique status of Louisiana's Indian population posed specific challenges to LOIA, which quickly discovered that federal guidelines were too rigid for their purposes. The primary problem was the requirement that a tribal group had to have maintained a historic connection to a particular geographic area for at least two hundred years. Given the migratory histories of most of Louisiana's tribal groups, coupled with the impact of the 1830s Removal policy, the criteria was modified to exclude this requirement because many groups could not trace their histories that far back.[83]

The overarching need to protect tribal interests from outsiders encouraged most Louisiana tribal leaders to support the commission's proposed criteria.[84] The decision posed a challenge to some leaders who remained fearful that their state acknowledgment petitions ultimately would be rejected. Others, however, took a hard-line view about the process. "If we're not eligible that's tough," argued one tribal representative. "I think it's a fair criteria. I think everyone can meet it. I think if it's a fortified Indian tribe, a bona fide Indian organization, there won't be no problems."[85] As someone who had experience with the ITC recognition criterion, Jeanette Campos tried to put everything into perspective. She pointed out that the recognition criteria were not intended as an affront to tribal identity but as a way to assess who was eligible for services. "I think there's a lot of confusion going [on] here about recognition," Campos argued. "If you are an Indian, you are an Indian. I don't care what the government says. The only reason that recognition [exists] is because there is set aside monies that are especially earmarked to service Indian communities." She explained that the procedures were not intended to question tribal legitimacy. Instead, they served to define the relationships be-tween tribes and the commission in the eyes of the federal government. For example: "the community comes up there and says 'we're Indian . . . and we want services, we want federal money.' The federal government turns to [the commission] and says 'is this indeed an Indian community, are they [a] bona fide recognized group that meets your criteria?' If they are not registered with the state office then they cannot be serviced by the federal government."[86] In essence, the recognition criteria offered a form of protection for LOIA and the communities it served, giving many groups far more than psychological benefits.

Urban Indian groups expressed the most anxiety over the recognition guide-lines. In particular, Sarah Peralta of the Baton Rouge–based Indian Angels worried that her group would not qualify for services under the criteria.[87] She voiced her feelings about the unfairness of non-tribal Indians being "denied their heritage."[88] Peralta's fears of exclusion from LOIA were rooted in a long history of tribal leaders creating a division between the more established and predominantly rural groups and newer urban "organizations." For example, Ernest Sickey emphasized this distinction in a 1977 letter to the editor of the *Baton Rouge Enterprise*. He outlined the difference between his Coushatta community and the Indian Angels: "I tend to view [the Indian Angels] as a group that has truly never experienced the real issue [of prejudice] on the level faced by traditional Native Americans. One does not have a temporary experience in expressing a tradition, culture or knowledge. Indian people live daily in the knowledge of their heritage—and possess these qualities until he or she meets the Creator."[89] Sickey and other tribal leaders questioned whether all Indians within the state were entitled to the same resources and level of representation within the state government. Yet because thousands of Indians by 1980 lived in cities around the state, commissioners decided to give them an opportunity to have their interests represented. Despite the concerns of a few tribal leaders, the commission changed its criteria to include "organi-zations" as candidates for resources. To qualify, however, these groups had to show at least 90 percent membership of individuals who were already mem-bers of recognized state or federal tribes.[90]

In addition to conflicts over acknowledgment and representation, state-level Indian affairs commissions faced structural challenges and restrictions associated with being government agencies. This frustrated groups that began to see their relationships with the state as "both confusing and growing in im-portance."[91] As the issues of recognition and representation demonstrated, commissions served to define and test tribal self-determination. In their attempts to assert control over these agencies and negotiate the parameters of tribal-state relationships, tribal leaders had to weather the realities of state bureaucracy.

State Indian affairs commissions fell under the purview of state law. As early as 1973, Ernest Sickey pushed for an independently funded LOIA in the hope that the imposition of legal restrictions would be minimal.[92] Yet when it became apparent that restrictions were unavoidable, Sickey figured out how to work successfully within the system. "It would be more advantageous to the Indians," he argued, "if we were able to understand any boundaries, limitation[s], restrictions and any other criteria that the office is mandated under."[93] The lack of clarity regarding legal mandates compelled tribal leaders to budget some LOIA funding for legal advisors to establish bylaws, provide instructions on meeting procedures, and give advice on building relationships with legislators.

State policies and funding also posed staffing problems throughout the 1980s. LOIA had difficulties with staffing during periods of state hiring freezes. The commission also had to obey civil service standards and requirements.[94] In 1988 commissioners pleaded with the governor for more funding so LOIA could operate more effectively. Louisiana commissioners complained: "There are eight tribes with a collective population of approximately 20,000 Native Americans. The job of representing the interests of the state with the tribes is too massive for only one person. Likewise, travel in FY 86–87 amounted to over 8,000 miles within the state (at the staff's own expense). It is humanly impossible for one individual to maintain this level of service as well as to maintain in-office operations such as grantsmanship and budget preparation with only clerical support."[95] The commissioners worried that funding restrictions made adequate representation of the state's Indian population impossible, and they feared for the future of the commission.

State restrictions often posed hardships for tribal representatives serving on the commission. According to Louisiana law, proxy voting was prohibited, so to ensure a quorum commissioners had to physically attend each meeting.[96] Most tribal leaders, however, served their communities on their own time. They held jobs during the week and fulfilled their tribal obligations in the evenings or on weekends. These already overburdened individuals— particularly tribal leaders, who traveled the farthest—found it difficult, therefore, to attend meetings.[97] As a result, some LOIA meetings were held on Saturdays so that all could attend. The commitment demonstrated by Indian leaders in working toward tribal development and stronger tribal-state relationships came with a price. Many became exhausted, and others sacrificed other aspects of their lives. For example, in June 1981 Apache-Choctaw leader Raymond L. Ebarb resigned his position as commissioner and tribal administrator, explaining that "this seems to be the proper time for I have been most unfair to my family and various properties by placing Indian Affairs ahead of everything else."[98]

Just as Alabama governor Fob James had appointed Dr. Hudson, the Louisiana governor's office also appointed outsiders, hampering LOIA's ability to function smoothly. For example, Charles Simpson, a Cherokee resident of Louisiana, wrote to Governor Treen in 1981 asking to be appointed to the commission. Soon afterward, LOIA was notified that Simpson was appointed to serve as a "member at large."[99] Although Simpson's role was minimal, his spontaneous appointment by the governor reflected the lack of control that tribal leaders had over LOIA representation.

Louisiana governors also impacted Indian affairs through their inaction on certain issues. After reviving LOIA in 1980, Governor Treen declared that he was in no rush to appoint an executive director to the commission. This crucial position was responsible for administering programs and coordinating grants. To Indian people across the state, it was imperative that someone be appointed quickly so that Indian communities could make full use of the resources available to them. Indian Angels leader Sarah Peralta publicly expressed her dissatisfaction when the position remained vacant for seven months. "Federal funding for Indian programs is being lost," Peralta argued, "because no one has been hired to look out for Indian affairs."[100] Although the governor's office disputed this claim, Peralta continued to pressure the governor to take action. In December 1980, she led a demonstration of more than fifty Indian activists to the governor's mansion. Although the war-painted demonstrators, referred to by newspaper journalists as "a group of angry Indians," received media attention, they failed to get the personal attention of the governor, who was not at home during the demonstration. As a result, the demonstrators gave the mansion's security guard a petition for the governor. When asked later about the incident, Treen showed little concern, stating, "Nothing around here surprises me anymore."[101]

The demonstrators' petition demanded that Treen appoint Diana Williamson, a Chitimacha tribal member, as the new executive director of the commission. The Indian Angels believed that Williamson, a former Miss Eastern American Indian pageant winner, could best represent their interests because of her polished public persona and recognition among other Indians across the region. Although she had ties to the Chitimacha reservation, she saw herself as an urban Indian from New Orleans. Growing up with an Indian father and a white mother, Williamson candidly admitted that, with the exception of an incident in college, "she suffered little prejudice or discrimination."[102] This admission, however, made her candidacy difficult for some to accept. Ruth Loyd Miller, who had been instrumental in the commission's creation in 1972, wrote to Treen's assistant John Cade after reading about the Indian Angels' demonstration at the governor's mansion. She voiced her opinion that Treen should avoid appointing Williamson because her commitment to the Indian movement was suspect. Miller questioned, "Where was Ms. Williamson in those dark and discouraging times?"[103] Miller believed that Williamson had never experienced the full brunt of discrimination as an Indian and therefore lacked the background and respect necessary to unify Indian interests.

Despite Miller's opposition, Treen agreed to consider Williamson for the position. Soon after, however, he announced that he was also considering Helen Gindrat, a Houma leader who already had a history of Indian affairs involvement.[104] Gindrat's candidacy, though, lacked widespread support from tribal leaders, who claimed she would not represent the state's entire Indian population. Her rural upbringing in a predominantly French-speaking Houma community in southern Louisiana distinguished her from urban Indians.[105] Also, detractors cited her tenure as executive director of the Houma tribe, along with her involvement with the ITC of Louisiana, as proof that she would represent solely the interests of rural or reservation groups.[106] Odis Sanders of the urban-based Louisiana Band of Choctaws wrote the governor: "Helen Gindrat is unacceptable as Director. Her close ties to the Inter-Tribal Council would assure the reservation Indian an undue advantage. The ITC at present recognizes only five of the nine tribes or bands living in Louisiana. Under Helen's administration about 75 per cent of the Indian population of Louisiana would be ignored as they are now by the ITC. . . . Before you choose, dig deeper and study the situation of Louisiana's Indians. We can be an asset to Louisiana and to its Governor, but only if treated fairly and as a whole."[107] The discussion about the executive director post provided an opportunity for old hostilities against the ITC's exclusionary practices to resurface. There was widespread concern that if appointed, Gindrat would deny commission representation to groups not recognized by the ITC. During the course of the debate, it became difficult to separate Gindrat and her intentions as the potential executive director of LOIA from the ITC itself.

Despite these concerns, Governor Treen appointed Gindrat executive director on December 19, 1980.[108] Members of the Indian Angels were furious and once again turned to the media to lash out. "I don't think Governor Dave

Treen knows what he has done," declared Peralta. "But he will know because he has lost 85 percent of the Indian vote." Peralta's claim that Indians would vote against Treen was indicative of problems other tribal leaders had with her tendency to speak on behalf of the entire Louisiana Indian population. Peralta even threatened that "lawsuits may be forthcoming if all Indians are not equally represented."[109] In addition to Peralta's public remarks, local newspapers received a series of letters accusing the governor of "deliberately overlooking the qualifications of the leading candidate, Ms. Diana Williamson, for the sake of political expediency."[110] Defending herself and the governor's decision to appoint her, Gindrat said the issues had been blown out of proportion and that she fully intended to represent the state's entire Indian population.[111]

Demonstrating how concerns about her appointment were unfounded, Gindrat, as LOIA executive director, brought various Indian groups together to discuss common concerns. A diverse range of tribal groups populated Louisiana, and just as in Alabama, a close look at the symbols that tribes used to represent themselves on formal stationery and tribal seals gives insight into how they see themselves and what they value. In 1983 a Baton Rouge newspaper published the images of seals from five different tribes in the state to draw attention to their shared struggles; however, from the seals clustered together above the headline one can also glean a sense of their individuality. The tribal symbols of the Tunica-Biloxi, the Coushatta, the United Houma Nation, the Jena Band of Choctaws, and the Chitimacha—although basic in their designs—portray culturally and politically meaningful messages. For example, the Chitimacha tribal seal depicts a historic scene of a meeting between a group of Native people and a European with the words "Sovereign Nation of the Chitimacha" framing the image. The emphasis on seeing the Chitimacha as a self-governing political entity that has a long-established history dominates this image. In contrast, the United Houma Nation's seal depicts a drawing of a crawfish, which calls to mind the more geographically specific unique Houma homeland. This particular seal does not make any overt political assertions, but it certainly identifies a cultural and, perhaps, economic symbol important to the Houma community.[112]

Gindrat faced the challenge of fielding tribal groups' desires to maintain a distinct political identity. For instance, the Jena Choctaw leaders questioned the ability of Clifton Choctaw leaders to call themselves "Choctaw."[113] Gindrat responded by arguing that Louisiana leaders should find common ground. She believed that the unification of tribal interests was the only way to economically empower tribal governments, even though by 1981 two of the eight groups were federally recognized. A consortium was necessary, she pointed out, for state block grant money to become "Indian money."[114] The woman whom many feared had only a few select tribes' interests in mind quickly proved to be a strong unifying force within the state.

Gindrat's vision went beyond securing funds for Indian communities. She wanted to create a cohesive political identity for the state's Indian population. Following a 1981 trip to Juneau, Alaska, where she participated in the Governors' Interstate Indian Council Conference, Gindrat returned to Louisiana with a new outlook on how to run a state commission. She reported that the way other state Indian affairs commissions established relationships with state government was "really fantastic." Commissioners met directly with governors, whom they presented with position papers outlining their needs. Gindrat felt strongly about following the example of other commissions. "The administration seems to be open to that right now," she argued to tribal representatives. "It seems to be a now or never situation. The governor is a Republican and his intention is to do something for the Indian."[115]

In April 1981 all tribal chairmen throughout the state convened in Jena, Louisiana, for a historic meeting. Gindrat viewed the meeting as the most significant step toward tribal unity the state had ever seen. She recalled, "I'll never forget it because it was the biggest day of my life, to see all the tribal chairmen sit around one table for the first time in their lives and [sit] there and really [talk] over the differences."[116] The meeting resulted in a formal "Declaration of Unity," in which each tribal leader promised to "enter into a spirit of common interest and dedication towards a goal of cooperation between all tribes in working towards what is best for the Indians of Louisiana."[117]

One month later, the group of leaders collectively titled the "Undersigned Sovereign American Indian Tribal Governments of Louisiana" distributed a position paper to Governor Treen and state legislators. It outlined the history of tribal-state relationships in the United States and defined Indian tribes as distinguishable from other "ethnic groups" because they "are units of government and should be treated as such by the state government of Louisiana."[118] Treen and lawmakers responded favorably, saying that it was the first time they had ever seen anything concrete come from the Indian affairs commission.[119]

LOIA entered a new phase in which tribal unity was the official policy and Indian leaders tried to look beyond historical rivalries. This position, however, was a delicate one and was easily disrupted. For example, the same year Louisiana tribal leaders created the "Declaration of Unity" and issued their position paper, a political action organization, called the Louisiana Indians for Equality (LIFE), was formed by a group of Houma. It was loosely modeled after the NAACP and was envisioned as an inter-tribal organization that included non-Indian members. The group, predominantly consisting of Houma tribal members, initially planned to band together with an African American organization but later discarded this idea because of the fear of conflicting interests. LIFE intended to help Indians politically by supporting them in elections and pushing bills through the legislature.[120]

LIFE members disrupted LOIA's delicate cohesion by using commission meetings as a forum to showcase tribal politics. For example, Houma leader and LIFE member John Billiot confronted Houma tribal chairman Steve Cheramie at an April 1982 meeting. Billiot accused Cheramie of working against him and his organization. "Pay back is hell," threatened Billiot, who also insinuated that he had influence within the Houma community and planned to use it against Cheramie.[121] The dispute between the two alarmed the rest of the commission, which wanted to avoid the reestablishment of tribal divisions and hostilities of years past.

Even more disturbing to other Indian leaders was Billiot's intention to land LIFE a seat on the commission, giving the organization access to tribal leaders and the governor's office. Gindrat, who worked tirelessly to develop a strong relationship between the governor's office and LOIA, recoiled at the prospect that her hard work would be undone—particularly by members of her own Houma community. She reminded Billiot that he would be undermining previous achievements.[122] Sickey agreed, adding, "I would think that you are infringing on tribal sovereignty. . . . The commission of Indian Affairs is created by the governor supposedly to act as an advocacy group to lobby and create support . . . but now you're having an organization that says I'm going to be lobbying in your behalf. Aren't you trying to circumvent the powers of the commission?"[123] Sickey did not want LIFE to use LOIA to further their agenda, which he thought would eventually harm the commission. As one tribal leader pointed out at a 1982 meeting, "It's only been just recently that we've been able to even trust each other around a table and the LIFE or any other organization coming in, I think, would confuse the issue."[124]

The unwillingness of tribal leaders to become involved with LIFE reflected the importance they placed on maintaining the unity that had evolved over many years. Although there had been initial concerns over Gindrat's appointment, her ability to unify tribal interests statewide was recognized by Indian leaders. In particular, Roy Procell of the Choctaw-Apache commended her in a 1982 letter, stating, "There are a lot of important needs being met for the Indian people, through the hard work being done by your office. We feel that you and your staff are doing an excellent job and we hope you will be there for a long time."[125] Nevertheless, Gindrat resigned her post as executive director the following year to focus on her own Houma community. The spirit of unity that developed under her influence, however, remained when Clyde Jackson became the new director. Prior to taking the position, Jackson had been chairman of the Jena Band of Choctaw for eight years and a board member of the ITC. His appointment did not incite the controversy of Gindrat's, for all of the eight state-recognized tribes supported him. The future seemed promising for Louisiana's Indian communities, and, as David Broome of the Louisiana Band of Choctaw claimed, "Presently there is a unity of the eight tribes in Louisiana that we have never enjoyed before. . . . This unity will become stronger with the leadership of Mr. Jackson."[126]

In Sum

The 1980s offered southern tribes an opportunity to reach a new level in defining their identities as tribal nations. The influence of the national movement toward self-determination, as well as the federal recognition of the Poarch Creek, Coushatta, and Tunica-Biloxi, instilled Indian groups in Alabama and Louisiana with newfound confidence. As state governments became more receptive to developing relationships with tribal groups, Indian leaders embraced the opportunity to create a strong Indian front and access resources through the development of state Indian commissions. Yet tribes found it difficult to agree on a unified vision because the specific needs of each community dictated their goals, the resources they sought, and the ways in which they conducted business in an inter-tribal forum.

In both states, the question of commission representation generated controversy in the early years. Although a single tribe controlled the Alabama commission, Louisiana's commission limited representation to the five tribal groups that made up the ITC. The Indian movement's increased public visibility generated many positive changes, but it also stirred up anxiety and suspicion. Indian groups that arrived late to the movement or became politically organized after the commissions were created faced the scrutiny of more established and publicly visible groups represented by Alabama's Tullis or Louisiana's Sickey.

While the Indian agencies were a positive step toward tribal self-determination, the development of recognition criteria in both states led to some unrest. The precarious position of southern Indians inspired leaders to protect the integrity and legitimacy of their own groups, often at the expense of other groups. Most tribes in Alabama and Louisiana viewed federal recognition as the ultimate goal, and they did not wish to jeopardize that opportunity. The question of who should have the authority to extend state recognition and commission representation remained. Both offices seemingly held the responsibility of recognizing new tribal entities, but in reality, state legislators thwarted tribal authority by proposing legislation to both recognize specific groups and restructure the commissions to be more inclusive. Conflict within the commissions proved destructive, encouraging the intervention of legislators and leading to the loss of funding for the SAIAC and causing LOIA to come to a "dead stop."

It was not until Alabama governor Fob James and Louisiana governor David Treen took office that the commissions were revived and restructured. The decade-long economic trend of downsizing government agencies and eliminating social programs made the states more receptive to supporting tribal self-determination because of the promise it held for relieving the state's financial responsibilities to impoverished Indian communities. Even with the second chance, however, Indian leaders in both states quickly learned that the commissions held vulnerable positions within the state governments. Ernest Sickey's fears were realized when it became clear that the level of funding LOIA received dictated the type and scope of work the agency could conduct. State policies also created legal and practical challenges for the commissions that at times made their continuation difficult. Finally, the governors' roles in appointing individuals to leadership positions within the Indian agencies had dramatic effects on the direction of Indian policy in both states. Commission chairmen and executive directors were supposed to represent tribal unity, but as governor-appointed positions, they were often highly contested.

Even more difficult to solve than disputes over state recognition—or the pressures of operating within the confines of state policies and bureaucratic restrictions—was unifying a diverse range of tribal interests. Tribes themselves posed the greatest challenge to state commissions, which were intended to serve as their single voice. As seen in Louisiana, maintaining cohesion was a delicate process that was easily disrupted by politically motivated groups such as LIFE. A similar pattern unfolded in Alabama as commissioners negotiated the balance of power within the newly organized AIAC. In the end, despite conflicting interests and external pressures, tribal leaders demonstrated an awareness that cooperation was in their best interest and came together "in the spirit of brotherhood."

3
Acknowledging Indians in a Bipolar South
Shifting Racial Identities

On May 16, 1981, Norman Billiot sat in an overcrowded cellblock in Louisiana's violent and tense Angola Prison. He was drafting a distressed letter to the state Indian affairs office appealing to Helen Gindrat, LOIA's new director and fellow Houma community member. He wanted Gindrat to help him with the "racial problem" he was experiencing. Billiot complained that despite the supposed decline of Jim Crow, prison officials continued to segregate inmates according to their race. African American and white inmates were housed in separate cellblocks, creating an uncomfortable situation for Billiot, who did not fit neatly into the prison's racial categories. He complained that guards forced him into the rigid biracial system by refusing to recognize him as an Indian. "I told them upon my arrival here . . . that I am Indian," Billiot explained. "The classification officer classified me as 'white' anyway."

The prison's race-based inmate counting procedures exacerbated Billiot's problems. Depending on the guard on duty, Billiot was frequently counted as African American during the daily counts despite his assignment to a white cellblock. He explained that "if the officer who makes the count is unfamiliar with me, he would count me as black. During the summer I get a really dark complexion, and with my hair being as bushy as it is I can easily be mistaken for black." On the occasions when Billiot was included in the African American counts, a panic stirred among the prison officials when discrepancies arose in the numbers, and recounts were issued until officers discovered the problem. This practice not only made Billiot unpopular with other inmates, who had to endure repeated headcounts, but it also led to intimidation from prison officials. "I've had officers stare at me a minute trying to figure out if I was black or white," he wrote. "I've had some walk in front of my cell back and forth three and four times trying to figure me out. Others even ask other inmates about my race. I could see in some officers' facial expressions that they were irritated by trying to figure my race." Billiot's anxiety prompted him to give himself the nickname "Indian" so inmates and prison officials would realize that he was neither black nor white.[1]

Billiot's situation reflected the continued invisibility of Indians in many areas of the South. He occupied an ambiguous racial space for which the region's political and social culture did not easily account. But even within a biracial system not designed to include them, Indians remained part of political and historical processes. As Alexandra Harmon points out in her study of the Puget Sound region, Indian identity is fluid and vulnerable to changing social conditions.[2] In the South, the perception that Indians no longer populated the southern states prevailed following the campaign that forced thousands of people to Indian Territory in the 1830s. Indians who returned or simply never left their homelands were accounted for in historical records in a variety of ways, depending on the locale. Most commonly, however, they were given the classification of "free people of color" to designate them as non-white but distinguish them from black slaves.[3] When the Jim Crow system of racial segregation took center stage in the 1890s, the category "free people of color" took on a different meaning and blurred the line that once divided Indians and African Americans. Particularly in communities where racial mixing had occurred, the postwar racial hierarchy had no other mechanism with which to deal with those of mixed heritage than to call them "colored."[4]

Under the pressures of Jim Crow, southern Indians were left to navigate through a system that either marginalized or mislabeled them. Most Indians rejected the stigma of being associated with African Americans, but others concentrated their efforts on "passing" as white to gain access to white privileges.[5] As the director of the Northwest Florida Creek Indian Council explained, "passing as white was seen as a matter of survival for generations."[6] But this was not always an option, much less a desire, of Indians who learned to live under the ill-defined racial category of "other."

Billiot's experience with the de facto segregation system within Angola Prison—one that continued into the 1980s—reveals the broader impact of the southern Indian movement of the 1970s and 1980s.[7] Billiot refused to embrace a white identity in a situation where an accommodating attitude would have made life easier for him. He continuously asserted his Indian identity even when facing the cruel reality of being singled out and "othered." His problems were further compounded because he did not belong to one of the few federally recognized tribal communities in the South, but Billiot convinced LOIA to advocate for him in an effort to help him out of his isolating and demoralizing situation. His experience was unexceptional, but the mere fact that he spoke up about his dilemma, and had somewhere to turn, was historic.

This chapter investigates one of the most significant effects of the southern Indian movement: the reintroduction of "Indian" as a meaningful and accepted form of racial identification. Tribal communities historically and inappropriately given labels that stressed their mixed ancestries—such as "hybrids," "mongrels," "Cajuns," "Sabines," or "Redbones"—underwent a social and political revolution as they sought new avenues to clarify and emphasize their tribal identities. Dozens of Indian groups throughout the region formed political organizations. These organizations were recognized not only by other Indian groups but also by their respective state governments. A movement toward writing—or rewriting—tribal histories also reflected the shifting racial landscape of the South. New generations of educated southern Indians, with the aid of non-Indian scholars, helped tribal leaders construct their own historical narratives. Tribes then used these histories to educate the public and prepare petitions for federal acknowledgment. While emphasizing their unique histories, tribal leaders also recognized the potential impact of creating a strong "Indian" constituency. They encouraged Indians to register to vote as "Indians." They also asked Native people to make sure that their driver's licenses and birth certificates accurately reflected their race and that the U.S. Census Bureau would count them as "Indians." With the success of these efforts in both Louisiana and Alabama, tribal leaders could introduce Indians to the public and state legislators as the "new minority."

"Sabines," "Cajuns," and "Others": Setting the Record Straight

When William Harlen Gilbert Jr. reported to the Smithsonian Institute in 1948 that Indians of the eastern United States were on the verge of "becoming extinct," he had no way to predict the onslaught of an Indian revival and tribal resurgence just a few decades later.[8] What happened? How does one account for this visible upsurge in eastern—and more specifically, southern—Indian political activity? Like others across the nation, southern Indian groups were impacted by the changing federal attitude toward Indian affairs, which abandoned the termination stance to support a tribal self-determination policy. The Federal Acknowledgement Project in the 1970s also invited and added an incentive for non-recognized, self-identified southern Indian groups to re-organize politically. The emerging southern Indian movement gained further momentum from the shifting racial politics of the region. Spurred on by de-segregation and the civil rights movement, this momentum allowed Indian groups to transcend their ambiguous racial categorizations and secure a more pronounced Indian identity.

The southern Indian movement, and the state Indian affairs agencies that developed apace, provided many racially elusive groups a forum in which to define themselves formally as tribal nations. This process, however, proved more difficult for some than others, revealing the diverse experiences of In-dians across the region. For example, the Poarch Creek of Alabama and the Coushatta of Louisiana gained public recognition as Indian tribes soon after the groups' leaders began actively campaigning for visibility. The U.S. gov-ernment acknowledged the status of these groups following the creation of the state Indian affairs commissions, which helped further the tribes' agendas. Other groups, however, struggled to gain wide acceptance as Indian tribes, a task made even more challenging by an increase in fraudulent claims. The Lumbee of North Carolina is the best-documented example of a group that consistently had to defend its Indian identity.[9] In the lower South, groups such as the Houma of Louisiana and Alabama's MOWA Choctaw also faced challenges. They confronted decades of inconsistent racial categorization by scholars, government officials, missionaries, and local non-Indians, which made them targets of suspicion and controversy when asserting themselves as Indian tribes. The southern Indian movement, however, ushered in a new era in Indian affairs, giving formerly marginalized groups an opportunity to dispute misinformation while establishing relationships with their respective states.

Although the experiences of the Houma and MOWA Choctaw were unique, distinguished by distance, culture, language (the Houma are pre-dominantly French speaking), environment (bayous versus dense forest), and local politics, the impact of being racially "othered" shaped remarkably simi-lar experiences in both communities. Like so many other southern Native groups, isolation and a history of intermarriage with other Indian commu-nities and non-Indian neighbors, along with Jim Crow politics and compe-tition over economic resources, complicated their recognized racial status at the state and local levels. Throughout the nineteenth and twentieth centu-ries, southern Indians demonstrated the fluidity of racial labels. They were readily identified as "Indians" in some contexts, but in other situations they were called "so-called Indians," "hybrids," or "mongrels"—or, in the specific cases of the Houma and MOWA Choctaw, "Sabines" or "Cajuns." Nevertheless, within a rigid system of segregation, and perhaps for political and economic reasons or for the sake of convenience, the Houma and MOWA Choctaw were frequently labeled "Negro" so that their children would be sent to the "appropriate" schools.

This classification, which mandated that Houma and MOWA Choctaw children attend black schools, met resentment from both groups, who maintained a strong sense of Indian identity. Even with the Houma's long history of migration and relocation, which brought them to their permanent settlements in Terrebonne, Lafourche, and St. Mary parishes, tribal members continued to view themselves as Indians.[10] The Alabama Choctaw, who reside in the Pine Hills Belt of the coastal plain in Mobile and Washington counties, also maintained strong ties to their Indian identity despite facing a history of racial ambiguity. As Jacqueline Anderson Matte points out, the group was deemed "the lost tribe" since they represented descendants of several Choctaw families—plus at least one Cherokee family and one Creek family—who avoided removal in the 1830s.[11]

In early attempts to assert their Indian identities—or more specifically, their non-black identities—Houma and MOWA Choctaw members used the court system to challenge the stringent biracial system within public education. For example, in 1917, Houma community member Henry L. Billiot refused to enroll his three sons in a black school, insisting they were not of the "Negro race." When local authorities refused to agree that Billiot's sons were of the "white race," the Louisiana Supreme Court took the case the following year. Judges supported the school board's position. Lending no credence to Billiot's argument, the court ruled that Billiot had some black ancestry and therefore could not send his children to an all-white school.[12] Court cases in Alabama had similar results when MOWA Choctaw members tried to integrate their children into all-white schools.[13] Previously labeled "free people of color," these groups found their efforts foiled even prior to arguing their cases before a judge.

Like those in many other Indian communities throughout the region and the nation, Houma and MOWA Choctaw families intermarried with other Indian groups, as well as with Europeans, European Americans, Africans, and African Americans. Despite the continuation of a dominant Indian identity and culture in these communities, the Louisiana and Alabama state court systems saw the issue from a purely biological standpoint and ignored the history of these groups, deeming them "racial hybrids." Southern courts operated under the "one drop" rule to determine black ancestry. Because of this policy, dozens of Indians fell victim to a legal system unwilling to consider an individual's self-identity in segregation cases or even to complicate race beyond the black-white paradigm.

While southern courts countered threats to the biracial system by suppressing "Indian" as a third racial category, scholars, missionaries, and local non-Indians debated the "true" identities of these "racial intermediaries." The varied outcomes of these inquiries demonstrate how racial constructions were often subject to economic, political, or religious agendas. For example, opponents of the Houma's quest for access to better educational resources refused to accept them as "white" and allow them admittance to white-only schools. These same critics, however, were also reluctant to acknowledge them as "Indians." As John d'Oney noted in an extensive history of the group, the Houma were "viewed by many non-Natives as a group of mixed white and African ancestry attempting to pass themselves off as Native."[14] Promoters of this argument felt justified by the 1911 assessment of the ethnohistorian John Swanton, who, without conducting rigorous research within the community, concluded that the Houma had very few Indian traits.[15]

Henry L. Bourgeois, superintendent of the Terrebonne Parish school board, led the charge against the Houma claim to an Indian identity. He resented Houma resistance to black schools and claimed that they had adopted an Indian identity as a way to avoid enrolling their children there. He was outwardly hostile toward the "so-called Indians of Terrebonne Parish" and their supporters, such as the ethnologist Dr. Frank Speck, who called the Houma a legitimate Indian tribe, as well as the Methodist, Baptist, and Catholic missionaries who worked with the group. "The 'Indians' of the parish have few, if any, of the earmarks of their boasted ancestry," Bourgeois argued. "And if Indian blood ever coursed through their veins, it has been washed thin with white and colored infusions."[16] Bourgeois's obsession with the Houma's racial classification reflected how far beyond the court system the fear of seriously challenging—and further complicating—the Jim Crow system extended. Bourgeois and other school administrators were threatened by both the expense of establishing schools to accommodate Indians and a new racial understanding. In an attempt to explain the underlying cause of such aggressive opposition from Bourgeois and others, Houma community members alleged that their critics secretly did acknowledge their Indian identities but deliberately impeded their educational opportunities because of the "white fear that an educated, literate Indian community would successfully seek the return of land taken fraudulently from them."[17] This notion was true for many

Houma community members who remembered a time when surrounding businesses clearly acknowledged their heritage by posting "No Indians Allowed" signs in store windows.[18]

The MOWA Choctaw also found themselves at the center of a debate over their true racial identities. Despite the state mandate that their children attend black schools, there was governmental acknowledgment of their unique racial status. In the 1880s, Alabama senator L. W. McRae attempted to account for this distinction, labeling them "Cajuns." Conveniently overlooking their self-proclaimed identity as Indians, he reasoned that the group shared many characteristics with and resembled the Louisiana Cajuns. Although a 1923 survey conducted by Hilary H. Holmes concluded that the MOWA Choctaw were *not* Cajuns, the local non-Indians widely adopted and perpetuated this mislabeling for decades.[19] Edward Thomas Price Jr., who wrote a chapter titled "Cajans of Southwest Alabama" in his 1950 Ph.D. dissertation, even used the term.[20] In his assessment of this "racial island," Price described them as racial hybrids who were a combination of white, black, and "possibly" Indian and concluded that they were nothing more than an isolated community of African Americans with some white ancestry. Price relied on racial stereotypes, emphasizing their "Negroid" features, such as "kinky hair," "wide nostrils," "thick lips," and "vein-covered eyeballs."[21] "In general," Price concluded, "there are among the Cajans more characteristics reminding one of Negroes than of Indians. . . . I have seen none who look strikingly like Indians."[22]

Like many scholars in the pre– and immediate post–World War II period who made their careers writing about "racial intermediaries" in the eastern United States, Price relied on his limited contact with the studied group and his preconceived notions of what Indians should look like. The self-proclaimed racial identity of an individual—or entire group—who cooperated with researchers frequently meant very little. Price demonstrated this lack of concern in his admission that the MOWA Choctaw resented being called "Cajuns." In fact, he noted that "some call themselves Indians if they think the white peak is out of reach."[23] Price perpetuated this false label, taking advantage of the culture of silence and suspicion that had developed within the MOWA Choctaw community. With little if any political power, groups like the Houma and MOWA Choctaw were vulnerable to the policies that were shaped and reinforced by the mounting literature that deemed them "outcasts or pariah peoples." Their vulnerability and ambiguity also made them susceptible to being characterized as "backward or superstitious" people who were both socially inferior and genetically flawed as a result of miscegenation.[24]

As the discussion over the racial identities of the Houma and MOWA Choctaw waged on in courtrooms, school board meetings, and academic forums, the only consistent conclusion was that both groups were in many ways distinct from their neighboring communities. Although it was still not widely accepted that their distinctiveness derived from their Indian identities, public officials felt pressure to incorporate these "othered" communities into the Jim Crow system—or at the very least, to adapt the system to fit them. By the 1930s, "Cajun schools" were built in Mobile and Washington counties in Alabama to accommodate the MOWA Choctaw. Federal officials felt similar pressure; they sent investigators into the Houma community to conduct surveys and issue recommendations.[25] Because of this attention, even the Houma's most outspoken critic was compelled to act. Louisiana school superintendent Bourgeois established a separate "Indian" school in Terrebonne Parish in 1944 and others in the area soon followed.[26]

Although the creation of separate schools for Indians across the South acknowledged their unique status, these schools did little to clarify the groups' Indian identities. Lacking tangible support from the federal government, the Houma and MOWA Choctaw suffered budget cuts and continuous pressures to give up their special schools and attend black schools. Indian communities were also concerned about the long-term effectiveness of the segregated, low-quality "special schools." Many people believed these schools were meant to appease the communities but contained little commitment to advancing the opportunities of Indians. As a result, Houma and MOWA Choctaw leaders worked toward better-quality Indian schools or, in some cases, continued trying to integrate their children into all-white schools.[27]

The dramatic social and political changes of the 1960s and 1970s caused by desegregation and the civil rights movement helped give the emerging southern Indian movement more momentum as Indian leaders encountered additional opportunities to improve their tribes' educational situations. Many non–federally recognized Indian groups took advantage of federal education grants and state aid to help maintain Indian schools and establish Indian education programs. These programs and grants enabled tribal communities, including the Houma, to celebrate their first college graduates in the 1970s.[28]

The opportunities created by the southern Indian movement also gave many groups the ability to take the first step toward clarifying a tribal identity by politically unifying scattered families and communities that shared a common culture and history.[29] Shifting regional and national racial policies, along with a new generation of educated leaders, made the unification of individuals under common tribal identities possible. For example, the Houma lacked historical cohesion because of competing visions and geographical isolation. Nevertheless, community leaders were able to find common ground in their desire to buttress economic infrastructures by establishing a shrimp cooperative. This newfound unity went beyond the economic realm as the joint forces melded into a single political entity to develop a relationship with the state government and other tribal groups. In 1977 the United Houma Nation, Inc., was created and soon afterward was granted state recognition.[30]

The MOWA Choctaw, who also lacked a central governmental structure prior to the 1970s, also managed to politically unify the interests of ten kin-based subdistricts of Choctaws.[31] In 1979, with the support of State Representative J. E. Turner, the MOWA Choctaw were officially organized and recognized through state legislation. When Governor Fob James formed the fourteen-member Choctaw commission the following year, it included representatives from both Mobile and Washington counties. James signed a bill acknowledging the group as a tribal nation, making them eligible for a variety of programs, and by 1983, the tribe had purchased 160 acres in north Mobile County.[32]

Organizing disparate Indian families into single tribal communities with offices and elected leaders not only made it easier for state governments to recognize the groups as tribal nations but also made them easily identifiable to other tribes throughout their own states. The inter-tribal networks that developed throughout the 1970s and 1980s proved invaluable to Indian leaders, who as a result felt less isolated in their struggles. For example, with the reestablishment of the Alabama Indian Affairs Commission (AIAC) in 1984 as a more democratically representative agency, the MOWA Choctaw benefited from the exposure that the Alabama commission afforded them. When community leader Gallasneed Weaver became commission chairman and was asked by three different Alabama governors to serve as a delegate to various national Indian conferences, Weaver brought additional visibility to his formerly mislabeled community.[33] Similarly, Houma leaders helped develop the Louisiana Office of Indian Affairs (LOIA) and the Inter-Tribal Council (ITC) of Louisiana, as well as national organizations including the National Congress of American Indians, the Coalition of Eastern Native Americans, and the American Indian Policy Review Commission.[34] In addition to providing tribal leaders the opportunity to link their communities to state and national Indian affairs, the commissions served as arenas for sharing frustrations and gaining support. "We want the right to tell a white man we're Indian people," explained Tommy Davenport of the Star Clan of Muscogee Creeks during an Alabama commission meeting.[35] Although he spoke on behalf of his own community, Davenport's comment reflected the sentiments of other tribal leaders who believed that state recognition was just the first step in gaining full acknowledgment and rights as Indian people.

To tribal leaders, the ultimate goal was formal acknowledgment from the federal government. Upon the creation of the Federal Acknowledgment Office in 1978, non–federally recognized Indian groups could petition the Bureau of Indian Affairs (BIA) for recognition. As demonstrated among eastern tribes—as well as others scattered throughout the nation—obtaining recognition was no easy task. One of the criteria petitioning Indian groups had to meet was to demonstrate—through documentation—that they had existed as an "Indian tribe" from historic times to the present.[36] This was a nearly impossible feat for many southern groups. Nevertheless, southern state Indian affairs commissions supported, and in many cases aided, state-recognized Indian groups with genealogical research and with filing federal petitions. The SAIAC staff hoped that "revitalization and retention of a once proud culture will surface as a result of this total tribal involvement to 'prove up.'"[37]

Proving long-term existence as a tribe required aggressive research. Indian communities had to demonstrate that they had maintained a distinct Indian identity, with external boundaries and internal cohesion, over a prolonged period of time. LOIA explicitly said that one of its purposes was to help state-recognized groups "initiate procedures for their recognition by the federal government."[38] Tribal researchers attended federal acknowledgment workshops and hired scholars to reinterpret census reports and other historical records.[39] With the legacy of prejudice and secrecy that characterized the southern Indian experience, however, many groups found that proving a credible Indian identity was nearly impossible using written records alone.[40]

Southern Indians who sought to clarify their Native identities—first through the state and then through the federal government—received aid from a variety of sources. The state commissions supported small-scale research projects to aid tribes in their pursuits. For example, in 1981 the SAIAC launched a research project made possible by the Summer Youth Employment and Indian CETA Program. The commission hired two high school students to serve as records research clerks, who were responsible for compiling genealogical data for tribes seeking state recognition. With pens and magnifying glasses in hand, the two students searched through microfilm and paper documents in the State Archives and History Building in Montgomery.[41]

Missionary groups and southern tribal communities also formed partnerships to conduct the genealogical research necessary to put together recognition petitions. The most successful example of this partnership was between the Poarch Creek, who achieved federal recognition in 1984, and the Lutheran World Ministries.[42] The Houma also drew upon the vast research experience of the Mennonite Central Committee, which helped them draft a federal acknowledgment petition, submitted in 1986.[43] Relationships with church groups initially developed under the duress of racial segregation and tribal struggles for equitable education, but they took on a new shape as the needs of Indian communities changed from seeking rights and services at the local level to lobbying on a national scale.

While churches were instrumental in the petitioning process for some groups, the MOWA Choctaw leaders turned to secular scholars and researchers to help them compile genealogical charts and tribal histories. In 1981 the group received a planning and development grant from the Alabama Committee for the Humanities to begin research for the eventual petition for federal recognition. One year later, tribal leaders sought the aid of Jacqueline Anderson Matte, a local historian and history teacher who had written a history of Washington County and later wrote a book on the MOWA Choctaw. In 1983 the tribe received another grant from the Administration for Native Americans and soon sent a letter of intent to the Branch of Acknowledgement and Research (BAR) division of the BIA.[44] After several years of arduous work, the group submitted its formal petition on April 28, 1988.

The southern Indian movement of the 1970s and 1980s also fostered regional inter-tribal coalitions to help Indian groups pursue recognition. Most notable was the Indian Information Project, a component of the Lumbee Regional Development Association, Inc., which organized a 1981 conference in Alexandria, Virginia, titled "Critical Issues Affecting Eastern Indians." The project was created in response to the shared concerns of more than one hundred eastern tribal groups who wanted to ensure that the federal and state governments did not continue to overlook them.[45] At the conference, tribal leaders developed a definition of "Indian" that would better reflect the unique history of unrecognized groups. Leaders hoped to remove the power of the federal government in determining Indian authenticity, which had been based on preconceived notions and stereotypes. The group determined that the definition should be broadened beyond the blood quantum rule, one difficult for eastern groups to follow given the lack of accurate records and decades of intermarriage. Instead, the conference attendees concluded that Indian identity should be measured in terms of recognition by state Indian commissions or other Indian groups. This, however, was not an uncomplicated matter, as tribal governments themselves were vested with the responsibility of "watching out for 'wannabes'" by closely monitoring their own tribal rolls.[46]

Although the conference had little impact on the federal acknowledgment process, the proceedings provided significant insight into the common issues and concerns of tribal leaders throughout the South and Northeast. The conference attendees stressed that eastern Indians were not looking for a "government handout" but a formal acknowledgment of their very existence. "It is a matter of pride," one representative said. "Our people have always been self-sufficient!"[47] As the Indian Information Project began to receive media attention, its director, Helen Scheirbeck, reiterated this sentiment, pointing out that "being recognized as an Indian has something to do with building self esteem and pride, not just dollars."[48]

The Indian Information Project became a source of guidance and support for petitioning groups. As Ella Thomas, a Narragansett tribal representative, commented, "[I]f denial comes, be prepared for it. Don't give up, come back again! Challenge them! Resubmit!"[49] Thomas's perspective reflected the attitude of conference attendees, who saw federal acknowledgment as a hurdle for established Indian tribes to confront, not the ultimate authority in determining Indian identity. The federal acknowledgment process was basically a game. In fact, the official conference motto was: "God made Indians, not the U.S. government. We are in a game, let's play it to win!"[50] Conference attendees discussed research strategies, learned from each other's experiences, and shared contact information for professional researchers and graduate students in anthropology and history.[51]

For many tribes, the effort that went into submitting a petition for federal acknowledgment, even if it was rejected, permitted them to construct their *own* tribal histories in their *own* words following decades of mislabeling and degradation. For example, in the previously mentioned work on the MOWA Choctaw by Jacqueline Anderson Matte, *They Say the Wind Is Red: The Alabama Choctaw Lost in Their Own Land,* she traces the group's struggle to survive in Alabama from the colonial period to the present. Although Matte relies heavily on historical and genealogical documentation in the group's federal petition, extensive oral histories comprise the bulk of the published book. Through Matte's work, the MOWA Choctaw community members spoke as "Indians" rather than "Cajuns."

Educating the public was also one of the goals of the United Houma Nation. In 1982 the tribe published a booklet based on excerpts from their federal acknowledgment petition "to acquaint the general public with age-old truths and centuries of Houma history." The acting tribal chairman, John Billiot, set the book's tone by stressing: "we maintain [a] very strong identity which is our own." Billiot rejected the historic characterizations of hybridity and mongrelization, which implied an absence of racial or cultural individuality. He asserted that the Houma were not just an Indian group but a tribal nation. He wrote: "As we move further into our tribe's 'Era of Change,' we realize that communication with non-Indians as well as other tribes is necessary to create an awareness of the nature of Houma Indians. We are a determined people working toward self-sufficiency, self-respect, self-government and, in the final analysis, self-determination."[52] The booklet was intended to "tell the tribe's story from the inside," combining oral histories with the established literature on the group to detail "discrimination, struggle and triumph in the years 1910 to 1981."[53]

Indian leaders took on increasingly prominent roles in constructing tribal histories, but academic works on southern Indians also exhibited pronounced shifts. The first generation of Indian college graduates—many of whom were the first to attend desegregated schools—added their insider perspectives on the decades-long academic discussion on the Houma and MOWA Choctaw. Individuals like Bruce Duthu, a Houma legal scholar, offered unique historical understanding and forced other scholars to challenge outdated notions of Houma history.[54] At the same time, the MOWA Choctaw leader Gallasneed Weaver, who earned a master's degree from the University of South Alabama, wrote several papers on the history of his community, including "Minority among Minorities" and "I Led Three Lives Because of Jim Crowism."[55] Other scholars, such as the ethnohistorian Hiram Gregory, worked extensively with Indian groups across Louisiana for decades and created a surge of interest in southern tribal history.[56] A new generation of scholars exposed the inadequacy of past works on southern Indian groups that were shaped by the prejudices of researchers and census takers and their preconceived notions of Indians. By the 1970s, most academic works had de-emphasized the "race question" and focused more on Indian resilience in the face of adversity.[57]

Newspaper reporters who had traded in the former categorizations of "Cajun," "Sabine," and "so-called Indians" also showed an identifiable shift in attitude and understanding when mentioning Indians in their writing. For example, in a story about the development of tribal enterprises, one Louisiana journalist admitted, "you probably couldn't tell from first glance they _are_ Indians."[58] Although the journalist was judging what Indians _should_ look like, the comment did not doubt the subjects' identities. It reflected the increasing public acceptance of Louisiana Indians. In fact, some newspapers even became ardent public supporters of their states' Indian residents, as demonstrated in such headlines as: "Baton Rouge Indian Woman to Be Honored on Saturday: Kicking the Stereotype," "Coushatta Tribal Head Is Proud of His People," and "Revive the Pride of the Choctaw Indians."[59]

The MOWA Choctaw also found support in unlikely places. An elementary teacher from Hubbertville School wrote a letter in 1989 to Alabama governor Guy Hunt on behalf of her fifth grade class. In the letter, Brenda Wyers expressed her class's concern for the economic and political status of the MOWA Choctaw, who were in the midst of petitioning for federal acknowledgment. The class enthusiastically supported the petition and even inquired as to how they could help tribal leaders pay for trips to Washington, D.C., to attend hearings.[60]

Although many southern Indian groups became increasingly empowered through their acceptance as Indians at the local and state levels, they found the federal government—specifically the BAR—less willing to acknowledge them as tribal nations. The experiences of the Poarch Creek of Alabama and the Coushatta and Tunica-Biloxi of Louisiana—who used their positions with the state commissions to gain support from governors and legislatures for their eventual federal acknowledgment—proved exceptional and difficult to replicate. Both the Houma and MOWA Choctaw successfully transcended their racial ambiguity and were acknowledged as tribal nations by their respective states, but the federal acknowledgment office ultimately denied their recognition. Despite Louisiana's claim that the United Houma Nation was an "authentic Indian community," members of the BAR disputed the nation's descendancy claim to the historic Houma tribe, arguing that members were ethnically French, German, and English in origin.[61] The BAR also argued that the MOWA Choctaw lacked adequate evidence tying them to a historic tribe. Despite the group's oral tradition, the BAR staff disregarded stories it believed could not be substantiated through documentation. The BAR concluded in its report on the MOWA: "the MOWA ancestors, most of whom were well documented, were not identified as American Indians or descendants of any particular tribe in the records made in their own life times."[62]

Both groups fell victim to the ultimate southern Indian irony. After successfully navigating through a biracial system that had marginalized them for decades, the Houma and MOWA Choctaw did not possess documentation to prove their continuous existence to the federal government. It seemed the nasty legacy of Jim Crow would leave a permanent impression on the region's Indian population.

Some scholars, however, argue that a lack of records was not the only reason the Houma and MOWA Choctaw were denied federal recognition. John Daniel d'Oney claims that the BAR did not interpret carefully all of the Houma's evidence. He disputes the fact that the tribe could be categorized with other groups because their dialect of French is distinctly different and they show significant cultural and physical differences from their non-Indian neighbors. He also points out how the BAR overlooked the fact that the group had maintained an understanding of themselves as Indians over time as evidenced in the court cases about educational segregation.[63] The historian Mark Miller further posits that the group simply "did not neatly fit the model of tribalism" that BAR members looked for and was therefore defeated from the start.[64] The BAR's 1994 ruling against the MOWA Choctaw repeated this pattern by emphasizing historic documentation identifying the group as "Cajun" or "Negro." In response, the tribe hired an anthropologist from the University of Arizona, Richard W. Stoffle, to conduct an ethnographic study of the community. Stoffle affirmed the MOWA Choctaw's claims, but his conclusions did nothing to reverse the BAR's decision.[65]

The Houma and MOWA Choctaw outcomes raise intriguing questions regarding differences in how federal and state governments construct Indian identity. As seen in the previous chapter, state recognition could be attained via two channels: (1) a direct legislative act or (2) a formal petitioning process reviewed by the state Indian agencies. States often granted tribal recognition with legislative acts to further political and economic interests. Tribal leaders on the commissions, however, began to construct stricter recognition criteria, and the state recognition process began to loosely mirror the federal process. Why, then, did groups like the United Houma Nation and the MOWA Choctaw find support and recognition from their state governments and Indian commissions when the BAR determined that their claims were unconvincing?

Federal and state officials used different assumptions to define an Indian tribe. Although southern states had suppressed Indian identity with Jim Crow laws, by the 1970s they were better equipped than their federal counterparts to understand the unique circumstances of Indians because tribal leaders had generated support and acceptance at the local and state levels. Despite inter-tribal conflicts, southern tribal leaders were more willing to accept Indian groups that had suffered the same types of oppression and marginality. The southern Native experience was by no means uniform, but the region's Indian movement stirred racial pride and unity among tribal leaders as they gained a more prominent place in the region's political arena.

Despite difficulties with the federal acknowledgment process, tribal nations obviously did not cease to exist. The value of state recognition therefore should not be minimized. By itself, state recognition did not lead to an economic revolution or social transformation, but it did lay the groundwork for change by giving non–federally recognized Indian groups the psychological benefit of being formally acknowledged by a governing body. The Poarch Creek leader Eddie Tullis expressed the value he placed on the tribal-state relationship: "[W]e have such a good relationship with the State of Alabama [and] we have had great support from both the governor and the legislature."[66] In addition to psychological satisfaction, state recognition also produced tangible benefits such as access to funding, the opportunity to create governmental alliances, and the freedom to rally political support to reclaim land and develop an economic infrastructure. State recognition was also valuable because it restructured the southern racial hierarchy, forcing it to accept and embrace a more diverse demography.

The southern Indian movement allowed many tribal groups to assert and clarify their Indian identities following decades of invisibility within a biracial system, and the Houma of Louisiana and the MOWA Choctaw in Alabama exemplified the difficulties that many southern groups faced in pursuing recognition. Indian claims of identity in the early twentieth century spurred lively courtroom debates, school board meetings, and academic forums as the racial identities of these groups were explored. The battles to assert racial distinctiveness were merely small steps, however, that resulted in the development of separate schools. Nevertheless, real success did not arrive until the southern Indian movement emerged in the 1970s, bringing a renewed public awareness of Indian issues to state governments. As Indian leaders shaped their communities into centralized tribal governments and constructed their own histories, this visibility slowly began to reshape the racial demography of southern states. The state Indian affairs commissions developing within this context further validated tribal communities through formal recognition by the states and other Indian groups.

Building Racial Unity

Indian communities recognized that to mount an effective challenge to the established southern racial order they needed to unite scattered and diverse Indian populations under a common racial identity. Unification was not an easy feat, however, given the tension surrounding the developing tribal acknowledgment process. As one Houma leader explained during a 1982 meeting: "It's kind of hard to affect legislation or anything else when you don't have a real large concentrated population."[67] Moreover, a regional culture of suspicion and silence obstructed the goal of unification under a common racial identity. The Indian movement profoundly changed southern Indians, but benefits did not immediately impact the lives of the average Indian person. Tribal leaders, however, had insights regarding unity that others did not. The leaders traveled to state capitols to help foster tribal-state relationships through the formation of commissions. These leaders' unique perspectives also arose from their direct exposure to counterparts in other tribal communities, inter-tribal organizations, and the broader regional and national pan-Indian movement.

The larger Indian population did not universally share the enthusiasm of elected leaders for the potential long-term benefits of becoming integrated into state politics. In fact, many Native people—both tribal and non-tribal—preferred to remain isolated and unseen. For many decades, invisibility had been a matter of survival. The isolated and secretive lifestyles that had developed had a significant impact on later generations that were suspicious of outsiders and people in positions of power—a common characteristic of impoverished southerners generally. An Alabama commission report acknowledged the challenges, stating: "Indian community members exhibit a low level of self-esteem, which directly contributes to a lack of motivation in participating in tribal affairs. Strong evidence of fear and distrust on the part of the Indian population toward county, state, and federal agencies places a tremendous burden on tribal leaders striving to effectively represent the group."[68] Deeply imbedded suspicions frequently frustrated state officials, but tribal leaders in privileged positions also found it challenging to gain the trust and respect of their own people. This distrust was evident when tribal members requested that small-scale advocacy organizations, such as Louisiana Indians for Equality (LIFE) or the Indian Angels, serve as intermediaries between themselves and government agencies. LIFE organizers claimed that many tribal elders were "scared to death" to call the governor's office, the Indian affairs commission, or even their own tribal chairman's office when they needed services.[69] A general distrust of government agencies pervaded many Indian communities, which was no surprise given the anguish and betrayal that Removal had caused.

The legacy of Jim Crow also thwarted efforts toward racial unification. An AIAC report complained that the Alabama Indian experience was a "peculiar" one because "Indian people have been compelled to exist within the state structure." With many Indians' birth certificates officially declaring them "colored" or "white," people were initially reluctant to challenge the established biracial order publicly. The report further clarified, "Indian heritage was once a source of danger for Indian individuals who lived in the world apart from reservations."[70] Parents often impressed upon younger generations the danger of being an Indian in the South. A member of the Cherokee Tribe of Northeast Alabama recalled her childhood in the 1930s and 1940s: "Mom was ashamed of letting anyone know her background—not because she was afraid of what someone would do to her, but because she thought people would look down on her. We were taught not to talk about our Indian background. We didn't openly bring it out. I'm proud to be an Indian now, but Mom wasn't back then. I wish that we had been taught to be proud—it would have helped our self-esteem."[71] The culture of silence that developed among many descendants of southern Indians who refused to move westward took a toll on their tribal cultures and languages. The AIAC called this the "curse" of many Indians who either took their cultural practices underground or abandoned them altogether. Despite the situation, "a number of groups have retained their community structures and, although their life ways are outwardly very much like their non-Indian neighbors, they have retained their unity and some unique customs."[72]

To earn the trust and promote the racial unity of Indian people statewide, staff members of both the Louisiana and Alabama commissions launched outreach campaigns. Following earlier efforts to unify tribal interests by people such as the Poarch Creek leader Calvin McGhee in the early 1960s, the Alabama commission of the 1970s and 1980s took a particularly aggressive approach in reaching out to the diverse Indian groups throughout the state.[73] The staff enhanced their agency's visibility by attending tribal gatherings and visiting schools, Indian churches, and tribal council meetings to have "firsthand contact [with] Indian people who . . . [demonstrated] reluctance . . . to interact with government bodies."[74] The Louisiana commission also recognized that "mercantilism, racial, and ethnic discrimination, and federal status denial have combined to hide much of the Indian culture of Louisiana from the general population." By reaching out to isolated Indian groups and increasing public awareness about Indian issues, LOIA staff reported a promising trend that began in the 1970s when more people marked "Indian" as their dominant racial identity on the U.S. census.[75]

In fact, southern states followed the upward national trend of self-reporting Indians.[76] According to the U.S. Census Bureau, Indian populations increased nationally by 71 percent between 1970 and 1980 alone.[77] Although the Native population in the South was smaller than that in western states, the South saw the largest upsurge in self-identified Indians since 1960—with Alabama and Louisiana having two of the largest population increases.[78] The rising population reveals a trend in racial clarification and transformation and displays several processes happening simultaneously. Historically self-identified Indians had found a more hospitable environment for their claim, while historically self-identified non-Indians made the choice to "identity switch" by adopting an Indian identity. No matter the status of an individual—tribally affiliated or not—southern Natives began to change the racial makeup of the region by pushing for the identification of "Indian."

Newsletters and pamphlets enhanced the commissions' outreach campaigns. Information not only kept readers abreast of important tribal issues at local and national levels, it also promoted racial unity by invoking historical memory. For example, traumatic recollections of the forced removal of thousands of Indians from their homes and families were dredged up in a 1981 issue of the *Alabama Indian Advocate*. The Creek psychologist Wayne Hodges argued that in light of "the conditions under which our people were ushered out of Alabama . . . it would be only natural for our people to develop strong emotions of resentment, fear, and anger toward the Non-Indian in general." Hodges also addressed how the intergenerational trauma of the removal experience caused many to adopt a posture of suspicion, which made inter-tribal cooperation difficult. Even more important, perhaps, these psychological defenses made it challenging for Indian people to see themselves as part of a larger racial group with a loosely shared past. Hodges argued that for the sake of the commission—and the broader movement—"we must grow and overcome such self-defeating defenses."[79] Similarly, a pamphlet produced by LOIA stressed that Indian people should come together because of their shared adversity. "These communities have all suffered," the pamphlet pointed out, "[and] rather than abandoning the ways of their ancestors . . . they have been strengthened . . . [to] work harder at preserving a [shared] heritage which Louisiana otherwise might have lost."[80]

Attempts to educate and unify Native people were also made through radio broadcasts. On November 12, 1981, the first Indian-owned commercial radio station in the South—and the second in the nation—went on air in Atmore, Alabama. WASG radio was a Poarch Creek family–owned venture with a range of about one hundred miles. The station included special programming to educate Indians about the regional movement and national issues related to tribal sovereignty.[81] The AIAC even scheduled a daily feature called the *Alabama Indian Journal*, a sixty-second radio program designed to empower

Alabama's Indian residents through history and information on local and national politics.[82]

Tribal leaders had learned from early Indian activists and had found that the key to building racial pride among their people was through forging connections with other Indian groups nationally. Representatives from Alabama and Louisiana participated in the National Congress of the American Indian, the National Indian Education Association Conference, and the Governors' Interstate Indian Conference. The AIAC even hosted the latter in 1990.[83] In addition to representing their tribes in national Indian conferences and organizations, leaders in both states unified their communities' interests with those of other groups throughout the South. For example, in 1988, the North Carolina Indian Affairs Commission hosted the Indian Unity Conference for more than a thousand participants from across the region who came together to promote pride among southern Native populations.[84] By involving the general Indian population—either directly or indirectly—in the formation of inter-tribal coalitions, leaders hoped to alleviate some of the anxieties associated with claiming an Indian identity. The objective was "to provide a climate in which people may be free to be Indian and express their heritage."[85]

Building racial unity also meant empowering Native people to become more visible through state-issued identification documents, which had historically failed to include "Indian" as a racial category. Several members of the Clifton Choctaw of Louisiana worked tirelessly to change the racial designations on their birth certificates from "colored" to "Indian."[86] At the same time, Alabama tribal leaders lobbied the state department of motor vehicles to include the label "Indian" on state-recognized tribal members driver's licenses. They argued that tribal enrollment cards should be sufficient proof of an individual's racial status. In 1990 Alabama attorney general Don Siegelman supported this argument in a formal statement, which permitted Native people to identify themselves as "Indian" on Alabama driver's licenses if they are members of one of Alabama's state recognized tribes.[87]

Portraying Indians as informed voters became an additional priority for the state commissions. Alabama commission newsletters published legislators' names and addresses, pointing readers toward their local representatives and recommending that they write letters to "make members of state government and private sector more sensitive to the employment, education, health, and social service needs of Indian people."[88] LOIA also worked to merge diverse tribal identities into a single racial identity in order to build a profile with politicians and impress upon them that Indians were an underserved minority.[89] "If you can tell a fellow you might be able to swing a few thousand votes his direction," explained one tribal leader, "he'll tell you what he will do for you."[90]

Although political influence was a common goal among tribal leaders, many held a deep concern that voter registration records misrepresented Indians, making it difficult to attract the attention of politicians effectively. In Alabama, Indians believed that "there is no listing of minorities other than Blacks on the State voter lists . . . only Black voters are counted, all 'others' are listed as white."[91] A similar situation existed in Louisiana, where the Houma leader Steve Cheramie claimed that Native voters were invisible because they were "mixed in with the blacks and the whites." He noted that even though he listed himself as Indian on his voter registration card, the courthouse records in Jefferson Parish indicated that he was black. "They changed it," Cheramie complained as he warned others to check into their own records to ensure accuracy.[92] Accurate voting registration records were viewed as a critical component in establishing a visible constituency. Native people in both states were encouraged to challenge a false racial label and to assert their identities as Indians.

A concentrated voting population was crucial if Indians were to have influence on local and state legislation. LOIA members recognized this problem in 1973 when they first set out to repeal the 1920 statute (LSA-R.S. 9:201) that outlawed marriage between Indians and African Americans and denied the children of these unions their inheritance.[93] Ironically, although the law was a remnant of Jim Crow it gave the commission footing to point out that the state in fact acknowledged the existence of Indians in an attempt to suppress "racial mixing." This recognition, however, had little impact on altering the biracial system that had become the norm in the South. Peggy Pascoe illuminates this contradiction in her study of twentieth-century American miscegenation laws, which reveals that by the 1920s American courts refused "to recognize obvious inconsistencies in legal racial classification schemes."[94] Because groups like the Houma and MOWA Choctaw complicated the established racial order, the acknowledgment of "Indians" in miscegenation laws was part of a larger effort to simplify the process of identification. Although the "one drop" rule was often employed to identify those of the "colored race," states such as Virginia, Georgia, and Alabama also passed laws during the 1920s declaring that "persons who have one-sixteenth or less of the blood of the American Indian and have no other non-Caucasic blood shall be deemed to be white persons."[95] Five decades after the passage of the 1920 statute, tribal leaders in Louisiana rallied behind the law to unify people around the common racial identity of "Indian." They believed the only way to counter racially discriminatory legislation was to speak out collectively as *the* targeted race.

In the end, the commissions succeeded in instilling trust in an otherwise distrustful population of Indian people. Commission members in both states aligned their agencies' purposes toward racial unity. They recognized that inter-tribal coalition building must reach beyond the leadership to develop outreach programs: commission staff attended tribal gatherings, circulated newsletters, and broadcast relevant issues over the airwaves. Through all of these efforts, they encouraged a broader involvement with national Indian organizations and suggested that Native people become more politically active and visible. Tribal leaders understood that the strength of the southern Indian movement must come from individual Indians themselves—people who could reach beyond false Jim Crow identities and grow together under a common racial category of "Indian."

A New Minority

Even though the southern Indian movement succeeded in building racial unity among Indians, most laws continued to recognize only whites and African Americans. Native leaders and activists argued that although tribal groups were a significant minority in the South they were unjustly denied any special consideration or assistance available to other minority groups. According to an Alabama Indian Affairs Commission report, "Because the American Indian in Alabama has never before had a voice in issues and concerns that affect their lives and their continued existence, their progress is some 50 to 60 years behind that of the non-Indian community."[96] Most states in the region still did not consider Indians a racial minority by the 1980s, so the positive steps taken by state-level Indian affairs commissions to establish a place for their people within the broader southern mosaic had limited effectiveness.

Indian affairs commissions in both Alabama and Louisiana understood the need to develop strategies to assert a minority status. In a 1975 report, LOIA members expressed hope that their most significant contribution would be to launch a public awareness campaign emphasizing Indians as the most neglected minority in Louisiana: "Although Indians claim a uniquely sentimental niche in historical Louisiana folklore, they are presently very socially and economically deprived, when compared to other groups in the state. In a time where public attention is being directed to minority groups, it is proper that we devote particular efforts toward improving the lot of our native Americans who are a minority in their own land." Without an official minority status, explained LOIA, southern Indians remained marginalized, impoverished, and underemployed. They were discriminated against because of their race but were unable to receive any advantages as minorities.[97] In 1980 the SAIAC reported a similar pattern: "The Indian people are caught between two societies. With no reservations in the state, the Indians are disconnected from their historical society and from the dominant contemporary society in which they live. Historically, they have been overlooked and ignored by the state and have survived without recognition as best they could, while other 'minority groups' have received special consideration and assistance. The Indian simply does not fit in; he has no place to go."[98] The commissions demonstrated that although many of the basic arguments used to promote change remained constant, the rhetoric describing the southern Indian experience shifted with the times. Instead of "racial intermediaries" or "outcasts" within a biracial system, southern Indians became the "overlooked minority" as the politics of the 1980s changed the terms of discussion.

Tribal communities remained some of the most disadvantaged people in their respective states. A 1970 report titled *American Indians of Louisiana: An Assessment of Needs* revealed that the median income for Indian families in Louisiana was $4,650—well below the statewide average. In addition, unemployment was high, housing was substandard, and 32 percent of Louisiana's Indian populations were illiterate.[99] A similar pattern of poverty and illiteracy existed among Alabama's scattered Indian communities. "What was somewhat surprising," admitted Charles Stevens in his 1983 master's thesis, "was the fact that the data indicate a literacy rate of the Indian population to be lower than that for the Black population."[100] It had been commonly thought that Indians held an intermediate social position between African Americans and whites in the South. After looking at the data he realized that an intermediate status was really nonexistent.

Nowhere was this false perception more evident than in employment. Until the 1970s, the MOWA Choctaw complained that local chemical companies refused to accept their job applications; the firms also maintained dressing rooms and water fountains for whites and African Americans only. Since the MOWA Choctaw claimed to be neither, there were no accommodations for them.[101] More recently, Indians were overlooked for work in many areas of Alabama where employers were "unaware and unreceptive to the acceptance of Indian people as a minority quota or employable population."[102] Many employers claimed that the only "real" Indians had gone to Oklahoma, eliminating Indians as a legitimate minority in Alabama.[103] Reflecting this pervasive attitude, an Alabama Indian affairs report assessed that in Mobile County, where surveyors had counted 1,162 Indians in the 1980 census, only one worked at a major industrial plant in the area. Of the four plants—with a combined workforce of 7,767—only one made any provisions for the inclusion of Indians under an affirmative action plan. Neighboring Washington County had a slightly better record; the single plant in that county employed 47 Indians out of a total workforce of 573.[104]

In the early 1980s, tribal leaders and commission staff in both states met with politicians to discuss reducing unemployment within their predominantly non–federally recognized communities. For example, following a 1981 LOIA meeting, Senator Bill Jefferson introduced legislation giving tax breaks to small industries that agreed to operate in impoverished areas throughout the state. Although the tax incentives targeted areas with particularly high concentrations of Indians, discrimination continued. Roy Procell of the Choctaw-Apache Community of Ebarb expressed his disappointment over how his people were treated by the small industrial plants in the area. "They came in, hired my people and then treated them like dogs," Procell said. Although workplace abuse was a common complaint among all southern factory workers—the nation's cheapest labor force—the experience convinced Procell that the only solution to persistent unemployment and maltreatment was to develop Indian-owned and Indian-run industries.[105] Daniel Darden of the Chitimacha tribe owned three businesses and gave preference to Indians in hiring. "I think the goal has to be to take care of ourselves [for] the future," he said.[106] Tribal leaders agreed that Senator Jefferson's program was a step in the right direction, but without a *specific* policy giving Indians hiring preference or significant regulation of program implementation, the potential for worker abuse was great. Many people instead began to ponder how to begin developing Indian-run businesses and reverse the economic depression in Indian communities.

Southern Indian leaders were also concerned about the continued scarcity of educational opportunities in their communities. They had noticed a link between high unemployment rates and limited education. For example, Chitimacha leaders complained that although many tribal members had graduated high school by the mid-1980s, few had the necessary resources to obtain a higher education or land lucrative employment. As a result, many people were consistently unemployed or took low-paying jobs in the construction industry or the oil fields of south Louisiana.[107] Commissioners realized that scholarships for college-bound Indian students were necessary and needed to be a high priority, but because commissions had few resources, members spent long hours strategizing how to raise money for this financial aid. At an Alabama commission meeting, the MOWA Choctaw leader Gallasneed Weaver suggested enlisting the aid of private enterprise. "I meet a lot of plant managers," he told other tribal representatives. "They said they'd be glad to contribute lots of money towards Indian funds in the state of Alabama to start scholarship programs [and] industrial training programs."[108] These brainstorming meetings resulted in a modest Alabama Indian scholarship fund that drew money from a variety of sources, including private donations and state discretionary money.

LOIA also managed to provide Indians with the opportunity to attend college by securing small sums of scholarship money. In 1981, however, the demand for scholarships increased at the same time that available funding decreased, and the commission found that there simply was not enough money to fill the need.[109] Nevertheless, leaders continued to pursue alternative sources of funding for college-bound Indians. In 1985 a desperate commission sent letters to every college and university in the state asking whether funds were available for Indian students. The responses were discouraging. Not a single school had earmarked money for Indian students, revealing that Indian needs remained largely unacknowledged despite the gains in opportunities and visibility.[110]

The difficulties that tribal nations continued to experience in securing employment and education for their members convinced leaders that promoting Indian visibility was not enough—they needed to establish a public image of Indians as a minority group that needed the benefits of affirmative action. In Louisiana, tribal leaders focused their attention on legislation that would officially label Native Americans, along with women and African Americans, as a minority for the purpose of employment breaks.[111] Because tribal unemployment rates were 30–40 percent, this legislation had broad political support, and on April 29, 1987, a bill sponsored by Republican senator Kenneth E. Osterberger passed without objection, officially adding Indians to the list of Louisiana's recognized minorities. Now Indians could receive employment preference based on race.[112]

Even though the bill passed easily, it led to tension between tribal leaders and African American leaders. This was no surprise, given that Louisiana's Black Legislative Caucus had initially resisted LOIA because of the competition it generated between black and Indian agencies for minority-based grants.[113] Following the passage of the Indian minority bill, African American Democratic senator Richard Turnley lashed out at LOIA member Diana Williamson, who identified herself as both white and Chitimacha Indian.

"You have the best of both worlds," he complained. "You're white and a minority."[114] Turnley raised some significant questions about the role that miscegenation and "passing" played in the racial hierarchy of the South. How should a minority be classified? Because many Indian communities had a history of intermarriage with both African Americans and whites, should that be considered when deciding who should benefit from affirmative action? How can discrimination be measured?

Determining minority status was complicated, and it was a sensitive issue for many of Louisiana's Indians who felt entitled to the status. "We're not trying to overshadow other minorities," explained the Jena Choctaw tribal chairman Jerry Jackson. "We feel like Native Americans are the original minority."[115] Attitudes on the issue were diverse, and in many cases southern Indians who campaigned for "minority rights" resented the criticism they received. In a letter to the editor of the Baton Rouge–based *State Times* in 1983, one Indian resident expressed his frustration: "In World War II, about 25,000 of my people served in the armed forces and one or two became heroes. Many just died while, back at home, many places still forced my people into white or black categories. They were still being murdered, ridiculed and were recognized as third class citizens. . . . You other so called minorities think about what I have said the next time you holler discrimination or someone has mistreated your children because of your color."[116] Amid the national debate on affirmative action, it isn't surprising that many Indian people took a defensive posture and were often more frustrated with the system itself than with their critics.

Aside from the poorly funded Indian commissions, there was no preexisting apparatus in place to deal with the unique historical experiences of tribal people who did not have the resources of the federal government at their disposal. Leaders chose to work within the state structure by turning to an existing affirmative action system and aiding other historically oppressed peoples. Although this decision understandably caused some anxiety within the African American community as it spread resources even thinner, it also created concerns within Indian communities whose ultimate goal was not to achieve a minority status but to assert a sovereign one. Many tribes viewed their newly defined minority status as a temporary necessity, repeatedly stressing that "unlike other minorities, state tribes have the potential to become federally recognized, and subsequently become sovereign nations."[117] Even so, tribal leaders realized that "there was also a strong possibility of losing our autonomy and becoming linked with the Division of Black Culture as a Division of Indian Culture."[118]

Nonetheless, Indians began to forge political alliances with their newly defined minority status. Tribal leaders recognized that self-determination not only established a foundation for tribal sovereignty but also helped them forge political alliances with the Republican Party. Strengthening tribal communities from within was "very important to our Republican friends," commented one Houma community leader. He clarified: "It would provide the tribes with means to contribute to the mainstream of the American society. As you know, the big word today is 'We don't want to be giving to the poor, all they do is take, take, take. They don't know how to put back.'"[119] Fully aware of the criticisms and concerns often used against African Americans, tribal leaders defended the need for an affirmative action plan for Indians. Carefully calling tribal groups "disadvantaged" rather than "poor," Indian affairs commissions emphasized the temporary nature of the situation and how assistance would accelerate their ability to develop a self-sustaining economic infrastructure. "Historically the American Indian has been a giver—never a taker," reported the SAIAC. "Traditional, Indian tribes, bands, or groups are not seeking give away or hand out programs and services . . . they are seeking guidance and direction in finding ways to become a more self supportive citizen . . . to increase tribal self sufficiency . . . striving toward Indian self-determination."[120] By appealing directly to the concerns of many politicians, tribal leaders gained widespread support for their efforts to obtain land, economic development opportunities, and, in some cases, federal acknowledgment.

As identified minorities, Indians in Alabama and Louisiana were introduced to more economic development opportunities by state agencies created to aid in minority business ventures. For example, the Louisiana commission worked closely with the Governor's Office of Minority Business also to help preexisting Indian-owned businesses reap new benefits.[121] Together, the two entities also met with entrepreneurs to discuss the feasibility of establishing craft markets, tanneries, mechanics shops, and alligator farms.[122]

According to the 1986–87 annual report, the AIAC and the Governor's Office of Minority Business held a series of meetings with unemployed Indians, small business owners, and tribal leaders. Soon afterward, the commission received a $35,000 grant from the Administration for Native Americans within the national Department of Health and Human Services. The money was used for a Tribal Employment Rights workshop at Auburn University for Alabama tribal leaders and Indian entrepreneurs.[123]

The workshop had several immediate results. Two Indian small business contractors were able to obtain legal certification, and several others were guided through the application process.[124] The U.S. Small Business Administration pledged to assist socially disadvantaged individuals—mainly American Indians, African Americans, and Hispanics—in developing businesses to compete in the American economy by having clear access to the federal procurement market.[125] In addition to helping small Indian-operated businesses, the Tribal Employment Rights workshop also helped the AIAC construct a minority rights certification procedure for Indians. By the end of 1987, seven Indian individuals had received employment based on their minority status. The AIAC also negotiated with individual companies and agencies—such as the Alabama Film Commission, General Electric Cooperative, Fort Rucker, and Ciba-Geigy Corporation—on behalf of Alabama's Indian population to pave the way for potential employment opportunities.[126] In addition, the AIAC trained tribal leaders regarding Indian minority rights while the Alabama Indian Small Business Association (AISBA) and the Alabama Indian Community Loan Fund (AICLF) were founded to develop tribal economic infrastructures statewide.[127]

Although self-determination through federal recognition remained the ultimate goal, tribal leaders understood that they needed to address the immediate concerns of their community members. Indians had to address the fact that they were among the most impoverished and poorly educated people in the states of Alabama and Louisiana. Without federal Indian services and resources, non–federally recognized communities found that embracing a minority status was the most effective way to jump-start social and economic development.

In Sum

The black civil rights movement made great strides in challenging the racially defined power hierarchy in the South, but the Indian rights movement complicated matters by confronting a categorization system that had mislabeled Indians for decades. For the first time in the twentieth century, ambiguously "othered" groups like the Houma and the MOWA Choctaw could publicly clarify their indigenous identities. As a result, the reorganization of tribal polities became a dominant theme of the 1970s and 1980s. Southern states willingly accepted the progressive shift from a biracial societal order and began recognizing tribal governments.

Tribal leaders and activists embraced the shifting politics of race by unifying scattered and diverse Indian peoples under a common racial identity. Because of the culture of silence and suspicion in many Indian families, however, eliciting cooperation was not easy. As a result, both the Alabama and Louisiana commissions sought out Native people through radio broadcasts and newsletters designed to educate Indians on contemporary issues, as well as tie them together under a loosely shared historical past. National and regional Indian organizations and conferences also linked the interests of the once isolated communities with the broader pan-Indian movement. In the end, a strong political force enabled Indians in both states to gain the support of politicians and affect policies at both the local and state levels.

As "Indian" became increasingly accepted as a racial designation, more Alabamans and Louisianans sought to change their race on birth certificates, driver's licenses, and voter registration cards. The resulting shift in racial demography generated more public awareness and enabled tribal leaders to access resources reserved for minorities. With a history of discrimination, poverty, and unemployment, many Indian communities found affirmative action strategically useful in promoting tribal development because it provided funding for college, created employment possibilities, and subsidized the establishment of Indian-owned and Indian-run businesses.

Despite the progress that shifting racial perceptions generated, change was slow in coming. No one knew this better than Angola Prison inmate Norman Billiot, whose plea to be recognized as an Indian went unheeded by prison officials. Although this situation caused Billiot much frustration and distress, he did not wage his battle alone. LOIA and the ITC acknowledged his plight and contacted state officials on his behalf.[128] It is unclear whether these advocacy efforts helped, but like so many other Indians across the state and region, the simple opportunity to affirm their identities proved empowering. The Houma councilman John Parfait perhaps said it best when he commented on how he was personally affected by the movement toward identity clarification: "We can show I am no more a Sabine, no more a Frenchman. I am an Indian."[129]

4
Starting from Scratch
Struggling to Improve Indian Lives

After she was fired from her job of fourteen years because of persistent absenteeism caused by health problems, Mildred Smith of the Louisiana Band of Choctaw found herself in a dire situation. A mother of four, Smith was burdened with sight and hearing impairments. Although resourceful enough to continue earning an income with a part-time position as a telephone operator at a law office, she was unable to procure quality health insurance coverage. In need of a new pair of trifocal glasses and set of hearing aids—a more pressing necessity given her difficulty hearing the phone ring at work—a desperate Smith wrote a hasty letter to the Louisiana Office of Indian Affairs (LOIA) in 1982. "Any help you give me would be greatly appreciated," Smith wrote after first recounting the other resources she had already explored. She reached out to LOIA as her last hope.[1]

A few weeks after Smith's letter arrived at the Louisiana Office of Indian Affairs (LOIA), an even more alarming letter came to the desk of the executive director. Elsie Billiot of the Houma community claimed to be at her "wit's end," as things seemed to be getting "steadily worse" for her, her ten-year-old son, and her two teenage daughters. There must be "some sort of program to help needy families," Billiot wrote after itemizing how she spent her monthly income of $463.20. With approximately $2.06 left after paying rent and utilities, the family could not afford adequate medical insurance or groceries. Also, with one of her daughters in need of medical care for a hearing problem and all of the children needing dental care, Billiot felt compelled to seek outside help. The most immediate concern, however, was the lack of food. "We are completely out of food except a few cans of vegetables," Billiot explained. "We have been having to go next door and eat with my sister."

Like Smith, Billiot also sought aid elsewhere before writing to the state Indian agency for help. She explained how she had applied for food stamps but could not wait the thirty-plus days necessary for her application to be processed. Fearing that her family would soon starve, Billiot stressed, "We need help now."[2]

As mothers, the primary source of income for their families, and members of non–federally recognized tribal communities, Smith and Billiot represented dozens of other women and men whose economic situations inspired them to pick up a pen and write to the Indian commissions for aid. These letters reflected not only the immediacy of their needs but also the success of tribal leaders in awakening Indians to the existence of state offices established to represent their interests. Even more telling than the letters, however, were the responses to them as commission staff revealed their struggles to provide even the most basic aid. Despite the strides made in the movement throughout the 1970s, the 1980s ushered in a new set of challenges in meeting the needs of Indian people. With the Reagan administration's budgetary cutbacks—particularly in programs and services most sought after by southern tribes—and the institution of a block grant system that gave funding discretion to state governments, state offices could do little to help people like Smith and Billiot.[3] The 1980s proved to be a difficult time for southern tribal development as leaders struggled with limited resources to build the economic and political infrastructures of tribal governments while responding to the immediate needs of their community members. "[Tribes] had fun in the 1970s," reflected one Louisiana tribal chairman who fondly remembered the "brainstorm meetings" and support rallies that marked the early years of the movement, but he continued, "hard times are here with us now."[4] Poarch Creek leaders agreed, calling the period a "crisis situation" that demanded strategic planning.[5]

Tribal leaders in Alabama and Louisiana maneuvered through this economic and political "crisis" by creatively procuring, coordinating, and delivering services to their Indian populations. Despite the diverse range of attitudes and approaches employed by tribal leaders, they agreed to focus on alleviating problems associated with poverty, poor health care, and housing, as well as limited education and unemployment in Indian communities. "We all have people that are in bad shape," recognized one Louisiana tribal chairman in a 1981 meeting.[6] The daunting questions, however, revolved around where to begin, whether tribal governments or consortiums should apply for grants, and who should administer grants after they were received. During a series of animated meetings aimed at answering these questions, tribal leaders plotted out the best approaches to address the immediate needs of their people while laying a foundation for the long-term social and economic growth of their governments. The tasks of identifying resources, applying for grants, administering programs, generating public support, and maintaining existing services proved overwhelming even for the most adept administrators and thus compelled community leaders to work together through state commissions, inter-tribal councils, and other organizations aimed at tribal development.

Although they were motivated to participate in inter-tribal coalitions, tribal leaders were equally driven to protect tribal self-determination from outside forces. As state agencies, Indian commissions held particularly precarious positions within Indian affairs. They were vehicles of change at the same time they held the strong potential of imposing on tribal sovereignty—the very thing they were initially intended to promote. Tribal leaders worried about the role that state Indian affairs agencies should play in the lives of tribal members. Alabama Poarch Creek chairman Eddie Tullis expressed this anxiety, stating: "Many people see state Indian commissions as being the cure-all to our ills. Commissions only provide mechanisms to see that people are served."[7] In fact, Indian leaders often envisioned southern Indian affairs agencies as bridges, go-betweens, or liaisons among state and federal agencies, tribal governments, and private individuals. As a result, the commissions not only negotiated for funds but also initiated and maintained important relationships with state and federal agencies on behalf of Indian communities. The 1980s, for many, was a time for state commissions to transcend a "historically familiar measure of appeasement" and become "vehicles for Indians to have control."[8]

This chapter examines the evolution of inter-tribal efforts in Alabama and Louisiana to answer the immediate and long-term needs of Indian people in the areas of education, employment, and social services against the backdrop of challenges presented by the Reagan administration's conservative economic policies. No matter their political affiliation or federal or state recognition status, tribal leaders struggled to find solutions to the larger problems of Indian poverty and political disempowerment. State commissions, inter-tribal councils, and other collaborative organizations assisted leaders in taking on the daunting task of promoting change. In 1981, AIAC chairman Leonard Hudson echoed the sentiments of others on the commission when he argued, "We have only scratched the surface of needs that have accumulated by more than 100 years of neglect."[9] Although the course of Indian affairs varied slightly in each state as leaders made decisions based on the specific needs of their people, the shared feeling of "starting from scratch" prompted an aggressive approach in both states. Leaders and supporters simultaneously promoted change from three different directions: from within state governments, from within tribal governments, and from within individual Indian families.

Change required several steps. Identifying the service population and documenting and measuring their needs were initial steps that tribal leaders implemented with varying degrees of success. This initial data collection was important, however, in building tribal-state relationships. Indian leaders also used the commissions to forge alliances with state agencies and legislators and to secure access to block grants. Meanwhile, the commissions strove to enhance tribal political and economic growth by acquiring funds and constructing support systems to offer advice and technical assistance. Communities in both states participated in workshops, forums, and demonstrations aimed at developing strong tribal leadership and promoting economic and political development to carry tribes into a more self-determining future. In the midst of crafting these far-reaching plans, tribal leaders still managed to meet the immediate needs of their people by obtaining funding—often on a piecemeal basis—to alleviate unemployment, enhance education, and increase the level of social services. Although certain programs proved temporary, some offered lasting benefits.

Despite the larger and often impersonal governmental forces and interests that converged to shape these accounts, this story centers on individuals like Mildred Smith, Elsie Billiot, and countless other Indian people who did or did not take the time to document their personal needs. Many of those not privy to the closed-door discussions that led to the initiation of new programs actually became driving forces behind them. Indian leaders served as ambassadors and negotiators for people who made their voices heard through letters, phone calls, public forums, private discussions, or survey responses. The heartfelt words of a struggling mother like Elsie Billiot, for example, conveyed a strong sense of urgency. In fact, soon after Billiot's letter reached LOIA, commission staff applied for and received an Emergency Food and Shelter Grant the following year in order to better respond to subsequent letters asking for help.

Measuring Indian Needs and Building Political Support

Indians were among the most impoverished and disadvantaged residents in Alabama and Louisiana. Tribal leaders knew this, and a few politicians even acknowledged it. Without an adequately documented and quantified level of need measured through community studies and surveys, however, commis-

6. House of a Louisiana Indian family at Bayou Grand Caillou, circa 1920s. (Courtesy of the State Library of Louisiana.)

sion staff members and tribal leaders found their efforts to promote change severely hampered. With no concrete statistical data, it was next to impossible to advocate for tribal services, submit grant proposals, or rally legislative support. As the AIAC reported: "There is a significant lack of awareness, in both private and public sectors, of the very existence of American Indians in this state. There is even less awareness of the needs, the issues and the concerns of Indian people."[10] Even as Indians became increasingly recognized as a racial minority in southern states, tribal leaders were eager to establish strong and lasting relationships with agencies and legislators. Crucial to this process was the identification of the unique requirements of Indian communities that distinguished them from other minority groups and demonstrated a need for special assistance.

The promise of assistance prompted the Indian commissions to give high priority to developing assessment instruments. With a scarcity of funding and lack of widespread cooperation, however, conducting a comprehensive study proved more difficult than anticipated. For example, in 1978 the Southwest Alabama Indian Affairs Commission (SAIAC) first attempted to conduct an informal needs assessment within the Poarch Creek community through volunteer interviews and mail surveys. The study supported earlier claims of a strong need for more employment opportunities and better educational resources, but because of its limited scope, the commission appealed to Governor George Wallace for funding to conduct a statewide assessment.[11] Also, because the federal government emphasized highly detailed documentation and statistical analysis, commission director Jennie Lee Dees lobbied the state to conduct a formal assessment of needs. She wrote the governor, "We must have more accurate, and therefore realistic, statistical data if we are to be effective in our continued efforts to acquire federal assistance to adequately meet American Indian needs."[12] When no funding came, a 1980 commission report reiterated: "Identifying needs of Alabama Indians is additionally difficult because of lack of statistics. Indians have previously been identified in Alabama as non-white or 'other' in most studies. In Washington County, reliable leaders claim that 50% of all Indians in that county live below the established income poverty levels. Of Indian youth entering school in 1969, 45% have dropped out and will become unemployable adults, lacking basic adult educational and life coping skills."[13]

Understanding the limited usefulness of vague statistics provided by tribal leaders and school enrollment records, the commission, along with other state agencies, developed an assessment instrument to be used in a comprehensive statewide study.[14] Without such a study, a commission report stated, Alabama Indians would continue to be excluded from "the plans of most local, state, and federal agencies for improved education, health and training services."[15] Although it was unclear whether the commission received the funds it requested for the study, by April 1981, commission leaders announced their intent to generate a needs assessment within the Jackson County Cherokee community, a group of about seven hundred people in Madison, Jackson, and De Kalb counties.[16]

The SAIAC's urgency in documenting the needs of Indians statewide complicates and illustrates the inter-tribal conflicts regarding equitable representation on the state commission in the early 1980s. While tribal leaders throughout the state argued that the Poarch Creek–dominated agency had blocked them in obtaining resources, SAIAC reports reflected an understanding that the agency's "responsibility is statewide." The problem, as reported to the governor's office, was that Alabama's diverse Indian population had "great variances in needs and problems."[17] The evidence demonstrates that the commission intended to use the data from the Poarch Creek community assessment to apply for grants and generate support for the general state Indian population, not just for the Poarch Creek. To succeed, however, Indian communities were expected to demonstrate a legitimate claim to such resources. This issue was a major source of contention among tribal leaders, who spent hours debating the point and its implications for tribal sovereignty.

They had become so embroiled in arguing with each other that the genuine needs of Indian people temporarily were forgotten. In 1982 Governor Fob James ended the fighting by defunding the commission, in effect eliminating any hope for implementing a comprehensive statewide needs assessment.

Although a large-scale survey was never conducted, the Alabama Indian Affairs Commission staff who ran the office after its restructuring in 1984 made use of the information they did have in annual reports: "Almost without exception, those counties in Alabama who have a high incidence of unemployment are also those counties where there is a high Indian population. Tribal governments, greatly impoverished because of their unique status since Indian Removal, struggle to maintain a governmental structure with little or no economic base."[18] Firsthand knowledge of the communities enabled the commission to speak in general terms about their needs, but it was unable to provide the detailed statistics the earlier agency had hoped to collect, which would have provided an even stronger argument.

LOIA and the Inter-Tribal Council (ITC) also placed a high priority on developing a needs assessment and collecting statistics. Just as the Alabama commission struggled with the logistics of conducting a large-scale study, Louisiana tribal leaders soon realized the difficulties of creating a high-quality and broadly encompassing report. In 1973 LOIA generated an "Assessment of Needs" report followed by a report in 1975 called "Elderly Indians of Louisiana and Their Needs" funded by the Bureau of Aging.[19] Although useful, the surveys were incomplete because they did not include every Indian group in the state. Plus, they only marginally unveiled the extent of need within communities.[20] In 1978 the ITC attempted to solve these shortcomings by sponsoring a research report entitled "A Survey of Rural Louisiana Indian Communities."[21] Unfortunately, tribal leaders also described this survey as "poorly done" because it only covered the five tribal communities belonging to the ITC. The council's director, Jeannette Campos, explained how the adult education grant proposal failed due to the lack of an accurate needs assessment. She stressed that the state needed data showing that Indians were in the lowest third of the socioeconomic scale. This proof was essential, she said, to compete with other organizations seeking aid, particularly those that had the advantage of political connections. For example, because Louisiana was a predominantly Catholic state, the Associated Catholic Charities had some "muscle" because of their longstanding relationships with legislators and grantors.[22]

In the 1980s, Louisiana tribal leaders delegated the task of assessing Indian needs to scholars who were particularly adept at drafting reports that painted a vivid picture of the conditions in the state's Indian communities. For example, John M. Roche, of the Catholic University of America, conducted an anthropological study in 1982 of the sociocultural impact of diabetes in the rural Choctaw-Apache Community of Ebarb.[23] From 1985 to 1986, John R. Faine, a professor at the University of Western Kentucky, collaborated with other scholars and Indian organizations to produce comprehensive reports on the Jena Band of Choctaw, the Chitimacha, the Apache-Choctaw, and the Tunica-Biloxi. Faine claimed that: "The Indian tribes of Louisiana have not shared in much of the progress of modernization. Today, Louisiana Indians suffer from high unemployment, low income, poor health care and education, and substandard housing. These conditions are exacerbated by the complexities of the culture of today and the difficulties of the tribes in receiving due recognition. Mercantilism, racial and ethnic discrimination, and federal status denial have combined to hide much of the Indian culture of Louisiana from the general population." Depending on the size of the community, each study consisted of interviews with 53 to 107 heads of household regarding economic conditions. The results were then compared to similar statistics from the surrounding non-Indian populations. The findings for each Indian community demonstrated varying degrees of need in housing, employment, education, transportation, and health care.[24] In sum, the studies confirmed, "Native Americans comprise a neglected segment of a population already suffering from extensive unemployment, illiteracy, and lack of job skills." Furthermore, "the plight of Louisiana's Indian population has worsened along with the state's economy."[25] Tribal governments could now use this information in prioritizing their communities' needs, and the ITC and LOIA utilized it when applying for grants.[26]

Tribal leaders in Alabama and Louisiana also recognized that they had to go beyond simply quantifying levels of need. The burden of meeting these needs was more pronounced for non–federally recognized groups, which had limited resources and had to compete with other non-Indian populations.[27] But even federally recognized groups such as the Chitimacha, Coushatta, Tunica-Biloxi, and Poarch Creek faced a finite pool of resources. In particular, Tunica-Biloxi representatives were concerned that the federal aid they had struggled to receive "will not begin for them until two years down the road after they have taken the opportunity to actually study and access and see what services are going to be needed." They complained that "even after federal recognition is granted, you've got to wait almost another two years for the government to come in and start intervening for you."[28] Jeannette Campos told a *State Times (Baton Rouge)* reporter that no tribe was guaranteed money because federally recognized tribes "still must compete against other federally recognized tribes for funds."[29]

Despite inter-tribal competition at the national and state levels, the reality of limited resources encouraged Alabama and Louisiana tribal leaders to build coalitions and tap into scarce funding sources by cooperating and sharing information, and state commissions became arenas in which to forge these relationships. In Alabama, for example, Indian leaders established an information exchange system among the commission, tribal governments, the private sector, and federal and state agencies. The stated goal was to negotiate with "relevant state agencies as advocates for Indian people in planning for economic development, and other subjects relevant to employment opportunities for Indians in Alabama."[30] The commission was responsible for creating a link between tribes and state agencies. Tribal leaders who had positioned themselves as overseers of the process believed that "[c]ommission staff are in a position to make members of state government and private sector more sensitive to the needs of Indian people. This will result in increased involvement of Indian leaders in statewide planning and more utilization of available services by Indian citizens. With such linkages between Indians and state agencies, the resources of both can be more effectively used to produce community development projects relevant and sensitive to the needs of the American Indian, thereby increasing Indian self-determination." In addition, Indian leaders wanted to establish a professional advisory board to aid them in community development. Without extensive knowledge or experience, Alabama Indians recognized that they needed help to build the social and economic infrastructures necessary for self-sufficiency.[31]

Tribal leaders in Louisiana also believed their state commission should be an "advocacy" agency to help promote the "mutual exchange of ideas and information."[32] Yet unlike the Alabama commission, which placed most of the responsibility on staff members, Louisiana's Indian leaders agreed that because the need was so overwhelming, each board member would take an active role in forging inter-agency relationships. As a result, they devised a plan in which LOIA would survey all state departments to find out what they could offer Indian people. Coushatta leader Ernest Sickey suggested that the commission split into three subcommittees to perform specific duties that would further the development of Indian affairs. "We should be a working unit," Sickey explained. "Each one of us has some kind of unique ability."[33] The subcommittees encouraged tribal leaders to collaborate and draw upon their talents for the greater good. As one Houma leader said during a 1982 meeting: "Before we can move on towards development, we have to know where we are. We have to know what our weaknesses are, we have to know what our strengths are. . . . Then, once we know our problems and what our resources are it would become our job to recruit professionally trained advisors and technicians. . . . We can't just be working out there in a void, there has to be an organizational structure."[34] Ernest Sickey volunteered to head the economic and industrial self-development subcommittee because of his experience developing the Coushatta craft industry. A second subcommittee monitored legislative issues relevant to Indian affairs, as well as the development of tribal-state relationships. Commission executive director Helen Gindrat and ITC director Jeannette Campos served on this committee because of their preexisting relationships with legislators. The third committee monitored federal block grants that the state received and ensured that tribes were able to tap into the grants for social services. Members of this committee became particularly skilled in learning the various available services and contacting the appropriate providers on behalf of the state's Indian population.[35]

Because of the shared responsibilities—and in an attempt to uphold the 1981 "Declaration of Unity"—LOIA held meetings at different locations. These meetings gave tribal chairmen from across the state the opportunity to have an "inside view of each tribe" while giving the host community a chance to educate other tribes, commission staff, and the media about the critical issues facing their particular communities.[36] For example, when the Jena Choctaw hosted a meeting in April 1981, Jena chairman Clyde Jackson provided his guests with a barbeque lunch, a photo session, and chances to mingle while he plied them with information regarding his community's housing shortage, high employment, and lack of roads.[37]

In addition to the cross-tribal relationships that were pivotal for promoting change at local levels, the Alabama and Louisiana commissions used their relationships with other state-level Indian agencies across the South to position themselves as the central link in a vast communication network. Tribal leaders involved in the 1981 Indian Information Project's conference titled "Critical Issues Affecting Eastern Indians" laid the groundwork for continued interstate connections. Southern tribal leaders commiserated as they wrestled with "a new Administration under President Reagan's leadership, new legislation, new service delivery patterns, and the controversial question surrounding federal and state recognition."[38] This discussion continued into 1987 when the Chitimacha tribe of Louisiana sponsored the United South and Eastern Tribes Inc. Convention. This meeting attracted one hundred members of more than sixteen different tribes who strategized about improving health, education, and economic development in their communities.[39] Throughout the 1980s, the AIAC maintained a strong connection to the Tennessee Indian Commission, which regularly shared funding information and offered aid in writing grant proposals.[40] Alabama Indian leaders were also invited to events hosted by the Florida Governor's Council on Indian Affairs and the North Carolina commission.[41] At the same time, in other parts of the country, state Indian commissions—like the Montana Indian Affairs Commission—looked to the Louisiana Commission as a successful model.[42]

Throughout the 1980s both LOIA and the AIAC focused on developing and maintaining relationships with agencies at the state and regional levels; however, they also still valued the national connections developed during the commissions' early years. In particular, tribal leaders continued to contribute to the dialogues generated by the nationally based Governors' Interstate Indian Council (GIIC). Budgetary cuts, however, made it difficult for tribal leaders and commission staff to attend annual meetings held across the nation.[43] Although New Orleans was originally scheduled to host the 1981 meeting, it was not until 1990 in Mobile, Alabama, that the deep South hosted a GIIC meeting.[44] The Inter-Governmental Committee on Indian Affairs, however, did host a meeting in 1983 for "various tribes in the Southwest" and extended an invitation to LOIA.[45]

In addition to an intermittent involvement with the GIIC, Alabama Indians remained visible within the ranks of the National Congress of the American Indian (NCAI) through the participation of Poarch Creek leaders such as Eddie Tullis, who was elected vice president, and Buford Rolin, who was elected NCAI treasurer in 1984.[46] Tullis and Rolin challenged the previously western-focused NCAI and helped Alabama and other southern tribes exploit a new network of resources and support. In fact, in 1984 and 1985, other tribal leaders in Alabama participated in two NCAI meetings, and by 1987 the commission had reported that every state-recognized tribe was an enrolled NCAI member.[47]

Even as tribal leaders in Alabama and Louisiana connected with other Indian communities and organizations, these efforts did not necessarily translate into meaningful contacts with legislators and other agencies. Cultivating these relationships occupied a significant amount of time and energy as commissions rallied for support within the state governments. Both commissions successfully drew upon resources by defining Indians as racial minorities, but they discovered that state officials were reluctant to acknowledge the unique status of Indians. In a 1981 letter to the BIA, for example, Governor Fob James boasted that "virtually all agencies of Alabama State Government are working with the Alabama Indian Affairs Commission to provide equitable services and consideration." However, he wrote, "The extent of services that may be available for Alabama's Indians as a specific group are uncertain at this time."[48] This uncertainty was not simply the reflection of a tight budget; it revealed legislators' inexperience with Indian affairs and a lack of understanding regarding the parameters of tribal-state relations.

Members of both commissions had to endure the frustrations associated with a lack of firm commitments from legislators and agency representatives. They "talked in circles," Helen Gindrat complained, and they were difficult to pin down.[49] For other leaders, problems stemmed from the historical neglect of Indian people. For example, LOIA board member and future director Clyde Jackson complained during a 1980 meeting: "Historically in this state, Louisiana has not been on the side of the Indian when it comes down to granting project dollars for projects. We have not been able to attract any direct dollars for programs from the state."[50] Jeanette Campos attributed this neglect to a lack of understanding of the status of Indian tribes. "When the state government or anybody looks at an Indian they think that you're sitting in the federal lap," she said. "They don't look at us [and consider] 'well this tribe is federally recognized, this tribe is terminated, this tribe is state recognized, this tribe has no recognition.' This is something that the general public has no conception of, and certainly the legislature doesn't. I've had an opportunity to testify before [legislative] committees and they know no more about what you're talking about with tribal sovereignty than if you're talking about the moon." Campos suggested that in addition to educating legislators, Louisiana Indians should follow the example of the Colorado River Tribes in Arizona, who did not approach the state with pleas for money. Instead, Arizona tribes entered into agreements with the state, "like one country dealing with another country." The establishment of mutual respect implied by a government-to-government relationship was particularly important for non–federally recognized tribes in order to avoid having a state assert authority over its tribal communities.[51]

The urgent need to attract the attention of state legislators and the funds under their control prompted the commissions in both states to follow tribal leaders such as Ernest Sickey and Calvin McGhee, both of whom had already worked with legislators on programs directly affecting their tribes. It took a concentrated and unified effort, however, to influence budgetary decisions on legislation. Even with the subcommittee devoted to the legislative aspects of Indian affairs, certain members of LOIA remained keenly aware that their comparatively small population faced an uphill battle in attempting to gain support.[52] In addition, the committee agreed to have each tribal council approve every decision to ensure that they accurately represented all tribal interests—a nearly impossible task given the diversity in needs and objectives.[53]

Despite all this, LOIA intended to "inundate the entire state with good feelings about Indians" by demonstrating a spirit of cooperation.[54] Executive director Helen Gindrat went a step further by "speaking for all Indians in Louisiana" and sending personal notes of appreciation to legislators who supported policies that benefited tribes in their drive toward self-determination.[55] At the same time, tribal leaders synthesized information for legislators who, according to Jeanette Campos, wanted the information watered down because "they are not going to sit and listen to the years of discrimination in the state."[56]

LOIA also welcomed outside recommendations from agency representatives, such as Daniel Lambardo from the Office of Health and Human Services, on how to increase LOIA's visibility and influence. Lambardo recommended that leaders continue to connect with legislators and befriend them so that tribes could simply make a phone call when they needed something.[57] He also recommended that Indians attempt to gain appointments to police juries and school boards in order to gain access to information. The idea, he continued: "[Is] to get your communities together to start making sure that your voice is one voice and that you start getting your representatives in key places. . . . If you as a group represent 1,100 voices, versus 1 or 2 people scattered with different needs, it's a very big difference. You become constituents and then you have to be dealt with as a people and as an entity."[58] Whether Lambardo's recommendations had any direct impact on the actions of Louisiana's tribal leaders was unclear, but the evidence reveals that many communities, such as the Clifton Choctaws, took a more personal approach to legislative relationships by inviting local politicians to their community.[59]

While LOIA established a committee to educate legislators on Indian affairs, the AIAC launched its own campaign to "ensure that Indians will be included in the planning and delivery of future services." According to a 1981 report, commission staff contacted both national and state legislative delegations and set up one-on-one consultations to educate delegates on the problems faced by Indians in the state.[60] A commission newsletter also encouraged individual Indians to "become acquainted with your local congressman and explain to him the benefits that would be derived from Indian people keeping their own land and developing their own resources." The newsletter continued, "Indian people should know their senators and congressmen practically by their first names. Sit down and talk with them. Tell them the problem as well as what we see as a resolution to the problem."[61] The commissions in both states hoped that change would be initiated when legislators had a clear plan of action to address the numerous concerns of Indians. Native leaders understood that they had to take extra measures to have any impact on state politics.

While individuals were encouraged to address their legislators, the commissions directed their primary efforts toward the governors' offices. Leonard Hudson, the first appointed chairman of the SAIAC, explained: "Indians were given a vehicle without a motor to keep it going. This is the first time in the history of Alabama that Indian citizens have had any form of representation in state government. The Alabama Indian Commission is now equipped to serve as that critically needed liaison or advocate for Alabama's Indians—the 'first citizens' of our state."[62] Louisiana tribal leaders also viewed their commission as a critical link to the governor's office, especially during times when budget meetings were held in Baton Rouge.[63] In 1987 Governor Edwin Edwards responded to the pressure put on his office by LOIA and created an advisory board for Native Americans to "address the social and economic needs of Louisiana's Native Americans."[64]

Two tactics were employed to encourage legislators to support the activities of the commissions. Some tribal leaders characterized the commissions as agencies representing an overlooked segment of the state's poor population. Ernest Sickey, for instance, fought for this strategy, arguing that the only way to achieve complete support from the administration would be to align Indian interests with those of the state. Then, he stressed how crucial it would be to involve LOIA in creating policies and procedures directly affecting Indian citizens.[65] Other tribal leaders emphasized the unique status of Indians, arguing that the commissions were not "bureaus" to be served but rather representatives of the interests of tribal nations.[66] MOWA Choctaw leader Framon Weaver took elements from each approach in a 1982 letter to Governor Fob James, arguing, "Indians in the State of Alabama are seeking, not a hand-out, but technical assistance and guidance in helping themselves to become more self-sufficient."[67] The Alabama state legislature widely embraced and supported this second tactic and repeatedly endorsed "efforts made by our Indian community toward self-determination for their people."[68]

Even as more legislators adopted the rhetoric of self-determination, tribal leaders questioned whether their supporters fully understood what it meant. While Indians defined this concept as upholding a semi-sovereign political status as tribal nations, legislators emphasized the economic aspects more than the political ones in the hopes of relieving the states' financial responsibilities to Indian communities. In addition to failing to grasp the meaning of self-determination, legislators also did not fully understand the parameters of tribal-state relationships. The Poarch Creek leader Eddie Tullis stressed the importance of this understanding, commenting that "states have an obligation to the unique needs of Indian people, and Indian commissions can best serve by seeing that the uniqueness of Indian communities [is] responded to."[69] Many Indian leaders agreed with Tullis and understood that state commissions occupied ideal positions to form bridges between tribal governments and state agencies. Building these bridges was crucial to securing resources, while simultaneously laying the foundation for tribal self-determination. The question was how to best construct such relationships. Key people within the Indian movement drafted position papers offering insights into how these relationships could evolve.

In 1980 Jennie Lee Dees, executive director of the Poarch Creek, sought consideration for the position of executive director for the SAIAC, arguing that her experience and enthusiasm could help Indians at the state level. As part of her application, Dees drafted a position paper entitled "A Two Year Plan of Development," which became the "foundation for commission activities."[70] The paper outlined a plan for communication between the state and tribal governments in which neither party was in control of the relationship but instead had a shared goal of understanding each other. The goal was to eliminate the need for any outside aid for tribal governments from non-Indian lawyers and advocates and allow "issues and concerns [to] come truly from Indian people!"[71] Furthermore, she wrote, every effort must be made to establish the Indian commission as "a viable AND VITAL asset to the State of Alabama." From this position, Dees argued, the commission could secure not only ongoing financial support but "conscience" support as well. This support would enable the commission, and ultimately tribal governments, to secure available resources, allowing them to become "largely self-supportive."[72]

Drawing upon the influence of the Dees treatise, Indian leaders challenged the state to look to the past as a way to plan for the future of tribal-state relationships. In other words, state officials were asked to appreciate the self-governing abilities of the tribal nations of the pre-Removal South and acknowledge the capability of modern tribal governments to follow suit. A 1980 Alabama commission report argued that if given the opportunity, "the traditional American Indian is capable and will strive toward tribal self-sufficiency and the improving of the socio-economic condition of tribal community members." Tribal leaders challenged the state to reconstruct a relationship with tribes that had been lost. "Unless and until a joint effort is firmly established," the report warned, "present problems are likely to continue, and may well even grow worse." Although the argument primarily emphasized the benefits that Indian communities would reap from the development of mutual relationships between tribes and the state, government officials were also enticed with how the "unique cultural differences" of Indian people were vital to the state's efforts to rebuild its public image.[73]

The Alabama commission identified the unique status of Indian tribes to legislators and state agencies by publishing discussions about tribal sovereignty in the commission's widely circulated newsletter. "Sovereignty," a 1981 issue offered, "is a difficult word to understand even though many people use it everyday. . . . Sovereignty refers to an attitude or strong feeling held by a people, a group, a tribe, or a nation. It cannot be seen."[74] Since the relationships between tribes and states were complex and uncertain, many Alabama tribal leaders defined sovereignty in terms similar to that of the federal-Indian relationship and, as a result, took a defensive posture against its historically paternal nature. For example, the Echota Cherokee leader Diane Weston snidely referred to the state legislature as the "Great White Father from Montgomery." She explained, "I, for one, am not a child, and I don't think any of you are either. We have resented for hundreds of years being treated as children, and I feel certain that our legislators resent their parental responsibility."[75]

While the Alabama commission struggled to define tribal-state relations, LOIA set the foundation for their future relationship with the state government. Specifically, tribal leaders identified a new era in Indian affairs, which positioned states to assume the trust obligation of the federal government for recognized tribes while providing non-recognized groups the opportunity to build a trust relationship. The evolving dynamic between tribes and states was articulated in a 1981 paper supported by many of the state's Indian leaders who came together as the "Undersigned Sovereign American Indian Tribal Governments of Louisiana." The paper, which was sent to the governor and state legislators, outlined the parameters of the federal trust obligation and discussed the transfer of this trust to the state. With President Reagan's $30–50 billion cutbacks on federal "entitlement programs," a relationship with the state government was crucial for the economic well-being of tribal governments in the early stages of redevelopment in the 1980s.[76] To facilitate the obligatory transfer, the paper offered LOIA as a resource to help transfer federal services to the state. To ensure that these services reached Indian communities, the commission recommended that tribal governments be given the same status as local governments, allowing them to become eligible for state subsidies.[77] As Jeanette Campos explained to a group of tribal leaders: "Tribal governments are a unit of government to be dealt with as a unit of government . . . we are not wards of the state. The state is not going to come in and dictate to you in your tribal communities you have to do it this way, this way and this way. We're going to negotiate government-to-government agreements."[78] Indian leaders hoped the governor would adopt this relationship as the official policy of his administration. "And then it would go on record like Nixon did when he began the federal recognition process," explained one tribal leader. "No governor in history has ever done that in a state."[79]

By September 1982, the legislature had demonstrated its receptivity to the commission's efforts by passing a resolution requesting a study to assess the important issues affecting Indian communities. The proposal required the House Committee on Governmental Affairs and the Senate Committee on Governmental Affairs to form a joint committee to analyze federal and state cooperation on these issues. Campos pointed out, "The state of Louisiana has very little knowledge or understanding of how Indians function. . . . So, with the fact that federal recognition has only been granted to 3 tribes here in the state[,] and even with that many of the relationships that have been extended between the federal government and federal tribes is starting to transfer somewhat to state government and their residents, we felt that it was very critical that our state be able to deal with Indians." LOIA and the ITC strategized on how best to address the special committee on Indian affairs. The ITC decided to employ the aid of the political lobbyist Charlie Smith, who made recommendations to tribal leaders on scheduling and organizational issues when working with the legislative committee. Ernest Sickey also recommended that tribes obtain legal counsel to represent them because they were going before a governmental body. "It is important that we don't go there unprepared," Sickey argued. He also urged leaders to discuss their overall objectives, research and construct their testimonies, and seek legal assistance for the technical aspect of the process. "We've got a lot of support. It's just putting our heads together and knowing what the devil we want them to support us on." Sickey requested that LOIA try to get somebody to summarize all the laws that deal with taxation so that tribal governments could participate in some of the programs and get the same funds that other municipalities or local governments did.[80]

Defining the parameters of tribal-state relationships was further complicated by the different levels of political status held by tribes in Alabama and Louisiana. The tendency of legislators, who knew little about Indian affairs, to make generalizations about the entire Indian population in their respective states led to misunderstandings about jurisdictional power. These tensions became particularly pronounced between the states and groups such as the Coushatta, Tunica-Biloxi, and Poarch Creek, who achieved federal recognition status in the early stages of developing tribal-state relationships. As these groups developed relationships with the federal government and began receiving the benefits of such a relationship—such as access to BIA services, federal trust land, and the potential to develop gaming—the terms of their relationships with the state governments shifted. The mounting tensions that accompanied these shifts often played out in the media, particularly with respect to law enforcement jurisdiction on reservations where Indian gaming facilities were developed. For example, a 1986 *Baton Rouge Magazine* article reported the problems that arose between the state of Louisiana and the Coushatta Tribe following the introduction of Indian bingo in 1984. This case forced the state legislature to realize, as one journalist put it, that "when a federal/Indian trust exists, law enforcement by the state or municipalities on a federally recognized reservation unless specifically authorized, is actually prohibited by federal law and can be viewed as an invasion of a sovereign Indian nation."[81]

Alabama tribes encountered similar problems and misunderstandings regarding gaming. In 1982 the SAIAC sent a memorandum to the state House of Representatives attempting to protect the future of the state's relationship with the six non–federally recognized tribes and their ability to tap into state funds by explaining how they "*do not* share in any way the profits or business ventures of the Poarch Creeks."[82] The danger of losing ground with legislators who didn't quite understand the unique and varied status of tribes presented an ongoing threat that commissions had to regularly address.

Building a Future: Initiating Tribal Development

In the midst of struggling to develop a long-term plan to promote change through needs assessments and political support at both the state and national levels, the Indian commissions continued receiving correspondence from individuals such as Bobby Joe Simmons of Baton Rouge, who in a 1982 letter insisted on learning the types of aid LOIA could give him as a non-reservation Indian.[83] Like Mildred Smith and Elsie Billiot, Simmons had immediate needs that remained unmet through the foundation-building activities of LOIA. Change was slow, perhaps too slow for tribal leaders in Alabama and Louisiana who remained troubled by the fact that their efforts did little—if anything—to alleviate the "human needs" of their people. As a result, Indian leaders in both states took a more aggressive approach to what they saw as their most serious community problems: poor education, lack of employment opportunities, and limited access to social services.

Throughout most of the twentieth century, poor educational attainment was the norm for southern Indians who did not neatly fit into the black-white Jim Crow system. Since their inceptions, both commissions had attempted to address educational inequalities. For example, in 1973, David Garrison, the first LOIA commissioner, wrote to Governor Edwin Edwards and expressed his frustration in lobbying for more educational resources on behalf of the state's Indian population. Garrison explained: "The average education of 2,300 Houma Indians is 2.9 years. The Coushatta Indian children speak Coushatta first and English second, yet there is not even a Head Start program available to them. When I went to the Department of Education and spoke to the officer who administers federal Title funds, which could pay for special Indian programs, he went into another room and laughed. I walked out."[84] Garrison may have walked out, but his action was not a concession of defeat. Rather, it was an acknowledgment of the continuing struggle that awaited Indian communities in the years to come.

Louisiana's tribes rose to the challenge. In 1975 LOIA supported a campaign to help keep Indian children in school with the development of Head Start programs. A few years later, they began focusing their efforts on developing special culturally relevant educational services for handicapped Indian students.[85] In Alabama, Indians actively pursued Title V funds through the Indian Education Act of 1972. Since local educational associations received Title V funds, cultural education and enhancement programs were "sponsored by local education entities, in individual counties or cities, through an agreement with an Indian tribal government." Grants were funded for one to three years and were "handled entirely through the federal arena,"[86] giving the state of Alabama no direct oversight. Parents, however, did have oversight. Indian parents residing within the funded county or city could serve on parent committees.[87] These committees helped craft culturally specific programs for students, including classes in "arts and crafts, dance, music and legends, as well as some Indian languages."[88] By 1980, Indian Education Programs operating under the Indian Education Act (Part IV A) existed in six counties throughout Alabama.[89] Several years later, that number had doubled, with twelve Title V Indian education programs serving more than ten thousand American Indian children.[90]

Although the Alabama commission had a limited role in Indian education in the initial stages of program development, in 1981 the agency began taking a more prominent role as technical advisor to the programs.[91] As one report indicated, "Education is now one of the commission's priorities and it is currently working with several county school systems on applying for federal funding available, due to the Indian children in their systems."[92]

One of the Alabama commission's most notable success stories involved the Jackson County school board. The commission provided organizational assistance to the board in its development of an ethnic studies program, which was funded by the U.S. Department of Education and focused on the study of the Jackson County Cherokee.[93] Alabama senator Jeremiah Denton promoted the program, stating the federal grant would be used to "study the legacy of the Cherokee in Jackson County" and thus help encourage state pride.[94] For the Jackson County Cherokee, the program arrived at a crucial moment in their development as they sought new sources of empowerment through cultural legitimization. In 1990 AIAC executive director Jane Weeks explained how Indian education programs "greatly assist our children in the restoration of their Indian birthright. . . . Because our communities do not reside on reservations, we feel very strongly that these programs, even as we realize their limitations, are absolutely a blessing to our tribal people and their children."[95] The same year that the Cherokee studies program developed, the Jackson County Cherokee took their cultural development efforts a step further by sending thirty-one delegates to Cherokee, North Carolina, to establish an annual tribal conference with the Eastern Band of Cherokee Indians.[96]

LOIA also positioned itself as a supporter of local Indian education programs by offering legitimacy to new applicants who needed official support. For example, in 1978 LOIA wrote a letter on behalf of the Indian Angels, who applied for Indian Education Act Title IV funds. Since the organization represented predominantly non–federally recognized Indians in the Baton Rouge area, LOIA felt compelled to send a letter to the Department of Education assuring that "this program is of vital necessity for the Urban Indians of Louisiana."[97] Like Alabama commission members, LOIA members attended Title IV Indian education workshops and provided technical and grant-writing assistance to tribes and school districts seeking funds specifically earmarked for Indian and bilingual education.[98]

Bringing educational opportunities to Indian communities was only part of LOIA's mission. Since the late 1970s, the agency had been educating Indian people about the largely untapped resources available to them. A 1977 report reflected this concern, stating: "Louisiana Indians are poorly educated, and the Indian communities have a history of not fully using available educational and social supportive services. In order to increase their educational level of achievement, it is imperative that Louisiana Indians begin to systematically seek and use both [state and federal] types of resources." The report stresses that by more successfully tapping into these resources, Indian communities can "alter critical elements in their environment, such as social isolation, employment, financial needs, and mental health."[99] The question was how to best educate the Indian population about these resources. The members of LOIA developed a plan for a Data Bank Assistance Program to serve more than nine thousand Indian residents in eight major communities. The intent was to create a systematic process by which Indians could learn about federal or state programs, resources, and services for which they might be eligible. With an illiteracy rate of 32 percent among Louisiana Indian adults, and only one in five with more than a fifth grade education, tribal leaders agreed that adult education was an important place to start. As a result, LOIA located and advertised all of the existing adult education programs established by the Department of Education within various districts. They even identified adult learning centers in close proximity to five tribal communities.[100]

While working to increase the number of high school graduates, tribal leaders also emphasized opportunities for Indian youth to attend college. Prior to securing higher education money for state-recognized Indians, however, LOIA started helping federally acknowledged students obtain federal Indian grants for school.[101] In 1979 the Louisiana legislature appropriated funds to establish an Indian Higher Education Assistance Program for Indians attending state public colleges or universities.[102] Because the funds were limited, LOIA gave priority to students who supported themselves through school. The goal, as one tribal leader explained, was "trying to find a way to give as many students as possible a chance to attend college."[103] To be eligible for assistance, students had to have "at least one-eighth degree of American Indian blood and be an enrolled member of a State or Federally recognized tribe, band, or group of Indians." With a $60,000 state allocation in 1981, LOIA provided tuition, room, board, and book fees for thirty-six Indian students from low-income families.[104]

Although the eligibility requirements appeared to be clear, poor grant management in the first years raised concerns. Grant applicants had to present proof of tribal enrollment and high school graduation, but it was later discovered that these pieces of information were never verified. When Helen Gindrat took over the LOIA executive director position, she called for a stricter monitoring process and identified numerous cases of fraud. After conducting background checks, she discovered that a number of grant recipients had lied about tribal membership. To make matters worse, many of the students' parents or guardians earned well above the income cutoff. These revelations were unsettling to other Indian leaders, such as Indian Angels founder Sarah Peralta, who addressed Gindrat's findings during a LOIA meeting in April 1982: "We worked very hard to get the $60,000 for education; it was with the understanding that it would go to the Indians that needed it the most. I didn't think that the money would be given out without discretion . . . I feel that the Indian children who were in high school, who would want to be a doctor, etc., should have that chance to go further if the money was available."[105] Gindrat's discovery prompted tribal leaders to adopt more stringent requirements for grantees. For example, tribal governments were now responsible for confirming a student's degree of Indian ancestry instead of LOIA staff, who were overwhelmed with requests. This way, the tribes themselves could screen the applicants to avoid fraudulent claims.[106] Other changes included raising the minimum qualifying grade point average from 2.0 to 2.5 and requiring that scholarship awardees carry full course loads.[107]

The need for stringent requirements became even more crucial when the LOIA scholarship fund was cut by 5.8 percent in 1983, making it impossible to accept any new students for the 1984–85 school year.[108] The commission staff planned to continue funding the students already receiving awards while lobbying the Interim-Emergency Board for additional funding.[109] Despite their best efforts, however, the program's budget tumbled from $60,000 to only $7,500 by 1984.[110] By 1985 the grant had been cut entirely and state officials requested that tribal leaders "seek other funding sources to replace state funds."[111] In their desperation, tribal leaders had a representative from the Department of Urban and Community Affairs send a heartfelt letter to Senator Leonard J. Chabert asking for help to reinstate the program. The letter argued, "In order to improve education and competition among the Indian population, funds, resources, and opportunities must be afforded. . . . This program is vital to the welfare of Louisiana's Native Americans; is fully utilized by all eight tribes; and, is needed more now due to proposed federal cuts in student aid."[112] All eight tribal leaders from state-recognized communities sprang into action with a "Declaration of Support" for LOIA to pursue funds from the federal Administration on Native Americans to continue the Indian Higher Education Assistance Grant. "As tribal leaders," the declaration stated, "we recognize that this program is vital in addressing the needs of our people [and] reflects a continuance of our dedication towards our goal of Indian Self-Determination of tribes."[113] By 1987 efforts to reinstate the Higher Education Assistance Program ceased to be mentioned in commission reports, but individual tribes continued to encourage youth to seek a higher education. For example, Bruce Duthu, a Houma community member and the director of the Dartmouth College Native American Program, met with tribal education leaders across the state and created a college recruitment program for high school students.[114] Indian leaders also continued to build self-esteem among their communities' youth by developing youth leadership programs.[115]

With little success in reinstating the Louisiana Indian Higher Education Assistance Program, LOIA began pursuing a Vocational Education Grant through the U.S. Department of Education. By February 1988, however, it became clear that this was a dead end when LOIA received notification that there were no funds for the grant.[116] Frustrated but determined, LOIA continued building relationships with various trade schools to secure internal sources of funding and encouraged Native people to attend these schools.[117]

While Louisiana Indian communities struggled to find funds for higher education, Alabama Indian communities engaged in a battle of their own. Like LOIA, the Alabama commission wanted to educate people about the resources already available to them. "Need Education Assistance?" read one headline in a 1981 commission newsletter that invited students to contact the commission for a hundred-page book on the subject. In addition to offering information, commission staff helped students write their applications and grant proposals.[118]

Alabama tribal leaders also turned to private donors in their efforts to secure education funding. For example, in 1980 the Poarch Creek Council successfully sought financial support from a wealthy donor for a scholarship to be awarded to that year's Poarch Creek Princess.[119] By 1984 the Alabama commission had collected enough private donations to create a scholarship program that awarded $80,000 to eighty-three students attending colleges, junior colleges, and trade schools.[120] However, it was difficult to sustain a healthy scholarship fund. The following year the AIAC wrote to Alabama attorney general Charles A. Graddick to ask whether some of the state funds the AIAC had received for operational expenses could be used for Indian scholarships. Graddick replied positively, adding that "scholarships would constitute a 'meaningful program' and could assist Indian communities in both social and economic development."[121] The state's willingness to help sustain the scholarship fund was a victory, but with annual budget cuts and the increased reluctance of private donors to part with their money, the AIAC found that they had fewer and fewer resources to offer students each year. In fact, by 1987 only about $15,000 was available for scholarships.[122]

By the end of the decade, tribal leaders recognized that they needed to take drastic measures to keep the Alabama Indian Scholarship Fund alive. As a result, in 1990, the AIAC convinced the Alabama legislature to allow residents to make a tax-deductible donation to the fund by checking a box on their state income tax form. The AIAC also circulated fifty-two thousand flyers in bank statements from Colonial Bank advertising the new item on the tax form. The strategy was successful on two fronts: (1) it generated enough cash to help forty-seven of the seventy students who applied for scholarships; and (2) it attracted scholarship opportunities from other sources. For example, as a result of these efforts, the University of West Alabama awarded one full scholarship and two partial scholarships to Indian students. Around the same time, George Wallace Jr. and AmSouth helped establish the Prepaid Affordable College Tuition (PACT) program, which provided scholarships to Indian students.[123]

Tribal leaders in Alabama and Louisiana shared a common concern regarding helping Native students fund their college education. They feared that after they received college educations they would take their skills elsewhere, away from the Indian community. This fear prompted the Houma Tribal Council to require certain scholarship recipients to sign an agreement stating that they would return for a few years to work for the tribe following graduation.[124] There is no evidence of any Alabama tribe going to this extent to keep educated tribal members in their communities, but the AIAC actively sought to inspire Indians to pursue careers to help their tribes. Individuals who did this were held in high regard and used as examples in the commission newsletter. For example, MOWA Choctaw member and deputy sheriff Jack Rivers, who patrolled both the paved streets and dirt roads of Washington County, was profiled in 1981. He was the only Indian in the state serving as a sergeant in a local sheriff's department. A member of the Choctaw Indian Political Affairs Committee, Rivers had been the first Indian to become employed in law enforcement under the Title III Indian CETA program administered by the Poarch Creek. More important than his singular status as an Indian law enforcement agent, however, was the fact that he chose to work within his own community. He patrolled areas within the MOWA Choctaw community where other officers traditionally had refused to work unless a major crime had been committed.[125] "It has helped when I'm working with other Indians," Rivers said, "since they place trust in one of their own people."[126]

In addition to combating poor education levels, tribal leaders also sought to alleviate the high unemployment rates that plagued their communities. In 1975 the Louisiana ITC became the prime sponsor of CETA and took on the responsibility of "providing employment and training services to un-employed, underemployed and economically disadvantaged American Indi-ans throughout the state."[127] Following in the footsteps of earlier federal at-tempts to provide employment assistance, CETA passed in 1973, marking the beginning of a trend to localize the decision-making process surrounding employment and training services.[128] Two separate assessments of the Loui-siana program in the 1970s claimed that the "project has successfully provided temporary employment, vocational training, and career information to eco-nomically disadvantaged Louisiana Indians." In particular, the Adult Learn-ing Project that the ITC operated in four tribal communities totaling ap-proximately 5,811 people "was effective in providing adult learners their high school diplomas, as well as information in the areas of occupational oppor-tunities, government, law, health and community resources."[129] In fact, only a few months into the ITC's operation, approximately fifteen Louisiana Indi-ans earned high school diplomas, and another ten received diplomas the fol-lowing year. By decade's end approximately six hundred Indians participated in job training in such fields as carpentry, clerical work, auto mechanics, cos-metology, drafting, and electrical engineering. According to a 1977 report, "this represents a significant increase in Indian participation in the skilled job market since 1975."[130]

By the late 1970s, the SAIAC also realized the urgent need to tap into CETA funding since their office was flooded with requests from unemployed Poarch Creek community members wanting immediate services that the of-fice was unable to provide.[131] Commission staff were aware that consistent employment was a concern for the MOWA Choctaw as well, a large number of whom worked in "part-time seasonal or day labor jobs such as agricul-ture, forestry, construction, or menial service jobs."[132] The agency's goal was to assess the employment and educational needs of those living within cer-tain geographic areas, not necessarily address them directly.[133] After the ur-gency of the need became clear, however, the U.S. Department of Labor des-ignated the Poarch Creek the prime sponsor of CETA funds, which were supplemented with subcontracts from various other sources.[134] In addition to jump-starting Alabama's first Indian job-training program, the SAIAC used the money to create a tribal media center to document Poarch Creek tribal history and employed community members in the center.[135]

To combat unemployment, Louisiana and Alabama tribal leaders focused on Indian youth, whom they saw as the future of their communities. The Poarch Creek Tribal Council merged CETA funds with another grant to focus on job training for Indian youth. The grants went toward developing the Summer Youth Employment Program, which provided young people with work experience, job search assistance, and job survival training while participating in Indian community improvement and public park facilities improvement activities.[136] The SAIAC explained its choice to focus on youth in a 1981 editorial in the *Alabama Indian Advocate*. Viola Peterson's vision for Indian youth swept across the front page: "We need to get our youngsters educated to the point where they can sit in these different decision making jobs. This will help upgrade the image of the American Indian. When an individual is educated he can provide for himself and his family. There is a need for not only the college educated; but also, there is a great need for the vocationally trained, the job ready individual."[137] The "job ready" individual would also be a role model and contribute to the broader vision of tribal self-determination. The SAIAC emphasized that through self-improvement all Indians could help their people.[138]

To further the objectives of the Summer Youth Employment Program, the Poarch Creek–controlled commission collaborated with the Tennessee Indian Council and the North Carolina Indian Affairs Commission in 1980 and coordinated the Deep South International Indian Job Fair held in Huntsville, Alabama.[139] The following year, the commission worked with the Alabama Department of Energy and Office of Employment and Training to offer a five-day career development training workshop to help participants develop job skills, such as preparing applications and résumés, interviewing, and dealing with rejection.[140] Although Indian youth between sixteen and twenty-one across the state were placed in temporary jobs, in which they essentially served as interns, during 1980 and 1981, the campaign strongly emphasized long-term career development.[141] "If you are in doubt about your future," read a 1981 commission newsletter, "consider the following data about the number of Indians holding different kinds of professional jobs." The newsletter encouraged readers to pursue specific career paths and increase the number of Native American doctors and librarians, for example. "Make sure Indians are well represented in all professions!" The newsletter's tone was hopeful, perhaps intended to help readers forget that shifting federal and state economic policies had all but shut the door on programs that would have helped Indians pursue better opportunities.[142]

By the time President Carter left office in January 1981, defeated by Ronald Reagan, the national unemployment rate had declined, but minority communities remained disproportionately underemployed. To make matters worse, the cost of living increased as inflation reached double digits and the federal government began eliminating social service funding. The federal government determined that states were not taking an active enough role in the coordination of local activities, so the administrative responsibilities for CETA were given to local agencies.[143] As the Reagan administration considered eliminating or consolidating social service programs to reduce the role of the federal government in administering these programs, CETA's value was called into question. Fearing the demise of the program, the Indian and Native American CETA Coalition, located in Washington, D.C., warned tribal leaders that the federal government wanted to kill all Indian CETA programs. "The Administration proposal would completely eliminate any guaranteed funding level for Indian workers," a coalition memo declared. More frightening to most southern tribal leaders, however, was the claim that it "would end all grants to off-reservation Indian groups."[144]

As southern tribal leaders struggled with the loss of an important funding source that had led to many positive changes through the 1970s, they also faced having to renegotiate their positions within a new funding system of block grants that defined tribal-state relationships. Through the 1981 federal Omnibus Budget Reconciliation Act, Reagan consolidated more than seventy categorical grants into seven block grants that provided 25 percent less funding than the programs being replaced.[145] Since block grant disbursement discretion was given to the states, state-recognized tribal leaders were pleased at the prospect of accessing money previously unavailable at the federal level, but they were also apprehensive about the dispersal of the funds.[146] Louisiana Indian leader Clyde Jackson particularly feared that tribes would have little claim to the money because certain tribal governments and organizations were not officially classified by the state as local governments, towns, municipalities, or villages.[147] Despite this apprehension, however, the block grant system did not close the door on funding tribal projects since state officials invited Alabama and Louisiana Indians to apply for Community Services Block Grants and the Energy Assistance for Low Income Families grant.[148]

Faced with new—though limited—opportunities, Louisiana's tribal leaders met throughout 1981 to discuss whether the tribes should attempt to obtain block grant funding and develop their own services or encourage individual community members to apply for services available to every citizen of the state.[149] In 1981 the *Alabama Indian Advocate* newsletter weighed in on the issue, arguing, "Many tribal leaders regard administration of direct grants as a continuation of the practice of tribal self-determination and at the same time, demonstrates the tribes' capability to manage its own affairs." Although many tribes wished to run their own programs, the newsletter reported that for smaller tribes, "proportionate shares of funding are not sufficient to administer a given program effectively," making it more cost-effective to receive direct services.[150]

For tribal communities applying for block grant money for Indian-run programs and services, other issues still had to be hammered out. What role should the commission, as a state agency, play in the administration of block grants? Initially many tribal governments—particularly the Coushatta, Jena Band of Choctaws, and Clifton-Choctaws—wanted to sidestep the commission and apply for direct funding.[151] Coushatta leader Ernest Sickey argued that although the commission should represent the interests of all tribal governments, "the tribes should deal directly with the state with or without the blessing of the commission."[152] Sickey did not want another layer of bureaucracy to act as a grant clearinghouse, and he and others argued that it was a sovereignty issue. Sickey said, "Each tribe has their own type of government. They would make their own decisions."[153]

Although the arguments in support of direct funding were strong, Richard Brazan, a legal consultant to LOIA, told Louisiana tribal leaders that the commission was "legally bound" to operate as a clearinghouse for state block grant money. He further argued that to use the commission as a clearinghouse would eliminate the need for tribes to compete for scarce resources and would allow tribal leaders to support the goals and needs of other communities. Brazan continued, "I'm not saying the board should control. I'm saying that you have a better chance of getting money when you speak as a group. When you are speaking for 8 Indian tribes, you just have a better chance. . . . Again, it's your board and you can do anything with it as long as you obey state law."[154] Most tribal leaders accepted these suggestions and admitted that the persistent funding cutbacks created competition that was best countered by coalition building.[155]

Tribal leaders wanted to revive the success of such 1970s programs as CETA by quickly securing the means to continue operating their own programs. In 1981 the Louisiana ITC and LOIA jointly applied for a community service block grant for a number of community needs, including a job-training program that, like CETA, could be administered by the council.[156] The following year, LOIA and the ITC pooled the money from the block grant and the few remaining CETA dollars to continue the much-needed job-training program. As Helen Gindrat explained, "There wasn't enough money to go out there to do just one thing . . . [so] the tribes have decided to go into consortium and go ahead."[157] The only tribe that opted not to enter into the consortium was the United Houma Nation (UHN), which, because of its large population, found it more beneficial to apply for direct funding.[158]

The block grant that the consortium obtained funded the first federal program to be administered by LOIA in cooperation with the Louisiana Department of Labor, which agreed to "maintain the integrity and dollar amount" of the funding.[159] Tribal leaders realized the benefits of working with the state labor office, an agency publicly committed to creative measures to employ and train people in order to remove them from the welfare rolls.[160] While LOIA supervised the grant by conducting on-site visits with tribal communities, the agency also educated Department of Labor employees who had misconceptions about Indians.[161] For example, the block grant, as spelled out by the Louisiana Department of Labor, required that recipients be federally recognized. "I think they thought everyone was federally recognized," postulated one commission staff member, "which really shocked me."[162] Because of misconceptions like this, LOIA worked with the state labor office to change the grant criteria wording to include both federally and state-recognized tribes.

Alabama tribal leaders also struggled to adapt to a shifting economic environment that gave state government control over a shrinking pot of money. As the dominant force on the commission during the early 1980s, the Poarch Creek Tribal Council resisted this transition, arguing that tribes should receive block grants directly from the federal government. Eddie Tullis, Poarch Creek chairman and vice president of the National Congress of the American Indians, argued that the states should not distribute funds. He believed that the federal government should deal directly with tribal governments, regardless of their federal recognition status.[163] Other Indian leaders throughout the state were more receptive to this economic shift because they saw an opportunity to more easily secure funding previously dominated by the Poarch Creek. Although the Poarch Creek did provide some limited assistance to the Jackson County Cherokee, the MOWA Band of Choctaw, and the Star Clan of Muscogee Creeks in the commission's early years, the larger conflict over equal representation hampered any large-scale success by CETA.[164] The final blow came in the summer of 1981 when the SAIAC was informed that their CETA funding had been slashed and that they would have to look elsewhere for supplemental aid.[165]

The Alabama commission turned to more creative measures to address unemployment. With the aid of the community service organization ACTION, which was initially authorized under the 1973 Domestic Volunteer Service Act, the VISTA Volunteer Project was established in 1982 to provide job training to Indian youth.[166] The program sought volunteers from within Indian communities who could help identify employment opportunities in the area.[167] Program coordinators believed that Indian youth would be more receptive to help from other Indians. "The results of this type of individualized service to Indian youth," stated one report, "may well determine what kind of leaders and citizens they become tomorrow."[168] Volunteers from the Poarch Creek, the MOWA Choctaw, and the Jackson County Cherokee attended training in Mississippi and identified disadvantaged youth within their communities. Leaders from these three tribes then formed advisory councils to recruit potential employers, conduct workshops, and organize tours of workplaces.[169]

With the VISTA project under way, several Alabama Indian communities developed more aggressive, community-specific programs to address the problems VISTA volunteers set out to tackle: unemployment and a lack of job training. For example, the MOWA Choctaw developed the Choctaw Indian Youth Community Conservation and Improvement Project, in which participants received an opportunity to perform work that matched up with their interests. The project also offered site tours of and job information about nearby companies.[170] Some participants learned carpentry; following a five-day workshop that included films and the hands-on experience of working on a model house, students were sent to the homes of community elders to provide home improvement services.[171] To tribal leaders concerned with funding cutbacks, training community members how to improve and maintain homes allowed them to "kill two birds with one stone."[172]

Tribal leaders in Louisiana also attempted to combat CETA cutbacks by coordinating a VISTA volunteer program. The Louisiana program, however, did not enjoy the success of the Alabama program. The main problem was that the predominantly non-Indian volunteers came from outside the tribal communities and Indian leaders did not think they grasped the needs of the Indian people. It also became burdensome to find lodging for volunteers. In addition, Houma Tribal Council members complained that VISTA workers entered their community without Houma consent or knowledge. "Nobody even bothered to go to the tribal government and request what their needs were," explained ITC director Jeanette Campos.[173] Other tribal leaders alleged that even when volunteers attempted to assess the extent of need in Indian communities, their youth and unfamiliarity with Indian cultures cast suspicion upon the program's efficiency. "The old people in our area don't like to talk to them young people," explained one tribal leader at a 1981 meeting. "They don't like a young kid coming up and asking questions. They resent it."[174]

Although the VISTA program had little success in Louisiana, tribal leaders remained determined to provide employment assistance through other means. In 1981 and 1982 the Louisiana ITC sponsored a summer youth conference to help high school students from five tribal communities develop job-hunting skills and leadership qualities. The nationally renowned counselor and motivational speaker Howard Rainer, of Taos Pueblo and Creek heritage, oversaw the conference as part of his "message to Indian youth that they can grow and learn in positive ways, and that their Indian heritage is something of which to be proud."[175] Under his guidance students spent hours studying and discussing self-esteem issues. Rainer also taught the students how to develop mini political campaigns, choosing candidates and selecting campaign managers. He wanted to help students identify problems unique to Indians and arrive at potential solutions. Candidates wrote speeches, presented their ideas, and delivered them to the entire group. As part of the conference, students traveled to the state capitol to observe the legislature. "I learned that I don't have to sit back and not speak up," said Anthony "Scooter" Fisher, from the Jena Band of Choctaws. Similarly, James Verdin of the Houma tribe reported that because of his experience, "I learned to have confidence in myself." As a mock political candidate, Verdin delivered his speech, entitled "What Is Real Indian Power," before the entire group at a banquet at the end of the conference. Worried that the trend toward decreasing educational funding was just the beginning, ITC director Campos and Jena Choctaw chairman Clyde Jackson, both of whom were at the banquet, asked conference attendees to find the power to be successful because the cycle of poverty worked against them.[176]

While the Louisiana ITC continued to provide employment assistance and training with a fraction of the previous funding, Alabama tribal leaders saw the benefit of forming an ITC of their own. By 1984 Alabama began a new chapter in Indian affairs when the Davis-Strong Act created a new state commission that represented more tribal interests and the Poarch Creek became the first tribe in the state to be granted federal recognition. Soon after, the remaining state-recognized tribal governments established the Alabama Inter-Tribal Council (AITC). Together, the Alabama commission and the AITC shared the responsibilities of helping individual Indian people, with the AITC specifically addressing the persistent problems of high unemployment. Since the Poarch Creek received all of the CETA funding for Indians in the state, the AITC had no funding to work with in providing services to other Indian communities.[177] As a result, AITC leaders petitioned the U.S. Department of Labor to reevaluate sponsorship of CETA funds, asking that the grant be administered by the Inter-Tribal Council instead of the Poarch Creek. It was not until 1990 that the Labor Department split the grant into two, awarding the Poarch Creek enough for three counties around their reservation and giving the remainder to the AITC for the rest of the state.[178] Although this compromise did not equitably distribute funds, it enabled tribal communities represented by the AITC to directly tap into this money for the first time.

Tribal leaders knew that creating more educational and employment opportunities for Indian youth was a crucial component of future development, but they also understood the need to promote tribal economic ventures. LOIA understood that each tribal community had different economic development capabilities, but it was "the consensus among the Indians, as well as the agencies, that tribal enterprises will be the long-term solution." Although each tribe in the state agreed with this assessment, only the Coushatta and Chitimacha demonstrated "a readiness to successfully plan and operate such enterprises." A 1975 LOIA report indicated that the Jena Band of Choctaw also was successfully planning and operating tribal enterprises, such as an arts and crafts center. Certain tribes, however, needed extra help. The commission targeted the Tunica-Biloxi and Houma communities as those in need of stronger leadership and communication skills to attempt such enterprises. The LOIA report stated that "the prevailing attitude among members of these tribes is 'give us our money.'" As a result of these perceived weaknesses, LOIA intervened and devised an "intensive program of on-site visits and meetings with residents and tribal leadership in order to foster a sense of involvement and conceptual understandings of cooperation, organizational unity and economic planning for these two tribes."[179]

This intensive program to aid some of the less economically developed tribes was not the first attempt by LOIA to promote tribal development. The previous year, LOIA determined that the Houma Alliance needed development aid for a problem with "timid and vacillating leadership" resulting from a failed shrimp cooperative business venture. Despite the fact that the shrimping season had been Louisiana's poorest in seventeen years, community members blamed their leaders for the failure of the business. According to LOIA, "[T]he leaders were intimidated by the criticism and were unable to agree on another project, although all tribal members agreed on the need for a craft and administrative center." Believing that intervention was the only way to unify the Houma, LOIA members sent a leadership-training specialist to help Houma leaders develop better organizational and administrative skills and to create a stronger relationship between the community and LOIA.[180] In 1979 the Choctaw-Apache Community of Ebarb took the initiative in developing leadership in its community when it applied for federal assistance for a "talent search" coordinator to identify those in the community who would be good candidates to take on leadership responsibilities.[181] Unlike efforts in the Houma community, which were initiated by LOIA, the Choctaw-Apache carried out their own efforts.

Alabama tribes also saw the benefit of developing strong leaders. By positioning itself as an advisor and advocate, the commission offered technical assistance and served as a liaison between tribes and the state government. As one SAIAC report assessed, "[T]ribal groups need specialized technical assistance to develop accountability and credibility necessary to develop and operate their own program, whether state, federal, or local economic development, to serve their own people."[182] The SAIAC strengthened tribal administration by partnering with individual leaders to develop projects promoting self-determination.[183] As funds were available, the commission provided tribal governments application materials and assistance in grant writing.

As in Louisiana, the Alabama commission's initial efforts to spark tribal economic development focused on an arts and crafts enterprise to provide jobs for individual craftspeople, especially women. On behalf of Indians statewide, the commission connected tribal enterprises to a global economic system by negotiating with local, interstate, and world trade markets.[184] The Alabama Bureau of Publicity and Information helped develop an export market for Alabama Indian-made products.[185] To further this enterprise, the Poarch Creek in 1981 used CETA funds to set up a sewing and design training center. Under the instruction of Mary Jane Tullis, participants learned basic sewing skills and used local and generic Indian designs in making patterns, designing quilts, and doing custom sewing. The last segment of the course concentrated on producing salable samples of beadwork, leatherwork, and basketry.[186]

In 1981 Kathleen S. Cottrell, executive assistant with the Alabama Bureau of Publicity and Information, traveled to England, Scotland, and Ireland to showcase tribal beadwork, sewing, leatherwork, and basketry. "People at every stop wanted to buy them," she said. "Everything [Indian made] was well received."[187] Cottrell learned that people were particularly interested in hair ornaments, a discovery that fueled a new export market: "Alabama Indian artisans' handiwork has been received with great enthusiasm by both the general public and by an import/export specialist who believes an export market could be established if these quality goods can be produced in sufficiently large quantity to satisfy the need."[188] Hoping to capitalize on the international interest, the commission arranged for Indian artisans to display their work at art exhibits and trade shows statewide.[189] A directory was also created for Alabama Indians who produced and sold traditional Indian crafts and other artwork.[190]

As the SAIAC continued to develop a craft market as part of its larger goals of encouraging cultural revitalization and establishing a broad economic base, Poarch Creek community members worried that the commission would impose stipulations on the self-determination of tribal governments.[191] In March 1981, commission chairman Leonard Hudson clarified the state's export trade development efforts, "emphasizing that the Commission is not serving as a middle man in market efforts, nor will it receive any compensation from export trade developments as a result of current efforts to provide samples of marketable items for showing." He described the commission's role as an advocate to help stimulate both domestic and foreign markets for Alabama Indian products, and he assured community members that Indian groups or individuals would be able to pursue potential markets without SAIAC interference.[192] The duty of the Indian agency, Hudson said, was to furnish tribal leaders with projected labor market statistics to aid them with community development plans.[193] Hudson felt that the commission should be involved only in the initial contact stage and then have nothing more to do with the process.[194] He also called for a "resolution prohibiting the exploitation or the utilization of the Commission by private enterprises and/or private individuals for personal gain."[195]

Despite massive budgetary cutbacks in the early 1980s, tribal leaders in Alabama and Louisiana remained optimistic that the changing times would open the door for more tribal enterprises to provide jobs to community members. To this end, commission meetings often became arenas for tribal leaders to share future economic plans. For example, in 1981 Daniel Darden explained to LOIA how the Chitimacha planned to buy an oil rig and operate it as the Chitimacha Drilling Company. "All I need," Darden explained, "is the money and I can get the contracts before I lay the first pipe."[196] The Coushatta also presented several proposals that involved subcontracting with the Houston-based Tenneco Oil Corporation and contracting with the Kodak Corporation, which would build a small plant in the community to assemble cameras.[197] Soon after, the Coushatta received a $10,000 state grant to construct a coin-operated laundromat, a convenience store, a car wash, and a self-service gas station and only tribal members were hired as construction workers.[198]

Even with such ambitious plans, however, tribal leaders soon faced budget cuts when the full impact of the Reagan administration's fiscal conservation was revealed. To counter these cuts, leaders called meetings to launch a more aggressive plan to promote tribal economic development. At a Houma Tribal Council meeting, Jeannette Campos and Clyde Jackson asked the council to support the creation of the Institute for Indian Development to promote economic growth in Indian communities. Filling the role that LOIA or the ITC was unable to do on its own, the institute focused exclusively on raising money for tribal governments to use in building economic infrastructures. In addition to applying for government grants, the institute invested time and energy into establishing contacts with executives at large businesses, potentially a major source of money and political influence.[199]

The institute also sought professional assistance on behalf of tribal governments from the public and private sectors. As one tribal leader explained: "What we would take these people and do is develop four steps with them to study the problems and resources in depth and develop a plan for the tribes along with your tribal leaders." The professional assistance would help tribal governments gain the knowledge needed to build sustainable tribal enterprises, but leaders continued to voice concerns about where to obtain the seed money for these projects. One idea was to raise money through a board of trustees consisting of people from the non-Indian community who represented business, industry, and government—"people who have influence and shape the state affairs." Another idea was to name this advisory board "Friends of Louisiana Indians" because organizations like the "Friends of Zulu," from New Orleans, were well-known throughout the state and were sources of support.[200] Tribal leaders understood the danger of inviting outsiders into Indian affairs, but their need for resources was so great that they took the risk despite the problems these relationships could pose for tribal sovereignty.

As part of their presentation to tribal leaders about the development of the institute, Campos and Jackson detailed plans to raise the funds necessary to launch the organization. During the first phase of the fund-raising campaign, they explained, tribal leaders would solicit the support of "some very good friends to the Indians that have supported tribes for years and years." Helen Gindrat created a list of possible benefactors from within the state who "were very excited by the possibility of this organization."[201] Many of these "friends of the Indians" also hosted parties in their homes to raise money for the institute.

The next phase of the campaign, which involved a statewide mailing of brochures, engendered the most debate. In particular, Steve Cheramie of the United Houma Nation questioned this approach and suggested that it likely would not be worth the return. Campos defended the mailing, stating that if the mailing list were selective—limited to about twenty individuals per tribal chairman—then the effort would be effective. The more personal the campaign was, Campos argued, the more successful it would be—especially because it would be competing with well-known organizations such as the Catholic Church and UNICEF.[202]

The final phase of the institute's fund-raising campaign involved public outreach through presentations to businesses, religious groups, and individuals, as well as benefits, concerts, and statewide Indian heritage festivals. The idea was to find a captive audience "interested in listening to our story."[203] Given the surge of interest in Indian culture and history throughout the region by the 1980s—as discussed in the next chapter—the institute found the final phase of their plan to be the most effective. For example, in October 1983 the institute made a presentation on the history of each tribe to the Kiwanis Club in Baton Rouge, which in turn made a donation.[204]

Organizers envisioned the institute as a launch pad for tribal development. In response to the criticisms aimed at the state commission and the threat it posed to tribal self-determination, institute leaders positioned the new organization as a resource, providing tribes with information they needed to grow independently. Institute founders also made it clear that their intent was "not the absorption of the tribes so they can no longer function on their own." Rather, the institute wanted to empower Indian communities to handle problems themselves by giving them the necessary tools to work toward self-determination. To facilitate this process, the institute offered the assistance of an economic planner with experience in setting up tribal enterprises.[205]

Many of Louisiana's tribal leaders supported the institute's inclusion of the private sector to promote economic development. Because the campaign to increase economic development was a collaborative effort of the institute, LOIA, and the ITC, however, Ernest Sickey argued that the commission should remain the main representative of Indian interests. Its position as a state agency, he felt, allowed tribes to more effectively pursue funding from the legislature and ultimately become more self-sufficient through alliances with the private sector. Sickey wrote in a 1982 letter: "These two areas will become an important step towards the state-Indian relationship and will enable us to work with the private sector in developing our own local initiative program."[206]

Concerns over equal representation in the institute were also raised. Since the ITC administrated the institute, old tensions concerning a lack of representation of some tribal communities resurfaced. Clyde Jackson explained that the institute's board of trustees would automatically consist of the five tribal chairmen already on the ITC board, and invitations would later be extended to the other three state-recognized groups not part of the ITC. "First," said Campos, "we want to get the organization strong and then we are going to start contacting them."[207] With the placement of the institute's offices in Baton Rouge where the ITC was located, however, some leaders expressed concern over the perceived inequity of the institute and unsuccessfully argued to relocate it to Lafayette, the location of the majority of the state's large businesses.[208]

Through efforts of the institute, the ITC, and LOIA, along with strong Indian leadership, Louisiana's Indian governments saw increased economic development opportunities by the mid-1980s. Some communities proposed tribal projects such as seafood processing, tribal ports, garment factories, and alligator farming, and others used their newly recognized racial minority status to gain benefits initiated by the state and given to minority-owned businesses.[209] LOIA worked with tribal governments to write grants as it also explored the potential of entering into government contracts so that "tribes and the state can work together to develop business relations to benefit both the Indian tribes and the state."[210]

In the midst of these developments, the Coushatta and Chitimacha continued to be role models for other communities statewide. In 1987 the Coushatta acquired a 124-acre industrial complex and negotiated with the BIA and outside investors to fund a tannery business.[211] The same year, the state's minority business director met with the Chitimacha to discuss a partnership in seafood processing and fur marketing.[212] Soon afterward, the governor signed the Chitimacha Economic Development Act, which secured state money for the tribe's economic ventures.[213]

As the Coushatta and Chitimacha developed new enterprises, other groups throughout the state worked on plans of their own. For example, the Jena Band of Choctaw started a furniture manufacturing plant and an auto repair shop.[214] The Tunica-Biloxi Tribal Council built a pecan-shelling plant where the shells were packaged and sold as flavoring for barbeque pits.[215]

While Louisiana's tribal leaders worked on providing more job opportunities to Indians, leaders in Alabama also jump-started development by establishing the Alabama Indian Community Loan Fund through an Administration for Native Americans (ANA) grant. Representatives went to meetings in North Carolina and Georgia regarding the formation of the fund and later made a presentation to the Alabama ITC. They also held a luncheon with business and professional leaders and attended a national meeting sponsored by the National Association of Community Loan Funds.[216] The AIAC wanted to raise money from foundations, organizations, and trusts willing to invest in minority business ventures that otherwise would have had a difficult time securing loans.[217]

In 1984 Tribal Economic Resource Officers (TERO) were appointed for each tribe in Alabama. These officers, along with guidance from the AIAC director, worked with their communities and the state government "to integrate Indian families and individuals into the existing system of social and economic services while maintaining their Indian identity and heritage."[218] This was the first such program for state-recognized tribal governments in the country; previous programs had been exclusively for federally recognized groups. In 1986 the AIAC used ANA funds to hire Darla Graves, a MOWA Choctaw leader, as a tribal development coordinator. She coordinated and implemented economic development projects for tribal governments and served as the tribal economic resource officer for the state.[219] That same year, the AIAC sponsored tribal economic development workshops for tribal councils, Indian entrepreneurs, and commissioners.[220] As a result of the meetings, the Cherokee of Southeast Alabama, with Graves's help, reached a contractual agreement with Houston County to allow the tribe to operate Omussee Creek Park.[221] By 1987 more than $100,000 was generated for other tribal governments and small businesses.[222]

Darla Graves's success as tribal development coordinator prompted the AIAC to continue expanding its efforts toward economic development. As a result, the agency hired Russell Baker as a tribal economic resource officer. Baker had more than eighteen years of experience with Indian programs, including those for Native Alaskans and the Mississippi Choctaw. When the initial ANA money for his position ran out, the AIAC received another grant from the federally funded Appalachian Regional Council (ARC) to extend the position.[223] The AIAC sought help from the council because the majority of Alabama's Indian population resided in the thirty-five-county area covered by the council in the Appalachian region. Although the ARC's focus did not necessarily encompass Indian communities, Graves successfully explained their problems and needs. As a result of these efforts, a segment of Alabama's Indian population received grants to help with community and economic development.[224] To improve matters further, by the spring of 1988, the Alabama ITC voted to establish the first Alabama Indian Small Business Association. Within the first year, the association identified approximately two hundred Indian entrepreneurs and contractors, and the numbers steadily grew, developing into two chapters that covered the northern and southern parts of the state.[225]

Tackling the Immediate Needs

Even with improvements in education, employment, and economic development, Indian communities remained plagued by social ills such as poverty, alcoholism, drug abuse, poor health care, and substandard housing. Tribal leaders' long-term goals were essential in laying the foundation for future tribal
development, but the immediate needs and concerns of Indian people were
inescapable. Letters from people such as Mildred Smith and Elsie Billiot
were reminders of the urgent need that still existed.

Without any special "set aside" money for Indians' welfare and social service needs, tribal leaders in both Louisiana and Alabama turned to research-
ing the availability of preexisting services. In 1981 LOIA sought the aid of
the Department of Health and Human Resources (DHHR) to devise strategies for providing services to their communities. They explored several federal programs, such as food stamps, legal aid, and medical and rehabilitation
services. They were instructed by a DHHR consultant to assign one person
within each tribal council to be responsible for learning about each service
and making contact with someone from their local parish welfare agency—
the main contact point for public assistance and social services. It was important that a tribal representative be involved in the process to make the experience more comfortable for those seeking assistance. The consultant was
candid in his advice, warning that "[l]arge bureaucracies especially like the
DHHR are extremely dehumanizing and impersonal and you are not going
to get the warmest most responsive kinds of services from the people who are
out there supposedly providing services."[226] Following this advice, tribal leaders educated themselves on welfare resources since many of their community
members were eligible for money and services but either lacked knowledge of
or were intimidated by the process. Tribal representatives intervened as intermediaries between individuals and aid agencies. LOIA director Helen Gindrat encouraged these intermediaries to do the actual legwork for needy community members. She instructed them to "go to your local welfare office, and
bring the social security number of the person that needs it and they will put
them into the computer." Gindrat also persuaded tribal leaders to aid elders
in applying for state care.[227]

The Alabama commission also encouraged Indian people to make use of
the preexisting services and aid system available to the state's low-income
residents. In 1981 the Poarch Creek and MOWA Choctaw began guiding
people through the system. This assistance was for people unable to afford

lawyers, but it also benefited those who did not trust outsiders. Legal aides helped people receive food stamps, Medicaid, and other social services. Tribal lawyers handled adoptions and helped protect the elderly from harassment by collection agencies and mistreatment in nursing homes.[228]

Tribes also attempted to deliver better health services to Indian communities. For example, in 1980 the Alabama commission negotiated with The University of Alabama School of Optics to conduct vision-screening in the Poarch Creek and MOWA Choctaw communities. The following year, the commission initiated similar programs in other Indian communities at the same time that an Indian Health Fair was held in north Mobile County. The fair, run by The University of Alabama Student Coalition for Community Health, provided health-screening services to more than nine hundred Indian attendees, including blood pressure readings, blood tests for anemia, diabetic screening, electrocardiograms, glaucoma tests, hearing screening tests, and lung function tests.[229]

Even with the free health screening, the dearth of adequate health facilities remained a pressing concern.[230] The MOWA Choctaw, for example, constructed a clinic in 1984 after receiving a DHHS grant.[231] Roy Procell of the Apache-Choctaw tribe of Louisiana also made a convincing argument for the expenditure of state block grant money on the construction of a tribal hospital in his community. He noted that the nearest hospital was twenty miles away and the closest maternity hospital fifty miles away. "Most of the expecting mothers do not see a doctor before delivery," Procell argued.[232]

Commissions in both Alabama and Louisiana sought programs that would provide food to needy Indian families. In 1980 the AIAC sponsored the Summer Youth Feeding Program for three Indian communities.[233] Similarly, the Louisiana Summer Food Program provided two meals and a supplemental snack to needy children under eighteen during the summer.[234] Tribal leaders clearly wanted to be able to do more than simply refer people to state welfare offices, so in addition to pursuing the sponsorship of the Summer Food Program they sought to administer other aid programs. LOIA coordinated the Emergency Food and Shelter Program, which distributed funds to each tribe for the purchase of food.[235] The AIAC also educated tribal leaders about the World Hunger Project, which gave Alabama tribes an opportunity to receive up to $25,000 in resources and services. From this project, the Star Clan of Muscogee Creeks, Ma-Chis Creeks, and Cherokees of Northeast Alabama received donated heifers, rabbits, beehives, and garden seeds, as well as assistance in the form of on-site visits and professional consultations.[236]

In addition to administering programs for needy families, the AIAC and

LOIA worked to alleviate housing and energy shortages in Indian communities. Louisiana established a governor-appointed Indian Housing Authority in the late 1970s to handle grants related to housing improvement.[237] Soon after, LOIA received federal assistance to launch the Energy Crisis Intervention Program for tribal elders on fixed incomes. The program provided funds for gas and electricity bills, as well as other items such as blankets, warm clothing, space heaters, and firewood.[238]

The establishment of home weatherization programs in both states also reflected attempts to improve living conditions. The state energy office awarded an initial contract to the AIAC to weather-proof a minimum of fifteen homes.[239] The weatherization process consisted of caulking, weather stripping, and insulating, as well as other emergency repairs to conserve energy. Although the commission was under Poarch Creek control when the initial grant was made in 1980, funding from the Alabama Department of Energy and supplemental funds went to the MOWA Choctaw community. The commission reported that the Alabama Office of Employment and Training provided six workers and a site supervisor through a contract with the Youth Conservation and Community Improvement Project. The program recruited all of its participants from the MOWA Choctaw community.[240] By April 1981, seven homes were completed and twenty-two people were assisted.[241] The majority of people who qualified were elderly or handicapped.[242] Just a few months later, the participants had completed five more homes before the project was suspended for a lack of available funds and tense Indian politics between the Poarch Creek and other tribal leaders in the state.[243] MOWA Choctaw chairman Framon Weaver wrote to Governor Fob James complaining that the Poarch Creek–dominated commission had prematurely cut off services to his community.[244] As a result, James soon handed the weatherization project to the MOWA Choctaw tribal office.[245]

In Sum

Although the southern Indian rights movement fueled great inspiration and change as it gained momentum in the 1970s, Indian activists and leaders were frustrated and heartbroken throughout the 1980s as President Reagan's economic plan tightened all aspects of applying for, receiving, and maintaining grants. For tribal leaders, responding to the needs of Indians was akin to waging a war that saw small successes followed by larger defeats. Successfully obtaining grants required organizational skills, the willingness of tribal leaders to work together and share resources, and political know-how. It was difficult to bring these crucial elements together, however, because relationships between tribal leaders were shaped by the needs of each community, their own particular agendas, and their willingness—or lack thereof—to relinquish their self-determining powers by allowing the commissions or intertribal councils to oversee grants.

Tribal leaders worked to improve their community members' lives by using the commissions or other Indian agencies as tools to develop relationships with states, create partnerships with legislators, and make valuable connections with service agencies. The commissions defined the rules, norms, and guidelines for tribal-state relationships, which both embraced the notion of rebuilding past government-to-government relationships and broke new ground in tribal relationships with states. While Indian leaders who worked through the commissions educated legislators about Indian affairs, they also responded to the basic needs of their people in improving educational and employment opportunities. Taking several approaches, leaders responded by applying for grants and creating Indian-run programs; issuing individual aid in the form of scholarships and job training; and helping people find and make use of preexisting social programs and services. Trying to meet educational and employment needs only partially solved the problem, however, because without a stable economic infrastructure or access to quality social services, Indian communities remained vulnerable to outside pressures. Yet despite their struggles and those of subsequent generations of Indian leaders, the unique relationships that tribes initiated with states sparked changes that continued to improve the lives of many Indians throughout the following decades.

5
A Regional Makeover
Tourism and How Indians Remade the South

In 1976 the romantic and harmonious lifestyle of southern Cherokees who managed to eke out an existence in the isolated stretches of the Appalachian Mountains captivated the nation. The critically acclaimed *New York Times* best-selling and self-identified memoir *The Education of Little Tree* by Forrest Carter represented an important evolution in the formation of southern identity. Carter incorporated the increasingly accepted knowledge that many Indians had hidden to avoid removal, perpetuating an image of southern pride, endurance, and exceptionalionalism.[1]

What many fans of *Little Tree* did not know, however, was that this new-age piece of literary history emerged from the politically charged imaginings of Alabama governor George Wallace's rabble-rousing speech writer Asa Earl Carter. Carter, who took his pen name "Forrest" from the Civil War general and founder of the Ku Klux Klan, Nathan Bedford Forrest, orchestrated a literary hoax that kept critics and scholars speculating years after Carter's true identity was revealed in 1991 by Emory University professor and biographer of George Wallace, Dan T. Carter.[2] Asa Carter, an anti-Semite and race-baiting organizer of the Alabama Citizens' Council and founder of his own KKK chapter, caused a stir by writing a "memoir" about a young Indian orphan raised by his grandparents in the isolation of Appalachia instead of staying true to his white supremacist roots.

The possible explanations for why Carter wrote the memoir are complicated and numerous. Some researchers claim that Asa "Forrest" Carter's use of Indian characters played an insignificant role in his attempt to tell a "southern story," but his decades-long history of spreading nativist and racist propaganda to the public through various mediums makes it difficult to dismiss

Little Tree as just a "good story."[3] As the author of the famous "segregation forever" speech delivered by George Wallace in 1963, Carter was keenly attuned to the changing political and cultural mood of the South and thought carefully about the manner in which he conveyed his message.[4] His seemingly innocent book was no exception.

The Education of Little Tree was more than just a simple appropriation of Indian identity that met national market demands for Indian-themed literature and films throughout the 1970s and 1980s.[5] The work showcased an evolving southern identity that Carter both created and reinforced. Although representations of Indians have always had a presence in the South—as seen by historical markers, museums featuring artifacts from mound-building cultures, and a seemingly infinite number of rivers, streams, mountains, and towns with Indian names—they had predominantly passive roles within the broader southern identity. In response to the changing social and political environment of the post–civil rights era, however, public figures and writers expressed a renewed interest in indigenous history and symbols as a way to transform the region's identity. Southerners who reveled in the romanticism of a distant Indian connection within their own family histories welcomed increased attention to Indian sites, history, and celebrated heroism. For many southerners, emphasizing the region's Indian past celebrated the bravery and endurance of thousands of Indians who escaped forcible removal.[6] This story of survival also reinforced a regional perception of victimization by the North, particularly the federal government.

Although Carter's characters embody the southern ideal of survival, they also are convenient analogs for his distrust, individualism, and anti-government sentiments that fueled his earlier KKK activities and career aspirations.[7] As Daniel Heath Justice points out, "Carter, who proudly acknowledged his lineage from fallen heroes of the Confederacy, found this Indian identity a useful tool in expressing his racist ideology."[8] In other words, *Little Tree* did not mark a turning point in his racism; it represented a new venue in which to disseminate preexisting attitudes and bolster white pride. Within the context of the 1970s, the book also was intended to deflect attention away from the awareness raised by the black civil rights movement by pointing out that African Americans were not the most mistreated or oppressed group in the South. The anxiety surrounding desegregation fueled southern nostalgia for Native Americans as "the link between the Southerner and the land," and a sense of entitlement was maintained through self-proclaimed indigenous connections. Carter himself even claimed he "was a white man with Indian blood."[9]

The continued popularity of *Little Tree* following its exposure as a hoax, however, revealed that promoting the region's indigenous history overpowered the need for authenticity. Thousands of American schoolchildren continued to read the book as an "accurate" testimonial of Native American values, and the story received even more attention when Paramount Pictures turned it into a movie in 1997. This interest in southern Indians did not diminish in the decades following the book's initial publication, as shown by the ongoing popularity of both fiction and nonfiction works on Indians in the post-Removal South.[10]

Indians and "Indian-themed" histories offered southern states an opportunity to redeem their tarnished image as the most racist and violent in the nation. Throughout the 1980s, many of the region's politicians expressed concern about the South's negative image and shared their ideas about a "remade South." For example, Louisiana governor Buddy Roemer spoke at the Southern Legislative Conference in 1988 on his vision for the South and "its potential to lead America." Acknowledging the state's scandalous and discriminatory past, Roemer vowed to help Louisiana "pull its act together" by investing more time and money in education and economic development for minorities. As part of his plan, Roemer promised to improve transportation so tourists could come to Louisiana to share in the rich cultural heritage of the state's African American, Creole, Cajun, and Native American communities.[11]

For tribal people across the South, the enthusiastic inclusion of Indians in the southern heritage industry during the last decades of the twentieth century was a prime example of "social forgetting."[12] Suddenly, despite decades of marginalization and discrimination within a biracial system that kept tribal leaders occupied with reintroducing "Indian" as an accepted form of racial identification, Indian identity became popular. Southerners from all walks of life wrote to state Indian affairs commissions seeking genealogical information. As Indian leaders struggled to draw attention to the social and economic problems in their communities, writers such as Carter promoted a particular brand of southern "Indian-ness," one of the noble survivor who was more fantasy than reality.

Indian leaders understood the need to generate awareness about the issues facing their communities and control the reproduction of their histories. Because Indians had become "popular," leaders and activists within the movement seized what one AIAC administrator identified as the chance to "promote a realistic image of the Native American to the non-Indian population to promote a climate in which Indians may be free to be Indian and to express their heritage."[13] Educating the public gave tribes many benefits, including collective pride and support for cultural revitalization. By actively shaping and protecting their historical and contemporary images, tribal leaders also protected Indian rights as more people—whether legitimately or not—began claiming an indigenous identity, while others desecrated gravesites and culturally significant areas in search of historical relics.

This chapter explores the steps tribal leaders in Alabama and Louisiana took throughout the 1970s and 1980s toward generating public awareness of their cultures and histories as the interest in southern Indian identity increased nationwide. State Indian affairs commissions often were liaisons between tribes and museums, tourism agencies, universities, and a variety of special interest groups. The state Indian agencies offered tribes the support needed to develop exhibits, festivals, documentaries, curriculum, public presentations, and educational booklets. Through the visibility generated by the commissions, Indians became involved in state efforts to attract tourism. Like the Eastern Band of Cherokee in North Carolina and the Florida Seminoles, Alabama and Louisiana Indians constructed their own public images while simultaneously promoting cultural and economic development by selling artwork, constructing tribal museums, and organizing public festivals and powwows.[14] Tribal leaders were invited to speak at schools and private organizations, collaborate on academic, archaeological, and archival projects, and appear at functions dedicating significant monuments or commemorating historical events in the region's history. Even with a receptive audience, however, Indian leaders understood that their role as public educators would compete with the romantic fantasy embodied in *Little Tree* for a prominent place in the region's identity.

Recognizing the Need for Public Education

After years of isolation, tribal leaders debated whether public support was crucial to their communities' futures. Although the tribes wanted to promote community interests by educating the public about their unique cultural characteristics, tribal leaders also believed that a collaborative inter-tribal effort would have a larger impact than would isolated efforts. A successful public awareness campaign required tribal leaders to transcend differences and collaborate on a common vision and set of strategies. "It's way past due that the tribes themselves try to help themselves in trying to educate the public," argued one Louisiana tribal leader in assessing the benefits of Indians taking control of their own public image.[15] Alabama tribal leaders reached the same conclusion. They faced a daunting task, as Jackson County Cherokee leader

H. L. "Lindy" Martin explained: "it is up to us to keep America reminded of the great heritage of our people."[16]

By the mid-1970s, Louisiana's tribal leaders had begun organizing efforts to generate public awareness. "It is recognized that without broad support in the state of the non-Indian population," one meeting report stated, "needed legislation and financial support of projects will be difficult to achieve."[17] To gain this support, Jeannette Campos, director of the ITC, declared it important that "Indians leave a good taste in people's mouths." She continued, "We want to tell our story, we want people to know that Indians in Louisiana have a contribution to make and that they have survived for all these years. That in itself is a major contribution. [We] not only [want] to let them know that we're here but to request their support, to get them to be helpful. I'm not talking about a hand-out or saying 'give us some money.'"[18] Campos and other Indian leaders wanted to avoid being portrayed as charity cases. Instead, they promoted Indians as citizens with both needs and talents who were in a prime position to develop a reciprocal relationship with the state.

As in other parts of the South, tribal leaders in Alabama and Louisiana recognized that tribal social and economic development and their states' tourism industries were connected. For example, the Alabama Poarch Creek leader Houston McGhee, like his father, Calvin McGhee, asserted that a strong interest in southern Indians made tourism an ideal economic opportunity for tribes. "The development of our Creek Indian Community," McGhee outlined in a 1974 letter to Governor George Wallace, "will enhance and enrich the cultural heritage of Alabama for all her citizens."[19] McGhee knew that Indians had much to gain—both monetarily and culturally—by becoming integrated into the region's revised identity and giving credence to the indigenization of this identity. The founding LOIA commissioner, David L. Garrison, also believed tourism was the first logical step in tribal development. "Tourism is a natural resource for them," Garrison explained to Governor Edwin Edwards. "Their craft and art [are] appreciated the world over."[20]

In addition to economic benefits, tribal leaders argued that public support and tourism also could instill pride within their communities. In fact, Alabama Indian leaders envisioned a statewide movement toward cultural revitalization and community building.[21] They assumed that public support would give Indian communities the confidence to overcome the "hiding" mentality they had endured since Removal. A similar argument waged in Louisiana because, as the Houma leader Steve Cheramie explained, "For many, many years, it was like a disgrace to be Indian. It was like you were subhuman or something."[22] Because of this mentality, many Native people often shied away from their Indian identities. As Leslie Lord complained in a 1981 letter to LOIA, "It is very difficult, in my family, to get anyone to talk about our Indian heritage."[23]

While leaders tried to reverse the psychological damage in their communities resulting from years of oppression and discrimination, administrators for state Indian commissions and inter-tribal councils noticed a rising interest among non–tribally affiliated southerners in claiming Indian ancestry. For example, Louisiana ITC director Jeannette Campos explained what she and LOIA commissioner Helen Gindrat were often told after revealing to people that they worked in Indian affairs: "'Oh, I'm part Indian,' or 'my husband is part Indian,' or somebody is part Indian, so people are very proud to be or to claim themselves as Indian."[24] The real-life needs of Indian communities, therefore, became convoluted as many southerners tried to determine how to benefit from the commissions.

In 1980 the southern Indian census population far exceeded the numbers officially enrolled in a tribe. This discrepancy created problems for the Indian commissions for two reasons. First, these numbers could mean that the commissions were losing touch with their service populations. Second, and more alarming, the numbers could mean that "we [tribal leaders] have to accept the fact that there are some people who want to be Indians that are not Indians."[25] Campos argued that Indian rights must be protected because "it has become very popular to claim Indian identity [and] people tend to feel that there are a lot of benefits wrapped into the package of being an Indian."[26]

The most common motivation for claiming Indian heritage was educational aid. For example, in 1981 Alvin Rainey Jr. wrote to LOIA requesting a tribal "number" so he could go to "school for a trade."[27] Similarly, Jo Whisenant requested information on her Indian heritage "in order to go back to school."[28] Such letters indicated a clear information gap, for without a full understanding of how to become a member of a tribe, Rainey and Whisenant mistakenly sought the aid of the commission not only to legitimate their Indian identities but also to gain access to educational resources.

The Alabama commission had a similar problem. In 1980 a United Southern Missionary Church member wrote the commission claiming that 90 percent of church members had "direct Indian heritage . . . [and] expressed a desire to lay claim to their heritage." Furthermore, the letter posited that it was the commission's "duty" to help these people in their pursuits.[29] Without mention of a tribal affiliation, however, commission director Jennie Dees had no way to guide the congregation members to the appropriate resources. She responded with a gracious letter expressing delight that "more and more people with Indian heritage are expressing pride in that fact," but, as Dees explained, the commission did not acknowledge individual claimants. Instead, she said, the Indian agency was constructing state recognition criteria for petitioning tribal groups. Dees replied with general information about the state and federal recognition process and recommended the church conduct research on Indian law.[30]

The commissions were also concerned that claimants intended to take advantage of the already limited state and tribal resources. As a result, Indian leaders agreed to take action. As Helen Gindrat complained, "Anybody can walk in and say 'I'm a Indian' and they can't find documents to back them up, nor are they able to say what tribe they belong to." Her solution was a campaign in cooperation with the governor's office to educate the public about state recognition and how to legitimately claim an Indian identity. "It's protecting ourselves on a state recognition basis," Gindrat pointed out.[31]

Tribal leaders blamed false and stereotypically romanticized representations of Indians perpetuated within schools as the primary reason why so many people began to claim Indian ancestry. In particular, the Alabama commission alleged that "many non-Indians were misinformed about Indian cultures, traditions and languages, [and] there was no concerted effort in the states to resolve this problem through the public school system."[32] Even museum exhibits about Indians, such as one set up at the Louisiana Arsenal Museum on the grounds of the state capitol in Baton Rouge in 1971, represented Native people as "primitive" and stuck in the past. Tribal leaders and commission administrators felt they had to reach out to the younger generations and show positive and accurate representations of Indians.

Protecting Indian gravesites and culturally significant areas was another motivating factor in developing a public awareness campaign. As one Louisiana newspaper explained, "Bulldozers have obliterated entire ancient neighborhoods throughout Louisiana, demolishing homes and turning human bones to dust—all without opposition."[33] In Alabama, similar occurrences prompted individuals to complain directly to the governor. In 1982 Governor Fob James received a letter from Mack White, the Principal Chief of the non-state-recognized Southeast Indian Confederacy. He claimed to speak on behalf of all Indian people in Alabama about the continued desecration of Indian gravesites throughout the state. Even though the majority of Alabama Indians were non–federally recognized, or non-state-recognized in his

7. Exhibit on Louisiana Indian history in Baton Rouge, 1971. (Courtesy of the State Library of Louisiana.)

group's case, White argued that they deserved to have their rights protected. He asked the governor to take a strong position against looting and grave desecration perpetuated by both amateur and professional archaeologists.[34]

Although most cases of gravesite destruction were not publicized, a few received media attention. Tribal leaders in Louisiana were outraged when contractors building the Indian Creek reservoir and recreation area in 1975 partially destroyed a Choctaw and Tunica-Biloxi graveyard. Saddened and angered by the news, LOIA representative Ernest Sickey said, "There's no way it should have been missed. It was a modern graveyard. There was a fence around it and it was clearly identifiable." Sickey viewed the incident as a prime example of the abuses waged against Indians in the state.[35] *Town Talk* reporter Jeff Cowart, who investigated the incident, wrote about the impact such destruction had on Indians. In recounting his conversation with an unidentified official concerning the matter, he reported that the official laughed and expressed an attitude of "who cares, anyway, it's just a bunch of old Indians." Attempting to generate public awareness and empathy, Cowart wrote: "Amateur archeologists, unconcerned officials and rabid artifact hunters sometimes don't realize that going back to gaze at the spot where one's ancestors are buried means a lot to some people." Besides arguing for the rights of Indians to preserve their cultural and historical integrity, Cowart also stated that "bona fide archeologists" should be able to salvage artifacts and preserve history. "Theirs is destruction with a purpose other than pleasure," he pointed out. "[Two hundred] years from now you can dig up my grandmother if it's the only means of helping others to learn more about my history. But don't bulldoze her for the sake of a boat ramp."[36]

Amateur archaeologists and Indian enthusiasts also posed a threat to gravesites and culturally significant areas. The AIAC stressed how "a deep and abiding concern exists among all members of the Indian community as to the care, treatment and preservation of Indian artifacts, burial sites, and quality archeological exploration and excavation." Most alarming, however, was the destruction by amateurs "who have no formal training or cultural interests in the items and sites they discover and desecrate."[37] Artifact collecting and site desecration demanded public awareness efforts by both the AIAC and LOIA. Because "most people who dig for artifacts do so for the thrill of discovery," wrote reporter Ray Formanek Jr., they needed to be educated about the destructive weight of their actions. Even more problematic were artifacts found on private property. "People are afraid that if they let someone know their find, the state will come in and restrict the use of their property," explained Kathleen Byrd, director of the archaeology division within the state's Department of Culture, Recreation and Tourism. "Others keep their findings secret because they think the artifacts are valuable."[38]

Along with teaching the public about site desecration, Indian leaders wished to have more influence over the use of historically significant sites in tourism. For example, Poverty Point, a site on the banks of Louisiana's Bayou Macon, drew much attention and debate. In 1977 the state purchased the three-thousand-year-old site from private owners. Designated as the Poverty Point State Commemorative Area, archaeologists thought the site contained the oldest group of ceremonial earthworks in North America. Budgetary cutbacks, however, forced the state to close the park in 1986. By the following year, archaeologists remained torn as to what should happen to the site. Many wanted it to remain under state jurisdiction, but others thought the site should be a national monument. Northeast Louisiana University professor Glen S. Greene told a reporter that the National Park Service's presence "would enhance the prestige of the site, make it better known to a wider spectrum of traveling Americans and Canadians, to say nothing of tour groups from other countries and in the long run significantly boost the local economy."[39] The site eventually was integrated into the state park system, and tourists were invited to "explore an ancient Indian village in Marksville."[40] The outcome was disappointing in that the involvement and perspectives of tribal communities continued to be overlooked.

Taking Control of Representations

Southern Indian leaders joined tribal leaders across the nation in a debate about the best ways to combat decades of cultural imperialism in which American Indian cultures were commercialized, exploited, and appropriated by non-Indians.[41] The Louisiana Coushatta leader Ernest Sickey was one of the first to express concern over the manner in which Indians were represented. "We don't want them on exhibition," he explained. "People of this state have to get rid of the feathers, drums and bells stereotype."[42] "Playing Indian" for white audiences nevertheless proved to be an effective strategy in some instances, such as Calvin McGhee's attempts to draw attention to the existence of his people or in the ploys of some southern Indian communities to attract tourism.[43] Critics like Sickey, however, argued that unrealistic and stereotypical images hindered progress because they prevented Indians from being taken seriously.

Many Native leaders in the 1970s and 1980s agreed with Sickey and sought to control their historic and contemporary representations by developing public exhibits featuring their unique cultural attributes and technological skills. The Coushatta in Louisiana are a good example of a tribe that successfully generated public interest through their basketry. In 1972 tribal members began working with the state to develop a tourism project to help weavers sell baskets and generate public support. The collaboration also allowed the state to advertise cultural diversity among its citizens.[44] Local newspapers contributed to the efforts by featuring stories about weavers and, in at least one case, publishing photographs of artisans laboring over intricately woven baskets.[45] Then, in 1973, LOIA opened a Coushatta exposition in New Orleans and invited the governor to attend. The basketry exhibition traveled to other parts of the state with the intent of educating the greater public.[46]

At the same time that the Coushatta made great strides in generating exposure, an Indian arts exhibit circulated throughout Louisiana. Backed by tribal leaders, the exhibit was on loan from the Louisiana Council for Music and Performing Arts, which had arranged with the Institute of American Indian Arts in Santa Fe, New Mexico, to display the works of contemporary Indian artists from across the country. Mrs. Edwin H. Blum, the council president, explained: "The purpose of the traveling exhibit is to show the American public that there is something in American Indian art which is viable, exciting and relevant to Americans today." The exhibit complemented the general awareness program of the state's tribal leaders to draw attention to Indian talent and contributions.[47]

The use of exhibits remained a common form of generating awareness about Indians because the public in general linked arts and crafts with Indians. For example, Dr. Robert W. Neuman, assistant director of the Louisiana State University (LSU) Museum of Geoscience, was the curator of a traveling exhibition called "Louisiana Indians Throughout the Ages." The free exhibit demonstrated the cultural contributions of prehistoric and more recent Louisiana Indians with texts, scale models, and photographs.[48] Another example was the American Indian Celebration exhibit, sponsored in 1983 by the Shreveport Regional Arts Council and the Institute for Indian Development. Tribal leaders statewide attended the event, which took place at the R. S. Barnwell Memorial Garden and Art Center. It featured arts and crafts exhibitions from various Indian communities and private collections. One of the primary displays included photographs of Louisiana Indians from the 1920s and 1930s and was part of the Swanton Collection, usually housed in the Smithsonian Institution. Contemporary photographs of Indian communities were also placed alongside the Swanton photographs. The LSU Museum of Geoscience also made a portion of their McIlhenny Collection of Chitimacha baskets available for display. The American Indian Celebration exhibit educated the public on Louisiana Indian history and culture and engendered cultural pride among Indians themselves.[49]

Many tribes also took control of their public images by opening their own tribal museums. For example, the Tunica-Biloxi operated a tribal museum containing pottery, jewelry, cooking utensils, and weapons.[50] In addition to publicizing their rich cultural heritage and technology, the tribe built the physical museum structure from cinder blocks to resemble a flat-topped Indian mound. To make the structure look like an actual earthen mound, architects planted English Ivy, which was positioned to grow over the structure and hide the blocks.[51] The Chitimacha and Coushatta tribes also built cultural centers in which tribal arts and crafts were displayed for purchase.[52]

The goal of exposing a wide range of Louisiana residents to the unique and vibrant tribal cultures within the state drove Indian leaders to organize many public presentations and Indian festivals. For example, in 1978 the Louisiana ITC sponsored a festival on the grounds of the old state capitol to teach the public about Louisiana Indian heritage.[53] Tribal leaders also partnered with the LSU chancellor to plan events on the university campus.[54] In 1982 the United Houma Nation worked with several New Orleans agencies, such as the Culture and Tourism Commission, the Tricentennial Commission, the Chamber of Commerce, and the Board of Trade, to hold a celebration at the City Park Stadium in New Orleans. The Tricentennial Indian Festival "celebrated the tricentennial of La Salle's visit into the Lower Mississippi River Valley and his 'discovery' of the Houma tribe." As the primary event organizers, the United Houma Nation asked LOIA for help planning the celebration and requested that the types of concessions and other goods to be displayed at the festival be authentic, such as Native foods and Indian-made art, crafts, and jewelry. To uphold the integrity of the event and promote a realistic image of Indians, organizers specified that "artisans must be Indian and present original work with an Indian theme." If the artwork violated these criteria, the festival committee could "require the removal of specific work." The care taken to present a respectable, authentic image to the public went beyond the concession stands, as screenings were also required for individuals who intended to participate in dancing, drumming, or any number of tournament challenges such as stickball, chungke, blowgun, and bow and arrow.[55] In addition to the Tricentennial Indian Festival, Native artisans received exposure through other statewide festivals and celebrations, such as the New Orleans Jazz Festival, which offered a prime opportunity for Indians to sell their artwork.[56]

Louisiana tribal leaders made great strides in educating the public about Indians through organized presentations. For instance, in 1982 LOIA sponsored a panel of tribal leaders to speak at a meeting of the Council of Catholic Women in New Orleans. The event gave the council a clear idea of the challenges facing their communities.[57] Louisiana Indians also had help exposing the public to the importance of including Indians in the discussion of the state's history by Dr. H. F. "Pete" Gregory, a Northwestern State University anthropology professor. Gregory organized and moderated an open discussion at the Lafayette Natural History Museum regarding the influence of Louisiana Indians. Coushatta and Tunica-Biloxi representatives spoke about "early settlement and lifestyle, the influences of the prairie, farming, language, landscape, culture, and the current status of Louisiana tribes." The discussion revealed that the public was largely unaware of what was being done—or not done—to preserve Indian cultures and the role the federal government played in the future of tribes. Gregory, who had collaborated with tribes across the state for more than twenty years, summarized the presentation: "Louisiana

Indian peoples are important to all citizens because they represent the original human adaptation to the diversity of Louisiana environments." In particular, Louisiana's Native traditions influenced the folk medicine and food of rural whites and African Americans. The discussion coincided with the exhibit "Dreams and Memories: The Louisiana Prairie Experience," which allowed teachers to borrow an "Indian suitcase" to supplement their curriculum. The suitcase contained clay balls, arrowheads, baskets, moss dolls, slides, and reading materials about Indian contributions to the state.[58]

Tribes throughout the South often expressed Indian identity through powwows and Indian princess contests.[59] As Patricia Barker Lerch notes in her study of state-recognized Indians in North Carolina, "powwow activities provide a way for the tribal community to publicly demonstrate its own commitment to its Indian identity."[60] For Indian communities that wanted to introduce themselves to the surrounding Indian and non-Indian communities, the adoption of music and dance from the northern and southern plains encouraged media exposure and invited others to share in a celebration of heritage and empowerment.[61] Beginning in 1970 the Poarch Creek hosted annual powwows on Thanksgiving to commemorate their community's endurance. The day marked a new year for the tribe—tribal elections were held, up-and-coming artists and craftspeople displayed their work, and the community crowned a new Creek Indian Princess.[62] As cultural ambassadors for their communities, Indian pageant winners represented the most "traditionally authentic" contestants, lending a sense of legitimacy to their communities as they were featured in newspapers and public appearances.[63]

Like the Poarch Creek, in the early 1980s the MOWA Choctaw began hosting an annual spring festival and powwow at a local public high school. The event, which became part of a larger powwow circuit, attracted Indian dancers from across the country to compete for prizes in four dance categories. The 1981 gathering, for example, highlighted the performances of Mississippi Choctaw and Lumbee dancers. There were even appearances by Susan Arkeketa (Miss Indian America from the Creek Nation of Oklahoma), Joe Bointy (a Comanche-Kiowa World Champion Fancy Dancer), and Tommy Ware (a Comanche flute player).[64]

As part of the festivities, the MOWA Choctaw also held a pageant for young MOWA Choctaw girls vying to be crowned "Indian princess." In 1981 representatives from the Mississippi Band of Choctaw, the Poarch Creek, and the Echota Cherokee, as well as Leonard Hudson of the Alabama Indian Affairs Commission, judged eight contestants. The judges tested the contestants' knowledge of tribal history and Choctaw culture and language, and evaluated their talent, poise, and traditional dress. In the end, Elizabeth Taylor won the title of Senior Princess by impressing the judges with her beautiful singing voice, which she had honed with lessons at Livingston State College. The Junior Princess title went to Lynn Weaver, who at the age of seven captured many hearts by reciting the Pledge of Allegiance in Choctaw. Taylor and Weaver later represented the tribe at public functions, such as local festivals and celebrations, and encouraged their community's youth to take a deeper interest in their history and culture.[65]

Powwows and Indian princess contests drew media interest and forged inter-tribal relationships. As an urban, inter-tribal organization, the Indian Angels, for example, regularly held powwows at the American Indian Center in Baton Rouge. The events attracted Indian dancers, drum circles, and artisans from all over the country, but the Indian Angels also used the gathering to invite Native leaders for discussions on common problems in Indian communities, as well as potential solutions. At a 1975 powwow, Sarah Peralta and other Indian Angels hosted a luncheon for Louisiana tribal leaders and representatives from the Northern Arapaho of Wyoming, the Montana Cheyenne, and the Navajo Nation to examine serious and pressing issues, including alcoholism and language revitalization.[66]

Rural Louisiana tribes also hosted powwows and Indian princess contests to foster pride within their communities and generate interest among the general public. For example, the Poverty Point State Park was the site of annual powwow celebrations featuring dancers and drum circles from across the country and showcasing pipe ceremonies and Choctaw traditional dances. As one organizer explained, "we let the public dance with us and we have a big turnout."[67] An annual powwow in the town of Houma drew as many as four thousand people—both Indian and non-Indian—from throughout the South. A 1987 article on the event cited Choctaw attendees from Louisiana, Mississippi, Alabama, and Oklahoma; Creeks from Oklahoma and Alabama; and Coushatta, Comanche, Apache, Seminoles, Tunica, and Chitimacha from across the region. Sixteen-year-old MOWA Choctaw pageant princess Tajuana Reed also appeared, stating that she came to give her community exposure because, as she put it, "I enjoy letting other people know what we are about."[68] Louisiana tribes also sought public recognition through beauty pageants. For example, in the early 1970s, the Coushatta began holding Miss Indian Princess contests.[69] Then the Houma followed suit and hosted a contest "designed as a boost to pride in a tribe once considered extinct."[70]

As tribes across the South organized or participated in exhibits, public presentations, festivals, powwows, and Indian princess contests, Indian-produced

8. Indian festival on the streets of Baton Rouge, 1983. (Courtesy of the State Library of Louisiana.)

literature and documentaries offered them a chance to shape their own historical narratives. For example, the Poarch Creek integrated the memory of Chief Calvin McGhee into Alabama's historical consciousness through the film *The Chief Calvin McGhee and the Forgotten Creeks*.[71] Lisa Larrabee's children's book *Grandmother Five Baskets* tells the story of a contemporary Poarch Creek girl learning about her history and culture.[72] Tony Mack McClure, a Tennessee Cherokee, also worked closely with the Alabama Cherokee of Northeast Alabama to promote public awareness about Cherokee history and culture by publishing a book and producing a television documentary on the tribe.[73]

The media also played a major role in generating public interest in Indian affairs. For instance, when Ernest Sickey was first appointed in 1972 as a consultant to the newly created LOIA, attorney Ruth Loyd Miller wrote the managing editor of the *Basile Weekly* to ensure that the media covered Sickey's appointment. "We have hopes," Miller explained, "that the interest will be sustained to a successful conclusion on behalf of the Indian tribes of Louisiana."[74] Agreeing to Miller's request, the paper featured a full-page article on Sickey several days later.[75]

Beyond the coverage of significant appointments, the media emerged during the 1980s as a strong ally of Louisiana tribes. In particular, Margrett Fels, the wife of a prominent German hotelier as well as a freelance journalist and Indian advocate, wrote several articles in the state's popular newspapers and magazines. Her 1986 article "Liberty and Justice for All?" for the *Baton Rouge Magazine* helped showcase Indians as "Louisiana's Living History." She also described their fight for the "preservation of their autonomy, cultural heritage, and basic civil rights."[76] Fels continued: "Living in palmetto huts and navigating their dugout canoes while fishing our waterways, Louisiana's Indians do not fit the stereotypical image of the savage on horseback circling a teepee village. Centuries of geographic isolation and cultural segregation from the white man resulted in proud Indians, independently governing their own sovereignties through a system of laws developed long before the signing of our Declaration of Independence."[77] Fels's journalistic celebration of the state's Native population included a detailed discussion of sovereignty and the unique position of southern tribes within the broader history of Indian affairs. As a result of the Indian rights movement, she maintained, "a strong Louisiana Indian image is emerging as they begin to demand their rights and are learning how to utilize the resources at hand. Louisiana's Indians are joining in an alliance with each other to produce a unified Indian voice." An intricate part of the state's historic and contemporary identity, "the Indians of today are saying: 'Know who we are, how we exist, and understand that the problems we face are no different from yours, because *we are part of you, Louisiana.*'"[78]

Alabama Indian affairs also received media exposure from Marie Cromer, editor of the *St. Clair News Press* and a close ally of the Echota Cherokee tribe. However, the exposure Cromer gave to Alabama Indians was not entirely positive as she thrust herself into the conflict over equal representation on the commission. In November 1981, Cromer began an aggressive campaign against the Poarch Creek with an article for the *Birmingham News* claiming that the commission was ineffective and "things seem to be bogged down in the ever familiar quagmire of politics and bureaucratic red tape." Painting the picture of an incompetent Indian agency, Cromer also accused the Poarch Creek of hoarding money and fueling "an existing rivalry and some lingering degree of bitterness between old enemies."[79] Cromer, who called herself an advocate and voice for the other Indian tribes in the state, disturbed Poarch Creek leaders and commission administrators such as Jennie Lee Dees, who responded to Cromer's article in an editorial in the *Birmingham News*. Try-ing to maintain a positive relationship with the rest of the journalistic com-munity, Dees wrote, "I have found Alabama's news media to be openly sensi-tive to the unique and long neglected problems experienced by Indian people, and to be supportive of our struggle to gain a meaningful and rightful place in this state. It is unfortunate that Ms. Cromer has elected to print miscon-ceptions and misinterpretations rather than reflect and report on the factual and very positive aspects of our efforts."[80] Cromer's involvement in Indian af-fairs went a step further when she began attending commission meetings as "a member of the press." For meetings she could not attend, however, she made her views known through open letters to the commission, such as the January 1982 meeting devoted to the commission's reorganization. Cromer asked that her letter be read aloud to the attendees. Recognizing her power in shaping public opinion, commission chairman Leonard Hudson suggested that tribal leaders take her request seriously "rather than antagonize the taxpaying mem-bers of the press."[81] In her letter, Cromer asserted her power as a journalist to expose problems in Indian affairs: "You can only go back to the public trough so many times, and unless these issues are settled equitably once and for all, prepare yourself for a backlash of non-Indian support in this state from the state legislature down to every non-Indian who has worked in support of the Indian movement for self-sufficiency and recognition. . . . The white com-munity looks on aghast, and my final words to all of you is start acting like true Indians."[82] This threat reveals the complexity of Indian leaders' relation-ships with the media in which journalists like Cromer imposed their own ex-pectations on how "true Indians" should behave. Although her writing gave tribes more exposure, Cromer did more than report on state Indian affairs— she actively tried to aid her Echota Cherokee friends by using her privilege as a member of the media, and as part of the non-Indian community, to try to influence the commission's organization. It is difficult to assess the extent of Cromer's influence on the events leading to the temporary closing of the commission; however, she succeeded in making tribal leaders aware of the importance of maintaining positive relationships with the local media.

While journalists like Fels and Cromer kept the public informed about tribal politics and progress toward community development, Indian leaders recognized that they needed to bridge the information gap more effectively. The flood of letters and calls to the commissions requesting information on the states' Indian communities prompted the Indian agencies to produce in-

formational booklets outlining tribal histories and providing genealogical assistance for individuals wishing to trace their family histories.

The Louisiana ITC first produced such a booklet in the late 1970s detail-
ing the history of each of the state's tribes. *Indians of Louisiana* helped inquiring individuals learn more about what they claimed as their own cultural heritage.[83] The booklet also proved useful when responding to a variety
of inquiries about Indian affairs. For example, fourteen-year-old Lee Wise
Jr. wrote for information, including a map of all Louisiana Indian reservations.[84] The booklet also reached Mrs. Bert Thornton, who wrote the commission in 1982 seeking information on Indians for a program she was planning.[85] Similarly, second grade teacher Sally Ann Liska requested materials
to help her construct a curriculum on Indians.[86] By 1983, however, LOIA's
limited budget made it impossible to continue furnishing free booklets to
everyone who sought information on the state's Indian populations.[87]

Determined to meet the demand for information, LOIA produced another booklet in 1989 entitled *Native Americans of Louisiana*, which also provided basic information for people seeking to prove their Indian heritage. Unlike the earlier booklet, this one addressed the numerous previous requests to
legitimate Indian identity. LOIA stressed that tracing Indian ancestry was
not the commission's responsibility because "there are no grants or programs
to finance (such individual) research." People were also asked not to submit
any information to the commission but rather to the appropriate tribe—to
which the commission could direct them—to be considered for enrollment.
The section of the booklet entitled "Tracing Your Family Tree" pointed out:
"It is important to note that you do not 'join' a tribe like a club or organization. Being a member of a tribe occurs as a birthright, you are a member of a
race of people. You cannot become a member of a race by choice, just as you
cannot stop being the race of your birth parents."[88] In response to the growing popularity of claiming an Indian heritage, the LOIA staff realized the
importance of discouraging the co-opting of Indian identity for personal gain
or psychological satisfaction. The public education campaign was intended to
promote a sense of respect for Indians—not to reinforce misconceptions and
stereotypes.

LOIA also disseminated the new booklet to elementary schools and libraries throughout the state to encourage further education.[89] Showing his
support of the commission, Governor Buddy Roemer wrote the booklet's
dedication, stating: "The Indians of Louisiana have played an important role in
the settling and development of our state, but they were victims of their own
hospitality.... These Native Americans of Louisiana now have overcome so-

cial and geographic isolation to become an outspoken, progressive minority."[90] An emphasis on contemporary Indian communities and the challenges they overcame was a common element found in educational materials throughout the region. For example, a similar booklet on contemporary Indians of South Carolina was published in 1985 to assert the perseverance of local Native people.[91]

Information about Indians that was either supported or produced by tribal leaders during this period represented Indian people as empowered after overcoming tremendous adversity perpetuated by the vanishing race image. As Dr. Gregory explained in 1988, the Indians of Louisiana had maintained their identity: "Their presence represents 300 years of resistance to assimilation for some of them—at least 200 for all of them. They have managed to survive Missionaries, government removals, tribal reorganization; schools and the coming of industrialization have all had their effects. Yet, somehow, the Indian peoples have clung to their own separate cultural heritages. In fact, they have seen their traditions borrowed by non-Indians, even as their own cultures were denied value."[92] This supports the narrative of tribal leaders who recount stories of resilience and perseverance during a time when tribal cultures were not lost but hidden until the time was right for them to resurface.

Alabama tribal leaders also emphasized their modernity while fighting the vanishing Indian image that remained prevalent in local publications throughout the 1970s. For example, the May 1972 issue of the *DeKalb Legend* featured an article on Granny Dollar, the "Famous DeKalb Indian" who lived on Lookout Mountain with her dog Buster until her death in 1931. The article stressed Granny's lonely existence in her Alabama home but downplayed the presence of other Indian families in the area.[93] By 1981, the Alabama commission had developed a forty-plus-page information booklet to combat these false representations of the state's demography.[94] The booklet described "the existence and purpose of the Alabama Indian Affairs Commission as well as provided information on Alabama's Indian tribes, bands, or groups." Like the Louisiana ITC and LOIA, the AIAC mailed the booklet to residents around the area seeking information on the state's Indian population.[95] Since many of the inquires came from teachers, the commission also reprinted the "Unlearning 'Indian' Stereotypes" segment from the "Indian Education" report produced by the Council on Interracial Books for Children. The segment suggested focusing on three questions: "are Native people shown in contemporary settings?; are different nations of Indians identified?; and does the book suggest that Columbus 'discovered' America, or that Squanto and Massasoit were the first and last 'good' Indians?"[96] Encouraging a proactive stance among Indian parents and teachers in the state, the commission republished an "Open Letter to Non-Indian Teachers," originally in the *Native Nevadan*, in the July–August 1981 newsletter. The passionate letter asked teachers to respect the intellectual and cultural needs of Indian children without "imposing your values on top of those."[97]

Tribal leaders in both states sought support and collaboration from government agencies as a final strategy to promote Indian visibility. For instance, LOIA commissioner David Garrison partnered with the Louisiana Tourist Commission in Baton Rouge, which launched projects in various communities—particularly the Houma.[98] LOIA also collaborated with the Louisiana Department of Commerce and Industry to attract business to the state by preparing a number of community profiles, including those with predominantly Indian populations, for distribution to governmental agencies and businesses as far afield as New York and Chicago.[99] The Alabama commission also attempted to foster economic development by bolstering fundraising efforts among tribes and improving their relationships with government agencies and the public.[100]

While the Alabama commission developed support for individual communities, it also made an ambitious attempt to unify the interests of different tribes and state agencies through the acquisition of Parker's Island. The island—rich with farmland, forests, historical and archaeological sites—was a rallying point for five of Alabama's tribal communities who saw themselves as "custodians of the past" and, as a result formed a legal consortium to protect and preserve the island.[101] In May 1981, H. L. "Lindy" Martin of the Jackson County Cherokees, Joseph Stewart of the Echota Cherokee Tribe, Framon Weaver of the MOWA Band of Choctaw, Tommy Davenport of the Lower Creek Muscogee Tribe, and Eddie Tullis of the Poarch Band of Creeks signed the Parker's Island Statement of Unity. Many tribal leaders viewed this act of unity as perhaps the most important step to date for Alabama Indians to reclaim their history while laying the foundation for developing tribal-state relationships.[102] The statement detailed plans to rally support and raise the $1.8 million needed to purchase the 1,800-acre tract, and it also named the state as the "trustee" of the Indian-owned property "for the benefit of all Indians in Alabama."[103] Although the state was unable to offer the tribes any money to help purchase the island, Governor Fob James publicly acknowledged the land's "great historical and archeological value" and offered to hold the property in state trust if tribal leaders raised enough money to purchase it.[104]

This initial support gave tribes the confidence to launch a full-fledged campaign called "Parker's Island: A Heritage for Sale," to rally broader support. The strategy, which made its debut in September 1981, included distributing pamphlets and presenting a slide show to representatives of various state agencies. The pamphlet made many claims, including the promise that the project would help visitors "unlearn Indian stereotypes."[105] In the end, the inter-tribal consortium persuasively argued that the project had economically benefited the entire state because it allowed the Indian population to "participate in the potential development of extensive employment opportunities" by establishing a Native American cultural center. The contribution that the island would make to state tourism, as well as refashioning its image as a culturally diverse place, won the consortium a captive audience. "This is one of the major chances we have in preserving our heritage and culture," argued Larry Oats, Alabama Historical Commission director. "I think we have an obligation to maintain and develop this historic site and cultural resource in a sensible way."[106] The commission reported that "the presentation was well received," as various state agencies requested additional viewings of the slide show.[107] In fact, at the Thirteenth Annual Alabama Environmental Awards Program, Parker's Island was the primary topic of discussion as the Indian commission's director spoke about the efforts to preserve the island. In a generous gesture of support, the wildlife artist Larry Martin announced his plan to donate a limited edition block of prints to the Alabama Environmental Quality Association, with sales proceeds to benefit the Parker's Island fund.[108]

Sadly, the campaign failed to raise enough money to purchase Parker's Island—a tragedy that many of the leaders in this charge never fully got over. However, the campaign had far-reaching effects in gaining additional exposure for Indian issues. The Alabama commission impressed the state and public with the need that existed in Indian communities and the desire of tribal governments for self-determination. Parker's Island represented more than just preserving tribal cultures; it also demonstrated tribal governments' desire to help themselves. The Parker's Island campaign revealed that the public and government agencies were indeed willing to support Alabama tribes in these pursuits.

Public Education Campaigns Pay Off

With the exception of the Parker's Island disappointment, tribal leaders saw significant results from their efforts to gain public recognition and support. For example, the Alabama Department of Tourism and State Travel expressed interest in working with the Indian commission to incorporate modern Indians into their tourism plans.[109] Also, Louisiana tribes made great strides in bringing tourists to their communities because of their relationships with local tourism agencies. In particular, the Coushatta drew visitors to their reservation through an agreement with the Acadiana Trailway Association, which donated a railroad depot building as a Coushatta cultural center and museum. The building appeared on local maps and pamphlets, and Mayor Mildred LaFleur enthusiastically supported the project, saying, "It is time the potential for attracting tourists to the Indian settlement is developed and I will help to accomplish this in any way I can."[110] As part of the local tourist scene, the city of Lake Charles also invited Coushatta weavers and artists to sell their works at the Festival of the Arts.[111]

By 1982 the United Houma Nation had entered into an agreement with the National Park Service for programs to preserve and interpret Houma culture in the Jean Lafitte National Historical Park region of south Louisiana. Like countless other tribal nations throughout the country, the Houma developed a complex relationship with the agency. While the Park Service had a tradition of displacing Indians to create an illusion of a pristine, untouched landscape, the agency also had a history, as seen in Yosemite National Park, of using Indians to promote tourism. Like the landscape, indigenous people were expected to stand still in time.[112]

The United Houma Nation attempted to avoid such a stagnant representation by requesting that a cultural committee be created to negotiate between the tribe and the Park Service to keep the tribe informed of "the general nature of its program objectives in the field of preservation and interpretation of Houma culture." The Park Service funded and maintained the exhibits, audio-visual programs, museum collections, and historic tours, which were designed and approved for historical accuracy by members of the United Houma Nation.[113] After the project was ready for visitors, tourists who came to New Orleans were encouraged to make a trip to Dulac to "become familiar with the Houma Indians." Also, the nearby Butler mounds were put on the National Register to be preserved and protected from the destructive dirt bikes that were frequently used in the area.[114]

The same year that the Houma entered into a cooperative agreement with the National Park Service, the Clifton Choctaw acquired a grant from the Louisiana Arts Council to revive traditional Native crafts with the help of Dr. Gregory as project consultant as well as the Mennonite missionaries living in the community. The tribe used the funds to "take inventory of crafts knowledge among older residents and to hold a series of workshops to pass along traditional techniques for producing baskets, quilts, blowguns, yucca whips, pottery, gourd dippers and tanned deer hides." Tribal members successfully marketed their products at local craft fairs, and seventy-year-old tribal member Luther Clifton commended the project for helping him relearn the art of basket making that his father had taught him as a child. "It all came back," he explained. "I hadn't made one for 50 years."[115]

While increased exposure helped certain Louisiana communities with cultural revitalization, others reaped the economic benefits of tourism. In 1987 the Louisiana legislature handed over the closed Butte LaRose rest stop along Interstate 10 to the Chitimacha, who reopened it as a tourism center. Legislation gave the tribe a fifty-year lease on the eleven-acre site in St. Martin Parish on the Atchafalaya River. The new rest stop, paid for with a BIA loan, not only reopened a boat ramp but also housed an interpretive center in which the tribe could construct and present their history to outsiders. Through exhibits (including a reconstructed village), theater productions, and a gift shop, the center depicted the life of the Chitimacha Indians in the Atchafalaya Swamp.[116] There are many other similar examples that demonstrate an increased willingness by non-Indians to celebrate and understand the state's Native population as distinct cultural groups, as well as the contributions they made to the construction of the broader "Louisiana culture."[117]

In 1982 one week in the fall was declared Indian Heritage Week in Alabama. The state decided to replicate the efforts of the Tallahassee Jr. Museum, which honored Florida's Native population on Indian Day.[118] By 2000 the Alabama legislature had voted to designate the second Monday in October American Indian Heritage Day in addition to Columbus Day, making Alabama the first state to create a dual observance.[119] Although this act generated bitterness among certain tribal leaders who saw this as a shallow gesture, Wilford Taylor of the MOWA Choctaw stated: "I see this as where this state is headed. We are trying to heal old wounds." Even Wabun-Inini, the national representative for the American Indian Movement, commended the state of Alabama "for their vision and reaching out to the Indian people. We would hope other states would follow the lead of Alabama."[120]

Alabama Indians were included in public events celebrating state heritage, especially those that incorporated Indians into the more general state history. For example, state officials invited representatives of the Echota Cherokee to the Horseshoe Bend National Military Park for the unveiling of a memorial plaque commemorating U.S. Army soldiers and their Cherokee and Lower Creek allies who died fighting against the Upper Creeks at the Battle of Horseshoe Bend during the Creek Wars of 1813–14. Park superintendent Walter Bruce introduced Chief Richard Bell of Blountsville and Clauda and

Diana Conn of Opelika as representatives of the nearly five hundred Cherokees who had fought in the battle and "played a decisive role in turning the
battle in favor of Andrew Jackson." The festivities began with an oral account
of the battle given by Judge Jack Coley of Tallapoosa County, who emphasized the role of Cherokees and Lower Creeks in breaking the Upper Creek
stronghold, thus allowing Andrew Jackson's forces to take the Bend. Reportedly, Cherokee Chief Junuluska saved Jackson's life. Years later, after Jackson
became president and forcibly relocated thousands of southern Native people
to Indian Territory, Junuluska stated: "If I had known that day at Horseshoe what I know now, I would have killed Jackson myself." In recounting
this famous local tale, Judge Coley de-emphasized the tragic removal history,
which caused deep resentment among some of the Indian people present, and
instead focused on the bravery of Indian leaders who helped Jackson. For an
event that had been frequently memorialized, the 1981 ceremony marked the
first time that Indians had participated; however, the event also reinforced the
need for the local historical narratives to be sensitized—if not complicated—
by Native perspectives.[121]

Later that year, the Alabama Environmental Quality Association (AEQA)
invited members of the Poarch Creek to Fort Toulouse to "explore the history of the past cultures that once thrived [there]" and to commemorate the
"Indian influence so prevalent [in] the area." Activities included a hike and
archaeological overview of the area around the fort, including a tour of a
nearby Indian mound adjacent to Parker's Island. While members of the
AEQA reflected on the historic contributions of Indians to the area, Poarch
Creek chief Eddie Tullis spoke instead about contemporary advances of Indian people in education, health, and self-determination.[122] Tullis's message
was clear: efforts to include Indians in reimaging the area's past were hollow
without acknowledging tribal gains and modern contributions.

The region-wide celebration of indigenous history continued into the 1990s
when the National Park Service officially recognized a series of road markers
designating the Trail of Tears route. Instead of honoring the Indian people
who suffered under Removal, however, the Park Service named the trail the
"Hood-Drane Route" after J. C. S. Hood, a wagonmaster who supervised the
march in 1838 when it left Ross's Landing, and Captain Gus Drane, an army
officer who rounded up Cherokees who had escaped to a site near present-day
Scottsboro, Alabama. Despite the disregard for what Native people thought
about the route's name, Indian leaders made their presence known at the Trail
of Tears marker unveiling on U.S. Highway 72 near Bridgeport, Alabama, and
about 1.5 miles from the Alabama-Tennessee border. AIAC director Darla

Graves spoke at the event to a large gathering of people, including representatives from both state and local governments. On behalf of Alabama's Indians, Graves thanked the state legislature for acknowledging the Hood-Drane
Route. She gave a few remarks about an Indian conference she had recently
attended in San Diego, commenting that "A lot of Indians throughout this
nation don't enjoy the kind of relationship with their legislatures that we have
in Alabama. They would be proud to live in a state like Alabama."[123]

To further commemorate the trail and bring visitors to the site, more than
a thousand motorcyclists, both Indian and non-Indian, left Ross's Landing—
a site in what is now Chattanooga, Tennessee, where more than a thousand
Indians were held in 1838 before being forced to march to Indian Territory. By
the time the motorcyclists reached Waterloo, Alabama, more than two hundred miles away from their destination, they had acquired nearly five thousand participants. Along the way, the group stopped in Bridgeport to attend
the dedication of a highway marker that bore the Alabama Indian Affairs
Commission logo designating the route.[124] The Trail of Tears route became
part of the National Park Service's brochure of national historic trails. Two
markers graced Alabama's roadways: one, funded by the Alabama Waterfowl Association, was placed near Waterloo, and the second trail marker, partially funded by the Alabama Harley Davidson organization and the Jackson County Historical Association, was placed in Bridgeport in Jackson
County.[125]

As the Indian commissions became more visible, the number of requests
by organizations, state agencies, and individuals for information and assistance increased exponentially. When the Georgia Department of Archives
and History applied for a grant from the National Endowment for the Humanities in 1980 to make a film on southern Indian history, the agency first
wrote to the AIAC for support. "After all," the letter read, "we share the goal
of enlightening the American public concerning the importance and value
of Indian history."[126] The following year, the AIAC received a letter from
Ina S. Trout, assistant librarian for the Smallwood Memorial Library in the
city of Chickasaw, informing the commission that the city had begun the
process of authenticating the city logo by "finally getting rid of the 'impos-
tor' in our City Hall" and replacing it with a "portrait of a real Chickasaw Indian."[127] The Chickasaw News-Herald explained how Trout found a likeness
of a Chickasaw Indian to replace the emblem, one that actually was an image
of an Indian native to the Midwest.[128] Realizing that Trout did not simply
wish to change the city logo but also wanted to include the Indian commission in the project, AIAC director Jennie Lee Dees wrote to Trout saluting

her "efforts to accurately portray the Indian image" in the city emblem. Dees even included recent issues of the *Alabama Indian Advocate* with her letter to encourage Trout to read more about tribal issues statewide.[129]

Like the AIAC, LOIA was a great storehouse of information. Throughout the 1980s, the agency received many letters from other agencies asking for assistance. For example, the Department of Defense's Galveston District Corps of Engineers in Texas asked for aid in "identifying Native American Indian tribes having aboriginal or historic ties to lands" in the Galveston area. The letter included a map and admitted unfamiliarity with "any tribes once occupying coastal Texas that have retained their cultural identity to the present."[130] The Congressional Research Service Department within the Library of Congress also sought the aid of LOIA in obtaining updated information on state tribal organizations in order to include them in a report titled "Indian and Indian-Interest Organizations."[131] In 1983 LOIA received a letter from Carol Wells of the New Orleans French Market Board asking for assistance to "include the Indian contribution to the French Market in our historic display either by reproduction of the old pictures or sculpturally." Indians were prominent in the market in the late nineteenth and early twentieth centuries, and the board contacted LOIA for a reaction to travelers' accounts describing Indians (predominantly Choctaws and Chickasaws) at the market, as well as comments on a series of photographs.[132]

New publicity also allowed tribes to tackle the problem of grave digging and looting by encouraging collaboration between Indian commissions and archaeologists. In Louisiana, LOIA brought tribes and archaeologists together "to come to a better understanding of each others' views and reconcile some of the differences experienced in the past." Archaeologists from several Louisiana universities negotiated with tribal governments to determine the necessary steps to serve the interests of both parties.[133] In the summer of 1987, Dr. Gregory, an archaeologist and close associate of LOIA, led a team of students on a survey of approximately 31,200 Indian artifacts from the Catahoula Basin, an area stretching across the parishes of Catahoula, LaSalle, Rapides, and northern Avoyelles. With a $23,000 grant provided by the National Park Service, the group raced "against bulldozers and art collectors" to locate important sites that could qualify for the National Register of Historic Places, which then protected the area for future study.[134]

The AIAC collaborated with its state historical commission to create a statewide comprehensive historic preservation plan, which set out do the following: "[F]oster an awareness of the value of historic structures, sites and objects that reflect the heritage of all Alabamians and to facilitate the preservation and documentation of these resources for the use, enjoyment and education of present and future generations." Like LOIA, the AIAC wanted to educate the public to respect historic sites and avoid the temptation to loot burial areas. In addition, the plan identified more sites for preservation.[135]

While tribal leaders in both states were instrumental in preserving sites and material cultures, they also helped reshape educational systems. By 1988, for example, LOIA had been invited to serve on the state Curriculum Board within the Department of Education. Diana Williamson, LOIA director during this period, pointed out to tribal leaders: "Some of you may recall that in the last legislature session a bill was passed that required the inclusion of minorities in the history taught in Louisiana." She went on to request, "If you would like to submit any information pertaining to your tribe for consideration in the curriculum please provide this office with that material."[136] For many Indian leaders, this invitation served as a welcome shift in public attitudes given that school curriculum was consistently identified as a perpetuator of racial stereotypes and misrepresentations about Indians.

Increased interest in studying Indians was reflected in the rise of specialized programs of study devoted to American Indians. In 1980 the Alabama commission coordinated with the state's Department of Education and the Department of Archives and History for an Ethnic Heritage Studies Program, a project developed by the Poarch Creek and A&M University of Alabama.[137] Then, by 1981, the state Education Department approved a grant to the Jackson County Board of Education for the development of a program to study the legacy of the Cherokee in Jackson County.[138] To support these plans, the tribe participated in a cultural festival during the following year's Indian Heritage week, where they celebrated "the courage and endurance of their ancestors who struggled so that they and their descendants might remain in their Alabama homeland."[139] Jackson County Cherokee representatives also prepared for the development of a cultural program by traveling to the Cherokee reservation in North Carolina and visiting the tribe's museum, which reportedly turned out to be "all and more than we had anticipated." After viewing the museum's extensive collection of artifacts, listening to traditional stories, and witnessing the various "mini theatre" productions, members of the Jackson County Cherokee left inspired by their "memorable venture."[140]

Soon after the trip, the tribe began working to establish its own museum. They wished to incorporate some of the displays depicting Cherokee culture that they had seen in North Carolina, along with some of their own memorials honoring former Alabama Cherokee leaders, including Chief John Justice, William Keys, James McCoy, and Claude Thornhill, who helped their people remain in their homelands despite hardships in the post-Removal South.[141]

In Sum

The South attracts thousands of travelers from all over the world seeking to immerse themselves in the "southern experience." From Civil War battle-grounds to monuments celebrating the black civil rights movement, curious tourists seek to reflect on the past. As Indians were prominently integrated into the tourism literature throughout the 1970s and 1980s, tribal leaders in Louisiana and Alabama seized the opportunity to generate public support through positive and realistic representations of Indians. The strategies for promoting these images varied. Exhibits representing the past and present, festivals and powwows, public presentations, literature, and documentaries were all leveraged to advance these perspectives. These efforts ultimately facilitated collaborative relationships with state, national, and private agencies to promote tourism and preserve historic sites.

Despite positive strides toward these objectives, however, the movement toward more public exposure for Indians also generated a backlash as southerners debated the authenticity question. For example, a 1984 article questioning the legitimacy of Echota Cherokee leader Joe Stewart resurfaced in a 1991 letter to Alabama governor Guy Hunt. The anonymous author—identified only as "a concerned taxpayer"—attached a copy of the article with the letter, claiming that the only legitimate tribes were federally recognized ones. Using Chief Stewart as an example, the letter's author asked the governor to "examine this whole Indian situation in the state of Alabama" and to be aware that with the exception of the Poarch Creek, "so called Indians are just a bunch of whites that haven't got any Indian in them and [they were] jiping [*sic*] the taxpayers of this state out of a lot of money."[142] The enclosed article published criticisms aimed at the Echota Cherokee by Robert Youngdeer, chief of the federally acknowledged Eastern Band of Cherokees. Youngdeer questioned where the Echota had been "back in the 1920s and 1930s when it was unpopular to be an Indian." The journalist allowed Chief Stewart to defend his community by explaining, "We've always been here, but we had to keep quiet to stay alive." He added that his group finally decided to enter the public eye to "promote the Indian cause."[143] Following this editorial attack, Stewart gave interviews to several Birmingham newspapers, taught lessons in Indian

9. Louisiana American Indian license plate.

history at local elementary schools, and set up exhibits at the Indian festival at the Red Mountain Museum. As a result of this article and others like it, it became clear that even with all of the public support Alabama tribes had garnered, not everyone was willing to embrace all state-recognized groups, giving individuals like Stewart even more reason to educate the public and assert their Indian identities.

Even with the ongoing public debates regarding the authenticity of certain southern tribes, Indians continued to develop public awareness in the 1990s and later. As they continued to host powwows, develop tribal museums, and partner with government agencies, Alabama and Louisiana Indian leaders devised new strategies to generate public awareness about the Indian presence throughout the region. Another way both states did this was through the introduction of Indian-themed vehicle license plates that would allow Native people to assert their identities and for non-Indians to demonstrate their support. The idea of generating a visible Indian presence on the roadways was exciting and heavily promoted by the Indian commissions. Today, the "Indian-themed" license plate is an option for Louisianans to purchase from the Department of Motor Vehicles. Unfortunately, however, the AIAC never got their specially designed Indian plate adopted.

By the turn of the twenty-first century, decades of work in rallying public attention and support paid off. The states of Alabama and Louisiana both identified a pronounced improvement in the inclusion of Indians in state pride celebrations. For instance, in 2002 the Alabama Bureau of Tourism and

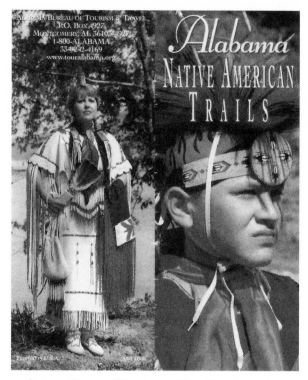

10. Alabama Bureau of Tourism and Travel brochure published in 2002.

Travel introduced a new pamphlet called "Alabama Native American Trails" into its repertoire of literature sent to tourists inquiring about popular destinations. While potential visitors were enticed to explore historic trails, village sites, "hide out caves," and burial mounds of the state's Indian inhabitants from centuries past, they also were introduced to Alabama's current Indian population. Joshua Rich, a Coushatta living in Alabama, and Laura Pyle, a Cherokee-Chickasaw, connected the two eras, bridging the past and present by appearing dressed in regalia on both the front and back of the pamphlet. Short biographies describe Rich and Pyle as "living history," Indians whose ancestors were tied to many of the historic places featured in the brochure.[144] Likewise, Louisiana Indians continued to play increasingly prominent roles in the state and local tourism industry as collaborative efforts and celebrations of the state's Native identity became more common. Similar activities region wide marked a profound shift in public awareness and served to challenge—if not complicate—the *Little Tree* character born out of Asa Carter's politically motivated imaginings. Southern Indians were no longer simply relegated to the pages of books or compelled to suppress their identities. They had taken on dominant roles in controlling their past and present images, and as the Houma leader Steve Cheramie so poignantly put it, "They are proud to be Indian again."[145]

Conclusion

> Let us not discount the value of having the state admit that we exist.
> —Southwest Alabama Indian Affairs Commission, "Comments
> Regarding Proposed Legislation," July 17, 1981

The Indian Rights Movement of the 1970s and 1980s is a story of transformation. As the regional political and economic culture shifted under the pressure of the black civil rights movement, industrialization, urbanization, and the growing influence of the Republican Party, marginalized southern Native populations joined other Indians in a national movement, one that promoted tribal development and self-determination. A region once bound by a biracial identity thus witnessed a rebirth in Indian awareness, spawning the development of tribal governments that became increasingly vocal while trying to assert political authority and rally public support.

Although this movement was by no means monolithic—it took on unique characteristics shaped by the political environment along with the specific needs of local Indian groups—this book's examination of Alabama and Louisiana reveals distinct patterns. Perhaps the most significant is the historic creation of relationships between tribal and state governments. Although Indian groups connected to states independently, inter-tribal efforts to establish state Indian affairs commissions provided the greatest impetus for these relationships to evolve. For the first time, previously marginalized Native people—particularly those who lacked federal recognition—found a voice within state governments and began to forge networks with local, state, and national agencies.

These relationships did not occur spontaneously; they were the fruits of charismatic Indian leaders with determination and political savvy. Although they followed different avenues to obtain legislative and public support for their endeavors—making personal appeals, donning Indian regalia for meetings and public appearances, staging demonstrations, allying with reporters—

they collectively strengthened the movement's momentum and impact. These individuals tell this story through letters and meeting transcripts, which provide the majority of evidence for this narrative. Indian leaders were the advocates for local Natives seeking the aid of tribal governments, Indian organizations, and commissions to, among other things, gain access to education, heat their homes, find employment, and validate their identity. The Indian movement addressed the needs of Indians statewide by bringing leaders together—for the first time—to share talents and knowledge, apply for grants, and build a strong political force.

Despite their good intentions, reaching common ground was no easy task. The seven Alabama tribes and eight in Louisiana represented in this study varied in appearance, political status, education, economic levels, and cultural maintenance. This diversity sparked inter-tribal rivalries and disrupted cooperative efforts. These tensions were further exacerbated by questions over tribal legitimacy, which in turn dictated who should have representation on the commissions and access to already scarce resources. Many Indian leaders also resisted involvement in any effort that might undermine tribal sovereignty, falling back on old suspicions of governmental agencies. In the end, inter-tribal cooperation proved difficult, as Indian leaders had the arduous task of simultaneously negotiating for power with both the states and other tribal interests.

These difficult negotiations were most evident in the commissions' early development. The Alabama Indian Affairs Commission and the Louisiana Office of Indian Affairs served the same purpose—to promote tribal economic, political, and social development—but they followed starkly different paths. The Alabama commission started as an extension of the Poarch Creek Council, which from 1978 to 1982 made all of the decisions on behalf of the state's Indian population. The persistent conflict between Poarch Creek officials and other Indian leaders throughout the state, followed by the introduction of legislation intended to restructure the commission, caused the agency to lose its funding for two years until it was revived in 1984.

The Louisiana commission had similar initial tumultuous circumstances, but instead of being controlled by a single tribe it evolved from a single man. Ernest Sickey, who rallied the support of lawyer Ruth Loyd Miller and businessman David Garrison, nearly single-handedly established the Louisiana commission in 1972. Although the agency in its early years was dominated by non-Indians, tribal leaders soon stepped into positions of power. As in Alabama, however, inter-tribal conflicts paralyzed the agency when only five of the eight organized tribes were represented on the commission until new leadership opened membership to other interests. By describing the origins and activities of the commissions, I do not intend to simply recount bureaucratic histories. Rather, I believe the findings of the previous chapters illuminate, as well as complicate, our understanding of the commissions as products of Indian activism.

The southern Indian movement did not exist within a vacuum. It was shaped and reshaped by political and economic changes at both the regional and national levels. Indian leaders and activists, for example, participated in the national drive for Indian rights. Alabama and Louisiana both sent representatives to the historic 1961 American Indian Chicago Conference, which set the tone for Indian activism over the next few decades. Throughout the 1970s and 1980s, leaders from both states also worked closely with other pan-Indian organizations such as the National Congress of the American Indian, the American Indian Movement, and the Coalition of Eastern Native Americans. Tribes throughout Alabama and Louisiana exhibited the influence of the national Indian movement through the adoption of powwows and Indian princess contests to promote Native pride and be more visible to their non-Indian neighbors.

The black civil rights movement also shaped the southern Indian movement and the tribal-state relationships that derived from it. Indian activists felt empowered by the revolution in race relations initiated by the civil rights movement, but reinforcement of a southern biracial image continued to marginalize them. In response, Indian leaders worked both individually and with the state commissions or other Indian organizations to fashion a public persona and become more visible to legislators and the public. As these leaders soon realized, however, a rapidly increasing interest in the South's indigenous identity gave tribal groups a unique opportunity to educate the public, as well as generate economic development through tourism. This interest was partially a result of a backlash toward the black civil rights movement and southerners' quest to explore their own genealogy. Writing tribal histories, rewriting local histories to include Indians, exhibiting Native artwork, constructing tribal museums, and hosting Indian festivals and powwows were just a few ways Indians gained visibility while countering the popular and stereotypical images of Indians in film and literature. With visibility came an increased acceptance of "Indian" as a valid racial category on birth certificates, driver's licenses, and voter registration cards. Indians became the new "racial minority" of the South, competing with African Americans for employment opportunities under affirmative action. Native people also were reflected in the white backlash to the black civil rights movement, becoming the unwilling participants in racist commentary as "concerned taxpayers" wrote to the state about how Indians were more deserving of resources than were African Americans.

While the black civil rights movement influenced Indian leaders who lobbied for the rights of individuals to self-identify as Indian, tribal leaders also used the commissions to validate tribal legitimacy. Regardless of the relationship—or lack thereof—with the federal government, the Indian Self-Determination and Educational Assistance Act of 1975 influenced every tribal government. This study has unveiled that the journey toward self-determination was not merely about receiving federal recognition. This status was the ultimate goal of non–federally recognized groups, but Indian leaders also used their relationships with state governments to negotiate power and promote a semi-sovereign status. As southern states increasingly acknowledged tribal governments—either by resolution or through commission by-laws—tribes began to assemble government-to-government relationships that validated their status and provided the opportunity to tap into state and federal funds.

This process drew the attention of Indians nationwide. Leaders of federally recognized groups, including Wilma Mankiller of the Cherokee Nation of Oklahoma, strongly disapproved of such arrangements, arguing that states had no business in Indian affairs.[1] Tribal leaders of non–federally recognized groups, however, were inspired. In a 1977 letter to Alabama governor George Wallace, Roy Crazy Horse, a representative from the Powhatan-Renape Nation of New Jersey, commended Wallace's administration, stressing that "the establishment of this [Alabama Indian affairs] commission is a meaningful inspiration not only to the Indians of Alabama, but to the Indian people nationwide, as recognition by the state of Alabama may be instrumental in convincing other state legislatures to follow your example."[2] Although Crazy Horse understood the power of tribal-state relations as early as the 1970s, it wasn't until 1995 that the New Jersey legislature created the New Jersey Commission on American Indian Affairs.[3]

Although this book emphasizes the benefits that tribes reaped from tribal-state relationships, the states of Alabama and Louisiana likewise benefited from their relationships with tribal governments. States could wield power by adjudicating Indian identity and allocating resources—traditionally federal responsibilities. Within a post–black civil rights movement context, alliances with Indian groups gave southern politicians a claim to diversity and social welfare at a time when they were villainized as supporters of white supremacy. Governors during the 1970s did not always fiscally support the commissions they helped create, but they were motivated to help tribal groups achieve federal acknowledgment because this status would bring more federal education and social service funding to the states. A shift in the national economic system in the 1980s, however, altered the dynamics of tribal-state relations. The federal block grant system redefined state power and ended the partnership. Tribes and states no longer had to cooperate to access federal resources, for states received the money directly, along with the discretion on how to distribute it. This served to further complicate matters, causing tribal leaders to have to request funding directly from the states, not the federal government. In the end, non–federally recognized tribes in Alabama and Louisiana did receive more grant money from the states than they ever did from the federal government prior to the 1980s. With the continued cutbacks, however, in the block grants targeting community development—those most frequently sought by Indian groups—tribal leaders had to employ creative tactics to continue securing funds.

This shift in power revealed the vulnerable status that tribes and commissions held within state governments. Indian leaders never wavered in their commitment to their people, but they exhibited tremendous flexibility in catering their strategies to a fluctuating political and economic system. Although the Indian movement of the 1970s generated visibility through public demonstrations and promoting Indians as an overlooked minority, leaders shifted their approaches in the 1980s and relied heavily upon the rhetoric of economic independence and tribal self-determination. Within an economically conservative environment, state officials supported programs that promised to be self-sustaining, thus relieving the threat that Indians would become a welfare burden.

As tribal-state relationships evolved during the 1990s and later, Indian leaders experienced a series of minor successes followed by larger defeats—a theme that defined the early years of the Indian movement. Like their ancestors who refused to leave their homes more than a century earlier, southern Indians showed resilience and strength, making significant progress in promoting economic and social development, acquiring land, revitalizing and preserving Native languages and cultures, and increasing their educational levels. Southern tribes entered the new millennium with confidence, summed up in an excerpt in a 1997 Cherokee Tribe of Northeast Alabama newspaper: "Remember our ancestors' nations were the first but greed and jealousy broke them down. Today our nations have grown and we are even stronger and this fact holds the truth, so accept it, OUR ANCESTORS WERE THE FIRST AND WE WILL BE THE LAST."[4]

Appendix
Other Tribes of the South

States are listed in chronological order of the creation of each state Indian commission.

*As the political landscape continues to evolve beyond the scope of this book, additional Indian communities and organizations may have formed or been recognized by their respective states and thus joined the ranks of the following groups.

North Carolina

Cherokee Indians of Hoke County
Cherokees of Robison & Adjoining Counties
Cherokee Powhatan Indian Association
Coharie Tribe (state recognized)
Coree Indians, Meherrin Indian Tribe (state recognized)
Eastern Band of Cherokee (federally recognized)
Faircloth Indian Tribe
Haliwa Saponi Tribe (state recognized)
Hattadare Indian Tribe (state recognized)
Hatteras Tuscarora
Kaweah Indian Nation, Inc.
Lumbee Tribe of North Carolina (state recognized)
Occaneechi Band of Saponi Nation (state recognized)
Person County Indians
Santee Tribe (White Oak Community)
Tuscarora Nation of North Carolina
Tuscarora Tribe

United Lumbee Nation of North Carolina and America
Waccamaw Siouan Tribe (state recognized)

Florida

Creeks East of the Mississippi
Florida Tribe of Eastern Creeks
Miccosukee Tribe (federally recognized)
Oklewaha Band of Seminoles
Perido Bay Tribe of Lower Muscogee Creeks
Seminole Tribe of Florida (federally recognized)
Topachula Tribe
Tuscola United Cherokees of Florida & Alabama, Inc.

South Carolina

Beaver Creek Indians (state recognized)
Catawba Indian Nation (federally recognized in 1943 and then voluntarily
    terminated in 1959)
Chaloklowa Chickasaw Indian People (state recognized)
Chicora-Siouan Indian People (state recognized)
Four Hole Indian Organization (Edisto Tribe) (state recognized)
Lower Eastern Cherokee Nation of South Carolina (state recognized)
Pee Dee Indian Nation of Upper South Carolina (state recognized)
Santee Indian Organization (state recognition)
Summerville Indian Group
Waccamaw Indian People (state recognized)

Virginia

Ani-Stohini/Unami Nation
Chickahominy Indian Tribe (state recognized)
East Chickahominy Indian Tribe (state recognized)
Monacan Indian Tribe (state recognized)
Nansemond Indian Tribal Association (state recognized)
Pamunkey Nation (state recognized)
United Rappahannock Tribe (state recognized)
Upper Mataponi Tribe (state recognized)

Tennessee

Aniyunweya Nation of Indigenous Native Indians of Tennessee
Cherokee of Lawrence County (Sugar Creek Band)

Chickamaka-Cherokee of the South Cumberland Plateau Region
Chickamauga Circle of Free Cherokee
Chota Nation
Cumberland Creek Indian Confederation
Deerclan of East Tennessee (Free Cherokee)
Eastern Cherokee of Tennessee
Elk Valley Council Band of Free Cherokees
Etowah Cherokee Nation (recognized by the governor in 1978)
The Far Away Cherokee
Original Cherokee Nation
Over-Hill Indian Nation
Red Clay Band of Southeast Cherokee Confederacy
Red Stick Confederacy
Stone Mountain Metis Indian Nation
TeeHahNahMah Nation
Tennessee Band of Cherokee (Earth Clan)
Tennessee Band of Eastern Cherokee (Polk County)
Tennessee River Band of Chickamauga
United Eastern Lenape Nation

Georgia

American Cherokee Confederacy, Inc.
Cane Break Band of Eastern Cherokee
Cherokees of Georgia, Inc. (state recognized)
Georgia Tribe of Eastern Cherokees (state recognized)
Lower Muskogee Creek Tribe East of the Mississippi (state recognized)
Southeastern Cherokee Confederacy, Inc.
United Creeks of Georgia

Notes

Preface

1. A few Indian groups did maintain relationships with their respective state governments prior to the 1970s. For example, the Pamunkeys and Mattaponies of Virginia and the Catawba of South Carolina remained under the protection of local and state governments following Indian Removal in the 1830s. In addition, the few tribes that still maintained their federally acknowledged status, such as the Chitimacha, the Eastern Band of Cherokee, the Mississippi Choctaw, and the Florida Seminoles, also had some dealings with their respective states as defined by the federal-Indian relationship.

2. In order to fully understand the extent of the Indian movement in the South, which included a massive tribal resurgence and organization, see the list of tribal groups from these states in the appendix.

3. For an extensive and interdisciplinary collection of literature on the South, see the *New Encyclopedia of Southern Culture,* edited by Charles Reagan Wilson, which was initially published in 1989. The most recent version was published in 2006 and 2007 and contains twenty-four volumes.

4. Gilbert, "Surviving Indian Groups of the Eastern United States," 430. For a complete list of tribal petitions for federal recognition, see "500 Nations: Petitions for Federal Recognition," http://500nations.com/tribes/Tribes_Petitions .asp (accessed 16 November 2010).

5. V. Deloria, *Custer Died for Your Sins.*

6. In this book I hope to contribute to the scholarship on the complex interplay among race, politics, religion, culture, and economics in both Alabama and Louisiana, which has inspired studies such as Carter, *The Politics of Rage;* Gaillard, *Cradle of Freedom;* and Fairclough, *Race & Democracy.*

7. In 1960, there were 1,276 American Indians in Alabama according to the census. By 1970, the number had increased to 2,443, by 1980 it was 7,583, and then by 1990 the number had jumped to 16,506. U.S. Census Bureau, Table 15: "Alabama—Race and Hispanic Origin: 1800 to 1990," http://www.census.gov/population/documentation/twps0056/tab15.pdf (accessed 22 May 2001).

8. The Louisiana Indian population was listed at 3,578 in 1960, 5,294 in 1970, 12,065 in 1980, and 18,541 in 1990. U.S. Census Bureau, Table 33: "Louisiana—Race and Hispanic Origin: 1810 to 1990," http://www.census.gov/population/documentation/twps0056/tab33.pdf (accessed 22 May 2001).

9. For the purpose of this book, I only included the Indian groups that were recognized by the late 1980s. Since the period covered in this study, the state of Alabama has officially recognized the Cher-o-Creek Intra Tribal Indians and Piqua Sept of Ohio Shawnee Tribe, while the state of Louisiana has recognized the Caddo Adais Indians and the Four Winds Cherokee Tribe.

10. Through the 1980s, the Chitimacha tribe comprised about 250 people, with another 400 who lived off of the reservation but returned to attend tribal gatherings. The reservation had its own school and council house, and by 1984 the tribe had entered into an agreement with the National Park Service for the development of a tribal museum. Although unemployment was high within the community, the largest source of employment was in the petroleum industry. With many of their traditions lost, the tribe set out to revive their language and cultural art forms such as cane basketry. See Faine and Bohlander, *The Chitimacha Indians*, and Mueller et. al., *Nations Within*, 7–13.

11. About 360 members strong, the Coushatta first drew the attention of the federal government in 1898 when 160 acres of land were placed into trust for them. In the 1930s, under the direction of Commissioner John Collier, the Bureau of Indian Affairs (BIA) established an elementary school within the community. In 1953, the tribe was unofficially terminated, which left them landless and in a state of poverty. Efforts toward redevelopment were made in the mid-1960s, but it was not until the early 1970s that any headway was made when tribal leader Ernest Sickey helped establish the state Indian commission and raised enough outside support to aid in the tribe's federal re-recognition. The Coushatta also blazed the path in economic development through the establishment of a craft association to sell tribal art to tourists. See Coushatta, "The Struggle Has Made Us Stronger" and "Red Shoes People."

12. The 1934 Wheeler-Howard Act—more commonly known as the Indian Reorganization Act (IRA)—renewed the trust relationship between tribes and the federal government after decades of harsh assimilationist tactics (i.e., ending treaty making in 1871, the Major Crimes Act of 1885, and the Allotment Act of 1887). Among many other things, the IRA provided a process for tribes to organize themselves into business corporations and offered them educational assis-

tance. The IRA impacted the Coushatta when the BIA assumed responsibility for the education of the community's children through the establishment of a grammar school. It was this relationship that provided the basis for the group to be re-recognized in 1973.

13. Having retained many of their cultural ways, the Tunica-Biloxi share a similar migratory history with the rest of the groups in their state. Upon first contact with Europeans, the Tunica resided on the Mississippi River, north of the mouth of the Arkansas River where they were heavily involved in European conflicts as a strong ally to France. The Biloxi were first encountered on the Gulf Coast of Mississippi in 1699 and after several moves motivated by their avoidance of the British, they settled on the Mississippi River across from the Tunica, with whom they soon formed an alliance. By 1780, the groups moved inland together toward the Avoyelles Prairie, where the Tunica were granted land by Spanish authorities. The Tunica and Biloxi eventually fused under one chief in the 1920s and then became incorporated as a legally defined group when the state of Louisiana recognized them in the 1970s. See Faine, *The Tunica-Biloxi;* Mueller et al., *Nations Within,* 41–45; and Juneau, "The Judicial Extinguishment of the Tunica Indian Tribe."

14. With about 950 members living in the area of Atmore, the Poarch Creek first piqued the interest of the ethnologist Frank Speck in the early 1940s, who saw them as a "lost" group. They descended from a group of "friendly Creeks" who provided aid to the United States against other Creeks during the Creek War (1813–14). As a result, they were permitted to stay behind during the Removal period only to be abandoned and forgotten by the federal government. The group managed to eke out an existence for themselves by cutting railroad ties, by dipping turpentine, and as sharecroppers. In 1947, tribal leader Calvin McGhee began to organize the community to combat racial discrimination in education and to file land claims. By 1971, the Creek Nation East of the Mississippi was incorporated under Alabama state law and began working to obtain resources for tribal development while constructing a petition for federal acknowledgment. Although conflict between the Poarch Creek and other tribal groups throughout the state surfaced during the 1970s and 1980s, the tribe played a major role in the establishment of the state Indian commission and initiated a campaign to draw the public's attention to the formerly forgotten Indian population within the state. See Paredes, "The Emergence of Contemporary Eastern Creek Indian Identity" and "Federal Recognition and the Poarch Creek Indians."

15. The MOWA Choctaw are descendants of those who lived in the six villages of the southeastern district of the original Choctaw Nation. Like other groups in the region, they went into hiding during and after the Removal period, where they remained essentially unnoticed until Reconstruction. When they did not neatly fit into the newly established segregation laws, the group was labeled

"Cajun" and sent into a racial limbo, which made it impossible to access resources. From 1887 to 1894 the Apache leader Geronimo and about seven hundred of his followers were held in a federal arsenal in Mt. Vernon, Alabama, where they came into frequent contact with the MOWA Choctaw community—and, in a few cases, intermarried. Despite their endurance, however, the MOWA Choctaw did not have any official claim to the land in which they squatted, and as timber companies and private citizens began purchasing the MOWA Choctaw homeland, they increasingly found their way of life threatened. A portion of their land eventually became the site of Birmingham-Southern College, a Methodist school. Once the group officially organized in 1979 and then obtained state recognition in the early 1980s, however, the college sold the land back to the tribe, which used it as a ceremonial area to help in their efforts toward tribal revitalization. As leaders in the development of Indian education and cultural revitalization, the group submitted a federal petition in 1982 and were forced to wait many years before they ultimately received a denial in 1994, a decision that shook the faith of the community in their leadership and forced a restructuring of the tribal government. Over the next few years, the new leadership of the MOWA Choctaw challenged the denial. See Matte, *They Say the Wind Is Red.*

16. The modern Houma mainly reside in Terrebonne, Lafourche, and St. Mary parishes in southeastern Louisiana; however, at the time of French contact in 1699, the Houma lived in central Louisiana along the Mississippi border. They were then driven to the edge of New Orleans until plantation owners and Cajuns who drove them deep into the bayous of the Mississippi Delta displaced them again. Although the group has consistently maintained an Indian identity despite external pressures to conform to a rigid biracial system, the Houma's quest for federal recognition was denied by the BIA in 1994 on the grounds that they were the result of a racial mixture of German, French, English, and African ethnicities—with only a small mixture of various Indian tribes. Responding to a history of isolation and institutionalized racism, Houma leaders have worked to empower their community members to seek better educational opportunities and job advancement—beyond their traditional low-paying jobs in factories, in oil fields, and on fish boats. See Bowman and Curry-Roper, *The Forgotten Tribe,* and d'Oney, "A History of the Houma Nation."

17. Phillip Martin (Mississippi Band of Choctaw) to the Honorable Eddie Brown (assistant secretary of Indian Affairs), 7 September 1990, Indian Affairs Files, Louisiana State Archives (hereafter LSA).

18. The Jena Choctaw is a band that originally belonged to the larger Choctaw tribe in Mississippi. As a result of hostilities between the British and French in the eighteenth century, the group moved into Spanish areas west of the Mississippi and eventually settled in Louisiana, where they were used to neutralize

"hostile tribes," such as the Comanche and Osage. Although the last tribal chief died in the 1930s, the Jena Choctaw community remained strongly bound because of close kinship ties and isolation; however, many of them fought poverty by becoming sharecroppers. In 1974, a tribal council was organized and began applying for tribal development grants. The Jena Choctaw were the last to submit a successful federal petition, making them the fourth federally recognized group in Louisiana. See Faine, *The Jena Band of Choctaws*, and Mueller et al., *Nations Within*, 101–7.

19. The Clifton community's history in their present location extends back two hundred years; remnants of old villages can be identified along the Old Spanish Trail. Although they did not retain as many cultural traits as did the Jena, the Clifton Choctaw remained isolated; it wasn't until the 1970s that a paved road led to their community. Most Choctaw had little education, although a one-room elementary school operated in the area from 1925 to the early 1960s. The community began the process of petitioning for federal recognition in 1978. See Spicker, Steiner, and Walden, "A Survey of Rural Louisiana Indian Communities."

20. The Choctaw-Apache Community of Ebarb number about 1,500 people strong—although some scholars estimate that there may be as many as 15,000 members who are not officially on the rolls. The modern tribe has been in the present area of Zwolle since the late eighteenth century after the Lipan Apache were enslaved and sold to the French after battling with the Wichita Indians in eastern Texas. They were then released in the 1790s in Natchitoches, where they intermarried with a Choctaw group living near the Texas border. As seen in other Indian communities, employment opportunities in the twentieth century were sparse, so many Choctaw-Apaches worked in sawmills and plywood mills, or took jobs in Shreveport. The educational level in the Ebarb community, however, was higher than in most other communities since they were one of the first Indian groups to receive a state-supported public school. As a result, they have a high percentage of college-educated members. See Faine and Gregory, *The Apache-Choctaw of Ebarb*.

21. The Louisiana Band of Choctaw is the most urban of all of the state's Indian groups. The group's recent organizational history is a reflection of its members' migration into Baton Rouge looking for work.

22. The Jackson County Cherokee (or CTNA) were descendents of Cherokees who settled in Alabama—a traditional hunting territory of the Cherokee Nation—in the early 1780s under the leadership of Chief Dragging Canoe, an opponent of the rest of the tribe's liberal policies in dealing with American encroachment. Under treaties in 1817 and 1819, a handful of Cherokee families were given "reserved" land in Alabama, which protected them from removal in the 1830s and provided safe refuge for others who were concealed by the exempt fami-

lies. The modern community derived from those who were exempt, those who hid, and those who traveled back to the area after being forced to move. In 1974, a federally funded Indian Education Program was established in Jackson County, which allowed the community to generate pride among their children while gaining some exposure among the public. Dr. H. L. "Lindy" Martin, who was born on the North Carolina-Virginia border to Cherokee-Powhatan parents, oversaw the development of the group's tribal council at North Sand Mountain High School in Higdon, Alabama. See Cromer, *Modern Indians of Alabama*.

23. Like the Jackson County Cherokee, the Echota Cherokee Tribe trace their ancestry to the Chickamagua Cherokee, a group that moved into Tennessee and Alabama to resist white encroachment after some chiefs within the Cherokee Nation signed a treaty ceding vast tracts of land to South Carolina. These descendants reorganized in 1980, adopting the word "Echota" as part of their tribal name because of the historical significance of New Echota, the former capital of the Cherokee Nation. By 1984, the Echota Cherokee, along with the other six Alabama groups covered in this book, became state recognized under the Davis-Strong Act. As the most rapidly growing community in the state, the Echota Cherokee reported 11,619 members by 1987. See Cromer, *Modern Indians of Alabama*.

24. Since the literature on the Cherokees of Southeast Alabama is sparse, it is difficult to discern the nature of their existence in southern Alabama. What is known is that they were first organized in 1982 under the leadership of Deal Wambles, who encouraged the community to actively celebrate their heritage through festivals, relearning art forms, and establishing Indian education programs. In 1984 the tribe held their first powwow, and the following year, the nearby Dothan's Landmarks Park was the site of an Indian Heritage Month Celebration. See Cromer, *Modern Indians of Alabama*.

25. The Star Clan of Muscogee Creeks (also known as the Creeks of Pike County) are descendants of Indians who fought in the last Indian battles in the area—such as the battle at Blood Island. Like their Cherokee neighbors, their ancestors resisted removal and many of their modern members trace their lineage back to Creek chiefs, such as William McIntosh and James Island, who signed treaties with the federal government. The Star Clan is affiliated with the Lower Tribe of Muscogee Creek East of Molino, Florida, a group with over ten thousand members, of which the Star Clan constitutes three thousand spread out over several counties. The group opened a craft store in 1981 as a tribally operated and owned venture. See Cromer, *Modern Indians of Alabama*.

26. At the time of organization, the Ma-Chis Creek had almost nine hundred members who benefited from the tribe's development of Indian Education Programs in their community. See Cromer, *Modern Indians of Alabama*.

27. Cromer, *Modern Indians of Alabama*, xiv.

Chapter 1

1. Ruth Loyd Miller to John Cade of the Louisiana Governor's Office, 16 December 1980, Indian Affairs: P1992-92, LSA.

2. Although there were approximately 250 Coushatta in Allen Parish in 1972, there were 600 members total throughout the United States. "Profile: Ernest Sickey," *(Jennings) Daily News*, 20 December 1972; "Editorial: Coushatta Tribe Gets Break," *Lake Charles American Press*, 24 June 1973.

3. David L. Garrison Jr. to Governor Edwin Edwards, 15 March 1973, Indian Affairs: P1992-92, LSA. In 1969, the median family income in the state of Louisiana was $7,527. In 1970, the national median family income was $9,867. See U.S. Census, http://www.census.gov/hhes/www/income/histinc/f06ar.html (accessed 1 September 2005).

4. Miller to Cade, 16 December 1980.

5. "Illiterate Alabama Dirt Farmer Led Creek in Struggle to Find and Restore Their Heritage," *Tampa Times*, 18 October 1976.

6. Houston L. McGhee, Chief of the Creek Nation East of the Mississippi, to Alabama governor George C. Wallace, 10 May 1974, 3, Wallace Papers, Alabama Department of Archives and History (hereafter ADAH).

7. Cowger, *The National Congress of American Indians*, 3.

8. Cornell, *The Return of the Native.*

9. Cowger, *The National Congress of American Indians*, 3; see also Fahey, *Saving the Reservation*, and Ablon, "The American Indian Chicago Conference."

10. National Congress of American Indians official site, http://www.ncai.org/About.8.0.html (accessed 11 October 2010).

11. Hauptman and Campisi, "Eastern Indian Communities Strive for Recognition," 464.

12. See Lurie, "The Voices of the American Indian" and "Sol Tax and Tribal Sovereignty."

13. *The Declaration of Indian Purpose* was printed in *New Directions in Indian Purpose.*

14. Brown, "'The Year One,'" 77.

15. Quoted in Hauptman, "There Are No Indians East of the Mississippi," 106.

16. Roster printed in appendix 8 of the AICC Indian Registration, *New Directions in Indian Purpose*, 45–51.

17. Miller, *Forgotten Tribes*, 188. Although the Houma sent delegates to the AICC, their names were not officially added to the conference roster.

18. For an alternative perspective on this act, see Esber, "Shortcomings of the Indian Self-Determination Policy."

19. Unger, *Indian Self-Rule*, 305; Miller, *Forgotten Tribes*, 38–39.

20. McCulloch and Wilkins, "'Constructing' Nations within States," 361.

21. Harmon, *Indians in the Making.*

22. See Blu, *The Lumbee Problem;* Lowery, *Lumbee Indians in the Jim Crow South;* and Campisi, *The Mashpee Indians.* For other significant works on the construction of Indian identity, see Clifton, *Being and Becoming Indian;* Nagel, *American Indian Ethnic Renewal;* and P. Deloria, *Playing Indian.*

23. By 1987, one-third (34) of the total of petitions for federal recognition (104) had come from groups in the Southeast. Many groups found their federal petitions for acknowledgment challenged by earlier government reports from the 1930s and 1940s that were prepared by anthropologists, ethnographers, and geographers who were sent to the Southeast to determine the authenticity of groups claiming Indian identity. These reports tended to downplay Indian identity, thus making later claims difficult. See Gilbert, "Surviving Indian Groups of the Eastern United States," and Price, "A Geographic Analysis" and "Mixed-Blood Populations."

24. Bruyneel, *The Third Space of Sovereignty,* 123–24.

25. Rountree, "Indian Virginians on the Move," 11.

26. Office of Indian Affairs, Louisiana Indian Community Development EDA No. 08-6-01537, "1974 Progress Report," 6, Indian Affairs: P1992-92, LSA; "Indians of the East Bear Many Burdens," *Fayetteville Times,* 16 October 1981, 7C.

27. Eagles, "The Civil Rights Movement," 461.

28. The 1964 Civil Rights Act built upon provisions in earlier legislation (1957, 1960) and barred discrimination in public places. This legislation also authorized the attorney general to compel cooperation in the desegregation of public places and schools through lawsuits. The act also addressed fair hiring practices and voting rights, the latter of which was later supported by the Voting Rights Act of 1965 that was designed to enforce the Fifteenth Amendment's securing of voting rights. The Civil Rights Act of 1968, which was enacted into law the day after Martin Luther King Jr. was buried in Atlanta, was a follow-up to the 1964 act that prohibited discrimination in housing. This was the only civil rights legislation that specifically mentioned Indians. Titles II–VII of Public Law 90-284 came to be known as the Indian Civil Rights Act.

29. See Fairclough, *To Redeem the Soul of America;* Eagles, *Outside Agitator;* Dent, *Southern Journey;* Self, *American Babylon;* Chafe, *Civilities and Civil Liberties;* Dittmer, *Local People;* de Jong, *A Different Day;* Thornton, *Dividing Lines;* T. Davis, *Weary Feet, Rested Souls;* Goldfield, *Black, White, and Southern;* Lowery and Marszalek, *Encyclopedia of African-American Civil Rights;* Belknap, *Federal Law and Southern Order;* and Jonas, *Freedom's Sword.* For other influential works on civil rights struggles in the post–World War II years, see Vargas, *Labor Rights Are Civil Rights,* and Crawford, Rouse, and Woods, *Women in the Civil Rights Movement.*

30. As Eagles describes, "The first *Eyes on the Prize* . . . contributed to the es-

tablishment of a canonical view of the movement that grew linearly from *Brown* through Montgomery and Little Rock, followed by the freedom rides and the sit-ins, to King's Albany, Birmingham, and Selma campaigns, and including Missis-sippi's James Meredith and Freedom Summer" ("The Civil Rights Movement," 464). See *Eyes on the Prize.*

31. Ferguson, *Contemporary Native Americans in South Carolina*, 5.

32. See Dial and Eliades, *The Only Land I Know*, and Blu, *The Lumbee Problem.*

33. Paredes, "Federal Recognition and the Poarch Creek Indians," 122; Miller, *Forgotten Tribes*, 187–88; Gregory, "The Louisiana Tribes," 174; Curry-Roper, "A History of the Houma Indians," 22; and Taukchiray and Kasakoff, "Contempo-rary Native Americans in South Carolina," 84.

34. Rountree, "Indian Virginians on the Move," 27.

35. Deloria and Lytle, *American Indians, American Justice*, 155.

36. Josephy, *Red Power.*

37. See Fixico, *The Urban Indian Experience in America.* For works on the pan-Indian movement, see Hertzberg, *The Search for American Indian Identity;* Fa-hey, *Saving the Reservation;* Peroff, *Menominee Drums;* V. Deloria, "The Indian Movement"; Josephy, *Red Power;* Smith and Warrior, *Like a Hurricane;* Johnson, Nagel, and Champagne, *American Indian Activism;* and Cobb and Fowler, *Beyond Red Power.*

38. Quoted in Miller, *Forgotten Tribes*, 190.

39. For a more complicated view on black activism, including the Black Power Movement, which was based on an ideology of separatism, see Ogbar, *Black Power;* Pinkney, *Red, Black, and Green;* O'Reilly, *"Racial Matters";* and Collier and Horowitz, *The Race Card.*

40. Winfrey, "Civil Rights and the American Indian."

41. Just ten years after its enactment, the Indian Civil Rights Act was chal-lenged by the landmark case *Santa Clara Pueblo v. Martinez*, which posed the dilemma of whether the rights of individuals were more significant than tribal self-determination. The Supreme Court ruled to support tribal sovereignty by eliminating the ability of individuals to call upon the jurisdiction of federal courts to force tribal governments to adhere to American civil rights codes. Bordewich, *Killing the White Man's Indian*, 85–87.

42. Gercken-Hawkins, "Authentic Reservations," 190–91.

43. The biracial construction of the South also denies the existence of large pockets of other groups, such as the Chinese, Lebanese, and Asian Indians in Mississippi, Vietnamese in Georgia, Mexicans in Alabama, Cubans in Florida, and Guatemalans in Texas. For scholarship that addresses the multiraciality of the South, see Cohen, *Chinese in the Post–Civil War South;* Loewen, *The Missis-sippi Chinese;* Quan, *Lotus among the Magnolias;* Mormino and Pozzetta, *The Im-migrant World of Ybor City;* Maloof et al., "Cultural Competence and Identity in

Cross Cultural Adaptation"; Mohl, "The Nuevo New South"; Soruco, *Cubans and the Mass Media in South Florida;* Jorge et al., *Cuban Exiles in Florida;* and Bettinger-Lopez, *Cuban-Jewish Journeys.*

44. Paredes, Introduction 4.

45. Taukchiray and Kasakoff, "Contemporary Native Americans in South Carolina," 101.

46. See Williams, *Southeastern Indians since the Removal Era;* Paredes, *Indians of the Southeastern United States in the Late 20th Century;* and Bonney and Paredes, *Anthropologists and Indians in the New South.*

47. Blu, *The Lumbee Problem* and "'Reading Back' to Find Community"; Lowery, *Lumbee Indians in the Jim Crow South;* Sider, *Lumbee Indian Histories;* and Dial and Eliades, *The Only Land I Know.*

48. Bowman and Roper-Curry, *The Forgotten Tribe;* Roberts, "Media Savvy Cajuns and the Houma Indians"; Brasseaux, *French, Cajun, Creole, Houma;* and Miller, *Forgotten Tribes,* 156–208.

49. Covington, *The Seminoles of Florida;* Weisman, *Unconquered People;* Kersey, *An Assumption of Sovereignty;* and West, *The Enduring Seminoles.*

50. Lofton, "Reclaiming an American Indian Identity"; Wickman, *The Tree That Bends.*

51. Matte, *They Say the Wind Is Red.*

52. Cromer, *Modern Indians of Alabama;* Kniffen, Gregory, and Stokes, *The Historic Indian Tribes of Louisiana.*

53. Clancy, *Just a Country Lawyer,* 171–81; Wise, *The Wisdom of Sam Ervin,* 67.

54. Grantham, *The South in Modern America,* 339.

55. Identifying as a "minority" is heavily debated across Indian country. While I argue that southern tribes utilized this label to gain access to certain resources, it was by no means uniformly accepted since many tribal leaders preferred to emphasize their status as members of their own sovereign nations.

56. See Black and Black, *Politics and Society in the South,* and Bass and DeVries, *The Transformation of Southern Politics.*

57. For a discussion on the nation's political right turn that has its roots in the politics of race, opposition to the civil rights movement, and the globalization of the American economy, see Troy, *Morning in America;* Hodgson, *More Equal than Others;* Berkowitz, *America's Welfare State;* and Berman, *America's Right Turn.*

58. "Sickey Waves No Flags in Indian Rights Move," *Basile Weekly,* 28 June 1972, Indian Affairs Files, LSA.

59. Ernest Sickey to John Hamilton Cade Jr., Special Assistant to Governor, [1979], Indian Affairs: P1992-92, LSA.

60. Fairclough, *Race & Democracy,* 464–65.

61. "Sickey Waves No Flags."

62. "A Red Man's Plea," *Winn Parish Enterprise,* 14 November 1973.

63. Coushatta Tribe, *Red Shoes People,* 2–4; "Senate Moves to Honor Coushattas," *Lake Charles American Press,* 10 July 1974.

64. "Bank Presents Donation for Indian Museum," *Lake Charles American Press,* 8 July 1974; "Jury to Aid Indian Tribe," [newspaper source unknown] 14 July 1974, Indian Affairs: P1992-92, LSA; "Sickey Waves No Flags."

65. "Coushatta Tribal Head Is Proud of His People," [newspaper source unknown], 6 January 1980, Indian Affairs: P1992-92, LSA.

66. "Editorial: Coushatta Tribe Gets Break," *Lake Charles American Press,* 24 June 1973.

67. Ruth Loyd Miller to unknown "Senator," 1974, Indian Affairs: P1992-92, LSA.

68. "Sickey Waves No Flags"; "Indians Learning Art of Basket Weaving through State Program," *(Jennings) Daily News,* 18 August 1972, 14.

69. "Sickey Waves No Flags."

70. Office of Indian Affairs, Louisiana Indian Community Development EDA No. 08-6-01537, "1974 Progress Report," 3; Miller to Cade, 16 December 1980.

71. Miller to Cade, 16 December 1980.

72. Ruth Loyd Miller to Governor Edwin Edwards, 11 April 1972, Indian Affairs: P1992-92, LSA.

73. Ruth Loyd Miller, "Resume," http://www.ruthmiller.com (accessed 15 September 2005).

74. Miller to Edwards, 11 April 1972.

75. Ruth Loyd Miller to Governor Edwin Edwards, 26 April 1972, Indian Affairs: P1992-92, LSA; Miller to Edwards, 11 April 1972.

76. Suggested letter to David Garrison Jr. from Governor-Elect Edwin Edwards, drafted by Ruth Loyd Miller, 11 April 1972, Indian Affairs: P1992-92, LSA.

77. Miller to Edwards, 11 April 1972.

78. Miller to Cade, 16 December 1980.

79. Ibid.; Official Statement from the Office of Governor Edwin Edwards, 11 December 1972, Edwards Papers, LSA.

80. Miller to Edwards, 11 April 1972.

81. David Garrison Jr. to Governor Edwin Edwards, 6 June 1972, Edwards Papers, LSA.

82. Watt, "Federal Indian Policy and Tribal Development in Louisiana," 170.

83. Miller to Cade, 16 December 1980.

84. David L. Garrison to Governor Edwin Edwards, 15 March 1973, Indian Affairs Files, LSA.

85. Ruth Loyd Miller to the Louisiana Political Educational Council, 1 December 1972, Indian Affairs: P1992-92, LSA.

86. "Coushatta Tribal Head Is Proud."

87. Miller to Cade, 16 December 1980.

88. Darryl Drewett, "Full Recognition Goal: Coushattas' Road a Long One," *Lake Charles American Press*, 3 July 1973, 6.

89. "Federal Government Services: Coushattas Deprived," *(Jennings) Daily News*, 21 December 1972, 16. By 1980, nearly 140 acres were placed into trust for the Coushatta.

90. "Coushatta Indians Gain Recognition," *Lake Charles American Press*, 29 June 1973.

91. "Re-recognition: Coushatta Observance," *Lake Charles American Press*, 3 July 1973.

92. Ernest Sickey, opening letter, "The Struggle Has Made Us Stronger."

93. By 1977, the Louisiana Office of Indian Affairs had increased their service population to nine thousand Indian residents in eight major communities. See Louisiana Department of Urban and Community Affairs OCS—Indian Affairs grant proposal for project entitled "Dissemination of Information and Technical Assistance Concerning Educational and Social Service Resources to Louisiana Indian Communities," 6 June 1977, Indian Affairs: P1992-92, LSA.

94. Office of Indian Affairs, Louisiana Indian Community Development EDA No. 08-6-01537, "1974 Progress Report," 4, 6, 8.

95. David L. Garrison Jr. to David B. Self (Louisiana state director, OEO), 27 November 1972, Indian Affairs: P1992-92, LSA.

96. Official Statement by Governor Edwards, 11 December 1972, Edwards Papers, LSA.

97. Ernest Sickey to Shelly Doise, 10 October 1979, Indian Affairs: P1992-92, LSA.

98. Sickey to Cade, [1979].

99. Gregory, "The Louisiana Tribes," 165.

100. "Indian Problems Discussed: Barnetts Attend Pow Wow," *The Observer (Baker, LA)*, 10 February 1975.

101. "Treen Won't Rush to Fill Indian Post," *Times-Picayune (New Orleans)*, 16 December 1980, sec. 2, p. 4; Capitol News Bureau, "Aide Says Money Lacking to Empower Indian Panel," news source unknown, [1980], Indian Affairs Files, LSA; "Indian Affairs Position Goes to Helen Gindrat," *Morning Advocate*, 20 December 1980.

102. Melinda Shelton, "Indian Rights Activist Loves U.S., Hates Discrimination," *(Baton Rouge) Sunday Advocate*, 7 August 1983, 9-B.

103. Ibid.

104. Written phone message to John Cade, 22 October 1980, Edwards Papers, LSA; "Treen Pick for Indian Post Rapped," Associated Press, [1980].

105. "Treen Won't Rush to Fill Indian Post"; Watt, "Federal Indian Policy and Tribal Development in Louisiana," 168.

106. Garrison to Edwards, 6 June 1972.

107. Russell Gross to John Hamilton Cade Jr., Special Advisor to Governor Treen, 19 March 1981, Treen Papers, LSA.

108. Jim Seale, "His Title Is Ceremonial: Creek Chief Dresses for TV," *Tampa Times,* 19 October 1976.

109. "Sickey Waves No Flags."

110. Miller to Cade, 16 December 1980.

111. "Coushatta Tribal Head Is Proud."

112. Garrison to Edwards, 6 June 1972.

113. Miller, *Forgotten Tribes,* 190.

114. Paredes, "The Emergence of Contemporary Eastern Creek Indian Identity," 65.

115. "Illiterate Alabama Dirt Farmer."

116. Ibid.

117. Paredes, "The Emergence of Contemporary Eastern Creek Indian Identity," 70.

118. Dewey McGhee, quoted in *The Chief Calvin McGhee and the Forgotten Creeks.*

119. Hugh Rozelle, quoted in *The Chief Calvin McGhee and the Forgotten Creeks.*

120. Paredes, "Kinship and Descent in the Ethnic Reassertion of the Eastern Creek Indians," 185, and Lofton, "Reclaiming an American Indian Identity," 124.

121. Paredes, "The Emergence of Contemporary Eastern Creek Indian Identity," 134. For an overview of black activism in Alabama, see Thornton, *Dividing Lines,* and Gaillard, *Cradle of Freedom.*

122. "Illiterate Alabama Dirt Farmer."

123. In January 1951, the Creek Nation East of the Mississippi set out to intervene in a suit brought by the Creek Nation of Oklahoma before the Indian Claims Commission for loss of land as a result of the Treaty of Fort Jackson.

124. Paredes, "The Emergence of Contemporary Eastern Creek Indian Identity," 73.

125. Olivette McGhee, quoted in *The Chief Calvin McGhee and the Forgotten Creeks.*

126. Jack Edwards, quoted in *The Chief Calvin McGhee and the Forgotten Creeks.*

127. Gercken-Hawkins, "Authentic Reservations," 306. For a discussion on how the Tiguas of Texas "played Indian," see Miller, *Forgotten Tribes,* 209–55.

128. Cowger, *The National Congress of American Indians,* 157.

129. Lofton, "Reclaiming an American Indian Identity," 139.

130. Paredes, "The Emergence of Contemporary Eastern Creek Indian Identity," 75.

131. Seale, "His Title Is Ceremonial."

132. History of the Poarch Band of Creeks, 6, Indian Affairs Files, ADAH.

133. Quoted in Eskew, "George C. Wallace," 220.

134. Ibid., 226. For more about George C. Wallace's shifting racial politics, see Carter, *From George Wallace to Newt Gingrich* and *The Politics of Rage*.

135. Martin Luther King Jr., *The Camera Never Blinks,* quoted in Carter, *The Politics of Rage,* 156.

136. John Lewis, interview by Dan Carter, 7 January 1998, cited in Carter, *The Politics of Rage,* 462.

137. Karen Kreamer to Governor George C. Wallace, 12 November 1973, Wallace Papers, ADAH.

138. Ada M. Godwin to Governor George C. Wallace, 13 April 1978, Wallace Papers, ADAH.

139. Hugh Shadduck to Governor George Wallace, 31 March 1971, Wallace Papers, ADAH.

140. Carter, *The Politics of Rage,* 208.

141. The school property was initially the site of an Indian mission that was built for the Poarch Creek in 1932 by Episcopal missionaries. By 1948, the Protestant Episcopal Church donated the twenty-acre property to the state of Alabama and an Indian school was built.

142. McGhee to Wallace, 10 May 1974, 2–3.

143. Ibid., 3.

144. Carter, *The Politics of Rage,* 457.

145. Governor George Wallace to Harry L. Weaver, Superintendent of the Escambia County Board of Education, 8 November 1974, Wallace Papers, ADAH.

146. Curtis C. Reding to Dr. Ted Mars, 12 December 1975, Wallace Papers, ADAH.

147. Deed to Real Estate and All Appurtenances from the Escambia County School Board to Governor George Wallace, 10 September 1975, Indian Affairs Files, ADAH.

148. George C. Wallace to Morris Thompson, Bureau of Indian Affairs Commissioner, 15 September 1975, Wallace Papers, ADAH.

149. Cromer, *Modern Indians of Alabama,* 180.

150. "Government Relationship to Tribes Seen As Critical Issue," *Alabama Indian Advocate* 1, no. 1 (May 1981): 2, Indian Affairs Files, ADAH.

151. Lofton, "Reclaiming an American Indian Identity," 144.

152. Coalition of Eastern Native Americans brochure (exact date unknown); "Government Relationship to Tribes Seen as Critical Issue," 2.

153. "Government Relationship to Tribes Seen as Critical Issue."

154. Phillip Rawls, "Creeks Differ over Bill to Create State Indian Affairs Commission," *Montgomery Advertiser,* 31 March 1977, 2.

155. Quoted in Cromer, *Modern Indians of Alabama,* 180–81.

156. Quoted in Rawls, "Creeks Differ over Bill."

157. Rawls, "Creeks Differ over Bill"; Cromer, *Modern Indians of Alabama*, 180.

158. Rawls, "Creeks Differ over Bill."

159. Mims Act (No. 677), Section 4, Regular Session, 1 May 1978.

160. Eddie Leon Tullis to Governor Fob James, 11 May 1979, James Papers, ADAH.

161. Barry A. Margolin (staff attorney with Pine Tree Legal Assistance, Inc.) to Cleve (Curtis) Reding, Esq., 17 November 1975, Wallace Papers, ADAH.

162. Cromer, *Modern Indians of Alabama*, xiv.

163. Tullis to James, 11 May 1979, Indian Affairs Files, ADAH.

164. Ibid.; Cromer, *Modern Indians of Alabama*, 181.

165. Southern states played a crucial role in the tensions between tribal nations, state governments, and the federal government in the early nineteenth century that culminated in the Supreme Court cases *Cherokee Nation v. Georgia* (1831) and *Worcester v. Georgia* (1832). The conflict over which sovereign was in charge of Indian policy was ruled on by Chief Justice John Marshall, who constituted tribes as "domestic dependent nations," which recognized that tribal nations maintained a degree of sovereignty that prevented states from exercising power over them, yet they were subject to the guardianship of the federal government. The Marshall cases served to define not only the federal-Indian relationship but the parameters of the state-Indian relationship as well. As federal Indian policy changed, however, so did the involvement of states in Indian affairs. The termination era (1953–68) provides the most notable example of this shift when in an effort to reduce federal assistance to Indians, federal legislation such as Public Law 83-280 was enacted to extend state jurisdiction to Indian reservations in the mandatory states of Alaska, California, Minnesota, Nebraska, Oregon, and Wisconsin (with ten other states exercising partial jurisdiction). In addition to PL 83-280, Congress passed laws terminating the federally recognized tribal status of more than one hundred tribes, subjecting them to the full jurisdiction of the state. See Fixico, *Termination and Relocation;* Bernstein, *American Indians and World War II;* and Pevar, *The Rights of Indians and Tribes.*

166. See O'Brien, *American Indian Tribal Governments,* 290; Wilkins and Lomawaima, *Uneven Ground;* and Biolsi, "*Deadliest Enemies.*"

167. "North Dakota Indian Affairs Commission Governors' Interstate Indian Council Survey" (1978), 9–10; Taylor, *The States and Their Indian Citizens,* 27–47.

168. O'Brien, *American Indian Tribal Governments,* 290; Wilkins and Lomawaima, *Uneven Ground,* 176; Deloria and Lytle, *American Indians, American Justice,* 203–15.

169. Wilma Mankiller to Governor Guy Hunt, 4 January 1992, Hunt Papers, ADAH.

170. Kerbs, "A Voice for Native Americans," 24.

171. Gulf South Research Institute, "American Indians of Louisiana."

172. See Taylor, *The States and Their Indian Citizens*, 40.

173. *Alabama Indian Advocate*, 1, no. 1 (May 1981): 1, 5, Indian Affairs Files, ADAH.

174. Ernest Sickey to Shelly Doise, 10 October 1979, Indian Affairs: P1992-92, LSA.

175. Charlie A. Duthu of the United Houma Nation to Ernest Sickey, 15 October 1979, Indian Affairs: P1992-92, LSA.

176. Official Meeting Minutes for the Louisiana Office of Indian Affairs, 24 September 1973, Indian Affairs: P1992-92, LSA.

177. Miller, *Forgotten Tribes*, 195.

178. Governor Edwin Edwards to Congressman David Treen, 20 April 1977, Edwards Papers, LSA.

179. See Miller, *Forgotten Tribes*, 209–55.

180. Duane Thompson, "Louisiana Indians Sue for Land, Money," *Times-Picayune (New Orleans)*, 8 January 1980, 2.

181. Duane Thompson, "Tribes Have Little Legal Pull," *Times-Picayune (New Orleans)*, 7 January 1980, 12.

182. Rawls, "Creeks Differ over Bill."

183. Official statement of Governor Edwards, 11 December 1972.

184. Miller to Cade, 16 December 1980.

185. Garrison to Edwards, 15 March 1973.

186. Ibid.

187. David Garrison to Ruth Loyd Miller, 23 May 1973, Indian Affairs: P1992-92, LSA.

188. Ernest Sickey, Louisiana Commission of Indian Affairs Meeting Transcript, [1980], Indian Affairs: P1992-92, LSA.

189. Kerbs, "A Voice for Native Americans," 24.

190. The southern border states of Virginia, Tennessee, Arkansas, Texas, and Florida occasionally elected Republican governors into office prior to the 1980s. It was not until the 1970s and 1980s that Republican governors took office in the Deep South (with the exception of Georgia). The Alabama governorship was dominated by Democrats until Republican Guy Hunt was elected in 1987. Louisiana's first Republican governor, David Treen, was elected in 1980.

191. Sickey, Louisiana Commission of Indian Affairs Meeting Transcript, [1980], 4.

192. Eddie Tullis quoted in "Government Relationship to Tribes."

193. Sickey, Louisiana Commission of Indian Affairs Meeting Transcript, [1980], 4.

194. Miller to Edwards, 26 April 1972.

195. Turner, "The Politics of Minor Concerns," 65.

196. Ron Grant, "Tunicas-Indian Author Are TV Subject," *Alexandria Daily Town Talk,* 4 December 1973, 1, sec. B.

197. Vine Deloria Jr., foreword to Matte, *They Say the Wind Is Red,* 11.

Chapter 2

1. Diane Weston, Southwest Alabama Indian Affairs Commission Meeting Transcript, 8 January 1982, 2, Indian Affairs Files, ADAH.

2. Thompson, "Tribes Have Little Legal Pull."

3. Weston, Meeting Transcript, 8 January 1982, 2.

4. Reo Kirkland, Southwest Alabama Indian Affairs Commission Meeting Transcript, 8 January 1982, Indian Affairs Files, ADAH, 10.

5. Eddie Tullis, Southwest Alabama Indian Affairs Commission Meeting Transcript, 8 January 1982, Indian Affairs Files, ADAH, 6.

6. Creek Nation East of the Mississippi, Inc., Tribal Council Announcement, 28 March 1978, Wallace Papers, ADAH.

7. Jennie Lee Dees to Governor George C. Wallace, 28 March 1978, Wallace Papers, ADAH.

8. Fob James was the only Alabamian to first be elected as a Democrat, in 1978, and later reelected as a Republican, in 1994.

9. CETA was a federal program enacted in 1973 to aid disadvantaged and unemployed populations. Block grants were given to state and local governments to establish job-training programs.

10. Official Minutes of the Southwest Alabama Indian Affairs Commission, 31 January 1980, Indian Affairs Files, ADAH.

11. Leonard Hudson, Southwest Alabama Indian Affairs Commission Meeting Transcript, 8 January 1982, 17, Indian Affairs Files, ADAH.

12. Southwest Alabama Indian Affairs Special Meeting Transcript, 20 January 1982, 2–3, Indian Affairs Files, ADAH.

13. Dr. Leonard Hudson, Official Minutes of the Southwest Alabama Indian Affairs Commission, 31 January 1980, 17, Indian Affairs Files, ADAH.

14. Hudson, Meeting Transcript, 8 January 1982, 17.

15. Tullis, Meeting Transcript, 8 January 1982, 17.

16. Poarch Creek Tribal Council to Governor Fob James, 11 May 1979, Indian Affairs Files, ADAH. The United Cherokee Tribe of Alabama was organized on 14 June 1978 in Daleville, Alabama. Chief Faulkner gained media attention when he first opposed the development of an industrial park on what he believed was a former Indian village site near Northport. A few years later, he publicly sought the reassignment of approximately three thousand Indian graves that were to be flooded by the Tennessee-Tombigbee Waterway Project.

17. Cromer, *Modern Indians of Alabama,* 71.

18. Tullis, Meeting Transcript, 8 January 1982, 22–23.

19. Members of the MOWA Band of Choctaw became involved in local politics in the late 1970s. Then, in the 1981 Democratic primary election, Gallasneed Weaver and Gilbert Johnston ran for seats on the Washington County commission. Although they lost, they still drew a lot of attention as the first Indians in the area to get as far as they did in a political election. Weaver had won his district with the Indian vote but lost the at-large vote across the county. See Matte, *They Say the Wind Is Red*.

20. Framon Weaver, Southwest Alabama Indian Affairs Commission Meeting Transcript, 8 January 1982, 20, Indian Affairs Files, ADAH.

21. J. E. Turner, Southwest Alabama Indian Affairs Commission Meeting Transcript, 8 January 1982, 7, Indian Affairs Files, ADAH.

22. Framon Weaver, Meeting Transcript, 8 January 1982, 14.

23. Framon Weaver to Governor Fob James, 11 May 1982, James Papers, ADAH.

24. Southwest Alabama Indian Affairs Commission, "Regulations Providing for Legal Recognition of Indian Tribes, Groups and Organizations by the State of Alabama," 1980, Indian Affairs Files, ADAH.

25. Tullis, Meeting Transcript, 8 January 1982, 6, 16.

26. Ibid., 6–7, 14.

27. Kirkland, Meeting Transcript, 8 January 1982, 10–11.

28. Gallasneed Weaver, Southwest Alabama Indian Affairs Commission Meeting Transcript, 8 January 1982, 33, Indian Affairs Files, ADAH.

29. Tommy Davenport, Southwest Alabama Indian Affairs Commission Meeting Transcript, 8 January 1982, 2, Indian Affairs Files, ADAH.

30. Ibid., 12.

31. Weston, Meeting Transcript, 8 January 1982, 13.

32. Gallasneed Weaver, Meeting Transcript, 8 January 1982, 14.

33. Hudson and Tullis, Meeting Transcript, 8 January 1982, 21–22.

34. Hudson, Meeting Transcript, 8 January 1982, 19.

35. Ibid., 18.

36. Tullis, Meeting Transcript, 8 January 1982, 5.

37. Cromer, *Modern Indians of Alabama*, 181.

38. Ibid., 182.

39. Ibid.

40. Governor Fob James to Marie West Cromer, 1 November 1982, James Papers, ADAH.

41. McGhee to Wallace, 10 May 1974.

42. Duane Thompson, "Louisiana Indian Tribes: 'Being a Tribe Is a Business,'" *Times-Picayune (New Orleans)*, 6 January 1980, 1.

43. Eddie Leon Tullis to Governor Fob James, 11 May 1979, Indian Affairs Files, ADAH.

44. Cromer, *Modern Indians of Alabama*, 73.

45. Ibid., 77.

46. "Cherokees of Jackson County File Petition for Federal Acknowledgment," *Alabama Indian Advocate* 1, no. 4 (September–October 1981): 4, Indian Affairs Files, ADAH.

47. Dr. "Lindy" Martin, Southwest Alabama Indian Affairs Commission Meeting Transcript, 8 January 1982, 3, Indian Affairs Files, ADAH.

48. Gallasneed Weaver, Meeting Transcript, 8 January 1982, 4.

49. Cromer, *Modern Indians of Alabama*, 187. By 1984, the Cherokees of Southeastern Alabama was added to the list of groups vying for commission representation.

50. Ibid.

51. Cromer, *Modern Indians of Alabama*, 193.

52. Ibid., 187–88.

53. "Sickey Waves No Flags."

54. As discussed in chapter 1, the ITC was incorporated in 1975 as a way to bring Indian communities together as a "formal unit" to apply for grants. It was founded by the Chitimacha, Coushatta, and Jena Choctaw. The Houma and Tunica-Biloxi were added to the membership a few years later.

55. Thompson, "Tribes Have Little Legal Pull," 12.

56. Gulf South Research Institute, "American Indians of Louisiana."

57. "Elton May Become 'The Indian Capital,'" *Jennings Daily News,* 27 December 1973.

58. Ernest Sickey, Louisiana Office of Indian Affairs, Indian Community Development Activity Report, 18 October 1974, 1; Dennis Evans, Louisiana Office of Indian Affairs, Indian Community Development Activity Report, 21 March 1975, 2, Indian Affairs Files, LSA.

59. Memorandum, David L. Garrison Jr. to commission members and government agencies, 22 December 1972, Indian Affairs Files, LSA.

60. Dennis Evans, Indian Community Development Activity Report.

61. Cheramie Sonnier, "Government Regulations Complicate Lives of Louisiana's Indians," *State Times (Baton Rouge),* 4 April 1985, 6-A; Inter-Tribal Council of Louisiana, Incorporated, Criteria for Tribal Membership, [1979], Indian Affairs Files, LSA.

62. Official Statement by Governor Edwards, 11 December 1972.

63. Thompson, "Tribes Have Little Legal Pull," 12.

64. Ibid.

65. Ibid.

66. Helen Gindrat, Louisiana Office of Indian Affairs Meeting Transcript, 3 April 1982, 35, Indian Affairs Files, LSA.

67. "Aide Says Money Lacking to Empower Indian Panel."

68. Margrett Fels, "Liberty and Justice for All?" *Baton Rouge Magazine,* November 1986, 17.

69. "Governor's Commission on Indian Affairs," date unknown, 1, Indian Affairs Files, LSA.

70. "State Has Indian Affairs Board," *Daily Iberian (New Iberia, LA),* 19 August 1981.

71. Jeannette Campos, Louisiana Office of Indian Affairs Meeting Transcript, 22 August 1981, 3, Indian Affairs Files, LSA.

72. Helen Gindrat, Louisiana Office of Indian Affairs Meeting Transcript, 17 December 1981, 3, Indian Affairs Files, LSA.

73. Thompson, "Tribes Have Little Legal Pull."

74. Helen Gindrat, Louisiana Office of Indian Affairs Meeting Transcript, 22 August 1981, 2, Indian Affairs Files, LSA.

75. Thompson, "Tribes Have Little Legal Pull."

76. Unknown speaker, Louisiana Office of Indian Affairs Meeting Transcript, 20 April 1982, 2, Indian Affairs Files, LSA.

77. Thompson, "Tribes Have Little Legal Pull."

78. There is no universally accepted definition of the concept "tribe," yet the most widely accepted "legal" definition comes from the legal scholar Felix Cohen. Culturally speaking, a "tribe" is a group of people with shared traditions and language. Politically speaking, a "tribe" is a group that has been recognized as such by the federal government—regardless if they are bound in a cultural sense—since the passage of the 1934 Indian Reorganization Act. It is the latter definition that the Louisiana state legislature attempted to impose on non–federally recognized groups. See Bordewich, *Killing the White Man's Indian;* O'Brien, *American Indian Tribal Governments;* and Wilkins, *American Indian Politics and the American Political System.*

79. Odis Sanders, Louisiana Office of Indian Affairs Meeting Transcript, 3 April 1982, 6, Indian Affairs Files, LSA.

80. Gindrat, Meeting Transcript, 3 April 1982, 7.

81. Thompson, "Tribes Have Little Legal Pull."

82. Unknown speaker, Louisiana Office of Indian Affairs Meeting Transcript, 3 April 1982, 2, Indian Affairs Files, LSA.

83. Helen Gindrat, Louisiana Office of Indian Affairs Meeting Transcript, 20 April 1982, 11, Indian Affairs Files, LSA.

84. Richard Brazan, Louisiana Office of Indian Affairs Meeting Transcript, 20 April 1982, 7, Indian Affairs Files, LSA.

85. Unknown speaker, Louisiana Office of Indian Affairs Meeting Transcript, 3 April 1982, 7, Indian Affairs Files, LSA.

86. Campos, Meeting Transcript, 3 April 1982, 8–9.

87. Sarah Peralta, Louisiana Office of Indian Affairs Meeting Transcript, 3 April 1982, 2, Indian Affairs Files, LSA.

88. Sarah Peralta, Louisiana Office of Indian Affairs Meeting Transcript, 20 April 1982, 2–3, Indian Affairs Files, LSA.

89. Ernest Sickey, letter to the editor, *Baton Rouge Enterprise,* 16–22 March 1977, 2.

90. Unknown speaker, Meeting Transcript, 3 April 1982, 2.

91. Undersigned Sovereign American Indian Tribal Governments of Louisiana, "Building Bridges: Old Problems—Present Issues," position paper, 31 May 1981, 5, Indian Affairs Files, LSA.

92. Louisiana Office of Indian Affairs Meeting Minutes, 24 September 1973, 3, Indian Affairs Files, LSA.

93. Memo, Ernest Sickey to Helen Gindrat, 1 September 1981, Indian Affairs Files, LSA.

94. Dennis Evans, Louisiana Office of Indian Affairs, Indian Community Development Activity Report, 21 March 1975, 6, Indian Affairs Files, LSA.

95. "Governor's Commission on Indian Affairs," Agency Summary, 1988, 1, Indian Affairs Files, LSA.

96. Richard Brazan, Louisiana Office of Indian Affairs Meeting Transcript, 17 October 1981, 1, Indian Affairs Files, LSA.

97. Campos, Meeting Transcript, 3 April 1982.

98. Raymond Ebarb to Apache-Choctaw Indian Community of Ebarb Tribal Council, 26 June 1981, Indian Affairs Files, LSA.

99. Press release, "Governor Names Simpson to Indian Affairs Commission," 5 November 1981; Gindrat, Meeting Transcript, 20 April 1982, 10.

100. "Aide Says Money Lacking to Empower Indian Panel."

101. "Treen Won't Rush to Fill Indian Post.".

102. Mary Ann Sternberg, "Baton Rouge Indian Woman to Be Honored on Saturday," *State Times (Baton Rouge),* 9 April 1975, 3-B.

103. Miller to Cade, 16 December 1980.

104. "Treen Won't Rush to Fill Indian Post."

105. Annabelle Armstrong, "On the 'Warpath' for Her People," *State Times (Baton Rouge),* [1981], Indian Affairs Files, LSA.

106. "Treen Pick for Indian Post Rapped," Associated Press, [1980], Indian Affairs Files, LSA.

107. Odis M. Sanders Sr. to Governor David Treen, 26 September 1980, Treen Papers, LSA.

108. Williamson, the popular candidate for urban Indians, was appointed to the position of assistant director of the commission in 1984 and then became executive director in 1986.

109. "Treen Pick for Indian Post Rapped."

110. Alice Hall, letter to the editor, "Treen and the Indians," *Times-Picayune (New Orleans)*, 6 January 1981.

111. "Treen Pick for Indian Post Rapped."

112. "After Hundreds of Years, Indians' Struggle Goes On," *Sunday Advocate,* 7 August 1983.

113. Clifton Choctaw Tribal Council to Diana Williamson, 3 December 1987; Diana Williamson to the Clifton Choctaw Tribal Council, 9 December 1987, both in Indian Affairs Files, LSA.

114. Gindrat, Meeting Transcript, 17 December 1981, 1.

115. Gindrat, Meeting Transcript, 22 August 1981, 2.

116. Gindrat, Meeting Transcript, 3 April 1982.

117. "Declaration of Unity," 11 April 1981, Indian Affairs Files, LSA.

118. Undersigned Sovereign American Indian Tribal Governments of Louisiana, "Building Bridges: Old Problems—Present Issues."

119. Gindrat, Meeting Transcript, 22 August 1981, 1.

120. John Billiot, Louisiana Office of Indian Affairs Meeting Transcript, 3 April 1982, 16–17, Indian Affairs Files, LSA.

121. Ibid., 23.

122. Gindrat, Meeting Transcript, 3 April 1982, 15.

123. Ernest Sickey, Louisiana Office of Indian Affairs Meeting Transcript, 3 April 1982, 17–18, Indian Affairs Files, LSA.

124. Unknown speaker, Meeting Transcript, 3 April 1982, 36.

125. Roy Procell to Helen Gindrat, 28 July 1982, Indian Affairs Files, LSA.

126. David W. Broome to Governor Edwin Edwards, 17 November 1983, Indian Affairs Files, LSA.

Chapter 3

1. Norman Billiot to Helen Gindrat, 16 May 1981, Indian Affairs Files, LSA.

2. Harmon, *Indians in the Making.* Also see Clifford, "Identity in Mashpee."

3. In a letter to Diana Williamson (Governor's Commission on Indian Affairs) from Elizabeth Shown Mills (American Society of Genealogists), 5 December 1987, the definition of "free people of color" was outlined as follows: "In the pre–Civil War South, this was a generic term that carried no specific ethnic identity. It merely meant that the individual: 1) was not in bondage, either as a slave or an indentured servant; and 2) was known in the community to have a significant degree of non-white blood. The term was applied to individuals of mixed Negro-white ancestry (but not pure-Negro ancestry) and to Indians; at times it

was also applied to Gypsies, Portuguese, Spanish, Mexican, Chinese, and various ethnic mixtures whose complexion appeared somewhat darker."

4. See Foster, *Negro-Indian Relationships in the Southeast;* Berry, *Almost White;* Forbes, *Africans and Native Americans;* Woods, *Marginality and Identity;* Dominguez, *White by Definition;* Lovett, "African and Cherokee by Choice"; Welburn, "A Most Secret Identity"; Jolivette, *Louisiana Creoles;* and Basson, *White Enough to Be American?*

5. For a discussion on identity politics and the benefits of whiteness, see Hall, *Whiteness;* Gabriel, *White Wash;* Hale, *Making Whiteness;* Lipsitz, *The Possessive Investment in Whiteness;* Mills, *The Racial Contract;* and Roediger, *The Wages of Whiteness.*

6. "Indians of the East Bear Many Burdens," *Fayetteville Times,* 16 October 1981, 7C.

7. Although the segregation practices of the Angola Prison were not supported by law, not all of the segregation laws were entirely removed from the books in states across the South. For a recent study on the persistence of segregation laws and practices, see Chin et al., "Still on the Books."

8. Gilbert, "Surviving Indian Groups of the Eastern United States," 430.

9. The Lumbee serve as a unique case; their formal acknowledgment by the state of North Carolina in 1885 had no immediate impact. It was not until 1956 that Congress passed the Lumbee Recognition Act, which acknowledged their existence, but it did not extend federal benefits and privileges to them as a tribal nation. See Blu, *The Lumbee Problem;* Lowery, *Lumbee Indians in the Jim Crow South;* and Sider, *Lumbee Indian Histories.*

10. The Houma lived in an upland environment at the time of French contact. They were then driven to the edge of New Orleans until they had to relocate again to the low country when that section of the Mississippi opened up to plantation culture. From there, Cajuns drove them deep into the bayous of the Mississippi Delta.

11. In 1830 the group that later became organized as the MOWA Choctaw still resided in their traditional lands, which were part of the southeastern district of the Choctaw Nation's territory. They were the descendants of residents from the Six Towns District who lived west of the Tombigbee and Mobile rivers, as well as various other dislocated Indian people fleeing from war, famine, forced removal, and white settlement in other areas. Following the Treaty of Dancing Rabbit Creek, the Choctaw who remained in the South legally lost their land and some had to turn to squatting while others managed to purchase some land titles. See Matte, *They Say the Wind Is Red.* For another example of an Indian community that was constructed as a result of culturally and linguistically different Indian people coming together, see Merrell, *The Indians' New World.*

12. *H. L. Billiot v. Terrebonne Board of Education* (143 La. 623, 79 So. 78). In the course of the case, it came out that Billiot had a grandfather who was a slave. It was never discussed in court whether the grandfather was an Indian or an African, yet the court drew its own conclusions for the purpose of the ruling.

13. MOWA Band of Choctaw Indians Recognition Act, 103D Cong., 1st Sess., Senate Report 103-193, 19 November 1993, 2; Matte, *They Say the Wind Is Red*, 71.

14. D'Oney, "A History of the Houma Nation," 179.

15. Swanton, "Indian Tribes of the Lower Mississippi Valley."

16. Bourgeois, "Four Decades of Public Education," 71.

17. Bowman and Curry-Roper, *The Forgotten Tribe;* d'Oney, "A History of the Houma Nation," 211.

18. Armstrong, "On the 'Warpath' for Her People," 4-G.

19. Matte, *They Say the Wind Is Red,* 118; Holmes, "The So-Called Cajan Settlement," a survey for Governor William W. Brandon, 1924.

20. Price, "Mixed-Blood Populations." See also Bond, "Two Racial Islands of Alabama"; Murphy, "Among the Cajans of Alabama"; Bailey, "The Strange Case of the Cajans"; Green, "Some Factors Influencing Cajun Education"; and Stopp, "The Impact of the 1964 Civil Rights Act."

21. Price, "Mixed-Blood Populations," 55–57.

22. Ibid., 54–56.

23. Ibid., 83.

24. See Parenton and Pellegrin, "The Sabines," and Roy, "Indians of Dulac." For an example of the more favorable works, see Speck, "The Houma Indians in 1940." For works on "racial hybrids," "racial islands," or "marginal peoples" of the eastern United States, see Berry, *Almost White;* Pollitzer, "The Physical Anthropology and Genetics of Marginal Peoples"; Gilbert, "Memorandum Concerning the Characteristics" and "Mixed Bloods of the Upper Monongahela Valley"; Beale, "American Triracial Isolates"; Price, "A Geographic Analysis" and "The Melungeons"; Johnson, "Personality in a White-Negro-Indian Community"; and Swanton, "Probable Identity of the 'Croatan' Indians."

25. Despite the attitude of Roy Nash, a special commissioner sent by the Office of Indian Affairs to the Houma community in 1932, who de-emphasized Houma needs and sympathized more with the school board's dilemma of a possible three-tiered segregation system, other government officials issued reports that took different positions. In 1938, after the ethnologist and Houma advocate Frank Speck met with Commissioner of Indian Affairs John Collier in Washington, DC, the anthropologist Ruth Underhill was sent to the Houma community where she discovered and reported a need for better educational facilities. Then, in 1942, Willard W. Beatty, director of Indian Education within the Office of Indian Affairs, conducted an educational survey of the state's Indian popula-

tion, discovering a need for Indian schools within the Houma community. See Bowman and Curry-Roper, *The Forgotten Tribe,* 40–45.

26. D'Oney, "A History of the Houma Nation," 205.

27. Ibid., 207; Price, "Mixed-Blood Populations," 76.

28. Matte, *They Say the Wind Is Red,* 87; Kniffen, Gregory, and Stokes, *The Historic Indian Tribes of Louisiana,* 310.

29. For more on tribal resurgence and ethnogenesis, see Nagel, "American Indian Ethnic Renewal," 947–65, and Roosens, *Creating Ethnicity.*

30. D'Oney, "A History of the Houma Nation," 231.

31. Matte, *They Say the Wind Is Red,* 80.

32. There were several childcare, education, eldercare, housing, health, and economic development programs that did not specify that a group had to be "federally recognized" to receive services. Southern state-recognized tribes took advantage of this ambiguity by tapping into these resources. Associated Press, "Alabama's MOWAs Seek Approval from U.S. as Indian Tribe," *Times-Picayune (New Orleans),* [198?], article clipping found in Indian Affairs Files, LSA.

33. Matte, *They Say the Wind Is Red,* 151.

34. Curry-Roper, "A History of the Houma Indians," 23.

35. Tommy Davenport, Southwest Alabama Indian Affairs Commission Meeting Transcript, 8 January 1982, 2, Indian Affairs Files, ADAH.

36. For a discussion on the complex nature of federal acknowledgment, see Miller, *Forgotten Tribes;* McCulloch and Wilkins, "'Constructing' Nations within States"; Weatherhead, "What Is an 'Indian Tribe'?"; Slagle, "Unfinished Justice"; Quinn, "Federal Acknowledgment of American Indian Tribes"; Greenbaum, "What's in a Label?"; Campisi, *The Mashpee Indians;* and Porter, *Strategies for Survival.*

37. Southwest Alabama Indian Affairs Commission, Comments Regarding Proposed Legislation, 17 July 1981, 3, Indian Affairs Files, ADAH.

38. United States of America, State of Louisiana Office of the Governor, Governor's Commission on Indian Affairs Functions and Responsibilities, 1973, Indian Affairs Files, LSA.

39. Greg Bowman to Helen Gindrat, 21 April 1982, Indian Affairs Files, LSA.

40. Louisiana Office of Indian Affairs Meeting Transcript, 20 April 1982, 11, Indian Affairs Files, LSA.

41. "Research Project Made Possible by Summer Youth Employment and Indian CETA Programs," *Alabama Indian Advocate* 1, no. 3 (July/August 1981): 5, Indian Affairs Files, ADAH.

42. "Lutheran World Ministries Offer Research Assistance to the Poarch Band of Creeks," *Alabama Indian Advocate* 1, no. 3 (July/August 1981): 7, Indian Affairs Files, ADAH.

43. Greg Bowman to Helen Gindrat, 11 June 1981, and United Houma Nation, Inc., Progress Report, 22 February 1981, both in Indian Affairs Files, LSA.

44. Matte, *They Say the Wind Is Red*, 153.

45. "Conference on Critical Issues Affecting Eastern Indians," *Alabama Indian Advocate* 1, no. 3 (July/August 1981): 8, Indian Affairs Files, ADAH.

46. Ibid., 9.

47. Report of the "Critical Issues Affecting Eastern Indians" Conference Proceedings (Alexandria, VA: Beverly Hills Community United Methodist Church, 1981), 4, Indian Affairs Files, ADAH.

48. "Indians of the East Bear Many Burdens," *Fayetteville Times*, 16 October 1981, 7C.

49. Report of the "Critical Issues," 10.

50. Ibid., 12.

51. Ibid., 10.

52. John Billiot to the Friends of the United Houma Nation, in Greg Bowman and Janel Curry-Roper, *The Houma People of Louisiana: A Story of Indian Survival*, compiled under the direction of the tribal council of the United Houma Nation (Lawrence: University of Kansas Press, 1982), Watson Library.

53. Ibid., 28–29.

54. See Duthu, "The Houma Indians of Louisiana," "Folklore of the Louisiana Houma Indians," and "Future Light or Feu-Follet?"

55. Cromer, *Modern Indians of Alabama*, 99.

56. Kniffen, Gregory, and Stokes, *The Historic Indian Tribes of Louisiana*, and Gregory, "The Louisiana Tribes."

57. See Curry-Roper, "A History of the Houma Indians"; Bowman and Curry-Roper, *The Forgotten Tribe;* Miller, *Forgotten Tribes;* Downs and Whitehead, "The Houma Indians"; Spiller, "The Houma Indians since 1940"; and Stanton, "Southern Louisiana Survivors."

58. Thompson, "Louisiana Indian Tribes."

59. Mary Ann Sternberg, "Baton Rouge Indian Woman to Be Honored on Saturday: Kicking the Stereotype," *State Times (Baton Rouge)*, 9 April 1975, 3-B; "Coushatta Tribal Head Is Proud"; Hope J. Norman, "Revive the Pride of the Choctaw Indians," *Alexandria Daily Town Talk*, 3 March 1982.

60. Brenda Wyers's Fifth Grade Class to Governor Guy Hunt, 5 May 1989, Indian Affairs Files, ADAH.

61. Congressman David Treen to Governor Edwin Edwards, 4 May 1977, Edwards Papers, LSA; Department of the Interior, Branch of Acknowledgement and Research, Bureau of Indian Affairs, "Proposed Finding against Federal Acknowledgment of the Houma Nation, Inc."

62. Department of Interior's Assistant Secretary of Indian Affairs (Kevin

Gover), "Final Determination against Federal Acknowledgment of the Mobil-Washington County Band of Choctaw Indians of South Alabama (MOWA)."

63. D'Oney, "A History of the Houma Nation," 227.

64. Miller, *Forgotten Tribes,* 157.

65. Matte, *They Say the Wind Is Red,* 159.

66. "Government Relationship to Tribes."

67. Unknown speaker, United Houma Nation Council Meeting Transcript, 5 June 1982, 6, Indian Affairs Files, LSA.

68. "Alabama Indian Affairs Commission Serving Indians in Alabama Report," 1980, 5, Indian Affairs Files, ADAH.

69. John Billiot, Louisiana Office of Indian Affairs Meeting Transcript, 3 April 1982, 16, Indian Affairs Files, LSA.

70. Alabama Indian Affairs Commission Annual Report, 1984–85, 7, Indian Affairs Files, ADAH; Louisiana Office of Indian Affairs Meeting Transcript, 20 April 1982, 7, Indian Affairs Files, LSA.

71. Wanda Light Tully, personal communication with the author, 28 April 2005.

72. Alabama Indian Affairs Commission Annual Report, 1987–88, 2, 17, Indian Affairs Files, ADAH.

73. Calvin McGhee created the Kinsmen of Indians for Liberty, Reform and Instructions in Civic Affairs (KILROI) in which he encouraged his own community, as well as the MOWA Choctaw, to vote. See Matte, *They Say the Wind Is Red,* 141–42.

74. Alabama Indian Affairs Commission Annual Report, 1984–85, 4.

75. State of Louisiana Governor's Commission on Indian Affairs, Community Services Block Grant Proposal, 1988–89, 2, Indian Affairs Files, LSA.

76. In 1900 approximately 250,000 American Indians were reported by the U.S. census. By 1990 the recorded population jumped to 2,000,000. See Snipp, "Sociological Perspectives on American Indians," and R. Thornton, *American Indian Holocaust and Survival.*

77. "Large Increase in Indian Population in 1980 Census," *Alabama Indian Advocate* 1, no. 2 (June 1981): 8, Indian Affairs Files, ADAH.

78. Louisiana Office of Indian Affairs, *Native Americans of Louisiana,* 1989, 31, Indian Affairs Files, LSA.

79. Wayne Hodges, "Let's Try Once More," *Alabama Indian Advocate* 1, no. 3 (July/August 1981): 5, Indian Affairs Files, ADAH.

80. Louisiana Office of Indian Affairs, *Native Americans of Louisiana,* 6.

81. "Indian Owned Radio Station Airing in Alabama," *Alabama Indian Advocate* 1, no. 4 (September/October 1981): 1–2, Indian Affairs Files, ADAH.

82. *Alabama Indian Journal* sample excerpts, 1981, Indian Affairs Files, ADAH.

83. Alabama Indian Affairs Commission Annual Report, 1990–91, 3, Indian Affairs Files, ADAH.

84. Alabama Indian Affairs Commission Annual Report, 1987–88, 5, Indian Affairs Files, ADAH.

85. Jennie Lee Dees, "Comments by the Executive Director," *Alabama Indian Advocate* 1, no. 2 (June 1981): 2, Indian Affairs Files, ADAH.

86. H. M. Westholz Jr. (State Department of Human Resources) to Anna Neal, 16 April 1987, and Anna Neal to Dianna Williamson, [1987], Roemer Papers, LSA.

87. Don Siegelman to Jane L. Weeks, 12 September 1990, Indian Affairs Files, ADAH.

88. Alabama Indian Affairs Commission Report, 1980, 14, Indian Affairs Files, ADAH.

89. Daniel Lambordo, Louisiana Office of Indian Affairs Meeting Transcript, 22 August 1981, 18, Indian Affairs Files, LSA.

90. Unknown speaker, Louisiana Office of Indian Affairs Meeting Transcript, 16 September 1982, 21, Indian Affairs Files, LSA.

91. Alabama Indian Affairs Commission Annual Report, 1984–85, 7.

92. Steve Cheramie, Louisiana Office of Indian Affairs Meeting Transcript, 3 April 1982, 25, 28, Indian Affairs Files, LSA.

93. Louisiana Office of Indian Affairs Meeting Minutes, 24 September 1973, 1, Indian Affairs Files, LSA. Also see Davis, "A Case of Identity."

94. Pascoe, "Miscegenation Law, Court Cases," 46.

95. Quoted in ibid., 53. See 1924 Va. Acts ch. 371, 1927 Ga. Laws no. 317, and 1927 Ala. Acts no. 626.

96. Alabama Indian Affairs Commission biannual progress report, 6 February 1981, 5, Indian Affairs Files, ADAH.

97. Dennis Evans, Indian Community Development Activity Report.

98. Alabama Indian Affairs Commission Report, 1980, 5.

99. Gulf South Research Institute, "American Indians of Louisiana," 2.

100. Stevens, "Demographic Variation and Ethnic Differentiation," 129.

101. Matte, *They Say the Wind Is Red*, 110.

102. Alabama Indian Affairs Commission Annual Report, 1984–85, 8.

103. Matte, *They Say the Wind Is Red*, 110.

104. "Alabama Indian Affairs Commission Serving Indians in Alabama Report," 1980, 4, Indian Affairs Files, ADAH.

105. Roy Procell, Louisiana Office of Indian Affairs Meeting Transcript, 17 October 1981, 14, Indian Affairs Files, LSA.

106. Daniel Darden, Louisiana Office of Indian Affairs Meeting Transcript, 17 October 1981, 15, Indian Affairs Files, LSA.

107. Fels, "Liberty and Justice for All?" 17.

108. Gallasneed Weaver, Meeting Transcript, 8 January 1982, 33.

109. Pat Schilling and Steve Cheramie, Louisiana Office of Indian Affairs Meeting Transcript, 17 October 1981, 17, Indian Affairs Files, LSA.

110. Curtis Johnson (University of Southwestern Louisiana) to Clyde Jackson (commission director), 14 February 1985; Donnie G. Copeland (Louisiana State University) to Clyde Jackson, 12 February 1985; C. B. Ellis (Delgado Community College) to Clyde Jackson, 11 February 1985; Charles McDonald (Northeast Louisiana University) to Clyde Jackson, 11 February 1985; Terry Faust (Northwestern State University of LA) to Clyde Jackson, 11 February 1985; Raymond Boswell (Louisiana State University of Alexandria) to Clyde Jackson, 6 February 1985; Frank Candalisa (Southeastern Louisiana University) to Clyde Jackson, 13 February 1985; Edgar Chase (Louisiana State University in Shreveport) to Clyde Jackson, 7 February 1985, all in Indian Affairs Files, LSA.

111. "Non-Indians Should Observe American Indians' Situation," *Morning Advocate (Baton Rouge)*, 5 April 1985, 3.

112. Louisiana Governor's Commission on Indian Affairs, Monthly Report, July 1987, Indian Affairs Files, LSA; "Bill Classifying American Indians as Minorities OK'd by Senate Panel," *Alexandria Daily Town Talk*, 30 April 1987.

113. "Indian Agency" news clip without full citation found in Indian Affairs Files, LSA.

114. Quoted in Bill McMahon, "Panel Approves Minority Status," *Morning Advocate (Baton Rouge)*, 30 April 1987.

115. Ibid.

116. John Strongbow, letter to the editor: "American Indians Have Suffered Great Pain," *State Times (Baton Rouge)*, 22 September 1983, 11-B.

117. "Governor's Commission on Indian Affairs," [198?], 1, Indian Affairs Files, LSA.

118. Louisiana Governor's Commission on Indian Affairs, Monthly Report, September 1986.

119. Unknown speaker, Houma Meeting Transcript, 5 June 1982, 8–9.

120. Alabama Indian Affairs Commission Report, 1980, 1.

121. "Governor's Commission on Indian Affairs," 2.

122. Governor's Commission on Indian Affairs, Monthly Report, November 1987, Indian Affairs Files, LSA; State of Louisiana Governor's Commission on Indian Affairs, Community Services Block Grant Report, 1988–89, 1, Indian Affairs Files, LSA.

123. Alabama Indian Affairs Commission Annual Report, 1986–87, 5, Indian Affairs Files, ADAH.

124. Ibid.

125. "U.S. Small Business Administration," http://www.sba.gov/8abd/ (accessed 12 September 2005).

126. Alabama Indian Affairs Commission Annual Report, 1986–87, 5.

127. Alabama Indian Affairs Commission Annual Report, 1989–90, 10; "Identification of Indian Business Owners," Alabama Indian Affairs Commission Annual Report, 1997–98, Indian Affairs Files, ADAH.

128. Jeannette A. Campos to Norman Billiot, 4 May 1983, Indian Affairs Files, LSA.

129. Quote from Curry-Roper, "A History of the Houma Indians," 8.

Chapter 4

1. Mildred Smith to Helen Gindrat, 6 April 1982, Indian Affairs: P1992-92, LSA.

2. Elsie Billiot to Helen Gindrat, 3 May 1982, Indian Affairs: P1992-92, LSA.

3. The LOIA staff admitted that they had nothing to offer the women at the time the letters were received and recommended that they inquire whether their tribal governments could provide aid. Patricia Schilling (Louisiana Office of Indian Affairs Administrative Assistant) to Mildred Smith, 20 April 1982, and Patricia Schilling to Steve Cheramie (United Houma Nation), 12 May 1982, both in Indian Affairs: P1992-92, LSA.

4. Quoted in Gregory, "The Louisiana Tribes," 181.

5. Unknown participant quoted in "Executive Summary of the Issue Management Forum for the Poarch Band of Creek Indians," prepared by the Center for Interactive Management, 14–17 July 1988, 2, George Mason University Library, Fairfax, VA.

6. Meeting between tribal chairmen of Louisiana, Clifton, LA, 22 August 1981, 10, Indian Affairs Files, LSA.

7. Eddie Tullis, quoted in "Tullis Re-Elected," *Alabama Indian Advocate* 1, no. 4 (September–October 1981): 5, Indian Affairs Files, ADAH.

8. Eddie Tullis, Southwest Alabama Indian Affairs Meeting Transcript, 8 January 1982, 6; Leonard Hudson, Southwest Alabama Indian Affairs Meeting Transcript, 8 January 1982, 17; Alabama Indian Affairs Report, [1980], 15, Indian Affairs Files, ADAH.

9. Leonard Hudson, quoted in "New Era for American Indians Begins in Alabama," *Alabama Indian Advocate* 1, no. 2 (June 1981): 1, Indian Affairs Files, ADAH.

10. Alabama Indian Affairs Report, [1980], 4.

11. Of the 354 Poarch Creek households surveyed, 55.08 percent had incomes below the poverty level, and of a possible workforce of 461 people, 20.61 percent were unemployed. In addition, the survey showed that 442 individuals were in need of dental service and 397 were in need of medical care. See "History of the Poarch Creek," [exact date unknown], 6–8, Indian Affairs Files, ADAH.

12. Jennie Lee Dees to Governor George C. Wallace, 28 March 1978, Indian Affairs Files, ADAH.

13. Alabama Indian Affairs Report, [1980], 5.

14. Ibid., 6.

15. Southwest Alabama Indian Affairs Commission, First Quarter FY81 Progress Report (1 October 1980–31 December 1980), 5–6, Indian Affairs Files, ADAH.

16. Southwest Alabama Indian Affairs Commission, Second Quarter FY81 Progress Report, April 1981, 2; Southwest Alabama Indian Affairs Commission, map of Indian populations by county, 1980, Indian Affairs Files, ADAH.

17. Alabama Indian Affairs Report, [1980], 5.

18. Alabama Indian Affairs Commission Annual Report, 1986–87, 5, Indian Affairs Files, ADAH.

19. "The Elderly Indians of Louisiana and Their Needs: A Report from the Office of Indian Affairs," Louisiana Health and Human Resources Administration Division of Human Services (1 December 1975), Western Michigan University Libraries, Kalamazoo.

20. While state Indian agencies struggled to document the needs of non-recognized communities, the BIA did report on the status of schools on the Chitimacha reservation in 1973. See Indian Education Resources Center, "Final Report."

21. This study found that non-Indian families in the state of Louisiana had an average annual income of $7,530, while the average Indian household included in the survey averaged $5,002. Although both of these figures were well below the national average, Indians were labeled as the "poorest of the poor." The study also found that over 40 percent of the Indian people interviewed for the study were unemployed. Finally, the highest grade completed in school for the general non-Indian population was twelfth grade while the Louisiana Indian population, on average, stayed in school only until seventh grade. See Spicker, Steiner, and Walden, "A Survey of Rural Louisiana Indian Communities," and Houma Meeting Transcript, 5 June 1982, 5.

22. Meeting between tribal chairmen of Louisiana, Clifton, LA, 22 August 1981, 22.

23. See Roche, "Sociocultural Aspects of Diabetes in an Apache-Choctaw Community in Louisiana."

24. See Faine, The Jena Band of Choctaws; Faine and Bohlander, The Chitimacha Indians; Faine and Gregory, The Apache-Choctaw of Ebarb; and Faine, The Tunica-Biloxi.

25. State of Louisiana Governor's Commission on Indian Affairs, Community Services Block Grant Report, 1988–89, 3, Indian Affairs Files, LSA.

26. In 1990 Dr. Dan Walsh and Debbie Hammond of Louisiana State University used the reports to write grants for tribes. See Louisiana Governor's Com-

mission on Indian Affairs Weekly Report, 14 September 1990, 1, Indian Affairs Files, LSA.

27. State of Louisiana Governor's Commission on Indian Affairs, Community Services Block Grant Report, 1988–89, 2.

28. Houma Meeting Transcript, 5 June 1982, 5–6.

29. Sonnier, "Government Regulations Complicate Lives of Louisiana Indians," 6-A.

30. Southwest Alabama Indian Affairs Commission, First Quarter FY81 Progress Report, 1–2.

31. The staff of the AIAC filled the advocacy role by initiating contact with agencies and laying the groundwork for future partnerships. See Alabama Indian Affairs Report, May 1981, 1; Southwest Alabama Indian Affairs Commission, First Quarter FY81 Progress Report, 2; Southwest Alabama Indian Affairs Commission, Progress Report, June 1981, 2; Cynthia Gloss (Georgia Department of Archives and History) to Alabama Indian Advocate Staff, 28 December 1981; Southwest Alabama Indian Affairs Commission, Budget Proposal, 9 February 1981, 2; Alabama Indian Affairs Report, [1980], 15.

32. Helen Gindrat to Lucretia Verdin, 19 October 1982, Indian Affairs Files, LSA.

33. Minutes from meeting of Board of Commissioners held at the Department of Urban and Community Affairs (DUCA) in Baton Rouge, 17 October 1981, 9, Indian Affairs Files, LSA.

34. Unknown speaker, Houma Meeting Transcript, 5 June 1982, 9–13.

35. Helen Gindrat, Louisiana Office of Indian Affairs Board of Commissioners Meeting, 16 September 1982, 23; Minutes from meeting of Board of Commissioners held at DUCA in Baton Rouge, 17 October 1981, 10; Meeting between tribal chairmen of Louisiana, Clifton, LA, 22 August 1981, 15.

36. Minutes from meeting of Board of Commissioners on Louisiana Indian Affairs, 17 October 1981, 3.

37. Louisiana Office of Indian Affairs Meeting Summary, 11 April 1981, Indian Affairs Files, LSA.

38. "Conference on Critical Issues Affecting Eastern Indians," *Alabama Indian Advocate* 1, no. 2 (July–August 1981): 8, Indian Affairs Files, ADAH.

39. "Tribes to Meet," *Sunday Advocate (Baton Rouge)*, 8 November 1987, 5B.

40. Memorandum, Southwest Alabama Indian Affairs Commission, Proposal for Second Year of Funding (1 October 1981–30 September 1982), ADAH; Alabama Indian Affairs Commission Annual Report, 1984–85, 4.

41. Invitation, Florida Governor's Council on Indian Affairs Open House, 14 April 1981; Alabama Indian Affairs Commission Annual Report, 1987–88, 5, Indian Affairs Files, ADAH.

42. James Parker Shield to Louisiana Office of Indian Affairs, 21 June 1982, Indian Affairs Files, LSA.

43. Governors' Interstate Indian Council Board of Directors for 1981, Indian Affairs Files, ADAH. In 1981 the SAIAC was unable to send representatives to the GIIC meeting in Juneau, Alaska. LOIA, on the other hand, managed to send Helen Gindrat to the meeting. The AIAC sent representatives to the 1984 meeting in Bismarck, North Dakota, and the 1988 meeting in Denver, Colorado.

44. Alabama Indian Affairs Commission Annual Report, 1990–91, 3, Indian Affairs Files, ADAH.

45. Clyde Jackson, "Executive Director's Report: Governor's Commission on Indian Affairs," 7 December 1983, 5, Indian Affairs Files, LSA.

46. Alabama Indian Affairs Commission Annual Report, 1984–85, 4.

47. Ibid.; Alabama Indian Affairs Commission Annual Report, 1986–87, 7.

48. Governor Fob James to Kenneth Payton (BIA), 13 November 1981, James Papers, ADAH.

49. Helen Gindrat, Louisiana Office of Indian Affairs Meeting Transcript, [1980], 2, Indian Affairs Files, LSA.

50. Clyde Jackson, Louisiana Office of Indian Affairs Meeting Transcript, [1980], 1–2, Indian Affairs Files, LSA.

51. Jeanette Campos, Louisiana Office of Indian Affairs Board of Commissioners Meeting, 16 September 1982, 12–13, Indian Affairs File, LSA.

52. Houma Meeting Transcript, 5 June 1982, 6.

53. Helen Gindrat, Louisiana Office of Indian Affairs Board of Commissioners Meeting, 16 September 1982, 24–25, Indian Affairs File, LSA.

54. Meeting between tribal chairmen of Louisiana, Clifton, LA, 22 August 1981, 4.

55. Helen Gindrat to Senator Anthony Guarisco Jr., 25 June 1982, Indian Affairs Files, LSA.

56. Campos, LOIA Board of Commissioners Meeting, 16 September 1982, 22.

57. Meeting between tribal chairmen of Louisiana, Clifton, LA, 22 August 1981, 23.

58. Ibid., 16–17.

59. Jackson, "Executive Director's Report," 7 December 1983, 2.

60. Southwest Alabama Indian Affairs Commission, Second Quarter FY81 Progress Report, April 1981, 1, Indian Affairs Files, ADAH.

61. "Peterson Declares Right Now Is Most Crucial Time in Indian History," *Alabama Indian Advocate* 1, no. 1 (May 1981): 1, Indian Affairs Files, ADAH.

62. Quoted in "New Era for American Indians Begins in Alabama," *Alabama Indian Advocate* 1, no. 2 (June 1981): 1, Indian Affairs Files, ADAH.

63. "Last Friday . . . Jena Band of Choctaws Host Governor's Group," *Times-Signal*, 24 February 1988, 2A.

64. Diana Williamson to unknown recipient, 30 September 1987, Indian Affairs Files, LSA.

65. Memorandum, Ernest Sickey to Helen Gindrat, 1 September 1981, Indian Affairs Files, LSA.

66. Southwest Alabama Indian Affairs Commission, Second Quarter FY81 Progress Report, 1.

67. Framon Weaver to Governor Fob James, 11 May 1982, James Papers, ADAH.

68. Governor Guy Hunt to the Administration for Native Americans, Department of Health and Human Services, 16 October 1987, Hunt Papers, ADAH.

69. Quoted in "Tullis Re-Elected."

70. Southwest Alabama Indian Affairs Commission Official Meeting Minutes, 18 October 1980, 3, Indian Affairs Files, ADAH.

71. Jennie Lee Dees to the Members of the Southwest Alabama Indian Affairs Commission, 1 May 1980, Indian Affairs Files, ADAH.

72. Jennie Lee Dees, "The Southwest Alabama Indian Affairs Commission: A Two Year Plan of Development," 1980, Indian Affairs Files, ADAH.

73. Alabama Indian Affairs Report, [1980], 15.

74. The Indian agency invited anyone who was interested in learning more about the nature and extent of tribal sovereignty to contact them and borrow a sovereignty resource kit produced by the Institute for the Development of Indian Law. An information guide accompanied the kit on treaties and the meaning behind trust responsibility. "What Do You Know about Indian Sovereignty," *Alabama Indian Advocate* 1, no. 2 (June 1981): 7, Indian Affairs Files, ADAH.

75. Diane Weston, Southwest Alabama Indian Affairs Meeting Transcript, 8 January 1982, 3, Indian Affairs Files, ADAH.

76. Meeting between tribal chairmen of Louisiana, Clifton, LA, 22 August 1981, 11.

77. Ibid., 1; Louisiana Office of Indian Affairs 1981–1982 Activities Report, 11 May 1983, 5; Undersigned Sovereign American Indian Tribal Governments of Louisiana, "Building Bridges: Old Problems—Present Issues."

78. Campos, LOIA Board of Commissioners Meeting, 16 September 1982, 12–13.

79. Meeting between tribal chairmen of Louisiana, Clifton, LA, 22 August 1981, 4.

80. Sickey & Campos, LOIA Board of Commissioners Meeting, 16 September 1982, 9–11.

81. Fels, "Liberty and Justice for All?" 18.

82. Memorandum, Jane L. Weeks to All Members of the House of Representatives, State of Alabama, 2 April 1982, Indian Affairs Files, ADAH.

83. Bobby Joe Simmons to Helen Gindrat (Governor's Commission on Indian Affairs), 2 April 1982, Indian Affairs, LSA.

84. Garrison to Edwards, 15 March 1973.

85. Charles J. Monlezun (Coordinator of Program Planning and Interagency

Liaison) to Peter Mora (Director of Indian Affairs), 17 January 1977, Indian Affairs Files, LSA.

86. Jane Weeks to Sheila Parson, 16 December 1992, 2, Indian Affairs Files, ADAH.

87. Ibid.

88. Alabama Indian Affairs Commission Annual Report, 1984–85, 5.

89. Alabama Indian Affairs Report, [1980], 7.

90. Jane Weeks to Luther Black Bear, 2 March 1990, Indian Affairs Files, ADAH.

91. Although the commission did not begin to take a more active role in Indian education until 1981, it had sponsored a 1979 "Deep South Indian Education Conference" at Gulf Shores, inviting more than "300 educators and administrators from all academic levels. . . . in an effort to again stimulate the interest of local education agencies, as well as community colleges and universities." See Jennie Lee Dees to James Chasteen (John C. Calhoun Community College), 23 April 1981; Dees, "The Southwest Alabama Indian Affairs Commission," 3.

92. In May 1981, the executive director of the SAIAC attended a three-day training workshop in Atlanta on Indian Education Act programs. Upon returning she met with Parent Advisory Committees of Indian Education Projects in Jackson, Pike, and Washington counties to share relevant information and materials collected at the meeting. The SAIAC also began providing technical assistance to local educational agencies and community colleges in filing applications for special Indian education programs. Kerbs, "A Voice for Native Americans," 24; Alabama Indian Affairs Report, [1980], 8; Southwest Alabama Indian Affairs Commission, Progress Report, June 1981, 1; Alabama Indian Affairs Commission Annual Report, 1984–85, 6.

93. Alabama Indian Affairs Report, [1980], 9; Southwest Alabama Indian Affairs Commission, First Quarter FY81 Progress Report, 2.

94. *Alabama Indian Advocate* newsletter advertisement, 1981, Indian Affairs Files, ADAH.

95. Weeks to Luther Black Bear, 2 March 1990.

96. *Alabama Indian Advocate* newsletter advertisement, 1981; "The Cherokees of Jackson County Establish Council," *Alabama Indian Advocate* 1, no. 2 (June 1981): 4; "First Annual Tribal Conference of Jackson County Cherokee," *Alabama Indian Advocate* 1, no. 1 (May 1981): 4, Indian Affairs Files, ADAH.

97. Peter D. Mora III (Director of Indian Affairs) to the U.S. Office of Education, 23 January 1978, Indian Affairs Files, LSA.

98. Jackson, "Executive Director's Report," 7 December 1983, 5; Louisiana Governor's Commission on Indian Affairs Monthly Report, April 1987, 1, Indian Affairs Files, LSA.

99. Louisiana Department of Urban and Community Affairs Office of Indian

Affairs, "Dissemination of Information and Technical Assistance Concerning Educational and Social Service Resources to Louisiana Indian Communities," 4 June 1977, 2, Indian Affairs Files, LSA.

100. Louisiana Office of Indian Affairs, Economic Development Administration Project Description, March–May 1975, 6; Louisiana Department of Urban and Community Affairs Office of Indian Affairs, "Dissemination of Information and Technical Assistance," 4 June 1977, 1.

101. "Indian Scholarship Granted to Brothers," *Lake Charles American Press*, 25 October 1973, 8.

102. Department of Urban and Community Affairs Office of Community Services Governor's Commission on Indian Affairs, "Higher Education Assistance Program Notice of Intent," 1979, 2, Indian Affairs Files, LSA.

103. Minutes from meeting of Board of Commissioners held at DUCA in Baton Rouge, 17 October 1981, 17.

104. Louisiana Office of Indian Affairs 1981–1982 Activities Report, 11 May 1983, 4.

105. Louisiana Office of Indian Affairs Qualifications & Certifications Meeting Minutes, 20 April 1982, 4–7, Indian Affairs Files, LSA.

106. Louisiana Board of Commissioners Meeting, 12 July 1983, 1, Indian Affairs Files, LSA.

107. Ibid.

108. Louisiana Governor's Commission on Indian Affairs Board of Commissioners Meeting Minutes, 29 December 1983, 1, Indian Affairs File, LSA.

109. Jackson, "Executive Director's Report," 7 December 1983, 6.

110. Sonnier, "Government Regulations Complicate Lives of Louisiana Indians," 6-A.

111. Clyde Jackson to Louisiana's Tribal Chairmen, 23 January 1985; Memorandum, Clarence Cunningham (undersecretary, DUCA) to Clyde Jackson, 7 February 1985, Indian Affairs Files, LSA.

112. Dorothy Mae Taylor (secretary of DUCA) to Senator Leonard J. Chabert, 6 March 1985, Indian Affairs Files, LSA.

113. "Declaration of Support," signed by Ernest Sickey (Coushatta), Larry Burgess (Chitimacha), Kirby Verret (United Houma Nation), Hester Escott (Apache-Choctaw Tribe), George Allen (Jena Band of Choctaw), Manuel Tyler (Clifton-Choctaw Community), David Broome (Louisiana Band of Choctaws), and Earl Barbry (Tunica-Biloxi), January 1985, Indian Affairs Files, LSA.

114. Louisiana Governor's Commission on Indian Affairs Monthly Report, September 1986, 1, Indian Affairs Files, LSA.

115. Louisiana Governor's Commission on Indian Affairs Monthly Report, December 1986, 1; Louisiana Governor's Commission on Indian Affairs Monthly Report, September 1987, 1, Indian Affairs Files, LSA.

116. Louisiana Governor's Commission on Indian Affairs Monthly Report, September 1987, 1; Memorandum, Louisiana Governor's Commission on Indian Affairs to the tribal chairmen, 26 February 1988, Indian Affairs Files, LSA.

117. Louisiana Governor's Commission on Indian Affairs Monthly Report, December 1987, 1, Indian Affairs Files, LSA.

118. "Need Education Assistance?" *Alabama Indian Advocate* 1, no. 3 (July–August 1981): 6, Indian Affairs Files, ADAH.

119. Southwest Alabama Indian Affairs Commission Executive Director's Report of Activities, October and November 1980, 3, Indian Affairs Files, ADAH.

120. Alabama Indian Affairs Commission Annual Report, 1984–85, 10.

121. Jean Alexandra Webb (assistant attorney general) to Jane Weeks, 7 October 1985, Indian Affairs Files, ADAH.

122. Alabama Indian Affairs Commission Annual Report, 1986–87, 5–6.

123. Alabama Indian Affairs Commission Annual Report, 1990–91, 3; Alabama Indian Affairs Commission Annual Report, 1994–95, 2, Indian Affairs Files, ADAH.

124. Minutes from meeting of Board of Commissioners held at DUCA in Baton Rouge, 17 October 1981, 18.

125. "American Indians at Work in Alabama: A Day with Deputy Sheriff Jack Rivers," *Alabama Indian Advocate* 1, no. 2 (June 1981): 4, Indian Affairs Files, ADAH.

126. Ibid.

127. Louisiana Office of Indian Affairs 1981–1982 Activities Report, 11 May 1983, 4; Dette Rainwater (chairperson of the Louisiana Band of Choctaws) to Alexander MacNabb (director of the Division of Native American Programs, U.S. Department of Labor Employment Training Programs), 22 February 1978; Raymond Ebarb (chairman of the Choctaw-Apache Community of Ebarb) to Alexander MacNabb, 24 February 1978; John Billiot (president of the Indian Angels) to Alexander McNabb, 20 February 1978; Amos Tyler (president of the Clifton-Choctaw Reservation) to Alexander McNabb, 24 February 1978, Indian Affairs Files, LSA.

128. Federal attempts to deal with unemployment and unskilled workers date back to the passage of the Vocational Education Program in 1917 and the Vocational Rehabilitation Act in 1920. Then, throughout the 1930s, the federal government funded a series of New Deal programs aimed at addressing the record high unemployment. World War II, the postwar boom, and the Korean War delayed further employment legislation. In 1962 the Manpower Development and Training Act (MDTA) was passed to retain workers whose jobs had been eliminated by technological advancements. The War on Poverty resulted in the 1963 Economic Opportunity Act (EOA), which was umbrella legislation encompassing programs such as Job Corps, Neighborhood Youth Corps, Community Action

Programs, and the Summer Youth Employment Program. The emphasis of these earlier programs was on training workers rather than increasing job availability. In 1971 President Richard Nixon changed this trend with the passage of the Emergency Employment Act (EEA), which provided increased job opportunities to the nation's unemployed. By the time CETA was passed a few years later, the federal government attempted to incorporate elements of the MDTA and EOA by providing training and employment availability. See U.S. Department of Labor, "Brief History of DOL," and New Mexico Department of Labor, "Workforce Investment Act History."

129. "Inter-Tribal Council of Louisiana, Inc." description, [1979], Indian Affairs Files, LSA.

130. The Inter-Tribal Council of Louisiana, "Indians of Louisiana," 1977, 24, Indian Affairs Files, LSA.

131. Jennie Lee Dees, Southwest Alabama Indian Affairs Commission Special Meeting Minutes, 20 January 1982, 10, Indian Affairs Files, ADAH.

132. Jennie Dees, "Comments by the Executive Director," *Alabama Indian Advocate* 1, no. 2 (June 1981): 2, Indian Affairs Files, ADAH.

133. Southwest Alabama Indian Affairs Commission, First Quarter FY81 Progress Report, 1.

134. "Employment and Training Opportunities of the Indian CETA Program," *Alabama Indian Advocate* 1, no. 2 (June 1981): 3, Indian Affairs Files, ADAH. To supplement their efforts in addressing unemployment, the Poarch Creek Council obtained assistance or subcontracts from the Division of Indian and Native American Programs (DINAP), the Department of Health, Education, and Welfare's Office of Indian Education and Human Development's Office of Native American Programs, and the Administration for Native Americans.

135. "Getting Recognized: Wade Black and Robert Thrower Co-Producers," http://www.mindspring.com/~bozartmt/GR.html (accessed 30 October 2005).

136. Alabama Indian Affairs Report, [1980], 10.

137. "Peterson Declares Right Now Is Most Crucial Time in Indian History," *Alabama Indian Advocate* 1, no. 1 (May 1981): 1, Indian Affairs Files, ADAH.

138. Southwest Alabama Indian Affairs Commission, First Quarter FY81 Progress Report, 5.

139. Alabama Indian Affairs Report, [1980], 8.

140. Alabama Indian Affairs Report, May 1981, 1, Indian Affairs Files, ADAH.

141. "Summer Jobs for Indian Youth," *Alabama Indian Advocate* 1, no. 2 (June 1981): 3, Indian Affairs Files, ADAH.

142. "Attention Indian Youth," *Alabama Indian Advocate* 1, no. 4 (September–October 1981): 8, Indian Affairs Files, ADAH.

143. See New Mexico Department of Labor, "Workforce Investment Act History."

144. Memo, Indian and Native American CETA Coalition to All Coalition Subscribers, 12 March 1982, Indian Affairs Files, LSA.

145. The newly formed block grants included: Preventive Health; Maternal & Child Health; Alcohol, Drug Abuse & Mental Health; Primary Care; Social Services; Community Services; and Energy Assistance. See Conlan, "Back in Vogue" and *New Federalism to Devolution;* minutes from meeting held at DUCA with the Dallas Regional Office, 24 September 1981, 1, Indian Affairs Files, LSA.

146. Minutes from meeting held at DUCA with the Dallas Regional Office, 24 September 1981, 2.

147. Clyde Jackson, Louisiana Office of Indian Affairs Meeting Transcript, [1980], 2, Indian Affairs Files, LSA.

148. Louisiana Governor's Commission on Indian Affairs Block Grant Forum, 7 December 1981, 1, Indian Affairs Files, LSA.

149. "Direct Block Grants to Indian Tribes," *Alabama Indian Advocate* 1, no. 4 (September–October 1981), 1, 7, Indian Affairs Files, ADAH.

150. Ibid., 7.

151. Louisiana Governor's Commission on Indian Affairs Block Grant Forum, 7 December 1981, 1.

152. Meeting of the Board of Commissioners on Louisiana Indian Affairs, 17 October 1981, Indian Affairs Files, LSA.

153. Ibid., 1.

154. Ibid., 6–7.

155. Meeting between tribal chairmen of Louisiana, Clifton, LA, 22 August 1981, 7.

156. Although CETA was replaced by the 1982 Job Training Partnership Act (JTPA), which provided some funding for the continuation of job-training programs, Indian leaders felt that they had lost some of the autonomy that they had enjoyed with CETA since the states took a more active role in the program. See Urban Institute, "Block Grants"; Farber, "Federalism and State-Local Relations," 27–50; and Patricia Schilling (administrative assistant) to Mildred Smith, 20 April 1982, Indian Affairs, LSA.

157. Helen Gindrat, Louisiana Office of Indian Affairs Board of Commissioners Meeting, 3 April 1982, 2, Indian Affairs Files, LSA.

158. Minutes from meeting of Board of Commissioners held at DUCA in Baton Rouge, 17 October 1981, 13; Louisiana Governor's Commission on Indian Affairs, 17 December 1981, 1, Indian Affairs Files, LSA.

159. Louisiana Office of Indian Affairs Meeting Minutes, 17 December 1981, 2, Indian Affairs Files, LSA.

160. Ibid., 11.

161. Louisiana Governor's Commission on Indian Affairs Block Grant Forum, 7 December 1981, 3.

162. Louisiana Office of Indian Affairs Meeting Minutes, 17 December 1981, 3.

163. "Government Relationship to Tribes."

164. Leonard Hudson, Southwest Alabama Indian Affairs Meeting Transcript, 8 January 1982, 18, Indian Affairs Files, ADAH.

165. Southwest Alabama Indian Affairs Commission, Progress Report, June 1981, 5, Indian Affairs Files, ADAH.

166. In 1993 the VISTA program, along with the National Civilian Community Corps Programs, were incorporated into the newly formed AmeriCorps program. See "Corporation for National and Community Service," http://www .nationalservice.org/about/role_impact/history.asp (accessed 4 June 2006).

167. Southwest Alabama Indian Affairs Commission, First Quarter FY81 Progress Report, 3.

168. Memorandum to SAIAC from Jennie Lee Dees, June 1981, Indian Affairs Files, ADAH.

169. Memorandum, Jennie Lee Dees to Southwest Alabama Commission Members, 22 February 1982, Indian Affairs Files, ADAH.

170. Some of these companies included the Olin Chemical Company, Alabama Dry Docks and Shipbuilding Company, the Alabama State Docks, the National Weather Service, the Federal Aviation Administration, Eastern Airlines, and the South Central Bell Telephone Company.

171. "Choctaw Youth Examine Career Opportunities," *Alabama Indian Advocate* 1, no. 2 (June 1981): 3, Indian Affairs Files, ADAH.

172. Southwest Alabama Indian Affairs Commission, Second Quarter FY81 Progress Report, 1.

173. Campos, LOIA Board of Commissioners Meeting, 16 September 1982, 16.

174. Meeting between tribal chairmen of Louisiana, Clifton, LA, 22 August 1981, 24.

175. Alabama Indian Affairs Commission Annual Report, 1989–90, 8.

176. Helen Gindrat to Charlie Smith, 11 June 1982, Indian Affairs File, LSA.

177. CETA was replaced by the Job Training Partnership Act (JTPA), which was then replaced by the Workforce Investment Act (WIA) in 2000.

178. Alabama Inter-Tribal Council, Workforce Investment Act flyer, 2001.

179. Louisiana Office of Indian Affairs, Economic Development Administration Project Description, March–May 1975.

180. Ibid., 9; Louisiana Office of Indian Affairs, Louisiana Indian Community Development Project Description, 1 June–31 August 1974, 2, Indian Affairs Files, LSA.

181. Choctaw-Apache Community of Ebarb, Summary of Community Needs, 29 July 1979, Indian Affairs Files, LSA.

182. Southwest Alabama Indian Affairs Commission, First Quarter FY81 Progress Report, 5.

183. Southwest Alabama Indian Affairs Commission, Proposed Budget, 9 February 1981, 1, Indian Affairs Files, ADAH.

184. Southwest Alabama Indian Affairs Commission, First Quarter FY81 Progress Report, 2.

185. Alabama Indian Affairs Report, [1980], 8.

186. "New Training Center Facility for the Poarch Band of Creeks," *Alabama Indian Advocate* 1, no. 2 (June 1981): 6, Indian Affairs Files, ADAH.

187. "Indian Crafts Received with Enthusiasm," *Alabama Indian Advocate* 1, no. 1 (May 1981): 3, Indian Affairs Files, ADAH.

188. Ibid.

189. "Comments by the Executive Director," *Alabama Indian Advocate* 1, no. 3 (July–August 1981): 2; Southwest Alabama Indian Affairs Commission, Official Meeting Minutes, 9 January 1981, 2, Indian Affairs Files, ADAH.

190. "Attention Indian Artists and Craftsmen," *Alabama Indian Advocate* 1, no. 4 (September–October 1981): 8, Indian Affairs Files, ADAH.

191. Southwest Alabama Indian Affairs Commission, Proposed Budget, 9 February 1981, 4.

192. Southwest Alabama Indian Affairs Commission, Official Meeting Minutes, 6 March 1981, 2, Indian Affairs Files, ADAH.

193. Alabama Indian Affairs Report, [1980], 14.

194. Southwest Alabama Indian Affairs Commission, Official Meeting Minutes, 9 January 1981, 2, Indian Affairs Files, ADAH.

195. Southwest Alabama Indian Affairs Commission, Official Meeting Minutes, 18 October 1980, 3, Indian Affairs Files, ADAH.

196. Darden, Meeting Transcript, 17 October 1981, 10.

197. Minutes from meeting of Board of Commissioners held at DUCA in Baton Rouge, 17 October 1981, 11.

198. Ernest Sickey to Senator John Saunders, 2 September 1982; Ernest Sickey to Clyde Jackson (LOIA), 14 September 1982, both in Indian Affairs Files, LSA.

199. Helen Gindrat, United Houma Nation Council Meeting Transcript, 5 June 1982, 20, Indian Affairs Files, LSA

200. Houma Meeting Transcript, 5 June 1982, 13.

201. Ibid., 19.

202. Jeanette Campos, United Houma Nation Council Meeting Transcript, 5 June 1982, 20.

203. Houma Meeting Transcript, 5 June 1982, 11–12.

204. Jackson, "Executive Director's Report," 7 December 1983, 3.

205. Houma Meeting Transcript, 5 June 1982, 1–2, 8, 14.

206. Ernest Sickey to Helen Gindrat, 22 April 1982, Indian Affairs Files, LSA.

207. Houma Meeting Transcript, 5 June 1982, 13. The first Institute of Indian Development Board of Trustees included Clyde Jackson (chairman), Ernest Sickey (vice chairman), and Earl Barbry (secretary/treasurer).

208. Ibid., 22.

209. Louisiana Governor's Commission on Indian Affairs, FY 1986–87 Governor's Report, 3, Indian Affairs Files, LSA.

210. Louisiana Governor's Commission on Indian Affairs Monthly Report, August 1987, 1, Indian Affairs Files, LSA.

211. Ibid.; State of Louisiana Governor's Commission on Indian Affairs, Community Services Block Grant Report, 1988–89, 1, Indian Affairs Files, LSA.

212. Louisiana Governor's Commission on Indian Affairs Monthly Report, May 1987, 1, Indian Affairs Files, LSA.

213. Louisiana Governor's Commission on Indian Affairs Monthly Report, July 1987, 1, Indian Affairs Files, LSA.

214. Louisiana Governor's Commission on Indian Affairs Monthly Report, August 1987, 1; State of Louisiana Governor's Commission on Indian Affairs, Community Services Block Grant Report, 1988–89, 1.

215. Louisiana Governor's Commission on Indian Affairs Weekly Report, 25 May 1990, 1, Indian Affairs Files, LSA.

216. Alabama Indian Affairs Commission Annual Report, 1984–85, 7.

217. Alabama Indian Affairs Commission Annual Report, 1989–90, 6.

218. Alabama Indian Affairs Commission Annual Report, 1984–85, 8.

219. Alabama Indian Affairs Commission Annual Report, 1986–87, 4.

220. Ibid., 5.

221. Ibid.

222. Ibid., 6.

223. Alabama Indian Affairs Commission Annual Report, 1987–88, 4.

224. Alabama Indian Affairs Commission Annual Report, 1988–89, 6.

225. Alabama Indian Affairs Commission Annual Report, 1987–88, 7.

226. Meeting between tribal chairmen of Louisiana, Clifton, LA, 22 August 1981, 10–12.

227. Gindrat, Louisiana Office of Indian Affairs Board of Commissioners Meeting, 3 April 1982, 13.

228. It was not until 1987 that at least three tribal governments in Alabama explored the possibility of opening care facilities for the elderly within their communities. See Alabama Indian Affairs Commission Annual Report, 1987–88, 7; "Discontinuation of Legal Services Corporation," *Alabama Indian Advocate* 1, no. 1 (May 1981): 4, Indian Affairs Files, ADAH.

229. "Health Fair Completed in Choctaw Indian Community," *Alabama Indian Advocate* 1, no. 3 (July–August 1981): 5, Indian Affairs Files, ADAH.

230. The urgent need for quality health care was reinforced following a 1985 Mississippi State University study of the Mississippi Choctaw, which concluded that the average American Indian lived approximately ten years fewer than the average white person in the United States (the average life span of an Indian was sixty-five years as opposed to seventy-five years for a white person). The study paid special attention to the social and psychological aspects that contribute to the average life span. See "Experts Study Indians' Lifespans," *Morning Advocate (Baton Rouge)*, 7 October 1985.

231. Alabama Indian Affairs Commission Annual Report, 1984–85, 7.

232. Minutes from meeting held at DUCA with the Dallas Regional Office, 24 September 1981, 1, Indian Affairs Files, LSA.

233. Jennie Lee Dees, "Synopsis of Status of Southwest Alabama Indian Affairs Commission," 10 April 1980, 2; Southwest Alabama Indian Affairs Commission, Official Minutes, 10 April 1980, 2, Indian Affairs Files, ADAH.

234. Louisiana Governor's Commission on Indian Affairs Monthly Report, December 1986, 1, Indian Affairs Files, LSA.

235. Louisiana Governor's Commission on Indian Affairs Board of Commissioners Meeting Minutes, 29 December 1983, 1; Louisiana Board of Commissioners' Meeting, 12 July 1983, 1; Governor's Commission on Indian Affairs Proposal for Emergency Food & Shelter Program, 13 July 1983, Indian Affairs Files, LSA.

236. Alabama Indian Affairs Commission Annual Report, 1986–87, 6.

237. Louisiana Office of Indian Affairs 1981–1982 Activities Report, 11 May 1983, 8; Memorandum, Matt Isch to Bill Nungesser, 28 July 1978, Indian Affairs Files, LSA; Louisiana Office of Indian Affairs Minutes, 24 September 1973; Garrison to Edwards, 6 June 1972.

238. Meeting between tribal chairmen of Louisiana, Clifton, LA, 22 August 1981, 9.

239. Southwest Alabama Indian Affairs Commission, Official Minutes, 29 May 1981, 2, Indian Affairs Files, ADAH.

240. "Carpentry Training and Energy Conservation," *Alabama Indian Advocate* 1, no. 1 (May 1981): 3, Indian Affairs Files, ADAH.

241. Southwest Alabama Indian Affairs Commission, Second Quarter FY81 Progress Report, 1.

242. "Carpentry Training and Energy Conservation," 3.

243. Southwest Alabama Indian Affairs Commission, Progress Report, June 1981, 2, Indian Affairs Files, ADAH.

244. Framon Weaver to Governor Fob James, 11 May 1982, James Papers, ADAH.

245. Southwest Alabama Indian Affairs Commission, Progress Report, June 1981, 2.

Chapter 5

1. F. Carter, *The Education of Little Tree.*

2. D. Carter, "The Transformation of a Klansman."

3. In a 1995 opinion paper, Central Washington English graduate student Clayton M. Darwin argued that Carter did not intend to misrepresent himself as an Indian but rather used an "Indian theme" to represent Appalachian cultural philosophies and worldview. See Darwin, "Now, This Is a True Story."

4. D. Carter, *The Politics of Rage,* 296.

5. Owens, *Mixedblood Messages,* 44; Gates, "'Authenticity' of the Lesson of Little Tree."

6. As Joel W. Martin points out, "Southerners associate Removal first and foremost with the Cherokees, thus displaying a selective historical memory. This bias is reflected in another way. Even when history and geography might suggest an Indian ancestor from a different group or none at all, an astonishing number of southerners assert they have a grandmother or great-grandmother who was some kind of Cherokee, often a 'princess.'" Martin, "'My Grandmother Was a Cherokee Princess,'" 143.

7. Asa Carter was connected to a 1956 attack on Nat King Cole during a Birmingham, Alabama, performance. He was also allegedly involved in the brutal beating and castration of Edward Aaron, an African American man targeted by Carter and his fellow Klansmen. Finally, police also connected Carter to the shooting of three former Klansmen who questioned his extremism.

8. Justice, "A Lingering Miseducation," 29.

9. Calvin Reid, "Widow of 'Little Tree' Admits He Changed Identity," *Publishers Weekly,* 25 October 1991, 16.

10. For example, see Hobson, *The Last of the Ofos,* and J. Ellis, *Walking the Trail.*

11. Speech by Governor Buddy Roemer to the Southern Legislative Conference, 24 August 1988, Roemer Papers, LSA.

12. The concept of "social forgetting" was initially developed by Iwona Irwin-Zarecka in *Frames of Remembrance,* 13–14. The term was then applied to the white-centric manner in which southern plantation museums glossed over slavery in order to celebrate white male culture in the antebellum period. See Eichstedt and Small, *Representations of Slavery,* 1.

13. "Comments by the Executive Director," 2.

14. See Neely, "Adaptation and the Contemporary North Carolina Cherokee Indians," and Mechling, "Florida Seminoles and the Marketing of the Last Frontier."

15. Unknown speaker, Houma Meeting Transcript, 5 June 1982, 21.

16. H. L. Martin, Alabama Indian Affairs Commission Meeting Transcript, 8 January 1982, 4, Indian Affairs Files, ADAH.

17. Louisiana Office of Indian Affairs Community Development Report, 1 March–31 May 1975, 9, Indian Affairs, LSA.

18. Campos, Meeting Transcript, 5 June 1982, 10–11.

19. Houston McGhee to Governor George Wallace, 10 May 1974, 3, Indian Affairs Files, ADAH.

20. Garrison to Edwards, 15 March 1973.

21. Alabama Indian Affairs Commission, FY81 proposed budget and program description, 9 February 1981, 5, Indian Affairs Files, ADAH.

22. "Tribes Gather in Houma for Pow Wow," *Morning Advocate,* 3 August 1987, 6A.

23. Leslie Lord to LOIA director of Indian affairs, July 28, 1981, Indian Affairs, LSA.

24. Campos, Meeting Transcript, 5 June 1982, 10–11.

25. Eddie Tullis, Alabama Indian Affairs Commission Meeting Transcript, 8 January 1982, 6, Indian Affairs Files, ADAH.

26. Jeannette Campos, Louisiana Office of Indian Affairs Meeting Transcript, 22 August 1981, 3, Indian Affairs, LSA.

27. Alvin Rainey Jr. to the Louisiana Office of Indian Affairs, 24 July 1981, Indian Affairs, LSA.

28. Jo. Whisenant to Helen Gindrat (LOIA), 13 October 1981, Indian Affairs, LSA.

29. Thomas E. Fleming, United Southern Missionary Church, to the Alabama Indian Affairs Commission, 3 November 1980, Indian Affairs Files, ADAH.

30. Jennie Lee Dees to Thomas E. Fleming, 25 November 1980, Indian Affairs Files, ADAH.

31. Helen Gindrat, LOIA Meeting Transcript from Clifton, Louisiana, 22 August 1981, 3, Indian Affairs, LSA.

32. "Indian Education: Problems in Need of Resolution," *Alabama Indian Advocate* (May 1981): 6, Indian Affairs Files, ADAH.

33. Ray Formanek Jr., "Loss of La.'s Past Causes Concern," *Sunday Advocate (Baton Rouge),* 3 February 1985, 5-D.

34. Mack White to Governor Fob James, 25 September 1982, James Papers, ADAH.

35. Jeff Cowart, "Indian Graveyard Reported Damaged," *Town Talk,* 3 March 1975.

36. Jeff Cowart, "Bulldozers and Graveyards," *Town Talk,* 9 March 1975.

37. Alabama Indian Affairs Commission Annual Report, 1984–85, 4.

38. Formanek, "Loss of La.'s Past Causes Concern."

39. Joe Atkins, "Mounds Have Day on Hill," *News-Star-World,* 8 April 1987, Indian Affairs, LSA.

40. "Bell Notes: Visit Louisiana's State Parks" Flyer (198?), Indian Affairs, LSA.

41. For a rich discussion on the impact of cultural imperialism, see Meyer and Royer, *Selling the Indian;* Bird, *Dressing in Feathers;* Stedman, *Shadows of the Indian;* P. Deloria, *Playing Indian;* Berkhofer, *The White Man's Indian;* and Churchill, *Fantasies of the Master Race* and *Indians Are Us?*

42. Sickey quoted in Thompson, "Louisiana Indian Tribes."

43. See Wilson, "Disputable Truths," and Brasell, "Imag(in)ing the American South in Documentary Film and Video."

44. "Sickey Waves No Flags."

45. "Indians Learning Art of Basket Weaving through State Program."

46. David L. Garrison to Ruth Miller, 23 May 1973, Indian Affairs, LSA; "Coushatta Indian Basket Exhibition to Open Sunday," *Times-Picayune (New Orleans),* 11 July 1973, sec. 2, p. 2.

47. "Indian Arts Show Opens at Museum," *Lake Charles American Press,* 13 October 1973.

48. "WBR Museum to Host Louisiana Indian Exhibit," *Sunday Magazine (Baton Rouge),* 12 April 1987.

49. Lane Crockett, "Indian Art Coming in SRAC Exhibition," *Times (Shreveport-Bossier),* 8 September 1983, 7-B.

50. Memorandum, Jack Faller to Suzian Martin, 25 May 1990, Indian Affairs, LSA.

51. Louisiana Governor's Commission on Indian Affairs weekly report, 21–25 May 1990, Indian Affairs, LSA.

52. Louisiana Governor's Commission on Indian Affairs, "Social and Economic Progress," in *Indians of Louisiana* (198?), 15, Indian Affairs, LSA.

53. Unknown speaker, Houma Meeting Transcript, 5 June 1982, 21.

54. Campos, Meeting Transcript, 5 June 1982, 21.

55. Joe Billiot (festival chairman) to Helen Gindrat (LOIA), 8 March 1982, Indian Affairs, LSA.

56. Louisiana Office of Indian Affairs report, 30 April 1990, Indian Affairs, LSA.

57. Louisiana Office of Indian Affairs Board of Commissioners Meeting Transcript, 16 September 1982, 25, Indian Affairs, LSA.

58. "Forum Will Cover Influence of Indians in South Louisiana," *Daily Advertiser,* 21 April 1987.

59. For a discussion on the origin and meaning of powwow culture, see Mattern, "The Powwow as a Public Arena," and C. Ellis, *A Dancing People.*

60. Lerch, "State-Recognized Indians of North Carolina," 77.

61. Rountree, "Indian Virginians on the Move," 21–22; Goertzen, "Powwows and Identity on the Piedmont and Coastal Plains of North Carolina."

62. "Thanksgiving Day Pow-wow," *Alabama Indian Advocate* (September–October 1981): 8, Indian Affairs Files, ADAH.

63. See Schackt, "Mayahood through Beauty"; Lisa Jones, "Crowning Miss Navajo," *New York Times Magazine* 150, no. 51535 (8 October 2000), 32, 2p, 1c; Banet-Weiser, *Most Beautiful Girl in the World;* Wu, "Loveliest Daughter of Our Ancient Cathay!"

64. "Mowa Choctaw Indian Spring Festival," *Alabama Indian Advocate* 1, no. 1 (May 1981): 2, Indian Affairs Files, ADAH.

65. "Mowa Choctaw Spring Festival," *Alabama Indian Advocate* 1, no. 3 (July–August 1981): 4, Indian Affairs Files, ADAH.

66. "Indian Problems Discussed: Barnetts Attend Pow Wow," *The Observer (Baker, LA),* 10 February 1975.

67. David Broome, Louisiana Office of Indian Affairs Board of Commissioners Meeting Transcript, 16 September 1982, 25, Indian Affairs, LSA.

68. "Tribes Gather in Houma for Pow Wow," 6A.

69. "Princess Contest," *Lake Charles American Press,* 22 September 1972.

70. "Indian Tribe Plans Beauty Pageant," *American Press,* 10 April 1987, Indian Affairs, LSA.

71. "Memorial Service Honors Chief Calvin W. McGhee," *Alabama Indian Advocate* (June 1981): 7, Indian Affairs Files, ADAH.

72. Larrabee, *Grandmother Five Baskets.*

73. McClure, *Cherokee Proud* and *Oowala.*

74. Ruth Loyd Miller to Elvira Evans, managing editor of the *Basile Weekly,* 18 December 1972, Indian Affairs, LSA.

75. "Sickey Appointed," *Basile Weekly,* 27 December 1972.

76. Fels, "Liberty and Justice for All?" 15.

77. Ibid., 17.

78. Ibid., 64.

79. Marie Cromer, "State's Indian Affairs Bogged in Red Tape," *Birmingham News,* 12 November 1981.

80. Jennie Lee Dees, letter to the editor of the *Birmingham News,* 19 November 1981, 2, Indian Affairs Files, ADAH.

81. Leonard Hudson, Alabama Indian Affairs Commission Meeting Transcript, 8 January 1982, 30, Indian Affairs Files, ADAH.

82. Marie Cromer, Alabama Indian Affairs Commission Meeting Transcript, 8 January 1982, 30–31, Indian Affairs Files, ADAH.

83. Inter-Tribal Council of Louisiana, *Indians of Louisiana* [197?], Indian Affairs, LSA.

84. Lee Wise Jr. to the Louisiana Governor's Office, 29 April 1982, and Helen Gindrat (LOIA) to Lee Wise Jr., 3 June 1982, both in Indian Affairs, LSA.

85. Mrs. Bert Thornton to the Louisiana Office of Indian Affairs, 3 August

1982, and Helen Gindrat to Mrs. Bert Thornton, 12 August 1982, both in Indian Affairs, LSA.

86. Sally Ann Liska (St. Mark's School) to the Louisiana Governor's Office, 25 March 1982, and Helen Gindrat (LOIA) to Sally Ann Liska, 18 May 1982, both in Indian Affairs, LSA.

87. Debbie Powell to the director of LOIA, 14 January 1983, and Helen Gindrat (LOIA) to Debbie Powell, 25 January 1983, both in Indian Affairs, LSA.

88. "Tracing Your Family Tree," *Native Americans of Louisiana* (1989), 31, Indian Affairs, LSA.

89. Memorandum, Diana Williamson (executive director, GCOIA) to Dennis Stine (commissioner, DOA), 3 August 1988, Indian Affairs, LSA.

90. Buddy Roemer, dedication to *Native Americans of Louisiana* (1989), 2.

91. Ferguson, *Contemporary Native Americans in South Carolina.*

92. Quoted in *Sunday Magazine (Baton Rouge),* 20 March 1988, 21, Indian Affairs, LSA.

93. "The Tale of Granny Dollar: Famous DeKalb Indian," *DeKalb Legend* (May 1972), 24, University of Alabama, Birmingham.

94. Alabama Indian Affairs Commission, Progress Report, April 1981, 1, Indian Affairs Files, ADAH.

95. Alabama Indian Affairs Commission, FY81 proposed budget and program description, 2.

96. "Unlearning 'Indian' Stereotypes," *Alabama Indian Advocate* (May 1981): 6, Indian Affairs Files, ADAH.

97. "Open Letter to Non-Indian Teachers," *Alabama Indian Advocate* (July–August 1981): 7, Indian Affairs Files, ADAH.

98. Garrison to Edwards, 6 June 1972, 2.

99. Louisiana Office of Indian Affairs Community Development Report, 1 March–31 May 1975, 2.

100. Alabama Indian Affairs Commission, Report of Activities, May 1981, 1, Indian Affairs Files, ADAH.

101. Southwest Alabama Indian Affairs Commission, First Quarter FY81 Progress Report, 2; "United to Save Parker's Island," *Alabama Indian Advocate* 1, no. 2 (June 1981): 2, Indian Affairs Files, ADAH.

102. "New Era for American Indians Begins in Alabama," *Alabama Indian Advocate* 1, no. 2 (June 1981): 1, 8, Indian Affairs Files, ADAH; Kerbs, "A Voice for Native Americans," 24.

103. "A Statement of Unity by American Indians in Alabama for the Acquisition of Parker's Island," 29 May 1981, Indian Affairs Files, ADAH.

104. Fob James quoted in "Parker's Island: Heritage for Sale" (presentation of the Alabama Indian Affairs Commission, [198?]); Alabama Indian Affairs Report, [1980], 8.

105. *Alabama Indian Advocate* pamphlet, 1981, Indian Affairs Files, ADAH.

106. Larry Oats quoted in "Parker's Island: Heritage for Sale."

107. Official Minutes of the Southwest Alabama Indian Affairs Commission, 18 September 1981; Southwest Alabama Indian Affairs Commission, Progress Report, June 1981, 1, Indian Affairs Files, ADAH. According to several reports in 1980 and 1981, the following agencies participated in the Parker's Island Acquisition Project: State Department of Conservation and Natural Resources, the Alabama Historical Commission, the Department of Archives and History, the State Environmental Quality Association, U.S. Administration for Native Americans, U.S. Department of Commerce, U.S. Department of Agriculture, the Nature Conservancy, and Alabama's Indian tribes, bands, and groups.

108. "Comments by the Executive Director," 8; "Contributions for Parker's Island," *Alabama Indian Advocate* (September–October 1981): 8, Indian Affairs Files, ADAH.

109. Southwest Alabama Indian Affairs Commission Meeting Minutes, 12 December 1980, 2, Indian Affairs Files, ADAH.

110. "Bank Presents Donation for Indian Museum," *LEAP,* 8 July 1974, Indian Affairs, LSA.

111. "Indian Ware Sale Set Saturday in Center," *Lake Charles American Press,* 22 September 1972, 42.

112. For more discussion on the relationships between Indians and the National Park Service, see Catton, *Inhabited Wilderness;* Spence, *Dispossessing the Wilderness;* and Keller and Turek, *American Indians and National Parks.*

113. National Park Service United States Department of the Interior, "Cooperative Agreement Between United Houma Nation, Inc. and Jean Lafitte National Historic Park," 15 July 1982, Indian Affairs Files, LSA.

114. Campos, Meeting Transcript, 5 June 1982, 25–26.

115. Hope J. Norman, "Revive the Pride of the Choctaw Indians," *Alexandria Daily Town Talk,* 3 March 1982.

116. "Indians Called Lafayette 'Home,'" [newspaper source unknown], 14 September 1987; "Chitimachas Plan Project," *Banner Tribune,* 13 May 1987; "Indians Consider Tourist Area," *State Times (Baton Rouge),* 18 May 1987, sec. C; "Panel Oks Indian Center at Rest Area," *Morning Advocate (Baton Rouge),* 28 May 1987, 11A; "House Votes to Give Rest Stop to Tribe," *Morning Advocate,* 12 June 1987, 13A; "Use of Area OK'd," *Morning Advocate,* 27 June 1987.

117. "Program on Louisiana Indians Presented," *Sunday Advocate,* 18 January 1985, 3-C.

118. Jan Tuveson (Florida Governor's Council on Indian Affairs) to "Friends," 10 June 1977, Indian Affairs Files, ADAH.

119. Since 1990 South Dakota has had an official holiday on the second Mon-

day in October for Native American Day, but the state does not recognize Columbus Day.

120. Phillip Rawls, "Alabama Makes Columbus Day Do Double Duty for Indians," *Associated Press State & Local Wire*, 1 June 2000; "Across the USA News from Every State," *USA Today*, 15 February 2000, 11A.

121. "Echota Cherokees at Horseshoe Bend," *Alabama Indian Advocate* (June 1981): 6, Indian Affairs Files, ADAH.

122. "Autumn Event at Fort Toulouse," *Alabama Indian Advocate* (September–October 1981): 6, Indian Affairs Files, ADAH.

123. Michael O'Hagan, "1,000 Bikes Follow Trail of Tears Route," *Chattanooga Free Press*, 21 September 1997, D1; "New Trail of Tears Marker Installed," *Chattanooga Times*, 19 September 1997, B6.

124. The first Trail of Tears Commemorative Ride was organized in 1993 with only about thirty participants. By 2000, the trip had become the largest organized motorcycle ride in the South.

125. Alabama Waterfowl Association, "Trail of Tears Designation," 6 May 1997, http://www.alabamawaterfowl.org/tot.htm (accessed 22 May 2001).

126. Dr. Robert Bouwman (Office of Indian Heritage, Georgia Department of Archives and History) to Jennie Lee Dees (AIAC), 9 December 1980, Indian Affairs Files, ADAH.

127. Ina S. Trout to Jennie Lee Dees, 26 September 1981, Indian Affairs Files, ADAH.

128. John Powell, "Chickasaw Hears Waste Report," *News-Herald (Chickasaw, AL)*, 27 August 1981.

129. Jennie Lee Dees to Ina Trout, 3 September 1981, Indian Affairs Files, ADAH.

130. Joseph C. Trahan (chief, Engineering and Planning Division of the Galveston District Corps of Engineers) to Clyde Jackson (LOIA), 23 April 1984, Indian Affairs, LSA.

131. Gilbert Gude (director of the Congressional Research Service, Library of Congress) to the Governor of the State of Louisiana, 10 February 1984, and LOIA to Richard Jones (Government Division of the Congressional Research Service), 16 February 1984, both in Indian Affairs, LSA.

132. Carol Wells to Helen Gindrat (LOIA), 19 May 1983, Indian Affairs, LSA.

133. Louisiana Governor's Commission on Indian Affairs Overview [198?], 2, Indian Affairs, LSA.

134. "Artifacts Survey Completed," *Sunday Advocate*, 16 August 1987, 2B; "Survey Near Completion on Indians," *Morning Advocate*, 25 June 1987, 6B.

135. Historic Preservation Planning Program, "Preserve Alabama."

136. Notes prepared by Diana Williamson on an informal meeting of the Board of Commissioners of the GCOIA, 26 February 1988, Indian Affairs, LSA.

137. Alabama Indian Affairs Commission, report of activities covering 1 October 1980–31 December 1980, submitted 6 February 1981, 4, Indian Affairs Files, ADAH.

138. "Senator Denton Announces Grant," *Alabama Indian Advocate* (June 1981): 7, Indian Affairs Files, ADAH.

139. "History of Alabama Indian Communities: The Cherokees of Jackson County," *Alabama Indian Advocate* (September–October 1981): 6, Indian Affairs Files, ADAH.

140. Notes from the Cherokees of Jackson County First Annual Meeting in Cherokee, NC, 27 March 1981, 1, Indian Affairs Files, ADAH.

141. "Cherokees of Jackson County" overview, date unknown, Indian Affairs Files, ADAH.

142. "A Concerned Taxpayer" to Governor Guy Hunt, August 1991, Indian Affairs Files, ADAH.

143. "Two Eagles Flying High," *Birmingham News,* December 1984, Indian Affairs Files, ADAH.

144. Alabama Bureau of Tourism and Travel, "Alabama Native American Trails," August 2002.

145. "Tribes Gather in Houma for Pow Wow," 6A.

Conclusion

1. Wilma Mankiller to Governor Guy Hunt, 4 January 1992, Hunt Papers, ADAH.

2. Roy Crazy Horse (Powhatan Nation) to Governor George C. Wallace, 23 March 1978, Wallace Papers, ADAH.

3. New Jersey Department of State, http://www.state.nj.us/state/american _indian/one/index.html (accessed 26 December 2006).

4. *Misty Mountain News* 1, no. 1 (July 1997): 3, emphasis in original.

References

Archival Materials

Alabama Department of Archives and History (ADAH), Montgomery

Alabama Indian Affairs Commission Files, 1977–90
Gov. Guy Hunt Papers, files on Indian affairs
Gov. Fob James Papers, files on Indian affairs
Gov. George C. Wallace Papers, files on Indian affairs
Digital Archives

Louisiana Secretary of State, Division of Archives, Records Management, and History, Baton Rouge (also referred to as the Louisiana State Archives [LSA])

Gov. Edwin Edwards Papers, files on Indian affairs
Louisiana Office of Indian Affairs, 1972–88, P1992-92, P1995-72
Gov. Buddy Roemer Papers, files on Indian affairs
Gov. David Treen Papers, files on Indian affairs

Louisiana State University, Baton Rouge

Louisiana Historical Photographs Collection of the State Library

Newspapers and News Agencies

Alabama Indian Advocate
Alexandria Daily Town Talk
Associated Press
Banner Tribune
Basile Weekly
Baton Rouge Enterprise
Birmingham News

Capitol News Bureau
Chattanooga Free Press
Chattanooga Times
Daily Advertiser
Daily Iberian (New Iberia, LA)
Fayetteville Times
Jennings Daily News
Lake Charles American Press
Misty Mountain News
Montgomery Advertiser
Morning Advocate (Baton Rouge)
News-Herald (Chickasaw, Alabama)
News-Star-World
New York Times
New York Times Magazine
The Observer (Baker, LA)
Publishers Weekly
State Times (Baton Rouge)
Sunday Advocate (Baton Rouge)
Tampa Times
Times (Shreveport-Bossier, LA)
Times-Picayune (New Orleans)
Times-Signal
Town Talk
USA Today
Winn Parish Enterprise

Films

Eyes on the Prize: America's Civil Rights Years. Dir. Judith Vecchione. WGBH Boston, Blackside, Inc., and the Corporation for Public Broadcasting. Alexandria, VA: PBS Video, 1986.

Oowala: Life and Light, Understanding and Friendship through Education. Dir. Tony Mack McClure. Somerville, TN: Chunannee Media Films, 2001.

The Chief Calvin McGhee and the Forgotten Creeks. Tuscaloosa: The University of Alabama Center for Public Television and Radio. 1995.

Other Sources Consulted

Ablon, Joan. "The American Indian Chicago Conference." *Journal of American Indian Education* 1, no. 2 (January 1962): 17–23.

Alabama State Senate. *MOWA Band of Choctaw Indians Recognition Act.* 103rd Cong., 1st Sess. Report 103-193 (November 1993).

Bailey, R. Clay. "The Strange Case of the Cajans." *Alabama School Journal* (April 1931): 8.

Banet-Weiser, Sarah. *Most Beautiful Girl in the World: Pageants and National Identity.* Berkeley: University of California Press, 1999.

Bass, Jack, and Walter DeVries. *The Transformation of Southern Politics: Social Change and Political Consequence since 1945.* New York: Basic Books, 1976.

Basson, Lauren L. *White Enough to Be American? Race Mixing, Indigenous People, and the Boundaries of State and Nation.* Chapel Hill: University of North Carolina Press, 2008.

Beale, Calvin. "American Triracial Isolates: Their Status and Pertinence to Genetic Research." *Eugenics Quarterly* 4, no. 4 (December 1957): 187–96.

Belknap, Michal R. *Federal Law and Southern Order: Racial Violence and Constitutional Conflict in the Post-Brown South.* Athens: University of Georgia Press, 1987.

Berkhofer, Robert F., Jr. *The White Man's Indian: Images of the American from Columbus to the Present.* New York: Vintage Books, 1978.

Berkowitz, Edward D. *America's Welfare State: From Roosevelt to Reagan.* Baltimore: Johns Hopkins University Press, 1991.

Berman, William C. *America's Right Turn: From Nixon to Clinton.* Baltimore: Johns Hopkins University Press, 1998.

Bernstein, Alison. *American Indians and World War II: Toward a New Era in Indian Affairs.* Norman: University of Oklahoma Press, 1991.

Berry, Brewton. *Almost White: A Study of Certain Racial Hybrids in the Eastern United States.* London: Collier Books, 1963.

Bettinger-Lopez, Caroline. *Cuban-Jewish Journeys: Searching for Identity, Home, and History in Miami.* Knoxville: University of Tennessee Press, 2000.

Biolsi, Thomas. *"Deadliest Enemies": Law and the Making of Race Relations on and off Rosebud Reservation.* Berkeley: University of California Press, 2001.

Bird, S. Elizabeth, ed. *Dressing in Feathers: The Construction of the Indian in American Popular Culture.* Boulder, CO: Westview Press, 1996.

Black, Earle, and Merle Black. *Politics and Society in the South.* Cambridge, MA: Harvard University Press, 1987.

Blu, Karen. *The Lumbee Problem: The Making of an American Indian People.* Cambridge: Cambridge University Press, 1980.

———. "'Reading Back' to Find Community: Lumbee Ethnohistory." In *North American Indian Anthropology: Essays on Society and Culture,* ed. Raymond J. DeMallie and Alfonso Ortez. Norman: University of Oklahoma Press, 1994. 278–95.

Bond, Horace M. "Two Racial Islands of Alabama." *American Journal of Sociology* 36 (January 1931): 552–67.

Bonney, Rachel A., and J. Anthony Paredes, eds. *Anthropologists and Indians in the New South*. Tuscaloosa: The University of Alabama Press, 2001.

Bordewich, Fergus M. *Killing the White Man's Indian: Reinventing Native Americans at the End of the Twentieth Century*. New York: Random House, 1996.

Bourgeois, Henry L. "Four Decades of Public Education in Terrebonne Parish." M.A. thesis, Louisiana State University, 1938.

Bowman, Greg, and Janel Curry-Roper. *The Forgotten Tribe: The Houma People of Louisiana*. Akron, PA: Mennonite Central Committee, 1982.

Brasell, Roger Bruce. "Imag(in)ing the American South in Documentary Film and Video." Ph.D. diss., New York University, 2000.

Brasseaux, Carl. *French, Cajun, Creole, Houma: A Primer on Francophone Louisiana*. Baton Rouge: Louisiana State University Press, 2005.

Brett, David. *The Construction of Heritage*. Cork, Ireland: Cork University Press, 1996.

Brown, Robert Paul. "'The Year One': The American Indian Chicago Conference of 1961 and the Rebirth of Indian Activism." M.A. thesis, University of Wisconsin–Eau Claire, 1993.

Bruyneel, Kevin. *The Third Space of Sovereignty: The Postcolonial Politics of U.S.-Indigenous Relations*. Minneapolis: University of Minnesota Press, 2007.

Campisi, Jack. *The Mashpee Indians: Tribe on Trial*. Syracuse: Syracuse University Press, 1991.

Carter, Dan T. *From George Wallace to Newt Gingrich: Race in the Conservative Counterrevolution, 1963–1994*. Baton Rouge: Louisiana State University Press, 1996.

———. *The Politics of Rage: George Wallace, the Origins of the New Conservatism, and the Transformation of American Politics*. Baton Rouge: Louisiana State University Press, 1995.

———. "The Transformation of a Klansman." *New York Times*, 4 October 1991, A31.

Carter, Forrest. *The Education of Little Tree*. 1976. Albuquerque: University of New Mexico, 1986.

Catton, Theodore. *Inhabited Wilderness: Indians, Eskimos, and National Parks in Alaska*. Albuquerque: University of New Mexico Press, 1997.

Center for Interactive Management. "Executive Summary of the Issue Management Forum for the Poarch Band of Creek Indians." Fairfax, VA: George Mason University, 14–17 July 1988.

Chafe, William. *Civilities and Civil Liberties: Greensboro, North Carolina, and the Black Struggle for Freedom*. Oxford: Oxford University Press, 1980.

Chin, Gabriel, et al. "Still on the Books: Jim Crow and Segregation Laws Fifty Years after *Brown v. Board of Education*: A Report on Laws Remaining in the Codes of Alabama, Georgia, Louisiana, Mississippi, Missouri, South Carolina, Virginia and West Virginia." *Michigan State Law Review* 2 (2006): 457–59.

Churchill, Ward. *Fantasies of the Master Race: Literature, Cinema and the Colonization of American Indians.* Monroe, ME: Common Courage Press, 1992.

———. *Indians Are Us? Culture and Genocide in North America.* Monroe, ME: Common Courage Press, 1994.

Clancy, Paul R. *Just a Country Lawyer: A Biography of Senator Sam Ervin.* Bloomington: Indiana University Press, 1974.

Clifford, James. *The Predicament of Culture: Twentieth Century Ethnography, Literature and Art.* Cambridge, MA: Harvard University Press, 1988.

Clifton, James, ed. *Being and Becoming Indian: Biographical Studies of North American Frontiers.* Chicago: Dorsey Press, 1989.

Cobb, Daniel M., and Loretta Fowler, eds. *Beyond Red Power: American Indian Politics and Activism since 1900.* Washington, DC: School for Advanced Research Press, 2007.

Cohen, Lucy M. *Chinese in the Post–Civil War South: A People without a History.* Baton Rouge: Louisiana State University Press, 1984.

Collier, Peter, and David Horowitz, eds. *The Race Card: White Guilt, Black Resentment, and the Assault on Truth and Justice.* Rocklin, CA: Prima Publishing, 1997.

Conlan, Timothy. "Back in Vogue: The Politics of Block Grant Legislation." *Intergovernmental Perspective* 7, no. 3 (1981): 8–15.

———. *New Federalism to Devolution: Twenty-Five Years of Intergovernmental Reform.* Washington, DC: Brookings Institution Press, 1998.

Cook, Samuel R. *Monacans and Miners: Native American and Coal Mining Communities in Appalachia.* Lincoln: University of Nebraska Press, 2000.

Cornell, Stephen E. *The Return of the Native: American Indian Political Resurgence.* New York: Oxford University Press, 1988.

Coushatta Tribe of Louisiana. "Red Shoes People." Elton, LA: Coushatta Tribe of Louisiana, 1999.

———. "The Struggle Has Made Us Stronger." Elton, LA: Coushatta Tribe of Louisiana, 1977.

Covington, James W. *The Seminoles of Florida.* Gainesville: University Press of Florida, 1993.

Cowger, Thomas W. *The National Congress of American Indians: The Founding Years.* Lincoln: University of Nebraska Press, 1999.

Crawford, Vicki L., Jacqueline Anne Rouse, and Barbara Woods, eds. *Women in the Civil Rights Movement: Trailblazers and Torchbearers, 1941–1965.* New York: Carlson, 1990.

Cromer, Marie West. *Modern Indians of Alabama: Remnants of Removal.* Birmingham: Southern University Press, 1984.

Curry-Roper, Janel. "A History of the Houma Indians and Their Story of Federal Nonrecognition." *American Indian Journal* 5, no. 2 (February 1979): 8–28.

Darwin, Clayton M. "Now, This Is a True Story." Information Analyses (070)—
Opinion Papers. December 1995. http://eric.ed.gov/PDFS/ED408117.pdf (accessed 21 April 2011).

Davis, Dave D. "A Case of Identity: Ethnogenesis of the New Houma Indians."
Ethnohistory 48, no. 3 (Summer 2001): 484–85.

Davis, Townsend. *Weary Feet, Rested Souls: A Guided History of the Civil Rights
Movement.* New York: Norton, 1998.

de Jong, Greta. *A Different Day: African American Struggles for Justice in Rural
Louisiana, 1900–1970.* Chapel Hill: University of North Carolina Press, 2002.

Deloria, Philip J. *Playing Indian.* New Haven: Yale University Press, 1998.

Deloria, Vine, Jr. *Custer Died for Your Sins: An Indian Manifesto.* New York: Mac-
millan Company, 1969.

———. "The Indian Movement: Out of a Wounded Past." *Ramparts* 13, no. 6
(March 1975): 28–32.

Deloria, Vine, Jr., and Clifford M. Lytle. *American Indians, American Justice.* Aus-
tin: University of Texas, 1983.

Dent, Tom. *Southern Journey: A Return to the Civil Rights Movement.* New York:
William Morrow and Company, 1997.

Department of Interior's Assistant Secretary of Indian Affairs. "Final Determination against Federal Acknowledgment of the Mobil-Washington County
Band of Choctaw Indians of South Alabama (MOWA)." Washington, DC.
http://www.doi.gov/bia/mowa-not.htm (accessed 16 December 1997).

Department of the Interior, Branch of Acknowledgement and Research, Bureau
of Indian Affairs. "Proposed Finding against Federal Acknowledgment of the
United Houma Nation." Washington, DC: Department of Interior, 22 December 1994.

Dial, Adolph L., and David K. Eliades. *The Only Land I Know: A History of the
Lumbee Indians.* San Francisco: Indian Historian Press, 1975.

Dittmer, John. *Local People: The Struggle for Civil Rights in Mississippi.* Urbana:
University of Illinois Press, 1994.

Dominguez, Virginia. *White by Definition: Social Classifications in Creole Louisiana.* New Brunswick, NJ: Rutgers University Press, 1986.

d'Oney, John Daniel. "A History of the Houma Nation, 1682–2002." Ph.D. diss.,
Arizona State University, 2002.

Downs, Ernest, and Jena Whitehead. "The Houma Indians: Two Decades in a
History of Struggle." *American Indian Journal* 2, no. 3 (March 1976): 2–18.

Duthu, Bruce. "Folklore of the Louisiana Houma Indians." *Louisiana Folklife* 4
(1979): 1–33.

———. "Future Light or Feu-Follet?" *Southern Exposure* 13, no. 6 (1985): 24–32.

———. "The Houma Indians of Louisiana: The Intersection of Law and History in the Federal Acknowledgement Process." *Louisiana History* 38, no. 4 (Fall 1997): 409–36.

Eagles, Charles W. "The Civil Rights Movement." In *A Companion to the American South*, ed. John B. Boles. Malden, MA: Blackwell, 2002: 461–73.

———. *Outside Agitator: Jon Daniels and the Civil Rights Movement in Alabama.* Chapel Hill: University of North Carolina Press, 2000.

Eichstedt, Jennifer L., and Stephen Small. *Representations of Slavery: Race and Ideology in Southern Plantation Museums.* Washington, DC: Smithsonian Institution Press, 2002.

Ellis, Clyde. *A Dancing People: Powwow Culture and the Southern Plains.* Lawrence: University of Kansas Press, 2003.

Ellis, Jerry. *Walking the Trail: One Man's Journey along the Cherokee Trail of Tears.* New York: Delta Trade Paperbacks, 1991.

Esber, George S., Jr. "Shortcomings of the Indian Self-Determination Policy." In *State & Reservation*, ed. George Pierre Castile and Robert L. Bee. Tucson: University of Arizona Press, 1992. 212–23.

Eskew, Glenn T. "George C. Wallace, 1963–1967, 1971–1979, 1983–1987." In *Alabama Governors: A Political History of the State*, ed. Samuel L. Webb and Margaret E. Armbrester. Tuscaloosa: University of Alabama Press, 2001: 216–34.

Fahey, John. *Saving the Reservation: Joe Garry and the Battle to Be Indian.* Seattle: University of Washington Press, 2001.

Faine, John R. *The Jena Band of Choctaws: An Assessment of the Status of a Louisiana Indian Tribe.* Baton Rouge: Institute for Indian Development, 1985.

———. *The Tunica-Biloxi: An Assessment of the Status of a Louisiana Indian Tribe.* Baton Rouge: Institute for Indian Development, 1986.

Faine, John R., and Edward Bohlander. *The Chitimacha Indians: An Assessment of the Status of a Louisiana Indian Tribe.* Baton Rouge: Institute for Indian Development, 1986.

Faine, John R., and Hiram F. Gregory. *The Apache-Choctaw of Ebarb.* Baton Rouge: Institute for Indian Development, 1986.

Fairclough, Adam. *Race & Democracy: The Civil Rights Struggle in Louisiana, 1915–1972.* Athens: University of Georgia Press, 1995.

———. *To Redeem the Soul of America: The Southern Christian Leadership Conference and Martin Luther King Jr.* Athens: University of Georgia Press, 1990.

Farber, Stephen. "Federalism and State-Local Relations." In *A Decade of Devolution: Perspectives on State-Local Relations*, ed. E. Blaine Liner. Washington, DC: Urban Institute Press, 1989, 27–50.

Fels, Margrett. "Liberty and Justice for All?" *Baton Rouge Magazine* (November 1986): 15, 17–18, 64.

Ferguson, Leland. *Contemporary Native Americans in South Carolina: A Photo*

Documentation Covering the Years 1983–1985. Charleston: Department of Anthropology, University of South Carolina, 1985.

Ferrara, Peter J. *The Choctaw Revolution: Lessons for Federal Indian Policy.* Washington, DC: Americans for Tax Reform Foundation, 1998.

Fixico, Donald L. *Termination and Relocation: Federal Indian Policy, 1945–1960.* Albuquerque: University of New Mexico Press, 1986.

———. *The Urban Indian Experience in America.* Albuquerque: University of New Mexico Press, 2000.

Forbes, Jack. *Africans and Native Americans: The Language of Race and the Evolution of Red-Black Peoples.* Urbana: University of Illinois Press, 1993.

Foster, Laurence. *Negro-Indian Relationships in the Southeast.* New York: AMS Press, 1978.

Gabriel, John. *White Wash: Racialized Politics and the Media.* New York: Routledge, 1998.

Gaillard, Frye. *Cradle of Freedom: Alabama and the Movement That Changed America.* Tuscaloosa: The University of Alabama Press, 2004.

Gates, Henry Louis, Jr. "'Authenticity,' or the Lesson of Little Tree." *New York Times Book Review* 24 (November 1991): sec. 7, 1.

Gercken-Hawkins, Rebecca. "Authentic Reservations: The Rhetorical War for Native American Identity." Ph.D. diss., University of Miami, 2001.

Gilbert, William Harlen, Jr. "Memorandum Concerning the Characteristics of the Larger Mixed-Blood Racial Islands of the Eastern United States." *Social Forces* 24 (1946): 438–47.

———. "Mixed Bloods of the Upper Monongahela Valley, West Virginia." *Journal of the Washington Academy of Sciences* 36 (1946): 1–13.

———. "Surviving Indian Groups of the Eastern United States." *Annual Report of the Smithsonian Institute.* Washington, DC, 1948.

Goertzen, Chris. "Powwows and Identity on the Piedmont and Coastal Plains of North Carolina." *Ethnomusicology* 45, no. 1 (Winter 2001): 58.

Goldfield, David R. *Black, White, and Southern: Race Relations and Southern Culture, 1940 to the Present.* Baton Rouge: Louisiana State University Press, 1990.

Grantham, Dewey W. *The South in Modern America: A Region at Odds.* New York: Harper Collins, 1994.

Green, Clatis. "Some Factors Influencing Cajun Education in Washington County, Alabama." M.A. thesis, The University of Alabama, 1941.

Greenbaum, Susan. "What's in a Label? Identity Problems of Southern Indian Tribes." *Journal of Ethnic Studies* 19, no. 2 (Summer 1991): 107–26.

Gregory, Hiram F. "The Louisiana Tribes: Entering Hard Times." In *Indians of the Southeastern United States in the Late 20th Century,* ed. J. Anthony Paredes. Tuscaloosa: The University of Alabama Press, 1992.

Gulf South Research Institute. "American Indians of Louisiana: An Assessment of Needs." Baton Rouge: Louisiana Office of Indian Affairs, 1972.

Hale, Grace Elizabeth. *Making Whiteness: The Culture of Segregation in the South, 1890–1940.* New York: Pantheon, 1998.

Hall, Michael, ed. *Whiteness: A Critical Reader.* New York: New York University Press, 1997.

Harmon, Alexandra. *Indians in the Making: Ethnic Relations and Indian Identities around Puget Sound.* Berkeley: University of California Press, 1998.

Hauptman, Laurence M. "There Are No Indians East of the Mississippi." In *Tribes & Tribulations: Misconceptions about American Indians and Their Histories.* Albuquerque: University of New Mexico Press, 1995, 93–108

Hauptman, Laurence M., and Jack Campisi. "Eastern Indian Communities Strive for Recognition." In *Major Problems in American Indian History,* 2nd ed., ed. Albert L. Hurtado and Peter Iverson. Boston: Houghton Mifflin, 461–71.

Hertzberg, Hazel W. *The Search for American Indian Identity: Modern Pan-Indian Movements.* Syracuse: Syracuse University Press, 1971.

Hill, Michael, ed. *Whiteness: A Critical Reader.* New York: New York University Press, 1997.

Historic Preservation Planning Program. "Preserve Alabama: Statewide Comprehensive Historic Preservation Plan." 12 July 1996. http://www2.cr.nps.gov/pad/stateplans/alabama.htm (accessed 29 July 2001).

Hobson, Geary. *The Last of the Ofos.* Tucson: University of Arizona Press, 2000.

Hodgson, Godfrey. *More Equal than Others: America from Nixon to the New Century.* Princeton: Princeton University Press, 2004.

Holmes, Hilary Herbert. "The So-Called Cajan Settlement in the Southern Part of Washington County, Alabama." Governors' papers (1923–27: Brandon), RC2: G156, Administrative Files Folder: "Cajan," ADAH.

Hudson, Charles M. "The Catawba Indians of South Carolina: A Question of Ethnic Survival." In *Southeastern Indians since the Removal Era,* ed. Walter L. Williams. Athens: University of Georgia Press, 1979, 110–22.

Indian Education Resources Center (Division of Program Review and Evaluation Branch of Curriculum). "Final Report: An Education Evaluation of the Choctaw and Chitimacha Schools." Evaluation Report Series No. 23 (14 December 1973). Linscheid Library, East Central University, Ada, OK.

Irwin-Zarecka, Iwona. *Frames of Remembrance: The Dynamics of Collective Memory.* New Brunswick, NJ: Transaction Publishers, 1994.

Johnson, Guy B. "Personality in a White-Negro-Indian Community." *American Sociological Review* 4 (1939): 138–55.

Johnson, Troy, Joane Nagel, and Duane Champagne, eds. *American Indian Activism: Alcatraz to the Longest Walk.* Urbana: University of Illinois Press, 1997.

Jolivette, Andrew. *Louisiana Creoles: Cultural Recovery and Mixed-Race Native American Identity*. Lanham, MD: Lexington Books, 2007.

Jonas, Gilbert. *Freedom's Sword: The NAACP and the Struggle against Racism in America, 1909–1969*. New York: Routledge, 2004.

Jorge, Antonia, et al., eds. *Cuban Exiles in Florida: Their Presence and Contributions*. Miami: Research Institute for Cuban Studies, 1991.

Josephy, Alvin M. *Red Power: The American Indians' Fight for Freedom*. New York: American Heritage Press, 1971.

Juneau, Donald. "The Judicial Extinguishment of the Tunica Indian Tribe." *Southern University Law Review* 7 (1980): 43–99.

Justice, Daniel Heath. "A Lingering Miseducation: Confronting the Legacy of Little Tree." *Studies in American Indian Literatures* 12, no. 1 (2000): 20–36.

Keller, Robert, and Michael Turek. *American Indians and National Parks*. Tucson: University of Arizona Press, 1998.

Kerbs, Dana. "A Voice for Native Americans: The Alabama Indian Affairs Commission." *Envirosouth* (July/September 1981): 6–7, 24.

Kersey, Harry A., Jr. *An Assumption of Sovereignty: Social and Political Transformation among the Florida Seminoles, 1953–1979*. Lincoln: University of Nebraska Press, 1996.

———. "Those Left Behind: The Seminole Indians of Florida." In *Southeastern Indians since the Removal Era*, ed. Walter L. Williams. Athens: University of Georgia Press, 1979, 174–92.

Kniffen, Fred, Hiram F. Gregory, and George A. Stokes. *The Historic Indian Tribes of Louisiana: From 1542 to the Present*. Baton Rouge: Louisiana State University Press, 1987.

Larrabee, Lisa. *Grandmother Five Baskets*. Tucson: Harbinger House, 1993.

Lerch, Patricia Barker. "State-Recognized Indians of North Carolina, Including a History of the Waccamaw Sioux." In *Indians of the Southeastern United States in the Late 20th Century*, ed. J. Anthony Paredes. Tuscaloosa: The University of Alabama Press, 1992, 44–71.

Lipsitz, George. *The Possessive Investment in Whiteness: How White People Profit from Identity Politics*. Philadelphia: Temple University Press, 1998.

Loewen, James W. *The Mississippi Chinese: Between Black and White*. Prospect Heights, IL: Waveland Press, 1988.

Lofton, Teresa Constance. "Reclaiming an American Indian Identity: The Ethnic Renewal of the Lower Muskogee Creek." Ph.D. diss., Georgia State University, 2000.

Louisiana Health and Human Resources Administration Division of Human Services. "The Elderly Indians of Louisiana and Their Needs: A Report from the Office of Indian Affairs." 1 December 1975.

Lovett, Laura L. "African and Cherokee by Choice." *American Indian Quarterly* 22 (Winter–Spring 1998): 203.

Lowenthal, David. *The Heritage Crusade and the Spoils of History.* Cambridge: Cambridge University Press, 1998.

Lowery, Charles D., and John F. Marszalek, eds. *Encyclopedia of African-American Civil Rights: From Emancipation to the Present.* New York: Greenwood, 1992.

Lowery, Malinda Maynor. *Lumbee Indians in the Jim Crow South: Race, Identity, & the Making of a Nation.* Chapel Hill: University of North Carolina Press, 2010.

Lurie, Nancy Oestreich. "Sol Tax and Tribal Sovereignty." *Human Organization* 58, no. 1 (1999): 108–17.

———. "The Voices of the American Indian: Report on the American Indian Chicago Conference." *Current Anthropology* 2, no. 5 (December 1961): 478–500.

Maloof, Valerie Miller, et al. "Cultural Competence and Identity in Cross-Cultural Adaptation: The Role of a Vietnamese Heritage Language School." *International Journal of Bilingual Education & Bilingualism* 9, no. 2 (2006): 255–73.

Martin, Joel W. "'My Grandmother Was a Cherokee Princess': Representations of Indians in Southern History." In *Dressing in Feathers: The Construction of the Indian in American Popular Culture,* ed. S. Elizabeth Bird. Boulder, CO: Westview Press, 1996, 129–48.

Matte, Jacqueline Anderson. *They Say the Wind Is Red: The Alabama Choctaw Lost in Their Own Land.* Montgomery, AL: New South Books, 2002.

Mattern, Mark. "The Powwow as a Public Arena for Negotiating Unity and Diversity in American Indian Life." *American Indian Culture and Research Journal* 20, no. 4 (1996): 183–201.

McClure, Tony Mack. *Cherokee Proud: A Guide for Tracing and Honoring Your Cherokee Ancestors.* Somerville, TN: Chunannee Books, 1999.

McCulloch, Anne Merline, and David E. Wilkins. "'Constructing' Nations within States: The Quest for Federal Recognition by the Catawba and Lumbee Tribes." *American Indian Quarterly* 19, no. 3 (Summer 1995): 361–88.

Mechling, Jay. "Florida Seminoles and the Marketing of the Last Frontier." In *Dressing in Feathers: The Construction of the Indian in American Popular Culture,* ed. S. Elizabeth Bird. Boulder, CO: Westview Press, 1996. 149–66.

Merrell, James H. *The Indians' New World: Catawbas and Their Neighbors from European Contact through the Era of Removal.* Chapel Hill: University of North Carolina Press, 1989.

Meyer, Carter Jones, and Diana Royer, eds. *Selling the Indian: Commercializing & Appropriating American Indian Cultures.* Tucson: University of Arizona Press, 2001.

Miller, Mark Edwin. *Forgotten Tribes: Unrecognized Indians and the Federal Acknowledgment Process.* Lincoln: University of Nebraska Press, 2004.

Mills, Charles. *The Racial Contract.* Ithaca: Cornell University Press, 1997.

Mohl, Raymond A. "The Nuevo New South: Hispanic Migration to Alabama." *Migration World Magazine* 30, no. 3 (2002): 14.

Mormino, Gary R., and George E. Pozzetta. *The Immigrant World of Ybor City: Italians and Their Latin Neighbors in Tampa, 1885–1985.* Gainesville: University Press of Florida, 1998.

Mueller, Tim, et al. *Nations Within: The Four Sovereign Tribes of Louisiana.* Baton Rouge: Louisiana State University, 2003.

Murphy, Laura Frances. "Among the Cajans of Alabama." *Missionary Voice* (November 1930): 22.

Nagel, Joane. "American Indian Ethnic Renewal: Politics and the Resurgence of Identity." *American Sociological Review* 60, no. 6 (December 1995): 947–65.

———. *American Indian Ethnic Renewal: Red Power and the Resurgence of Identity and Culture.* New York: Oxford University Press, 1996.

Neely, Sharlotte. "Adaptation and the Contemporary North Carolina Cherokee Indians." In *Indians of the Southeastern United States in the Late 20th Century,* ed. J. Anthony Paredes. Tuscaloosa: The University of Alabama Press, 1992. 29–43.

New Directions in Indian Purpose: A Project and Publication of NAES College. Chicago: Native American Educational Services, 1988.

New Mexico Department of Labor. "Workforce Investment Act History." http://www.wia.state.nm.us/WIA_history.html (accessed 9 May 2002).

O'Brien, Sharon. *American Indian Tribal Governments.* Norman: University of Oklahoma Press, 1989.

Ogbar, Jeffrey O. G. *Black Power: Radical Politics and African American Identity.* Baltimore: Johns Hopkins University Press, 2004.

O'Reilly, Kenneth. *"Racial Matters": The FBI's Secret File on Black America, 1960–1972.* New York: Free Press, 1989.

Owens, Louis. *Mixedblood Messages: Literature, Film, Family, Place.* Norman: University of Oklahoma Press, 1998.

Paredes, J. Anthony. "The Emergence of Contemporary Eastern Creek Indian Identity." In *Social and Cultural Identity: Problems of Persistence and Change,* ed. Thomas K. Fitzgerald. Athens: Southern Anthropological Society Proceedings, No. 8, 1974, 68–80.

———. "Federal Recognition and the Poarch Creek Indians." In *Indians of the Southeastern United States in the Late 20th Century,* ed. J. Anthony Paredes. Tuscaloosa: The University of Alabama Press, 1992, 120–39.

———, ed. *Indians of the Southeastern United States in the Late 20th Century.* Tuscaloosa: The University of Alabama Press, 1992, 1–8.

———. Introduction to *Anthropologists and Indians in the New South,* ed. Rachel A. Bonney and J. Anthony Paredes. Tuscaloosa: The University of Alabama Press, 2001.

———. "Kinship and Descent in the Ethnic Reassertion of the Eastern Creek Indians." In *The Versatility of Kinship: Essays Presented to Harry Basehart,* ed. Linda Cordell and Stephen Beckerman. New York: Academic Press, 1980, 165–94.

Parenton, Vernon, and Roland Pellegrin. "The Sabines: A Study of Racial Hybrids in a Louisiana Coastal Parish." *Social Forces* 29 (December 1950): 148–54.

Pascoe, Peggy. "Miscegenation Law, Court Cases, and Ideologies of 'Race' in Twentieth-Century America." *Journal of American History* 83, no. 1 (June 1996): 44–69.

Peroff, Nicholas C. *Menominee Drums: Tribal Termination and Restoration, 1954–1974.* Norman: University of Oklahoma Press, 1982.

Pevar, Stephen L. *The Rights of Indians and Tribes: The Basic ACLU Guide to Indian and Tribal Rights.* Carbondale: Southern Illinois University Press, 1992.

Pinkney, Alphonso. *Red, Black, and Green: Black Nationalism in the United States.* Cambridge: Cambridge University Press, 1976.

Pollitzer, William S. "The Physical Anthropology and Genetics of Marginal Peoples of the Southeastern United States." *American Anthropologist* 74, no. 3 (June 1974): 719–34.

Porter, Frank W., III, ed. *Strategies for Survival: American Indians in the Eastern United States.* New York: Greenwood Press, 1986.

Price, Edward Thomas, Jr. "A Geographic Analysis of White-Negro-Indian Racial Mixtures in the Eastern United States." *Annals of the Association of American Geography* 43, no. 2 (June 1953): 138–55.

———. "The Melungeons: A Mixed Blood Strain of the Southern Appalachians." *Geographical Review* 41 (1951): 256–71.

———. "Mixed-Blood Populations of the Eastern United States as to Origins, Localizations, and Persistence." Ph.D. diss., University of California, 1950.

Quan, Robert Seto. *Lotus among the Magnolias: The Mississippi Chinese.* Jackson: University Press of Mississippi, 1982.

Quinn, William W. Jr. "Federal Acknowledgement of American Indian Tribes: The Historical Development of a Legal Concept." *American Journal of Legal History* 34 (October 1990): 331–64.

Roberts, Timmons J. "Media Savvy Cajuns and the Houma Indians: Fighting an Oilfield Waste Dump in Grand Bois." In *Chronicles from the Environmental Justice Frontline.* Cambridge: Cambridge University Press, 2001, 137–64.

Roche, John M. "Sociocultural Aspects of Diabetes in an Apache-Choctaw Community in Louisiana." Ph.D. diss., Catholic University of America Anthropological Series, No. 55, 1982.

Roediger, David R. *The Wages of Whiteness: Race and the Making of the American Working Class.* New York: Verso Press, 1994.

Roosens, Eugeen E. *Creating Ethnicity: The Process of Ethnogenesis.* Newbury Park, CA: Sage Publications, 1990.

Rountree, Helen C. "Indian Virginians on the Move." In *Indians of the Southeastern United States in the Late 20th Century,* ed. J. Anthony Paredes. Tuscaloosa: The University of Alabama Press, 1992, 9–28.

Roy, Edison Peter. "Indians of Dulac: A Descriptive Study of a Racial Hybrid Community in Terrebonne Parish, Louisiana." M.A. thesis, Louisiana State University, 1959.

"Ruth Loyd Miller." http://ruthmiller.com/ (accessed 2 September 2001).

Schackt, Jon. "Mayahood through Beauty: Indian Beauty Pageants in Guatemala." *Bulletin of Latin American Research* 24, no. 3 (July 2005): 269–87.

Self, Robert O. *American Babylon: Race and the Struggle for Postwar Oakland.* Princeton: Princeton University Press, 2005.

Sider, Gerald. *Lumbee Indian Histories: Race, Ethnicity, and Indian Identity in the Southern United States.* New York: Cambridge University Press, 1993.

Slagle, Alogan. "Unfinished Justice: Completing the Restoration and Acknowledgement of California Indian Tribes." *American Indian Quarterly* 13, no. 4 (1989): 325–45.

Smith, Paul Chaat, and Robert Allen Warrior. *Like a Hurricane: The Indian Movement from Alcatraz to Wounded Knee.* New York: The New Press, 1996.

Snipp, Matthew. "Sociological Perspectives on American Indians." *Annual Review of Sociology* 18, no. 1 (1992): 351–71.

Soruco, Gonzalo. *Cubans and the Mass Media in South Florida.* Gainesville: University Press of Florida, 1996.

Speck, Frank. "The Houma Indians in 1940." *American Indian Journal* 2, no. 1 (January 1976): 4–15.

Spence, Mark. *Dispossessing the Wilderness: Indian Removal and the Making of the National Parks.* New York: Oxford University Press, 1999.

Spicker, Jean R., Halla R. Steiner, and M. Rupert Walden in cooperation with the Inter-Tribal Council of Louisiana, Inc. "A Survey of Rural Louisiana Indian Communities." Baton Rouge: Louisiana State University, School of Social Welfare, 1977.

Spiller, Milton. "The Houma Indians since 1940." *American Indian Journal of the Institute of the Development of Indian Law* 2, no. 4 (April 1976): 16–17.

Stanton, Max. "Southern Louisiana Survivors: The Houma Indians." In *Southeastern Indians since the Removal Era,* ed. Walter L. Williams. Athens: University of Georgia Press, 1979, 90–109.

Stedman, Raymond William. *Shadows of the Indian: Stereotypes in American Culture.* Norman: University of Oklahoma Press, 1982.

Stevens, Charles John. "Demographic Variation and Ethnic Differentiation: A Comparative Demographic Analysis of the Poarch Creek Indians and Their Neighbors in the 1900 United States Census of Selected Precincts of Escambia and Monroe Counties, Alabama." M.A. thesis, Florida State University, 1983.

Stopp, George Harry, Jr. "The Impact of the 1964 Civil Rights Act on an Isolated 'Tri-Racial' Group." M.A. thesis, The University of Alabama, 1971.

Swanton, John. "Indian Tribes of the Lower Mississippi Valley and the Adjacent Gulf of Mexico." *Bureau of American Ethnology Bulletin* 43. Washington, DC: GPO, 1911.

——. "Probable Identity of the 'Croatan' Indians." Washington, DC: Office of Indian Affairs, 1933.

Taukchiray, Wesley DuRant, and Alice Bee Kasakoff. "Contemporary Native Americans in South Carolina." In *Indians of the Southeastern United States in the Late 20th Century,* ed. J. Anthony Paredes. Tuscaloosa: The University of Alabama Press, 1992, 72–101.

Taylor, Theodore W. *The States and Their Indian Citizens.* Washington, DC: Department of the Interior, 1972.

Thornton, J. Mills, III. *Dividing Lines: Municipal Politics and the Struggle for Civil Rights in Montgomery, Birmingham, and Selma.* Tuscaloosa: The University of Alabama Press, 2002.

Thornton, Russell. *American Indian Holocaust and Survival: A Population History since 1492.* Norman: University of Oklahoma Press, 1987.

Trouillot, Michel-Rolph. *Silencing the Past: Power and the Production of History.* Boston: Beacon Press, 1995.

Troy, Gil. *Morning in America: How Ronald Reagan Invented the 1980s.* Princeton: Princeton University Press, 2005.

Turner, Charles C. "The Politics of Minor Concerns: Congressional Dynamics and American Indian Legislation, 1947–1998." Ph.D. diss., Claremont Graduate University, 2000.

Unger, Stephen. *Indian Self Rule: First-Hand Accounts of Indian-White Relations from Roosevelt to Reagan,* ed. Kenneth R. Philp. Logan: Utah State University Press, 1995, 305.

United States Census Bureau. http://www.census.gov/hhes/www/income/histinc/f06ar.html (accessed 22 August 2005).

United States Commission on Civil Rights. *Report of the United States Commission on Civil Rights.* Washington, DC: GPO, 1959.

——. *Report of the United States Commission on Civil Rights.* Washington, DC: GPO, 1963.

U.S. Department of Labor, Office of the Assistant Secretary for Policy. "Brief History of DOL." http://www.dol.gov/asp/ (accessed 21 March 2003).

Urban Institute. "Block Grants: Historical Overview and Lessons Learned." No. A-63 in series. "New Federalism: Issues and Options for States." http://www.urban.org/url.cfm?ID=310991 (accessed 1 May 2004).

Vargas, Zaragosa. *Labor Rights Are Civil Rights: Mexican American Workers in Twentieth-Century America.* Princeton: Princeton University Press, 2005.

Watt, Marilyn J. "Federal Indian Policy and Tribal Development in Louisiana: The Jena Band of Choctaw." Ph.D. diss., Pennsylvania State University, 1986.

Weatherhead, L. R. "What Is an 'Indian Tribe'? The Question of Tribal Existence." *American Indian Law Review* 8, no. 1 (1980): 1–47.

Weisman, Brent Richards. *Unconquered People: Florida's Seminole and Miccosukee Indians.* Gainesville: University Press of Florida, 1999.

Welburn, Ron. "A Most Secret Identity: Native American Assimilation and Identity Resistance in African America." In *Confounding the Color Line: The Indian-Black Experience in North America,* ed. James F. Brooks. Lincoln: University of Nebraska Press, 2002, 292–320.

West, Patsy. *The Enduring Seminoles: From Alligator Wrestling to Ecotourism.* Gainesville: University Press of Florida, 1998.

Wickman, Patricia R. *The Tree That Bends: Discourse, Power and Survival of the Maskoki.* Tuscaloosa: The University of Alabama Press, 1999.

Wilkins, David E. *American Indian Politics and the American Political System.* Lanham, MD: Rowman and Littlefield, 2002.

Wilkins, David E., and K. Tsianina Lomawaima. *Uneven Ground: American Indian Sovereignty and Federal Law.* Norman: University of Oklahoma Press, 2001.

Williams, Walter L. "Patterns in the History of the Remaining Southeastern Indians, 1840–1975." In *Southeastern Indians since the Removal Era,* ed. Walter L. Williams. Athens: University of Georgia Press, 1979, 193–210.

———, ed. *Southeastern Indians since the Removal Era.* Athens: University of Georgia Press, 1979.

Wilson, Pamela S. "Disputable Truths: *The American Stranger,* Television Documentary and Native American Cultural Politics in the 1950s." Ph.D. diss., University of Wisconsin–Madison, 1996.

Winfrey, Robert Hill, Jr. "Civil Rights and the American Indian: Through the 1960s." Ph.D. diss., University of Oklahoma, 1986.

Wise, Bill M. *The Wisdom of Sam Ervin.* New York: Ballantine Books, 1973.

Woods, Sister Frances Jerome. *Marginality and Identity: A Colored Creole Family through Ten Generations.* Baton Rouge: Louisiana State University Press, 1972.

Woodward, C. Vann. *The Burden of Southern History.* Baton Rouge: Louisiana State University Press, 1960.

Wu, Judy Tzu-Chun. "Loveliest Daughter of Our Ancient Cathay!: Representations of Ethnic and Gender Identity in the Miss Chinatown U.S.A. Beauty Pageant." *Journal of Social History* 31, no. 1 (Winter 1997): 5–31.

Index

Acadiana Trailway Association, 162
Administration for Native Americans (ANA), 80, 96, 135
affirmative action, 93–96, 98, 174
Alabama Bureau of Publicity and Information, 131
Alabama Citizens' Council, 141
Alabama Committee for the Humanities, 31, 80
Alabama Coushatta of Texas, 4, 37
Alabama Creek Indian Council, 29–30, 43, 49
Alabama Department of Energy Office of Employment and Training, 124, 139
Alabama Department of Tourism and State Travel, 161, 169–70, *170*
Alabama Department of Urban and Community Affairs, 58
Alabama Environmental Quality Association, 161, 164
Alabama Film Commission, 97
Alabama Historical Commission, 161
Alabama Indian Affairs Commission (AIAC), xiii, xviii, 43–56, 69, 78–79, 86–89, 92, 96–97, 101, 103–4, 109, 111–13, 116, 118, 121–24, 127, 131–32, 135–36, 138–39, 143, 149, 159, 164–67, 169, 173, 212n31, 215n91. *See also* Southwest Alabama Indian Affairs Commission (SAIAC)
Alabama Indian Community Loan Fund (AICLF), 97, 135

Alabama Indian Advocate, 124–25, 166
Alabama Indian Journal, 88
Alabama Indian Scholarship Fund, 121–22
Alabama Indian Small Business Association (AISBA), 97, 136
Alabama Inter-Tribal Council (AITC), xix, 129–30, 135, 137
"Alabama Native American Trails," 170
Alabama Office of Employment and Training, 139
Alabama Waterfowl Association, 165
Alcatraz Island occupation, 20
American Civil Liberties Union (ACLU), 7
American Indian Celebration exhibit, 151
American Indian Chicago Conference, 3, 24, 30, 174. *See also Declaration of Indian Purpose*
American Indian Heritage Day, 36
American Indian Movement (AIM), 8, 20–21, 39, 163, 174
American Indian Policy Review Commission (AIPRC), 4, 78
American Indian Center in Baton Rouge, 154
Appalachian Regional Council (ARC), 136
Associated Catholic Charities, 105
Association on American Indian Affairs, 18

Baker, Russell, 136
Bayou Grand Caillou, *103*
Billiot, Elsie, 99–100, 102, 116, 137
Billiot, Henry L., 74, 204n12

Billiot, John, xxi, 67, 82
Billiot, Norman, 70–72, 98
Black Legislative Caucus, 94
Black Power Movement, 8, 189n39. *See also* civil rights movement
block grants, 38, 66, 100, 102, 108, 125–27, 138, 176, 219n145
Bourgeois, Henry L., 75, 77
Branch of Acknowledgment and Research (BAR), 5, 80, 83–84. *See also* Office of Acknowledgment
Brazan, Richard, xxi, 126
Breaux, John, 17
Broome, David, xxi, 68, 216n113
Bureau of Indian Affairs (BIA): tribal recognition, xi–xii, 3–5, 32, 34, 48, 57, 69, 74, 115; land trusteeship, 1, 12, 116; services, 2, 5, 106–7, 116, 135, 163, 211n20. *See also* Office of Acknowledgment
Butte LaRose rest stop, 163
Byrd, Kathleen, 149

Cade, John, 64
Campos, Jeanette, xxi, 57, 60, 105–6, 108, 110–11, 114–15, 128–29, 133–35, 145–46
Carter, Asa Earl "Forrest," 141–42, 143, 171; *The Education of Little Tree* by, 141–43, 171, 224n3, 224n7; use of the pen name "Forrest," 141
Carter, Dan T., 141, 181n6
Carter, Forrest. *See* Carter, Asa Earl "Forrest"
Carter, President Jimmy, 124
Catahoula Basin, 166
Cheramie, Steve, xxi, 67, 90, 133, 145, 171, 210n3
Cherokee Tribe of Northeast Alabama, xiii, *xv*, xviii, 87, 176. *See also* Jackson County Cherokee (CTNA)
Cherokees of Southeast Alabama, xiii, *xv*, xviii, xxi, 32, 55, 186n24
Chief Calvin McGhee and the Forgotten Creeks, 155
Chief Junuluska, 164
Chitimacha Economic Development Act, 135
Chitimacha Tribe, xi, *xv*, xix, xxi, xxii, 1, 18–20, 36, 56–57, 63, 65, 93–94, 106, 108,

130, 132, 135, 151, 154, 163, 181n1, 182n10, 199n54, 211n20, 216n113
Choctaw-Apache Community of Ebarb, xii–xiii, xix, 20, 57, 67, 93, 106, 130–31, 185n20
Choctaw Indian Political Affairs Committee, 122
Choctaw Indian Youth Community Conservation and Improvement Project, 128, 220n170
Ciba-Geigy Corporation, 97
civil rights movement: activism, 8, 188n30; impact on Indian rights movement, 8–9, 24, 32–33, 97, 77, 172, 174, 188n28; national attention, 6, 8; politics, 5, 7; white backlash, 9, 27–28, 33, 142, 174
Clifton Choctaw Tribe, xii, *xv*, xix, 57, 65, 89, 111, 126, 162–63, 185n19, 216n113
Clifton, Luther, 163
Coalition of Eastern Native Americans (CENA), 6, 30, 39, 44, 78, 174
Cold War, impact of, 3
Coley, Jack, 164
Colorado River Tribes of Arizona, 110
Comprehensive Education and Training Act (CETA), 31–32, 38, 45, 56, 58, 79, 122–23, 125–29, 131, 197n9, 218n128, 219n156
Cottrell, Kathleen S., 131
Council of Catholic Women, 152
Council on Interracial Books for Children, 159
Coushatta Craft Association, 14, 182n11
Coushatta Tribe, xi–xii, xix, xxii, 1, 4, 12–15, *13*, 17–20, 31, 34, 37, 39, 42, 56–57, 61, 65, 68, 73, 83, 106–8, 116–17, 126, 130, 132, 135, 150–52, 154, 162, 170, 182n11, 183n12, 187n2, 199n54, 216n113
Crazy Horse, Roy, 175
Creek Nation East of the Mississippi, xii, 1, 22–24, 26, 31–33, 183n14, 193n123. *See also* Poarch Band of Creek Indians
Creek wars, 163–64, 183n14, 186n25
Creekmore, Roger, xix, 55
Cromer, Marie, xiv, xix, 156–57
cultural imperialism, 150

Darden, Daniel, xxi, 93, 132
Data Bank Assistance Program, 119

Davenport, Tommy, xix, 41, 49, 55–56, 79, 160

Davis, Pat, xix, 55

Davis-Strong Act, xix–xx, 55, 129

Declaration of Indian Purpose, 4, 24

Declaration of Unity, 66, 108

Deep South International Indian Job Fair, 124

Dees, Jennie Lee, xx, 44–45, 80–81, 104, 113, 120, 129, 138, 146–47, 154, 157, 165–66

Deloria, Vine, Jr., xi, 39–40

Denton, Jeremiah, 118

Dion, William T., 16

Division of Black Culture, 95

driver's licenses, 72, 89, 98, 174

Duhon, Mike, 16

Duthu, Bruce, xxi, 82, 121

Eastern Band of Cherokee, xiii, 4, 11, 118, 144, 167–68, 181n1

Ebarb, Louisiana, xii, xix, 57, 93, 106, 130–31, 185n20

Ebarb, Raymond, 63

Echota Tribe of Cherokee, xiii, *xv*, xviii, xx, xxi, 41, 46, 49, 51, 53–55, 114, 153, 156–57, 160, 163, 168, 186n23

Education of Little Tree, The, by Asa Earl "Forrest" Carter, 141–42, 144, 171

Edwards, Edwin W., xxi, 11, 14, 16, 19, 21–22, 29, 36–37, 40, 56, 112, 117, 145

Edwards, Jack, 25

Emergency Food and Shelter Program, 138

Energy Crisis Intervention Program, 139

Ervin, Sam J., Jr., 9–10

Escambia County School Board, 23–24, 28–29

Faine, John, xxi, 106

Faulkner, B. J., xx, 46–47, 197n16

Fels, Margrett, xxi, 156–57

Fisher, Anthony, 129

Florida Governor's Council on Indian Affairs, 109

Folsom, Jim, 23

Forrest, Nathan Bedford, 141

Fort Rucker, 97

Four Holes community, 7

"Friends of Louisiana Indians," 133

Garrison, David L., Jr., xxi, 14–22, 37, 56–57, 117, 145, 160, 173

General Electric Cooperative, 97

Gilbert, William Harlen, Jr., x, 72

Gindrat, Helen, xxi, xxii, 59, 64–68, 70, 108, 110–11, 119–20, 126, 133, 137, 146

Governors' Interstate Indian Council, 35, 66, 89, 108–9

Graddick, Charles A., 121

Grandmother Five Baskets, 155

Granny Dollar, 159

Graves, Darla, xx, 136, 164–165

gravesite desecration, 46, 144, 147–49, 166

Greene, Glen S., 149

Gregory, H. F. "Pete," xxi, 82, 152, 159, 162, 166

Gulf South Research Institute (GSRI), 16

Haliwa tribe, 4; Haliwa Saponi Tribe (state recognized), 177

historical markers, 142, 164–65

Hodges, Wayne, 88

Holley, Jimmy, 36

Holmes, Hilary H., 76

Hood-Drane Route, 164–65

Horseshoe Bend National Military Park, 163

Houma of Louisiana, xii, 4, 7, 9, 19, 78, 130, 184n16, 199n54, 203n10, 204n25. *See also* United Houma Nation

Hudson, Leonard, xx, 45–46, 50–51, 63, 101, 112, 132, 153, 157

Hunt, Guy, xx, 34, 83, 168, 196n190

Hunter, Edwin, 16

Indian activism, 3–4, 9, 11–12, 20–23, 29, 33, 39–40, 42, 63, 174, 112, 172, 174, 176, 181n2; "Red Power," 8; schools, ix, 7, 211n21

Indian Angels, Inc., xix, 20–22, 39, 61, 63–64, 86, 118, 120, 154

Indian and Native American CETA Coalition, 125

Indian Civil Rights Act, 8, 10, 189n41

Indian Creek reservoir, 148

Indian gaming, 11, 36, 116

Indian Heritage Week, 163, 167

Indian Higher Education Assistance Grant Program, 119–21

Indian identity, xii, 5–7, 19, 26, 70–71,
  80, 89, 146, 153, 158–59, 171, 175, 188n23,
  200n78; identity switching, 88, 143, 158;
  legitimacy issues, 42, 46, 48, 53, 57, 61,
  65, 68, 104, 119–20, 144, 146–47, 168, 173;
  racial designation, 72–77, 79, 89–90, 97,
  174, 190n55; state recognition, 47–49,
  59–60, 79, 205n32; unification efforts,
  52–54, 56, 66, 84–91, 97, 111, 156; urban
  Indians, 61, 118
Indian Information Project, 6, 80–81, 108
Indian princess contests, 121, 153–54, 174
Indian Removal, 8–9, 22, 24, 33, 60, 71, 74,
  86, 88, 105, 141–42, 145, 159, 164–65, 167,
  224n6
Indian Self Determination and Education
  Assistance Act, 4, 117–18, 175
Indian Unity Conference, 89
Indians of Louisiana, 158
Institute for Indian Development, xix,
  xxii, 133–34, 151
Institute of American Indian Arts, 150–51
Inter-Governmental Committee on In-
  dian Affairs, 109

Jackson, Andrew, 164
Jackson, Clyde, xxi, xxii, 68, 108, 110, 125,
  129, 133–34
Jackson County Cherokee (CTNA), xiii,
  xviii, xx, 32, 41, 46, 51, 53, 55, 104, 118,
  127–28, 144, 160, 167, 185n22, 186n23.
  See also Cherokee Tribe of Northeast
  Alabama
Jackson County Historical Association, 165
Jackson, Jerry, xxii, 95
James, Fob, Jr., xx, 32, 38, 45–47, 52, 55, 58,
  63, 69, 78, 105, 109, 112, 139, 147, 160,
  197n8, 197n16
Jean Lafitte National Historical Park, 162
Jefferson, Bill, 93
Jena Band of Choctaws, xii–xiii, xv, xix,
  xxii, 18–20, 56–57, 65–66, 68, 95, 106,
  108, 126, 129–30, 135, 184n18, 199n54,
  216n113
Jim Crow, 6, 11, 73–77, 83–84, 86, 90–91,
  95, 117, 142, 174; prisons, 70–71, 203n7;
  schools, 7, 23–24. *See also* race and politics
Johnson, Lyndon, 4

Kennedy, John F., 4, 24, 25, 44
King, Martin Luther, Jr., 27, 37, 188n28,
  189n30
Kirkland bill, 52
Kirkland, Reo, xx, 44, 49, 52
Kniffen, Fred, xxii, 16
Ku Klux Klan, 49, 141–42
Kushner, Jaynn, 55

Lafayette Natural History Museum, 152
LaFleur, Mildred, 162
Lambardo, Daniel, 111
land claims and acquisition, 24, 28–29, 36,
  59, 75, 78, 116, 160
Langley, J. D., 16
license plate, *169*
Louisiana Arts Council, 162
Louisiana Band of Choctaws, xiii, *xv,*
  xix, xxi–xxii, 57, 59, 64, 68, 99, 185n21,
  216n113
Louisiana Bureau of Aging, 105
Louisiana Council for Music and Perform-
  ing Arts, 150
Louisiana Culture and Tourism Commis-
  sion, 152
Louisiana Department of Commerce and
  Industry, 160
Louisiana Department of Economic Op-
  portunity, 16
Louisiana Department of Health and Hu-
  man Resources (DHHR), 137
Louisiana Department of Health, Educa-
  tion and Welfare, 57
Louisiana Department of Labor, 57, 127
Louisiana Department of Urban and
  Community Affairs, 120, 192n93
Louisiana Indians for Equality (LIFE),
  xix, xxi–xxii, 19, 67, 69, 86
Louisiana Indian Housing Authority,
  58, 139
Louisiana Inter-Tribal Council (ITC), xix,
  xxi, xxii, 19, 35, 56–60, 64, 68, 78, 98,
  105–6, 108, 115, 122–23, 126, 128–29, 133–
  36, 145–46, 151, 158–59, 199n54
Louisiana Office of Economic Opportu-
  nity, 57

Louisiana Office of Health and Human Services, 111
Louisiana Office of Housing and Urban Development, 57
Louisiana Office of Indian Affairs (LOIA), xix, xxi–xxii, 14, 16, 19, 35, 42, 56–67, 69–70, 72, 78–79, 87–94, 98–99, 102, 105–12, 114–21, 126–27, 130–35, 137–39, 145–46, 148–50, 152, 155, 158–60, 166–67, 173, 192n93, 210n3
Louisiana Political Educational Council, 17
Louisiana State University: Museum of Geoscience, 151
Louisiana Summer Food Program, 138
Louisiana Tourist Commission, 160
Lumbee tribe, 4–7, 9–10, 53, 73, 80, 153, 177, 203n9
Lutheran World Ministries, 80

Ma-Chis Lower Creeks, xiii, xv, xviii, 138, 186n26
Mankiller, Wilma, 34, 175
Margolin, Barry, 32
Mars, Ted, 29, 32
Martin, H. L. "Lindy," xx, 41, 43, 53–54, 145, 160
Martin, Larry, 161
Mashpee tribe, 5
Matte, Jacqueline Anderson, xx, 74, 80–81
McClure, Tony Mack, 155
McCormick, Neal, 26
McGhee, Calvin, xx, 1–2, 4, 22–26, 25, 30, 32–34, 39, 41, 44, 87, 110, 145, 150, 155, 183n14
McGhee, Houston, xx, 1–2, 26–30, 33, 34, 52, 145
McRae, L. W., 76
media, 51, 88, 91, 116, 148, 153–57
Mennonites, 162; Mennonite Central Committee, 80
Miller, Ruth Loyd, xxii, 1, 11–22, 15, 37, 39, 64, 155–56, 173
Mims Act, xx, 31, 38, 41, 43–44, 46–48, 50–51, 55; Amendment, 51. See also Southwest Alabama Indian Affairs Commission (SAIAC)
Mims, Maston, xx, 31

minority status, 10, 12, 14, 17, 27, 37, 55, 72, 82, 89, 91–97, 103, 124, 135–36, 159, 174, 176
miscegenation, 8, 71, 73–74, 77, 90, 95
Mississippi Choctaw, xii–xiii, 4, 9, 11, 136, 153, 181n1, 223n230
Mitchell, Wendell, 29
Montana Indian Affairs Commission, 109
Mora, Peter, xxii, 57–58
MOWA Band of Choctaws, xii, xv, xviii, xx, xxi, 9, 32–33, 40–41, 44, 46–49, 51, 55, 73–74, 76–78, 80–85, 90, 92, 94, 97, 112, 122–23, 127–28, 136–39, 153–54, 160, 183n15, 198n19, 203n11
museums and exhibits, 142, 147, 148, 150–51, 154, 161–64, 224n12; tribal, 151, 167–69, 174
Muskogee Creeks of Georgia and Florida, 9, 24, 26, 30. See also Northwest Florida Creek Indian Council

National Association for the Advancement of Colored People (NAACP), 7, 67
National Association of Community Loan Funds, 135
National Congress of the American Indian (NCAI), 3, 25–26, 30, 39, 44, 78, 89, 109, 127, 174
National Indian Education Association Conference, 89
National Indian Youth Council, 8
National Park Service, 149, 162, 164, 165, 166, 182n10, 229n112
Native Americans of Louisiana, 158
Native American Rights Fund (NARF), 7–8, 18
needs assessments, 44–45, 56, 92, 100, 102–16, 118, 128
Neuman, Robert W., 151
New Jersey Commission on American Indian Affairs, 175
New Orleans French Market Board, 16
Nixon, Richard, 115
North Carolina Indian Affairs Commission, 35, 59, 89, 109, 124
North Dakota Indian Affairs Agency, 34
Northwest Florida Creek Indian Council, 71

Oats, Larry, 161
Office of Acknowledgment, 5, 59, 72, 79–
    81, 175. *See also* Branch of Acknowledg-
    ment and Research (BAR)
Omnibus Budget Reconciliation Act, 125
Omussee Creek Park , 136
Osterberger, Kenneth E., 94

Parfait, John, 98
Parker's Island, 160–61, 164, 229n107
Peralta, Sarah, xxii, 20–22, 34, 39, 61, 63, 65,
    120, 154
Perdido Band of Friendly Creek Indians
    of Alabama and Northwest Florida.
    See also Creek Nation East of the Mis-
    sissippi
Peterson, Viola, 35, 124
Pittman, Loretta, 55
Poarch Band of Creek Indians, xii–xiii,
    xv, xviii, xix, xx, 4, 7, 9, 22–24, 26, 28–
    34, 41, 43–55, 59, 68, 73, 80, 83, 85, 87–88,
    100–101, 103–4, 106, 109, 113, 116, 121–
    24, 127–32, 137–39, 145, 153, 155–57, 160,
    164, 167–68, 173, 183n14, 194n141, 210n11,
    218n134. *See also* Creek Nation East of
    the Mississippi
Poverty Point State Commemorative
    Area, 149, 154
powwows and Indian festivals, 21, 26, 144,
    151–54, *155*, 167–69, 174, 186n24
Prepaid Affordable College Tuition
    (PACT) Program, 122
Price, Edward Thomas, Jr., 76
Procell, Roy, xxii, 67, 93, 138
public image and awareness, 39, 68, 72–73,
    85, 87, 89, 94, 98, 101, 110, 114, 116, 127,
    144–45, 147, 155, 166–70, 172, 174: Loui-
    siana Indians, 12, 16–17, 21, 63, 65, 81–83,
    91, 111–12, 134, *148*, 148–49, 151–52, 154,
    158, 160, 163, 168–71, *169*; Alabama In-
    dians, 24–26, 83, 103, 112, 159–61, 163,
    165, 168–71, *170*

race and politics, 6–10, 40, 72–73, 85, 92,
    97, 174, 189n43, 190n55, 190n57, 202n3;
    Alabama, 23, 27; Louisiana, 11, 203n7.
    See also Jim Crow
Rainer, Howard, 129

Ray, James E., xx, 51
Reagan, Ronald, 11, 38, 45, 100–101, 108,
    114, 124–25, 132, 139
Reding, Curtis, 29, 32
Rivers, Jack, 122
Roche, John M., 106
Roemer, Buddy, xxii, 143, 158–59
Rolin, Buford, 109
Rozelle, Hugh, 23

Sanders, Odis, xxii, 59, 64
Saunders, John, 59
Scheirbeck, Helen Maynor, 10, 81
Seminoles of Florida, 9, 11, 144, 154, 178,
    181n1
Shreveport Regional Arts Council, 151
Sickey, Ernest, xxii, 1–2, 11–14, 16–22, 29,
    33–40, 42, 53, 56–58, 61–62, 67–69, 107–
    8, 110, 112, 115, 126, 134, 148, 150, 155–56,
    173, 216n113
Siegelman, Don, 89
Simmons, Bobby Joe, 116
Simpson, Charles, 63
Smith, Charlie, 115
Smith, Mildred, 99, 102, 116, 137
Society for the Preservation of American
    Indian Culture (SPAIC), xix, 53–54
South Alabama Regional Planning Com-
    mission, 31
southern Indian identity: claims of Chero-
    kee or Cherokee "princess" ancestry,
    224n6; distinctiveness, x, 9–10, 28, 33,
    34, 53, 60, 64, 65, 68, 71, 73, 76, 77, 79, 84,
    85, 103, 141–42, 156, 163; emphasis on in-
    digenous roots, xii, 9, 30, 33, 52, 61, 114,
    118, 141–45, 159, 161, 170–71, 174
Southern Legislative Conference, 143
"Southern Manifesto," 10
southern politics: Republican Party, 10, 38,
    42, 45, 66, 96, 172, 176, 196n190, 197n8;
    Democratic Party, 10–11, 197n8
Southwest Alabama Indian Affairs Com-
    mission (SAIAC), xviii, xix, xx, xxi, 31–
    33, 35, 38, 42–54, 69, 79, 92, 96, 103–4,
    113, 116, 123–24, 127, 131–32, 215n92. *See
    also* Alabama Indian Affairs Commis-
    sion (AIAC)
sovereignty: tribal, 8, 34, 36, 38, 43, 45, 47–

48, 52, 59, 61, 65, 67–68, 72, 82, 88, 95–
    96, 101–2, 104, 107, 110–14, 116, 120, 124–
    27, 131, 133–43, 140, 156, 161, 164, 172–73,
    175–76, 195n165, 214n74; state, 35
Speck, Frank, 75, 183n14, 204nn24–25
Star Clan of Muscogee Creeks, also known
    as the Eufaula Star Clan or Troy Creeks,
    xiii, xv, xviii, xix, 29–31, 41, 43, 46, 49,
    51, 55, 79, 127, 138, 186n25
state Indian affairs commissions: benefits
    to states, 31, 33–34, 40, 64, 69, 145, 161,
    175–76; challenges, 62, 69, 108–10, 115–
    16, 124–28, 132, 140; purpose and func-
    tions, x, 10, 34, 42, 87–88, 107, 112–13,
    118–24, 126–27, 130–32, 140, 144, 146,
    158, 160–61, 173, 212n31; representation,
    50, 61, 65, 104, 111, 127, 156–57, 172–74;
    state relations, 113–15, 134, 140, 145, 165,
    172; tribal recognition, 10, 33, 36, 44,
    46, 48, 50, 57–60, 68–69, 73, 79, 84–85,
    147, 175
Stewart, Joseph, xx, 54–55, 160, 168–69
Stoffle, Richard W., 84
Strickland, W. J., 39
Strong, Frances, xx, 55–56
Summer Youth Employment Program,
    123–24
Summer Youth Feeding Program, 138
Swanton, John, 75, 151

Tax, Sol, 3
Taylor, Wilford, 163
Tennessee Indian Commission, 109, 124
termination policy, xii, 3, 12, 34, 72
Terrebonne Parish, 74, 77, 184n16; school
    board, 75, 204n12
Thomas, Ella, 81
Thomley, Wesley, 26
Thompson, Lenore, 23
tourism, 143–45, 149–50, 161–63, 168, 170, 174
Trail of Tears route, 164–65, 230n124
Treen, David, xxii, 11, 36, 58, 63–66, 69, 196n190
tribal development, 54, 58, 98, 101, 107, 173,
    176; arts and crafts industry, 12–13, 18,
    108, 131–32, 150, 162–63, 186n25; culture,
    118, 132, 136, 143, 145, 154, 161–63, 166;
    economic development, 35, 65, 85, 93,
    96, 114, 130–36, 144–45, 152, 160, 163, 174;

education, 77, 93–94, 103, 117–22, 124,
    118n134; employment, 32, 92–94, 97, 103,
    122–24, 127–29, 132, 217n128, 218n134,
    219n156; government and leadership, 85,
    102, 109, 111–15, 121, 130–31, 136, 172; re-
    lationship with states, 29, 89; social ser-
    vices, 108, 126, 128, 137–39, 222n228
Tribal Economic Resource Officers
    (TERO), 136
tribal histories, 72, 81–82, 113, 123, 134, 143–
    45, 149, 152–55, 158–61, 163–71, 174
Tri-State Creek Council, 26, 30
Tullis, Eddie Leon, xx, 30–34, 38–41, 43–
    44, 46–53, 55–56, 68, 85, 101, 109, 113, 127,
    160, 164
Tullis, Mary Jane, 131
Tunica-Biloxi Tribe, xii, xv, xix, 1, 36, 39,
    56–57, 65, 68, 83, 106, 116, 130, 135, 148,
    151–52, 154, 183n13, 199n54, 216n113
Turner, J. E., xx, 47, 78
Turnley, Richard, 94–95

"Undersigned Sovereign American Indian
    Tribal Governments of Louisiana,"
    66, 114
United Cherokee Tribe of Alabama, xiii,
    xx, 32, 46–47, 197n16
United Houma Nation, xv, xix, 35–36, 78,
    216n113. See also Houma of Louisiana
United Negro College Fund, 54
United Southeastern Tribes, Inc., 6, 108
United Southern Missionary Church, 146
United States Census Bureau, xi, 87–88,
    182n7–8, 187n3, 207n76
United States Department of Education,
    117–19, 121
United States Department of Labor, 123, 129
United States Small Business Adminis-
    tration, 97
University of Alabama, The: School of
    Optics, 138; Student Coalition for
    Community Health, 138

Vilcan, Archie, 16
Virginia Cherokee, 4
VISTA Volunteer Program, 38, 127–28,
    220n166
Voting Rights Act, 10, 33

Wallace, George C., xxi, 2, 11, 27–29, 32–33, 40, 44–45, 55–56, 104, 122, 141–42, 145, 175
Wambles, Deal, xxi, 55, 186n24
Weaver, Framon, xxi, 41, 43, 47, 48, 55, 112, 139, 160
Weaver, Gallasneed, xxi, 41, 43, 49–50, 54–56, 78, 82, 94, 198n19
Weeks, Jane L., xxi, 56, 118
Weston, Diane, xxi, 41–43, 49, 114
Wheeler-Howard Act, also known as the

Indian Reorganization Act (IRA), xii, 182n12, 200n78
White, Mack, 147
Williamson, Diana, xxii, 63–65, 94–95, 167, 201n108, 202n3
World Hunger Project, 138
World War II, impact of, 3, 76, 95

Youngdeer, Robert, 168
Youth Conservation and Community Improvement Project, 139